TERM PAPER RESOURCE GUIDE TO MEDIEVAL HISTORY

TERM PAPER RESOURCE GUIDE TO MEDIEVAL HISTORY

Jean Shepherd Hamm

GREENWOOD PRESS

An Imprint of ABC-CLIO, LLC

A B C CLIO

Santa Barbara, California • Denver, Colorado • Oxford, England

Library of Congress Cataloging-in-Publication Data

Hamm, Jean S.
    Term paper resource guide to medieval history / Jean S. Hamm.
        p. cm.
    Includes bibliographical references and index.
    ISBN 978-0-313-35967-5 (alk. paper) — ISBN 978-0-313-35968-2 (ebook : alk.
paper)
    1. Middle Ages—Study and teaching. 2. Civilization, Medieval—Study and
teaching. 3. Middle Ages—Bibliography. 4. Civilization, Medieval—Bibliography.
I. Title.
    D118.H235 2009
    940.1—dc22   2009036249

ISBN: 978-0-313-35967-5
EISBN: 978-0-313-35968-2

14 13 12 11 10   1 2 3 4 5

This book is also available on the World Wide Web as an eBook.
Visit www.abc-clio.com for details.

ABC-CLIO, LLC
130 Cremona Drive, P.O. Box 1911
Santa Barbara, California 93116-1911

This book is printed on acid-free paper ∞
Manufactured in the United States of America

Contents

Introduction

The centuries now grouped under the title Middle Ages received their name during the Renaissance. Scholars of the Renaissance thought that the period between the fall of Rome in 410 BCE and their own enlightened age from the late 15th through the 17th century were unproductive years of intellectual and cultural stagnation. Nothing was distinctive about this period—it was just a space between two cultural pinnacles. Some of that attitude lingers today. The earlier part of the medieval period is referred to as the Dark Ages, and the word *medieval* often has negative connotations. Empires did crumble during the Middle Ages, but some of the greatest empires in history were built as well—in Europe, the Americas, Asia, and Africa. A great deal of learning was lost, but mathematics, science, architecture, and agriculture all advanced. Fear and superstition were rampant, but the world's great religions grew and offered hope and solace. Old governments were conquered, but new governments took their places and slowly laid the foundations of law and justice that are still in place today. The Middle Ages were fraught with war, pestilence, famine, and persecution. They were not all romance—knights in shining armor and courtly love. Yet, they were not a time of stagnation. The human experiment of civilization was undergoing a period of trial and error, but above all it was a time of growth, which makes it a fascinating time to study.

This book is designed for students who are engaged in the study of medieval history and who will be writing research papers. The text is organized around 100 significant events from the Middle Ages, providing traditional and alternative term paper suggestions for each event, and recommending primary, secondary, Web, and multimedia resources. Information for the Advanced Placement World History course from Educational Testing Service (ETS) guided the selection of events and the term paper suggestions. ETS divides world history into five broad chronological periods. For this book, the dates of the medieval period have been extended slightly, using 410 to 1485, instead of 600 to 1450 (unless noted otherwise, all dates are CE). Historians designate a variety of starting and ending dates for the Middle Ages, but agree that the period began after the fall of the Roman Empire and ended with the dawn of the Renaissance. The year 410 was selected here because it is the traditional date for Alaric's sack of of Rome. The Empire was not entirely obliterated in that year, but after the devastation in the capital, it was never able to regain its power. The date beginning the Renaissance is also debated, but scholars point out it began earlier in Italy than in the rest of the world. For this book, 1485 was selected because that year marks the end of the Wars of the Roses in Britain and the significant changes that began under the Tudor monarchy. Britain was the last European power to move into the Renaissance.

Choosing only 100 events from over 1,000 years of history from four continents posed a challenge. This volume includes events from the entire period from Europe, Africa, Asia, and the Americas, but it is not intended to be a comprehensive history of the age. An effort was made to include related incidents not listed among the 100 in the suggested term paper topics. Readers and students of history will no doubt think of additional significant events for further research.

Three types of essay questions appear on the Advanced Placement test. Document-based questions require students to analyze the contents of primary sources, consider the author's purpose and audience, reflect on the wider implications, and construct a reasonable argument. Other questions emphasize continuity and change over time and drawing comparisons between cultures. These types of questions are represented throughout the term paper suggestions.

Exact dates for many medieval events can be difficult to ascertain. Recordkeeping, sporadic at best, was often not precise. The use of different calendars by various cultures complicates the determination of dates. Very reputable sources may list conflicting dates. For instance, the beginning of the Spanish Inquisition is listed in different sources as 1478, 1479, and 1480. Both the site and date of the first European university are spread over a wide area. Dates given for the 100 entries help establish the order of events and are those believed to be the most accurate.

The invention of the printing press in 1450, near the end of the medieval period, helped to standardize spelling. Earlier writers and scribes often spelled words however they wished, sometimes varying their spelling within a single document. For example, John Wycliffe's last name appears in different sources as Wycliff and Wyclif. The most common spellings were chosen in this book and are consistent, except when a resource title may use a variation. Suggested resources found on the Web were selected using four criteria: reliability of authority, lack of bias, likelihood to remain active, and extent of information. Most of the sites listed are maintained by universities, research centers, libraries, museums, and study associations. These are both less likely to present a biased picture of the topic and more likely to remain active. The commercial sites listed are identified as such. However, researchers should always take into account possible biases from any resources they use. Sites suggested generally have a large body of information, not a single article, and refer the researcher to even more resources. The Web is a dynamic entity with more resources added daily, yet it is also true that researchers will find that sites have been removed or have become inactive.

For an area of study such as the Middle Ages, primary documents can be difficult to obtain. The Web makes it possible to access many more of these than were available only a few years ago. This book references many primary documents that can be found in suggested Web sites and suggests other documents that are fairly easy to obtain through libraries. In most cases, if a book is very old, it is either available digitally or as a reprint. Search engines and online resources such as Amazon.com and BN.com are useful in locating rare, primary documents. Documents are being added daily to resources such as The Gutenberg Project (www.gutenberg.org) and The Internet Archives (http://www.archive.org).

Information and suggestions provided here are intended to provoke students' curiosity, not to limit them to one narrow topic. The purpose of this book is to aid students in their journey through a fascinating period of human history.

1. Barbarian Invasions of Europe (Beginning c. 410)

By 150 the Roman Empire had extended its boundaries throughout most of the western world, from Northern Africa to England, and from Constantinople to the Iberian Peninsula. The government of Rome worked because of the well-oiled, administrative bureaucracy it established. Even when the emperors were poor rulers, Roman aristocrats and soldiers were able to carry on. Garrisons throughout the empire were manned by Roman soldiers who kept order and helped administrators enforce Roman law. Many Roman citizens sent into conquered territories as soldiers or bureaucrats stayed to make the territories their homes, and their ties to the imperial city weakened. By the end of the fourth century, the nature of the army had also changed. The disciplined legions were no longer filled with loyal and well-trained Roman citizens. Many of the soldiers protecting Roman territories were members of the tribes that were harassing Roman borders and were more interested in pay than in the stability of the empire.

In 410, Alaric, king of the Visigoths, mounted an offensive that resulted in his capturing and sacking the city of Rome. This defeat marked the beginning of the end for one of the world's greatest civilizations. When it became obvious that Rome could be conquered, other barbarian tribes, eager for Rome's wealth, began to move into Roman territory. First, the Visigoths, who controlled most of Gaul (France), then the Vandals, Huns, Ostrogoths, and other Germanic tribes all carved off pieces of the Roman Empire, leaving only vestiges of Roman rule in the West. The empire collapsed in varying degrees in various places and it never regained its unity and power. Without a centralized government, regional powers rose and fell during the period called the Dark Ages, but this paved the way for a new civilization to emerge in Europe that was built on the ruins of the Roman Empire. Knowing what the Barbarian invaders destroyed and what they brought to the former Roman territories provides insight into the next era, the Middle Ages.

TERM PAPER SUGGESTIONS

1. In *The Decline and Fall of the Roman Empire,* British historian Edward Gibbon wrote that the Roman Empire collapsed under its own weight. Research the structure of imperial institutions in the last years of the Empire. Discuss the extent to which Rome's internal problems led to its demise.

2. How did Roman military policies in the late Empire contribute to the success of barbarian invasions?

3. Compare *The Visigoth Code* to Roman law.

4. Choose one of the significant leaders of a barbarian tribe, such as Alaric, Gaiseric, or Atilla, and discuss why and how he became a successful leader.

5. Research the training a Roman legionnaire received. Compare his training to that of a barbarian, a knight, or a modern soldier.

6. The term *barbarians* is used to cover a large number of different groups that fought against the Roman Empire. Research the social and cultural structures of some of these groups. Is the term, with the connotation we now associate with it, appropriate? Were the barbarians less civilized than the Romans? In what ways?

ALTERNATIVE TERM PAPER SUGGESTIONS

1. Prepare an interactive PowerPoint presentation with maps to illustrate the extent of the Roman Empire at the beginning of the fifth century and how and when its territory was lost.

2. Create a multimedia presentation comparing and contrasting the state, military organization, and life style of two or more of the Germanic tribes that invaded Europe. Use primary sources such as Jordanes, Ammianus Marcellinus, Priscus, and Salvian in your research.

Primary Sources

The Medieval Sourcebook. http://www.fordham.edu/halsall/source. Provides translated excerpts from Priscus (who wrote about the court of Attila the Hun), Jordanes, and accounts of Pope Leo's meeting with Attila.

Jordanes. *The Origins and Deeds of the Goths,* trans. by Charles C. Mierow. Gloucester, UK: Dodo Press, 2007. A full translation of sixth-century Roman historian Jordanes' work about the Goths.

The Visogoth Code. http://libro.uca.edu/vcode/visigoths.htm.

Secondary Sources

Bury, J. B. *Invasion of Europe by the Barbarians.* New York: W. W. Norton & Company, 2000 (1967). Considered a standard resource on the barbarian invasions. Chapter one, called a *lecture,* provides valuable background understanding, with a discussion of the Germanic tribes before they began their invasions.

Craughwell, Thomas J. *How the Barbarian Invasions Shaped the Modern World: The Vikings, Vandals, Huns, Mongols, Goths, and Tartars Who Razed the Old World and Formed the New.* Beverly, MA: Winds Press, 2008. This highly readable and well-researched volume covers invaders of Europe from 410–1242. Illustrations, maps, timelines and other readers' aids are plentiful. Chapters 1–7 deal with Rome's invaders.

Frye, David G. "Rome's Barbarian Mercenaries." *Military History Quarterly.* Spring 2007. http://www.historynet.com/romes-barbarian-mercenaries.htm. The article discusses the effects of replacing Roman legionnaires with barbarian mercenaries.

Heather, Peter. *The Fall of the Roman Empire: A New History of Rome and the Barbarians.* New York: MacMillan, 2005. Although much of this book discusses Rome before the invasions, it is an engaging narrative that offers students insight into how historians work, as well as providing many facts and details of the time.

King, P. D. *Law and Society in the Visigoth Kingdom.* Cambridge: Cambridge University Press, 2006. Includes topics such as royal government, the king and the law, the church, and the economy, plus two appendices and an index to the laws cited.

Randers-Pehrson, Justine Davis. *Barbarians and Romans: The Birth Struggle of Europe, A.D. 400–700.* Norman, OK: University of Oklahoma Press, 1983. Covers early medieval history from Britain in the north, to the steppes of Asia in the east, and Africa in the south.

World Wide Web

Elton, Hugh. (1996). "The Collapse of the Roman Empire–Military Aspects." ORB Online Encyclopedia, http://www.nipissingu.ca/department/history/muhlberger/orb.

Jordanes. *The Origins and Deeds of the Goths.* http://www.ucalgary.ca/~vandersp/Courses /texts/jordgeti.html. The Medieval Sourcebook.

Multimedia Sources

Attila the Hun. Episode of *Warriors.* 2008. The Military Channel. DVD, 60 minutes. Dramatization of Attila's life and major battles that attempts to separate fact from fiction.

Barbarians. 2004/2006. The History Channel. 200 minutes. A two-DVD series that uses reenactments, footage of historic sites, narration, and interviews with experts to detail the lives of the barbarian invaders of Europe. Includes two additional programs, "Modern Marvels: Axes, Knives and Swords" and "Weapons of the Barbarians." A number of short clips from the programs are available at http://www.history.com/bn.do?action =clip&id.

Decisive Battles of the Ancient World. 2004. The History Channel. 380 minutes. A three-DVD set that includes episodes about the Gothic invasion of Rome in volume 1 and Attila the Hun in volume 2.

Del Imperio Cristiano a los Reinos Barbaros. 2004. Films for the Humanities and Sciences. DVD. 44 minutes. 3-D animation, reenactments, and filming on location highlight the barbarian invasions on the Iberian Peninsula and life under the Visigoths. In Spanish with English subtitles.

The Germanic Tribes. 2009. Kultur Films. Two-disk set; four parts; 269 minutes. Uses reenactments and 3-D animation to portray the lives of the Germanic conquerors of Rome.

2. Leo I and the Medieval Papacy (440)

Leo I, also called Leo the Great, was pope from 440 to 461. He established the supremacy of Rome over other bishoprics, instituted a formidable central administrative system, and greatly enhanced the importance of the office of the pope. The strength and influence of the papacy that developed as a result of Leo's work affected every aspect of medieval life.

Probably born in Tuscany around 400, Leo figured prominently in the church before he was elected pope. His election occurred while he was away from Rome on a diplomatic mission, and he was consecrated on September 29, 440. Immediately, he set out to consolidate his power throughout the western world. By integrating ecclesiastical law and Roman authority, he increased the importance of his position. In 452, Leo met with Attila the Hun and convinced him not to sack the city of Rome, thereby saving some of the city's treasures from destruction.

The legacy of Leo I in centralizing the power of the church and papacy facilitated the efforts of later popes such as Gregory I (590–604) and Innocent III (1198–1216) to extend control of the church in both sacred and secular realms. Gregory I administered the entire city of Rome and raised an army to protect it from the Lombards (the Germanic tribe which controlled most of Italy). Later popes excommunicated secular and religious authorities, ruled on individual claims to a throne, assembled armies for the Crusades, and issued interdicts against whole nations, which, in effect, led to the overthrow of rulers. Kings and queens appealed to the pope for decisions concerning political matters, and commoners accepted his edicts as being directly from God.

Popes sometimes misused the enormous power that accompanied the office for their own ends. Popes such as Sergius III (904–911) and John XII (955–964) were notorious for the corruption of their reigns, but the papacy's power, for good or ill, permeated medieval society.

TERM PAPER SUGGESTIONS

1. Discuss how the Council of Chalcedon in 451 and Leo I's *Tome* (449) resulted in the increasing power of the papacy.

2. Research the Pseudo-Isidorian Decretals, which appeared between 833 and 857. Discuss how the papacy used these documents to establish the legitimacy of its authority.

3. Gregory I consolidated the lands controlled by the papacy into what would become the "Papal States." These territories expanded and were significant political entities until the 19th century. Research the development of the Papal States and their significance on political life in the Middle Ages.

4. Discuss the relationship between a member of the papacy and a medieval European monarch. How did their conflicts and/or collaboration affect the political developments of the time?

5. Investigate the conflicts between the Roman church and the Eastern church in Byzantium. Were the tensions based on theology, power, or personality?

6. The period of 330–665 is called "the Age of the Fathers" in church history. Discuss the influence of the popes of this age on present-day Christianity.

ALTERNATIVE TERM PAPER SUGGESTIONS

1. Using information from primary and secondary sources, reenact the meeting between Attilla and Pope Leo for the class. Provide an introduction that establishes the significance of this meeting. You may choose to do this live or as a pod cast.

2. Create a multimedia presentation comparing and contrasting the state, military organization, and life style of two or more of the Germanic tribes that invaded Europe. Use primary sources such as Jordanes, Ammianus Marcellinus, Priscus, and Salvian in your research.

Primary Sources

Cantor, Norman E., ed., *The Medieval Reader*. New York: HarperCollins, 1994. This collection of almost 100 original documents was compiled by one of the leading authorities on medieval studies. In addition to literature, the volume contains letters and documents important in state and church historical perspectives.

"The Definition of Chalcedon." 451. http://www.iclnet.org/pub/resources/text/ history/creeds.chalcedon.txt. A number of additional documents from the Middle Ages are accessible through this site.

Leo I. *Letters and Sermons,* collected in *Nicene and Post-Nicene Fathers, Series II, Vol. XII.* http://ccel.churchdocs.org/fathers2/npnf212/toc.htm. Also includes a biography of Leo.

Voragine, Jacobus de. *The Golden Legend or The Lives of Saints,* Vol. 4. Although not strictly a primary source, this historical document was compiled in 1275 and first published in 1470. A collection of biographies is available in the translation by F. S. Ellis at http://www.ccel.org/v/voragine/. The life of Leo the Great is included in the volume.

Secondary Sources

Bredero, Adriaan H. *Christendom and Christianity in the Middle Ages: The Relations between Religion, Church and Society.* Grand Rapids, MI: Eerdmans, 1994. Bredero's work concentrates primarily on the later medieval period, but the first chapter, "Religion and Church in Medieval Society," provides a strong overview of the importance of the church.

Brown, Peter. *The Rise of Western Christendom: Triumph and Diversity AD 200–1000.* Cambridge, MA: Blackwell Publishers, 1996. This comprehensive volume provides a perspective on the Latin and Greek forms of Christianity, with views of Coptic, Syriac, Celtic, and Central Asian churches as well.

Canning, Joseph. *A History of Medieval Political Thought, 300–1450.* New York: Routledge, 1997. Canning discusses the influence of the church on secular and political institutions in the Middle Ages.

Herrin, Judith. *The Formation of Christendom.* Princeton, NJ: Princeton University Press, 1987. This is a thoroughly researched resource on the first 1,500 years of church history. The maps and chronology included are especially helpful.

Ullmann, Walter. *The Growth of Papal Government in the Middle Ages: A Study in the Ideological Relation of Clerical to Lay Power.* 3rd ed. Cambridge: Cambridge University, 1970. This classic study of the bond between the papacy and ruling class is available through ACLS Humanities E-Books.

Volz, Carl A. *The Medieval Church: From the Dawn of the Middle Ages to the Eve of the Reformation.* Nashville: Abingdon Press, 1997. Volz's work covers developments in Christianity throughout the Middle Ages, with pertinent information on how church authority was interwoven with secular power.

World Wide Web

Feltoe, Charles Lett. *The Letters and Sermons of Leo the Great, Bishop of Rome.* http://www.ccel.org/ccel/schaff/npnf212.toc.html. Excerpts are also available at http://www.mb-soft.com/believe/txud/leo24.htm.

The Internet Sacred Text Archive. Translations of the writings of Popes Leo I and Gregory I. http://www.sacred-texts.com/chr/ecf/212/2120.001.htm.

The Medieval Sourcebook. http://www.fordham.edu/halsall/sbook.html. A number of church-related documents from the papacies of Leo and Gregory.

The ORB: Online Reference Book for Medieval Studies. http://the-orb.net. Articles and links to a variety of early medieval resources.

"The Letter of Pope Leo to Flavian, Bishop of Constantinople, about Eutyches: Commonly known as the 'Tome of Leo.'" http://www.crossroadsinitiative. com/library_article/526/Tome_of_Leo_St._Leo_the_Great.html. This letter led to the Council of Chalcedon formulating the doctrine of the dual nature of Christ. The site also includes other translations of the works of Leo.

Multimedia Sources

Early Church Fathers. 2007. Logos Bible Software. CD-ROM. Charles Scribner's Sons published 38 volumes of writings by the early church fathers in 1900. Now on CD, the set includes works by Leo I, Augustine, Ignatius, and many others.

Popes and the Papacy: A History. 2006. DVD. The Teaching Company. A series of thirty-minute lectures by Thomas F. X. Noble on various aspects of the papacy.

Saints and Sinners: The History of the Popes. 1997. DVD. The History Channel. 50 minutes each. Six-part television series investigates the lives of church leaders and the dilemmas they faced. Based on the book with the same title by Eamon Duffy, published by Yale University Press.

Sign of the Pagan. 1954. DVD. Universal International Pictures. 92 minutes. Movie production directed by Douglas Sirk. A fictional account of the meeting between Attila and Pope Leo I.

3. Anglo-Saxon Conquest of England (c. 449)

The lasting influence of obscure Germanic tribes on English culture has led to the term *Anglo-Saxon* being used almost synonymously with *British*. The people we now call Anglo-Saxons, however, did not identify themselves as such; it was only after the Norman Conquest that the term began to be used for the conquered English.

When Rome conquered most of Great Britain in 43, Celtic inhabitants were either driven into the northern and western highlands or enslaved to work in Roman cities and villas. In the late fourth century, Rome began withdrawing its legions from Britain because they were needed to defend continental lands and the imperial city itself, leaving Britain without protection. Verdant forests, fertile crop land, coasts with abundant marine life, and rich mineral deposits attracted invaders to this vulnerable island. Chief among numerous raiders were three Germanic tribes: the Angles, Saxons, and Jutes.

Although corroborating evidence is ambiguous, the *Anglo-Saxon Chronicles* report that in 449, King Vortigen of the Britons invited the Saxon leaders Hengest and Horsa to Britain to help him fight against the Picts. Afterwards, they returned to their homeland and brought tribe members to settle in England. The Anglo-Saxons settled among the native Celts in the areas that became modern-day Scotland, Wales, and Cornwall. The Celtic populations kept their native languages, which eventually developed into the Gaelic and Cymric languages still spoken today.

The early Anglo-Saxons were warlike people living in tribes led by an elected chieftain. They brought with them their Scandinavian gods, a legal system based on vengeance, an established *wergild* or "man-price" based on social standing, a well-established oral literary tradition, and a respect for the legal status of women. By the late seventh century, the tribes had settled into a more stable but stratified society of villages, and they recognized the hereditary rights of kings.

TERM PAPER SUGGESTIONS

1. The early Middle Ages saw large urban centers decline and be replaced by a decentralized, rural society. Describe how this change is reflected in the government, economy, and institutions of Anglo-Saxon England.

2. Compare and contrast Celtic Christianity with the Roman Christianity that Augustine brought to the British Isles in 597.

3. What role did women have in the social and political life of Anglo-Saxon England? What was the extent of their power? The limits of their power? What rights did they possess?

4. The *scop (skop)* or gleeman was more than a simple poet in Anglo-Saxon society. Research the roles and responsibilities of the *scop*. How do you account for the honor accorded a man of words in a society that set such a high premium on warfare? Cite examples from the literature to support your conclusions.

5. Research the law codes of Anglo-Saxon England prior to King Alfred. What do they reveal about the social structure of the culture and the nature of royal power?

6. Explain the importance of the development of the *bretwalda*, or overlord, in the political system of Anglo-Saxon England.

7. In what ways did the Anglo-Saxons establish the basis for modern English political and social structures?

8. By all accounts, early Anglo-Saxon society was filled with violence. What were the forms of this violence? What social and cultural functions did the violence serve?

ALTERNATIVE TERM PAPER SUGGESTIONS

1. Using images of Anglo-Saxon artifacts, such as those discovered in the Sutton-Hoo burial ship, create a visual argument proving that the English people of the fifth through eighth centuries were skilled artisans.

2. Prior to the Norman Invasion in 1066, Great Britain had already been conquered by the Celts, the Romans, and the Anglo-Saxons. Study place names on the island and create maps detailing the influence of each of these groups based on the place names.

3. A number of archeological sites have provided information about the Anglo-Saxon culture. Historic reconstructions of buildings and entire villages share much of that knowledge with the general public. Visit Web sites of both the digs and the reconstructions and consult reference materials to prepare a multimedia presentation about the culture.

Primary Sources

The Anglo-Saxon Chronicles. A number of modern English translations of these early records of English history are available in print. A Web-based reproduction is available at http://omacl.org/Anglo/. The text was originally produced under orders from Alfred the Great around 890. Additions were made at various locations throughout England until about the time of the Norman invasion.

Bede. *Ecclesiastical History of the English Church and People.* Written in 731, this Latin work provides our best source of information on Anglo-Saxon England. English translations are readily available. Bede, a monk at Jarrow, is considered the "father of English history."

Nennius. *History of the Britons.* Trans. J. A. Giles. Whitefish, MT: Kessinger Publishing, 2003. Nennius was a monk and historian in eighth-century Wales who provides much of our early information about King Arthur. This is a reprint of Giles's 1948 translation of his work.

Winterbottom, M., ed. *Arthurian Period Sources: Gildas: The Ruin of Britain and Other Documents.* London: Phillimore & Company, 1980. This includes translations of Gildas' and other contemporary British documents. Monk and saint, Gildas wrote sermons that give insight into the life of sixth-century Britain.

Secondary Sources

Blair, Peter Hunter. *Roman Britain and Early England 55 B. C. to A. D. 871.* New York: W.W. Norton and Company, 1966. Chapter 13, "The Nature of Early Anglo-Saxon Society," provides a helpful overview of the culture after the tribes settled in England.

Blair, Peter Hunter, and Keynes, Simon. *An Introduction to Anglo-Saxon England.* 3rd ed. Cambridge: Cambridge University Press, 2003. After two chapters on the history of the age, Blair devotes the remaining chapters to social institutions: the church, the economy, the government, and letters.

Campbell, James, John, Eric, and Wormald, Patrick. *The Anglo-Saxons.* New York: Penguin, 1991. Ten chapters, each by one of the three authors, cover Britain from the end of the Roman occupation to the Battle of Hastings.

Charles-Edwards, Thomas, and Langford, Paul. *After Rome (Short Oxford History of the British Isles).* Oxford: Oxford University Press, 2003. This book focuses on England and Ireland from the withdrawal of the Romans to the Viking invasions of the late eighth century. Political, religious, and cultural developments are analyzed.

Hindley, Geoffrey. *A Brief History of the Anglo-Saxons: The Beginnings of the English Nation.* Philadelphia: Running Press, 2006. Hindley focuses on the influences of the Germanic invaders on the English character and nation.

Stenton, Frank M. *Anglo-Saxon England (Oxford History of England).* Oxford: Oxford University Press, 2001. This reissue of Stenton's original 1943 work offers over 600 pages of comprehensive history of the period. The author draws heavily on primary sources and early historians.

Trupp, John. *The Anglo-Saxon Home: A History of the Domestic Institutions and Customs of England, from the Fifth to the 11th Century.* New York: Adamant Media, 2005. A facsimile reprint of the 1862 classic study of Anglo-Saxon domestic life. It begins with an extensive chapter on "The Wife" and her rights and responsibilities.

World Wide Web

Ages of English Timeline. Interactive resource produced by BBC that provides a number of links to resources and games. It has audio links to language recordings and an audio story of the English language. http://www .bbc.co.uk/history/british/launch_tl_ages_english.shtml.

The Avalon Project: Documents in Law, History, and Diplomacy. http://avalon .law.yale.edu/medieval/saxlaw.asp. Yale Law School provides translations of many historic documents, including *The Anglo-Saxon Chronicles,* excerpts from laws from the Anglo-Saxon period, and *History of the Britons (Historia Brittonum)* by Roman historian Nennius.

Early Manuscripts at Oxford University. http://image.ox.ac.uk/. Contains digital reproductions of more than 80 early manuscripts in Latin and Old English, housed in various colleges at Oxford. The texts are interesting to look through.

Regia Anglorum. http://www.regia.org/main.htm. Regia Anglorum is a society that attempts to preserve the history of Anglo-Saxon, Viking, and Norman Britain through reenactments and living history presentations. Their Web site offers articles on many subjects related to Anglo-Saxon England.

Multimedia Sources

Dark Age England. Vol. 3 in *Histories Ancient Legacies.* 2001. DVD Set. Produced by PBS. Deals with legends and facts from the end of Roman domination until about 1000. Shows that Anglo-Saxon England was a time of great political, social, and artistic development.

The End of Rome, the Birth of Europe. 2002. DVD. Films Media Group. 52 minutes. Part of the video series *The Wandering Tribes of Europe,* this video covers sixth-century kingdoms of the Ostrogoths, the Merovingians, and the Anglo-Saxons.

A History of Britain. 2001. A five-volume set of DVDs from PBS. Covers British history from pre-historic times to the 20th century. Hosted by historian Simon Schama.

Life in Anglo-Saxon Times. 2006. DVD. Kultur Video. Fifty-minute video featuring reenactments of life in an Anglo-Saxon village.

4. Developments in Arms and Warfare (450–1450)

Constant warfare, from short-lived skirmishes between neighboring lords to international conflicts persisting for decades, characterized the Middle Ages. Economic gains in war could be substantial, but so could the costs, especially for the lower classes. Historians lament the terrible costs of war to the peasantry, but recognize it was inevitable because of nobles who continually sought land, riches, and power.

In the mid-fifth century, the large professional armies of the Roman Empire suffered under the attacks of the less-organized barbarian infantry and mounted cavalry. From that time on, there was an increasing militarization of medieval culture. Germanic tribes that settled in former Roman territories generally treated all free men as equals, with an equal obligation to perform military service. Since the safety of one's person and property was continually under threat, men had to always be prepared to fight. Technological advances in weapons and improved military strategies made warfare more deadly and more costly. Swords, lances, and later, armor and horses were out of the reach of commoners, so professional armies of knights evolved. To effectively defend against attack, lords built well-fortified structures and kept them manned. Originally little more than wooden poles enclosing the lord's home and valuables, these structures soon developed into medieval castles.

Thick stone walls, drawbridges, moats, and towers made breaches of the castle difficult, so the use of sieges increased. Additional advances in weaponry provided offensive tools such as the trebuchet, mangonel, siege tower, and ballista. Similar tools were used throughout the medieval world, especially during the Crusades. Fighting on the field also continued throughout the Middle Ages with weapons such as swords, axes, polearms, crossbows, and the long bow, which was first used effectively during the Hundred Years War.

Wars led to innovations in weaponry, to the reshaping of power and authority, and to changes in the control of kingdoms. Fighting also resulted in shifting loyalties and, eventually, in the development of a sense of nationalism in many lands.

TERM PAPER SUGGESTIONS

1. Choose one of the major weapons developed during the Middle Ages and discuss the changes it brought about in the nature of battle.

2. Explain the different functions of soldiers, such as infantryman, archers, and cavalry, in battles taking place around 1000.

3. Analyze the conditions, decisions, and outcomes of a major battle of the medieval period. What would have been necessary for the results to have been different?

4. Using primary resources and literature from the Middle Ages, discuss the ethos of the warrior and its influence on the entire culture.

5. Research the role of naval power in the Middle Ages.

6. Many soldiers during the Middle Ages were fighting out of loyalty to their lord, their country, or their God. However, mercenary soldiers were common. Research the influences of these soldiers for hire.

7. Research the role of the mounted soldier in medieval warfare.

8. What role did women play in medieval armies and warfare?

9. Compare Japanese military organization and strategies with those of the Western military in the Middle Ages.

ALTERNATIVE TERM PAPER SUGGESTIONS

1. Create working models of one or more medieval weapons and demonstrate the uses.

2. Construct a model of a medieval castle showing its strategies for defense.

3. Create a multimedia presentation showing the development of medieval weapons.

4. Write a series of letters between one of the foot soldiers and the woman who stayed home waiting for him to return. Choose a specific battle or campaign, and include details of the fighting, and in the other letters include details of the life at home. Remember that the Middle Ages covers about 1,000 years. Choose authentic details from the time you select.

Primary Sources

Bruno of Merseburg. *The Saxon War.* Translation of excerpts by the School of History at Leeds University. http://www.leeds.ac.uk/history/weblearning/MedievalHistoryTextCentre/medievalTexts.htm.

Episodes of Medieval Warfare from the History of the Franks by Gregory of Tours. Translation by O.M. Dalton. Oxford, 1927. http://www.deremilitari.org/resources/sources/tours.htm.

The Siege of Amida in 502, According to Pseudo-Joshua the Stylite. Translation by William Wright. Cambridge, 1882. http://www.deremilitari.org/resources/ sources/pseudojoshua.htm.

The Siege of Tarsos in 965, According to Leo the Deacon. Translation by Alice-Mary Talbot and Denis F. Sullivan. Washington, DC, 2005. http://www .deremilitari.org/resources/sources/leodeacon.htm.

Secondary Sources

Contamine, Phillipe. *War in the Middle Ages.* Oxford: Blackwell Publishers Ltd.,1984. Background on the place of war in the early, middle, and high Middle Ages. One chapter in the Perspectives section discusses the judicial, ethical and religious aspects of war. Extensive bibliography provided.

Dahmus, Joseph Henry. *Seven Decisive Battles of the Middle Ages.* Chicago: Nelson-Hall, 1983. Describes seven battles and their importance, including Crecy and Hastings.

Davidson, Hilda Ellis. *The Sword in Anglo-Saxon England: Its Archaeology and Literature.* Woodbridge, UK: Boydell Press, 1998. Davidson devotes the first half of her book to the information gained from swords found in burial mounds and bogs and the second half to literary information regarding Anglo-Saxon swords.

DeVries, Kelly. *Infantry Warfare in the Early 14th Century: Discipline, Tactics, and Technology.* Woodbridge, UK: Boydell, 1996. Detailed descriptions of the tactics involved in fourteen major battles of the Hundred Years War.

DeVries, Kelly. *Medieval Military Technology.* London: Broadview Press, 1992. This volume contains a comprehensive survey of the technology of warfare.

France, John. *Western Warfare in the Age of the Crusades, 1000–1300.* Ithaca: Cornell University Press, 1999. Covers battles, technology, tactics, and armies involved in the Crusades.

Friday, Karl F. *Samurai, Warfare and the State in Early Medieval Japan.* London: Routledge, 2004. Makes extensive use of primary resources to discuss the meaning, organization, tools, science, and culture of Japanese warfare.

Haldon, John. *Warfare, State, and Society in the Byzantine World, 565–1204.* London: Routledge, 1999. Haldon looks at topics such as the Byzantine attitude toward war and the organization of the army. Contains appendices with helpful information about the actual operation of campaigns.

Holmes, George. *The Oxford History of Medieval Europe.* Oxford: Oxford University Press, 1988. A comprehensive history of the age, the book provides maps, a detailed bibliography, and a useful chronology.

Kagay, Donald J., and Villalon, L.J. Andrew, eds. *The Circle of War in the Middle Ages: Essays on Medieval Military and Naval History.* Woodbrigde, UK: Boydell Press, 1999. Collections of essays from scholars on many aspects of medieval war.

Keen, Maurice, ed. *Medieval Warfare: A History.* Oxford: Oxford University Press, 1999. Fourteen essays by leading researchers on all aspects of medieval warfare, from the Carolingians to the introduction of gunpowder.

Nicholle, David, and Thompson, Sam. *Medieval Siege Weapons (1): Western Europe AD 585–1385.* (2): *Byzantium, the Islamic World & India AD 476–1526.* Wellsborough, UK: Osprey Publishing Ltd., 2002. This two-book series is heavily illustrated and thorough in its explanation of the mechanics of medieval weapons.

Nicholson, Helen J. *Medieval Warfare: Theory and Practice of War in Europe, 300–1500.* New York: Palgrave Macmillan, 2004. Thorough presentation of medieval war, including military theory and land and naval tactics.

Nossov, Konstantin. *Ancient and Medieval Siege Weapons: A Fully Illustrated Guide to Siege Weapons and Tactics.* London: The Lyons Press, 2005. Includes three sections: the history of siege warfare, siege weapons, and methods of attack and defense, along with extensive appendices and a glossary. Black and white illustrations are numerous.

Oakeshott, Ewart. *Records of the Medieval Sword.* London: Boydell Press, 2007. Filled with photographs, this book provides an extensive history of the development of swords in the Middle Ages.

Santosuosso, Antonio. *Barbarians, Marauders, and Infidels: The Ways of Medieval Warfare.* Boulder, CO: Westview Press, 2004. Eighteen chapters on all aspects of fighting in the Middle Ages, including women at war and "How to Conquer a Castle."

World Wide Web

Blumenburg Associates: Purveyors of Rare Historic Images to the Publishing Trades. http://www.ahrtp.com/MedievalWarfareOnLine/medievalwarvideos1.htm. This site has a large number of short video segments and discussions of medieval weaponry.

De Re Militari: The Society for Medieval Military History. http://www.deremilitari.org/. Maintained by an international association of scholars, the site offers articles on many aspects of medieval warfare, links to other sites, a bibliography, and book reviews.

Middle Ages. http://www.middle-ages.org.uk/index.htm. This site has a number of advertisers and doesn't reveal the author(s), but the information on many topics, including weapons and warfare, seems to be accurate.

Regia Anglorum. http://www.regia.org/main.htm. Regia Anglorum is a society that attempts to preserve the history of Anglo-Saxon, Viking, and Norman Britain through reenactments and living history presentations. Their Web site offers a great deal of information on war and weapons.

Société de l'Oriflamme. 2005. http://xenophongroup.com/montjoie/oriflam.htm. This site, devoted to medieval warfare, provides links to many other sites and articles on the subject.

Multimedia Sources

Braveheart. 1996 . Paramount Pictures. Commercial film. Directed by Mel Gibson. Based on the historic Scotsman William Wallace, the movie takes liberty with historic facts, but the fighting and weapons are quite realistic.

Horsepower: Harnessed for War. 2009. DVD. Insight Media. 54 minutes. Examines the ways horses have been used in battle and their influence on the nature of warfare; includes the use of horses by Japanese Samurai, Roman soldiers, Huns, knights, and Mongols.

Medieval Siege. 2000. NOVA. 60 minutes. Examines warfare in medieval Britain by visiting many actual sites and examining the weapons used in siege warfare. Special attention is given the trebuchet, both its construction and its effects in battle.

Medieval Warfare. 2001. Kultur Films. 50 minutes, each program. Three-volume set that uses reenactments, maps, art work, and weapons to discuss several major battles of the Middle Ages.

Secrets of the Samurai. 2000. Disney Channel. 50 minutes. Views the Samurai from military and personal standpoints. Includes a segment on the metallurgy and production of Samurai swords.

5. Merovingian Dynasty Begins (480)

By the time Clovis I ascended to the Frankish throne in 480, the Franks had conquered most of Gaul and proceeded to unite the people into the nation that became medieval France, the first major political authority established after the fall of Rome. Remnants of Roman rule continued to persist in Gaul for some time after the collapse of the Empire, even after invasions by the Visigoths, who seemed for a time the most powerful force in Europe. Although they were barbarians, the Visigoths admired Roman skill in administration and taxation and kept much of the infrastructure intact in conquered territory. However, they were not able to conquer all of Gaul, in part because of defenses mounted by the Gallo-Roman Syagrius, who received aid from the Salian Franks. The last Visigoth kings, Euric and his son Alaric, might have been able to finish the conquest of Gaul, except for their persecution of the Roman Catholic population. As Arians, they were never able to establish a political base among the people of Gaul.

Little is known with certainty about the origins of the Franks. Gregory of Tours, relying on the resources of his times, writes that the founder of the Franks was Chlodio, and the poet Sidonius Apollinaria tells of Chlodio's attempt to capture territory in Artois around 431. Chlodio was succeeded by Merovech, who was considered the founder of the Merovingian family. When Clotilde (r. 460–481) became king of northern Frankish Gaul, he maintained good relationships with the remaining Gallo-Romans, Christians, and Frankish leaders in other parts of Gaul. In 481, Clotilde's son Clovis inherited the throne and set about establishing himself as ruler of adjacent Frankish kingdoms. His power increased around 496 when he converted to Christianity and won the support of the Church. Clovis mounted a campaign against and defeated the Visigoths in 507. As a result, Clovis received the title Augustus from the Byzantine Emperor Anastasius I (r. 430–518) and was recognized as the ruler of all Gaul. Clovis established the capital of his kingdom in Paris.

Following the Germanic custom, the kingdom was divided among Clovis's four sons at his death, then was reunited and divided at various times until the end of the Merovingian dynasty around 751. In spite of these divisions, Clovis's legacy was to unify a large area of Europe under a leadership with similar beliefs and policies. By the mid-eighth century, however, King Childeric III had become no more than a figurehead. He renounced his throne and retired to a monastery, allowing Pepin the Short to become king, thus ending the Merovingian dynasty.

TERM PAPER SUGGESTIONS

1. Discuss the social and political forces during Merovingian rule that encouraged the development of the European feudal system.
2. Discuss the rights of women in Merovingian France. How much direct responsibility for a decline in the status of women did the church bear?
3. Research the various means by which Clovis I was able to unite the diverse tribes in control of areas of Gaul.

4. Both Emperor Constantine I (r. 306–337) and King Clovis were converts to Christianity. Were their motives purely religious? How did the conversions affect the kingdoms they ruled?

5. One of the achievements of Clovis was the codification of law in the *Lex Salica* (Salian Laws; http://www.shsu.edu/~his_ncp/371eq.html). Research this document and its influence on the laws of the Holy Roman Empire.

6. Trace the development of French nationalism from the reign of Clovis to the 14th century.

ALTERNATIVE TERM PAPER SUGGESTIONS

1. Between 480 and 751, the various kingdoms and territories within Gaul and parts of Germany were united, divided, and reunited under a number of leaders. Create a PowerPoint presentation showing how these kingdoms were configured during those years.

2. Clovis I was converted to Christianity around 496. Some historians credit his Christian wife Clotilde with influencing his decision. Others point to political reasons for his making this choice. Create a dramatic monologue for presentation to the class in which Clovis discusses his reasons for and against changing his religion. Or create a dialogue between Clovis and Clotilde concerning his conversion.

Primary Sources

"The Conversion of Clovis: Two Accounts, 496." http://www.fordham.edu/halsall/source/496clovis.html. Two contemporary descriptions of the conversion of Clovis, one from Gregory of Tours, the other by St. Denis.

Gregory of Tours. *History of the Franks: Books I–X*. Trans. O. M. Dalton. (2 vols.) 1927. Oxford: Clarendon Press. A well-respected translation that includes extensive commentary and criticism in the Introduction.

"The Law of the Salian Franks." http://www.fordham.edu/halsall/source/salic-law.html. Excerpts from the collection of laws by Clovis.

Secondary Sources

Bachrach, Bernard S. *Merovingian Military Organization, 481–751*. Minneapolis: University of Minnesota, 1972. Traces the military operations of Merovingian rulers from Clovis I to the Mayors of the Palace.

Bury, J. B. *The Invasion of Europe by the Barbarians*. New York: W.W. Norton & Company, 2000. Reprint of 1967 publication. Lectures XII and XIII concern the Merovingian Dynasty and the rule of Clovis.

Geary, Patrick J. *Before France and Germany: The Creation and Transformation of the Merovingian World.* Oxford: Oxford University Press, 1988. Chapter 3 concerns Clovis and the creation of the Merovingian empire, and chapter 7 is a thorough discussion of the influences of Frankish culture.

James, Edward. *The Origins of France: From Clovis to the Capetians, 500–1000.* London: Palgrave Macmillan, 1982. James devotes the first half of the book to the political and social institutions of sixth-century Gaul, including the reign of Clovis I and the Merovingians.

Santosuosso, Antonio. *Barbarians, Marauders, and Infidels: The Ways of Medieval Warfare.* Boulder, CO: Westview Press, 2004. Chapter 4 deals with the emergence of the nation of France under the Frankish kingdom.

Wood, Ian. *The Merovingian Kingdoms 450–751.* Harlow, UK: Pearson, 1994. Extensive history of the entire Merovingian dynasty, from the invasions of Roman territory to its replacement by the Carolingians. Includes discussions of church relations, the development of laws, and civil wars that threatened the kingdom.

World Wide Web

Nelson, Lynn H. "Lectures for a Medieval Survey: The Rise of the Franks." (1999). http://www.the-orb.net/textbooks/nelson/franks_rise.html.

Medieval Sourcebook: Early Germanic States. http://www.fordham.edu/halsall/ sbook1f.html#Non-Christian%20Germans. This section of the Sourcebook contains a variety of primary and secondary resources on the Merovingian Franks.

Order of the Merovingian Dynasty. http://www.merovingiandynasty.com. Maintained by a group of private individuals who are interested in the history of the Frankish kings and their genealogy. In addition to historical information, the site provides images of a number of artifacts from the period.

Multimedia Sources

Barbarians. 2006. DVD. The History Channel. 100 minutes. Second DVD in series uses reenactments, footage of historic sites, narration, and interviews with experts to detail the lives of the barbarian invaders of Europe, including the Franks. A number of short clips from the programs are available at http://www.history.com/media.do?action=clip&id.

The End of Rome, the Birth of Europe. 2002. DVD. Films Media Group. 52 minutes. Part of the video series *The Wandering Tribes of Europe,* this video covers sixth-century kingdoms of the Ostrogoths, the Merovingians, and the Anglo-Saxons.

6. Agricultural Development (500–1200)

Throughout the medieval period, agriculture remained the principle occupation, with as much as 80 percent of the population directly involved in food production. Farming was also the primary source of wealth, and excess crops were always in demand.

With the fall of the Roman Empire, an orderly system of agricultural production ended. Instead of farming well-managed villas with irrigation, field rotation, and crop variety, the more nomadic invaders used the slash-and-burn method of clearing crop land. In an age when land was plentiful and population was sparse, barbarian tribes were easily able to move when land was too exhausted to produce food.

As medieval people became more settled and the population grew, farmers developed different techniques of farming and new tools, such as the wheeled plow and horse harnesses. When settled villages became the norm, the surrounding lands were held in common. In addition to a small garden plot attached to their hut, each family was allotted a certain amount of land on which to grow grain, the main staple of the diet. Planting was a cooperative effort, since a single villager could not afford a plow and oxen.

At first, villages practiced the two-field system, allowing one-half of the land to lie fallow each year. Vassal lords demanded portions of each crop in return for protection of the villages. When the farmers could not meet their payments, they often adopted the three-field system, leaving only one-third of the land fallow each year, which allowed for increased production, but also depleted the land more quickly. The burden of payments to lords, less fertile land, and fluctuating climate conditions caused widespread hunger for much of the medieval period, especially during late winter and early spring.

By the 13th century, the feudal system was firmly established in much of Europe, and the villagers had become serfs instead of the free land holders.

TERM PAPER SUGGESTIONS

1. The availability of arable land is necessary for adequate food production. Examine the patterns of fertile farmland in a territory or country of Europe during the Middle Ages, and discuss how the pattern influenced social and cultural developments in that area.

2. How did the change from the village agricultural system to the feudal system affect agricultural production and development? Was the feudal system a positive or negative development for agriculture?

3. Discuss the way villages of the early Middle Ages operated an autarkic (self-sufficient, independent) economy. What developments led to the change to a market economy?

4. Research the agricultural production patterns of the sixth through 11th centuries. What were the reasons for increases and decreases in the food supply? How did these increases and decreases affect the population?

5. Choose one or more technological advances in agricultural methods between the sixth and 14th centuries and discuss the ways in which the technology influenced farming.

ALTERNATIVE TERM PAPER SUGGESTIONS

1. Create a model of an early medieval farming village showing how the houses and buildings were grouped and how the fields were utilized. Indicate crops that were produced, appropriate for the area of Europe you choose.

2. Create a model of a typical feudal manor showing the manor house, the homes of serfs, and how the land was utilized. Indicate the crops that were produced in the area of Europe you choose.

3. Describe a typical diet of the farmer during the early Middle Ages. How does the diet change during the high Middle Ages? How does the farmer's diet compare to a nobleman's during the latter period? Plan weekly diets for the nobility, the clergy, and the peasants during the high Middle Ages.

Primary Sources

British History Online. http://www.british-history.ac.uk/catalogue.aspx. A repository of many primary and secondary documents, including manorial records. Most are from the Renaissance and later, but some medieval documents are accessible.

The Medieval Sourcebook. http://www.fordham.edu/halsall/sbook1j.html. The section entitled "Economic Life" has many primary documents concerning agriculture.

Secondary Sources

Adamson, Melitta Weiss. *Food in Medieval Times.* Westport, CT: Greenwood Press, 2008. Provides a detailed account of foodstuffs, cooking, regional cuisines, eating, drinking, celebrations, and health and diet restrictions, with recipes and menus. Different classes of people are considered.

Astill, Grenville, and Langdon, John. eds. *Medieval Farming and Technology: The Impact of Agricultural Change in Northwest Europe.* The Netherlands: Brill, 1997. Incorporates information derived from recent archeology as well as primary sources.

Campbell, Bruce. "Economic rent and the intensification of English agriculture, 1086–1350." In *Medieval Farming and Technology: The Impact of Agricultural Change in Northwest Europe.* G. Astill and J. Langdon, eds. Leiden, The Netherlands: Brill, 1997, pp. 225–250.

Campbell, Bruce M. S. *English Seigniorial Agriculture, 1250–1450.* Cambridge: Cambridge University Press, 2000. This scholarly and comprehensive volume makes use of many primary sources in providing information about the types of tools used, the amount of land farmed, and the crops planted and their yields. Contains many tables, charts, and illustrations.

Claster, Jill. *The Medieval Experience: 300–1400.* New York: New York University Press, 1982. Intended as an introductory text for college students, this volume looks at economic factors, especially agriculture, in depth.

Duby, George. *Rural Economy and Country Life in the Medieval West.* Trans. Cynthia Postan. Philadelphia: University of Pennsylvania Press, 1998 (1968). Duby's landmark study of the complexities of agricultural development takes in all of Europe.

Dyer, Christopher. *An Age of Transition?: Economy and Society in England in the Later Middle Ages.* Oxford: Oxford University Press, 2005. Dyer covers many aspects of economic development in the Middle Ages, including agriculture.

Dyer, Christopher. *Making a Living in the Middle Ages: The People of Britain 850–1520.* New Haven: Yale University Press, 2002. Medieval scholar Dyer traces developments such as the growth of towns, feudalism, population expansion, and the spread of disease on economic expansion and decline.

Hamerow, Helena. *Early Medieval Settlements: The Archaeology of Rural Communities in North-West Europe 400–900.* Oxford: Oxford University Press, 2003. Contains two chapters dealing with agriculture: "Land and Power" and "The Forces of Production."

Le Goff, Jacques. *Medieval Civilization 400–1500.* Trans. Julia Barrow. London: Blackwell Publishing, 1991. Comprehensive overview of life in the Middle Ages by a renowned French scholar.

Lopez, Robert S. *The Commercial Revolution of the Middle Ages, 950–1350.* Lopez traces the development of agriculture and ties its progress to the commercial and trade advances of the later Middle Ages.

Postan, M. M., ed. *The Cambridge Economic History of Europe from the Decline of the Roman Empire: Volume 1, Agrarian Life of the Middle Ages*. Cambridge: Cambridge University Press, 1966. This classic study in agricultural history contains chapters by experts on various areas of Europe from Scandinavia to the Mediterranean. Postan contributed the chapter on English agriculture.

Postan, M. M. *Essays on Medieval Agriculture and General Problems of the Medieval Economy*. Cambridge: Cambridge University Press, 2008. A collection of 22 essays published over five decades by medieval scholar Postan.

Price, T. Douglas, ed. *Europe's First Farmers*. Cambridge: Cambridge University Press, 2000. Although the ten chapters in this volume concern premedieval times, they contain useful background information for the study of the age that followed.

Stone, David. *Decision-Making in Medieval Agriculture*. Oxford: Oxford University Press, 2005. Using primary sources such as account rolls, Stone reconstructs the world of the farmer in the Middle Ages.

Sweeney, Del. *Agriculture in the Middle Ages: Technology, Practice, and Representation*. Philadelphia: University of Pennsylvania Press, 1995. One of the most thorough resources on agriculture available.

World Wide Web

Castle Learning Center: Medieval Tools. http://www.castles-of-britain.com/castlezc.htm. Lists medieval tools and their uses for agriculture and other purposes.

E-Museum at Minnesota State University. http://www.mnsu.edu/emuseum/history/. This site has brief, informative articles, images, and links to other resources.

Medieval Technology Pages. http://scholar.chem.nyu.edu/tekpages/Technology.html. Contains descriptions and images of agricultural tools.

Virtual Museum of the Strong Collection. http://talbotsfineaccessories.com/cgi-bin/Strong_Collection.cgi. A searchable collection of images from the collection of Doug and Amy Strong that concentrates on objects from the Middle Ages.

Multimedia Resources

The Medieval Plough. 1973. DVD. University of Toronto: Information Commons. 19 minutes. Using drawings, diagrams, and selections from medieval art, this short film examines the importance of the heavy-wheeled plow in agricultural production.

Medieval Times: Life in the Middle Ages (1000–1450 A.D.). 1992. Streaming
video. 28 minutes. Discovery Education. United Streaming. Contains
segments about life in a medieval village, feudalism, and serfs.

Tools in Medieval Life. 1981. Video. Centre for Medieval Studies, University of
Toronto. 30-minute video exploring how new tools changed agriculture
and manufacturing.

7. Battles of Mt. Badon (516) and Camlan (537)

During the years immediately following Rome's withdrawal from Britain,
the island attracted many invaders looking, first, for easy plunder and, later,
for good land on which to settle. More and more, the native Celts were in
danger of losing their property or their lives. One-hundred years had passed
since the Romans left, and Britain was struggling to keep from being swal-
lowed up by Germanic tribes and losing their traditions and way of life.
From among the ranks of the Celts arose a powerful leader who united
many of the Celtic tribes. This leader was able to lead his army to defeat the
Germanic troops at the Battle of Mt. Badon in 516. The sixth-century historian Gildas identified him as Ambrosius Aurelianus in Latin, and he may
have been the foundation of legendary "King Arthur."

The victory at Mt. Badon energized the Celts, and they continued to
fight against the Saxons for two decades. Gildas reported that Ambrosius
was killed in this battle, along with many of his best soldiers. The later
defeat at Camlan effectively brought an end to organized Celtic opposition to the Saxons. But the stories of Ambrosius/Arthur did not end.
Since these two events were recorded by Gildas, hundreds of writers have
found the story of Arthur fascinating, as have their audiences. Throughout the history of England, Arthur has been considered the consummate
English king. His life and legend have been retold time and time again,
each time with more and different details added, but always reflecting the
best qualities in man. Beyond developing an ideal for kingship, the
Arthurian legend influenced medieval thought about romantic love, personal freedom, and about the individual's desire to achieve self-fulfill-
ment, even in a hierarchal society that valued power and tradition.

The Arthurian legend grew to encompass not only his immediate companions, but also a long list of characters, who are often connected to
Camelot. These stories are largely responsible for the concept of the ideal

knight who lives by the code of chivalry that so influences the high Middle Ages and the Crusades. Symbols developed within the legends have become part of the Western tradition in literature, history, and art. It is for this reason that King Arthur and the major battles in which he fought are a significant part of any study of the period, whether one accepts his actual existence or not.

TERM PAPER SUGGESTIONS

1. Discuss the juxtaposition of the pagan and Christian in the stories of Arthur. How does the myth relate to the reality of sixth-century England?

2. In what ways does the Arthurian legend challenge the social and religious hierarchy of the Middle Ages?

3. Consider the various representations of Arthur in literature and history. Discuss whether he embodies the ideals of his own time (if he did exist) or of a later time.

4. What was the importance of the Battle of Mt. Badon, the Battle of Camlan, and King Arthur in the British resistance to invasions and settlement by Germanic tribes?

5. Some literary critics consider the Arthur legends are romance literature. Research the characteristics of romance literature and make a case for or against the Arthur legends as romances.

6. Camelot has often been held up as an ideal place. Consider Camelot as utopia. As presented in literature about King Arthur, was it ideal?

7. How could the Arthurian legends be said to have both increased the status of women and to have justified the double-standard of differing, acceptable sexual behaviors for men and women?

8. Historians are interested in factual information, yet many early records are laced with legend and myth. Research the difficulties and methods historians use to extract truth from these early written records and oral traditions.

9. Why, after 1,500 years, do we continue to read the stories about an obscure Celtic warrior? Why do stories about Arthur and the Knights of the Round Table continue to be written or produced? What do these stories tell us about ourselves?

10. Assume King Arthur died at the Battle of Camlan. In what ways did his death affect the Britain he ruled? What has been the significance of his death on later generations?

11. Choose two versions of the same part of the Arthur legend and compare them. Why do you think the authors chose to present the story as they did? What purposes did they have in retelling the story, and how did they achieve these purposes?

ALTERNATIVE TERM PAPER SUGGESTIONS

1. The Arthurian legend has inspired artists as well as writers. Create a multimedia presentation showing how artistic representations of the King Arthur stories have evolved. Include references from writers of the same time period as the art.

2. Working with other students in your class, prepare a formal debate in which you argue for or against the historicity of Arthur.

3. Using literature about Arthur, information about medieval castles, and information gathered by archeological researchers, create an image or model of Camelot as it may have been. Use quotations from these resources to support the details you include. For example, Camelot is sometimes referred to as "many towered." If you make your castle/city with many towers, find a quotation that you can cite as support for these.

Primary Sources

Aneirin. *Y Gododdin.* http://www.britishhistoryclub.com/bhc/sources/aneirin/gododdin.html. Translation of a sixth-century Welsh poem that extols King Arthur's prowess in battle.

Annales Cambriae, 447–954. http://www.britishhistoryclub.com/bhc/sources/ac/a_c.html. One of the earliest Welsh histories, the *Annales* records the Battles of Mt. Badon and Camlan.

Gildas. *De Excidio Britanniae (On the Ruin of Britain).* Modern English translation. http://www.britishhistoryclub.com/bhc/sources/gildas_deb.html. Gildas wrote one of the earliest histories of Britain and mentions Arthur and the Battles of Mt. Badon and Camlan.

Nennius. *History of the Britons.* Trans. J. A. Giles. Whitefish, MT: Kessinger Publishing, 2003. This is a reprint of Giles's 1948 translation of Nennius' sixth century work.

Winterbottom, M., ed. *Arthurian Period Sources: Gildas: The Ruin of Britain and Other Documents.* London: Phillimore & Company, 1980. This book includes translations of Gildas and other sixth century British documents.

Secondary Sources

Ashe, Geoffrey. *The Discovery of King Arthur.* New York: Henry Holt and Company, 1985. Arthurian scholar Ashe follows threads of evidence back to the earliest mentions of Arthur and presents a case for the existence of a real person behind the legends.

Busby, Keith and Dalrymple, Roger. eds. *Arthurian Literature XIX: Comedy in Arthurian Literature.* Suffolk, UK: Boydell & Brewer, 2003. Fourteen essays by various Arthurian scholars concerning elements of humor found in various retellings.

Castleden, Rodney. *King Arthur: The Truth Behind the Legend.* New York: Routledge, 2000. Castleden examines historic and literary documents, archeological evidence, and resources about sixth-century Celtic life to find elements of truth amid the legend. Appendices, maps, diagrams, and illustrations are provided.

Ingham, Patricia Clare. *Sovereign Fantasies: Arthurian Romance and the Making of Britain.* Philadelphia: University of Pennsylvania Press, 2001. Looks at the influence of Arthurian literature on the British sense of nationalism.

Lupack, Alan. *The Oxford Guide to Arthurian Literature and Legend.* Oxford: Oxford University Press, 2005. Covers the legend from the earliest mentions of Arthur by Gildas and Bede through modern retellings. Also discusses stories related to Arthur and includes an extensive bibliography.

Markale, Jean. *King of the Celts: Arthurian Legends and Celtic Tradition.* Trans. by Christine Hauch. Rochester, VT: Inner Traditions, 1994. Examining the many legends of Arthur, Markale searches for the Celtic warrior-king that lies at the bottom and places him within the context of the society in which he may have lived.

Shichtman, Martin B. and Carley, James P. eds. *Culture and the King: The Social Implications of the Arthurian Legend.* Albany: State University of New York Press, 1994. Eighteen essays on issues with the Arthurian legends, from the validity of historic sources to a prediction for the future of writing about the Knights of the Round Table.

Snyder, Christopher. *The World of King Arthur.* London: Thames and Hudson, 2000. With more than 200 illustrations, this thoroughly researched volume presents Arthur as he has appeared in literature, history, and art for 1,500 years. Snyder also discusses recent archeological discoveries and the light they have shed on the legendary king.

White, Richard. *King Arthur: In Legend and History.* New York: Routledge, 1998. A thorough examination of histories and literary works from Gildas to the late Middle Ages. Includes a bibliography, a list for further reading, and a chronology of Arthurian texts.

World Wide Web

Arthurian Studies at *The Labyrinth.* http://labyrinth.georgetown.edu/. An extensive list of links to Arthurian Web resources.

The Camelot Project of the University of Rochester. http://www.lib.rochester.edu/camelot/cphome.stm. Provides Arthurian texts, a glossary of characters, links to scholarly texts and projects, and a searchable collection of digitized images by artists and illustrators.

The Great King Arthur Index. http://www.britishhistoryclub.com/bhc/arthur/arthurdex.html. Maintained by The British History Club, this site is so thorough that it is the best place to start research on Arthur.

King Arthur's Realm. http://geocities.com/westenskowdorf/arthur.html. An interactive site that allows linear or nonlinear exploration of stories and videos about the Arthur legend.

Multimedia Sources

Camelot. 1967. Warner Brothers/Seven Arts. Director, Joshua Logan. 179 minutes. Based on T. H. White's *The Once and Future King,* this musical was written for the stage and adapted to film.

Dark Age England. 2001. Vol. 3 in *History's Ancient Legacies* DVD Set. PBS. 50 minutes. Includes segments about King Arthur.

Excalibur. 1981. Orion Pictures. Director, John Boorman. DVD or videocassette. 140 minutes. Faithful retelling of Thomas Malory's *Le Morte de Arthur.* Rated R.

King Arthur. 2004. Touchstone Pictures. Director, Antoine Fugua.126 minutes. Ignores much of the traditional legend, but good to use in a comparison between older versions and a 21st century representation. The atmosphere created by on-location filming in parts of the British Isles is effective. Rated R, but a PG-13 version is available.

King Arthur: His Life and Legends. 2005. A&E Home Video. 50 minutes. Explores the facts and the fictions of the Arthurian legend.

King Arthur: The Truth Behind the Legend. 2004. Delta Entertainment. 90 minutes. Looks for the man who grew into the legend.

King Arthur's Britain. 2005. Acorn Media. 186 minutes. Three-part series hosted by archeologist Francis Pryor.

The Knights of Camelot. 2006. The History Channel. 60 minutes. Archeologists and historians travel through Britain tracing the development of the legend of Camelot.

Legend of King Arthur. 2006. Kultur Video. Approximately 180 minutes. Includes three videos exploring the Arthurian stories: King Arthur, Camelot, and Merlin.

The Mystery of King Arthur. DVD. 2004. The British History Club. Six 35-minute programs. Includes guest appearance by Arthurian scholar Geoffrey Ashe, and goes on location throughout Britain to explore the origin of and truth behind King Arthur.

Quest for King Arthur. 2008. The History Channel. 120 minutes. Historians and archeologists discuss the evidence about King Arthur's existence.

8. Justinian Attempts to Reunite Eastern and Western Roman Empires (527)

The area known as the Byzantine Empire was once part of the vast Roman Empire. In 364, the Emperor Jovian died suddenly and the general Valentinian was chosen to replace him. To better manage the extensive territory under his rule, the new emperor divided the kingdom into East and West and sent his brother Valens to rule the East. Valentinian chose Byzantium (later Constantinople and now Istanbul) as the second capital of the Empire. During the next 200 years, the Western Empire disintegrated under internal pressure and through attacks from barbarian tribes, but the Eastern Empire continued to develop, although along a different path.

The first notable Byzantine emperor was Justinian I (r. 527–565), who also made the last attempt to reunite the Eastern and Western Roman Empires. Justinian's totalitarian reign was marked by warfare, political upheaval, and theological disputes, but it also produced a monumental codification of Roman law *(Corpus Juris Civilis)* and the rebuilding of Constantinople.

The nephew and heir of the previous emperor, Justin I, Justinian had been educated in theology, science, military strategy, political science, architecture, and art. As emperor, he began extensive military campaigns under his generals Belisarius and Narses, regaining much of the former Roman Empire, including Italy and parts of Northern Africa and Spain. The expenses of war, along with the tribute he paid to Persia to maintain the "endless peace," and an extensive building program, continually placed the empire in financial difficulties. Justinian levied additional taxes, which contributed to the unrest that provoked the Nika Revolt of 532. When the emperor was ready to abandon the capital to a mob, his wife, Empress Theodora, a commoner Justinian had married when he was a very young man, convinced him that he should stay and deal with the revolt. He ordered Belisarius and Narses to attack the Hippodrome, where the opposition was gathered. More than 40,000 people were killed, but Justinian's power and his reputation for brutality were firmly established.

During the Nika Revolt, Constantinople's Hagia Sophia cathedral was destroyed. Justinian had already planned to rebuild the church, but the revolt gave him the opportunity to do so on an even grander scale. Work began only 45 days after the revolt was put down. The rebuilt church is considered the finest example of Byzantine architecture in existence.

Ironically, the emperor who tried to reunite the Roman Empire dispensed with Latin as the official language of government and commerce, thus driving another wedge between the Eastern and Western Empires.

The political division also intensified conflict over ecclesiastical authority between Rome and Constantinople, which was to last for centuries. Disagreements over theology led to a number of smaller schisms before the final and Great Schism of 1054. For 37 years, from 482 to 519, the churches were involved in a rift called the Acacian Schism. The major disagreement was between the orthodox belief that Christ was both divine and human and the Monophysite assertion that Christ's only nature was divine. Empress Theodora was a Monophysite, and Justinian was determined to reunite the two factions. One of the successes of his reign is that he brought a temporary halt to this disagreement.

The history of Justinian's reign was recorded in detail by the writer Procopius. There is some doubt about the accuracy of Procopius' works, particularly his *Secret History*, but they remain as important resources in the study of the golden age of Byzantine. Justinian died in November 656 and was succeeded by his nephew Justin II, to whom he left a complex, but vital empire.

TERM PAPER SUGGESTIONS

1. During the century following Justinian's death, the Byzantine Empire experienced great difficulties. To what extent do you attribute these difficulties to Justinian's policies and actions?

2. Justinian's codification of the laws *Corpus Juris Civilis* (Codex) became the foundation of law in the Western world. What were Justinian's purposes for commissioning this work? What is the relationship of the *Codex* to Justinian's desire to reunite the Roman Empire? Did the *Codex* have the effect he wished?

3. What important aspects of the *Corpus Juris Civilis (Codex)* helped to establish civil law throughout the western world? In particular, how have these become part of the American civil justice system?

4. What effects did the natural disasters Constantinople went through during Justinian's reign (two outbreaks of plague, a devastating earthquake, a disastrous flood) have on the course of his rule?

5. Research the Acacian Schism. Why was this dispute important to Justinian? What influence did it have on his reign?

6. Discuss the effectiveness of Justinian's campaign against the Goths, Franks, Vandals, and others who had captured former Roman lands.

7. The Byzantine Empire faced many of the same challenges that were faced in the West. Why did Byzantium last nearly a thousand years longer?

ALTERNATIVE TERM PAPER SUGGESTIONS

1. Procopius gives a detailed, and probably highly imagined, account of a dialogue between Justinian and Theodora during the Nika Revolt. Research the circumstances leading to the revolt and the dialogue Procopius describes. Recreate the discussion between Justinian and Theodora when he is thinking of abandoning Constantinople and his throne. Also, imagine a discussion between the two after he acts to put down the revolt. Present your dialogue for the class.

2. Study the art of the Byzantine Empire. What forms were used? What is definitive about the styles? What media were available? What are some of the most famous works of art? Create a multimedia presentation about your findings.

Primary Sources

The Digest of Justinian. Trans. Alan Watson. Philadelphia: University of Pennsylvania Press, 1998.

The Institutes of Justinian, Trans. by J. B. Moyle. Reprint of 1913 edition. Charleston: BiblioBazaar, 2006.

Justinian's Institutes. Trans. Peter Birks and Grant McLeod. Ithaca: Cornell University Press, 1987.

Propocius. *History of the Wars, Secret History and Building.* Trans., ed., and abridged by Avernil Cameron. Great Histories Series. New York: Great Histories Series, 1967.

Propocius. *The Secret History.* Trans. by Peter Sarris and G. A. Williamson. New York: Penguin Classics, 2007.

Secondary Sources

Allen, Pauline. "Contemporary Portrayals of the Byzantine Empress Theodora (A.D. 527–548)," in *Stereotypes of Women in Power: Historical Perspectives and Revisionist Views,* Barbara Garlick, Suzanne Dixon, and Pauline Allen, eds. Westport, CT: Greenwood Press, 1992, pp. 93–103. Uses primary sources to analyze the personality and power of Theodora.

Allen, Pauline. "The 'Justinianic' Plague." *Byzantion* 1979 *49,* 5–20. Extensive article about the effects of this early outbreak of the bubonic plague.

Baker, G. P. *Justinian: The Last Roman Emperor.* New York: Cooper Square Press, 2002. This reprint of the 1931 biography of Justinian has become a standard for the study of Byzantium. It traces Justinian and Theodora's rise to power and their attempts to reunite the Roman Empire.

Cameron, Averil, *The Mediterranean World in Late Antiquity, AD 395–600.* London: Routledge, 1993. Includes a chapter on the reign of Justinian. A valuable resource for background on the Byzantine Empire, including its culture and social institutions.

Cameron, Averil. *Procopius and the Sixth Century.* London: Routledge, 1996. This volume is organized in three sections: a critical appraisal of Procopius as a writer, a closer look at individual parts of his work, and a discussion of the historical context of his work. Includes maps and an extensive bibliography.

Daube, David. "The Marriage of Justinian and Theodora. Legal and Theological Reflections," *Catholic University Law Review* 16. 1967, pp 380–399. Considers how Justinian's marriage to a commoner influenced his reign and how Theodora shaped his position on religious minorities.

Downey, Blanville. *Constantinople in the Age of Justinian.* Norman: University of Oklahoma Press, 2000. Discusses the city, its institutions, and its people. Nika Revolt discussed at length.

Evans, James Allan. *The Emperor Justinian and the Byzantine Empire.* Westport, CT: Greenwood Press, 2005. Introduction to the age of Justinian, includes a discussion of the state of the Eastern Empire when Justinian came to power and chapters about the major events during his reign. Has a number of annotated primary sources and an extensive bibliography.

Evans, J. A. S. *The Empress Theodora: Partner of Justinian.* Austin: University of Texas Press, 2002. Byzantine scholar Evans created a portrait of Theodora and her role in the events of her husband's rule.

Evans, J. A. S. "The 'Nika' Revolt and the Empress Theodora," *Byzantion* 54. 1984, p. 380. Discusses the part Theodora played in the revolt.

Metzger, Ernest. ed. *A Companion to Justinian's Institutes.* Ithaca: Cornell University Press, 1999. Begins with a discussion of the sources for Justinian's laws, then describes the contents and effects of laws concerning persons, marriage, property, succession, obligations, and actions.

World Wide Web

Brownworth, Lars. *12 Byzantine Rulers: The History of the Byzantine Empire Podcast.* www.anders.com/lectures/lars_brownworth/12_byzantine_rulers. Series of 12 podcasts by Brownworth covering twelve significant emperors of Byzantium, including Justinian.

De Imperatoribus Romanis: An Online Encyclopedia of Roman Rulers and Their Families. http://www.roman-emperors.org/. Has many links to additional sites. Provides timelines, genealogies, some biographical essays, and other information about Roman emperors, both East and West.

The Dumbarton Oaks Research Library and Collection, an Institute of Harvard University. http://www.doaks.org/. Dumbarton Oaks sponsors research on Byzantine culture and history and makes many research articles and other resources available on line. Choose the library link from the homepage to access more than 500,000 images related to Byzantium. Choose the publications link for articles.

The Glory of Byzantium. http://www.metmuseum.org/explore/Byzantium/byzhome.html. Online, interactive exhibit hosted by the Metropolitan Museum of Art. Includes images, a timeline, and articles.

Hildinger, Erik. "Gothic War: Byzantine Count Belisarius Retakes Rome." *Military History.* October 1999. http://historymedren.about.com/gi/dynamic/ June 12, 2006.

The Medieval Sourcebook. http://www.fordham.edu/halsall/sbook1c.html. Contains a large selection of translations from Justinian's reign, including much of the work of the historian Procopius and parts of the Codex.

Multimedia Resources

The Byzantines. Vol. IV of *Engineering an Empire.* 2007. A&E Home Video. Host Peter Weller. Discusses the rise of Byzantium and the Eastern Empire from the standpoint of their greatest engineering achievements.

Byzantium-The Lost Dream. 1997. TLC/Discovery Channel production. 209 minutes. Hosted by historian John Romer. Two-disc set.

Byzantium: The Lost Empire. 1997. Koch Vision; The Discovery Channel. Two 50-minute videos. Volume 1 tells of the growth of the Byzantine Empire through the late 1400s; volume 2 discusses the empire's fall.

The History of Orthodox Christianity. 2006. Vision Video. DVD. Three parts, 90 minutes total. Second part concerns the church in Byzantium.

Justinian. 2001. Volume 6 of the *Hail Caesar* series. A&E Home Video. DVD. 50 minutes. Explores the reign of Justinian with reenactments, visits to historic sites, interviews, and computer graphics.

9. St. Benedict Founds Western Medieval Monasticism (529)

Although forms of monasticism had existed since the earliest days of Christianity, it wielded little influence in the Western Church until Benedict of Nursia founded the Abbey of Monte Cassino around 529. St. Benedict's *Rule* became the standard by which monasteries were organized and operated for the next five centuries. Monasticism was a significant factor in medieval society; monks maintained centers for learning, converted thousands of pagans, strengthened papal power, and provided security for those who entered their ranks.

As a very young man, Benedict's wealthy parents sent him to Rome to complete his education. Here, he witnessed the worldly pursuits of his fellow students and decided that dedication to a godly life was more appropriate for him. He spent three years living in a desolate cave, but word of his virtue spread. A group of nearby monks asked him to be their abbot, even after he told them he would be too strict for them. The monks soon learned that Benedict had been truthful and tried to poison him. He discovered their plot and left, but founded twelve other monasteries of twelve monks each. After a while, he left these monasteries to found Monte Cassino on land given by the wealthy father of one of Benedict's students. At Monte Cassino, Benedict gathered monks into one large community and established rules for their living together. His sister Scholastica settled nearby in a convent that adhered to Benedict's teachings.

Benedict's *Rules* were revolutionary for his time. Anyone serious about his faith was welcomed into the monastery, poor as well as wealthy. There was no distinction in rank in an otherwise hierarchical world. In addition, everyone was expected to engage in manual labor, not only for the benefit of the monastery, but for the benefit of their bodies and souls. Although Benedict did not stress physical deprivation and suffering as a means of gaining God's favor, he did believe that manual labor was a worthy endeavor for all. Monks spent much of their day in study and prayer. Benedict called for a life of *ora et labora* (prayer and labor). Daily reading and contemplation of scripture and the study of church writings required that monks be literate. In fact, it is estimated that more than 90 percent of the literate population of Europe at the end of the first millennium lived in monasteries. Use by large number of monks required numerous volumes; therefore, Benedict established a scriptorium in the monastery where monks could reproduce texts. A number of volumes produced in monasteries are the only extant copies of ancient writings. Most of these are religious works, but the only Old English manuscript of *Beowulf* is one produced in a monastery. The libraries that developed in Benedictine monasteries throughout Europe attracted many of the greatest thinkers of the age to them for study. Thus, monasteries became the primary educational institution of the Middle Ages.

Benedictine monasteries spread throughout the West, and in 817 the Carolingian king, Louis the Pious, directed that all monasteries in his kingdom follow the Rule of Benedict. In 970, the same requirement was established in England. However, by this time, some monasteries were already drifting away from strict adherence to Benedict's principles, especially since they were rapidly developing into some of the wealthiest property owners in Europe.

TERM PAPER SUGGESTIONS

1. Discuss the economic impact monasteries had on medieval life.

2. Monasteries were for the most part self-sufficient, taking care of all their own needs. Discuss the assortment of gardens a typical monastery might have and how these provided not only food, but various other essentials for the monks.

3. Compare and contrast the Benedictine order with another order of Catholic monks.

4. Compare and contrast Christian monasticism with Buddhist monastic life.

5. Although the *Rule of Benedict* directed monks to engage in work, not all monks did the same work. Research the life within a medieval monastery and discuss the various occupations one might find and how these contributed to the overall well-being of the community.

6. Discuss the social and cultural conditions that drew so many medieval people into monasteries and convents.

7. Discuss the role of monasteries as institutions of social service.

8. How did monasticism and the production of illuminated manuscripts impact the development of art in the Middle Ages?

9. What part did monasteries play in the survival of Western culture?

10. Compare the lives of monks with those of women in the monastic life.

ALTERNATIVE TERM PAPER SUGGESTIONS

1. Interview a member of the Benedictine order today and prepare a paper or multimedia presentation on what you learn.

2. Construct a model of a typical medieval monastery that includes the various buildings and other structures. Be prepared to explain how the layout of the monastery fostered the aims of monastic life.

3. Create a multimedia presentation about illuminated manuscripts from the Middle Ages.

Primary Sources

Benedict of Nursia. *The Rule of St. Benedict.* http://www.osb.org/rb/text/toc .html#toc. Complete English translation by Leonard Doyle, arranged by chapters.

Benedict of Nursia. *The Rule of St. Benedict.* Trans. by Timothy Fry. Collegeville, MN: Liturgical Press, 1982.

Betterson, Henry, and Maunder, Chris, eds. *Documents of the Christian Church.* New York: Oxford University Press, 1999. Extensive collection of translated church documents, both before and after Benedict. Includes *Rule.* Especially useful in placing Benedict and monasteries within context of total church history.

Secondary Sources

Brooke, Christopher. *The Rise and Fall of the Medieval Monastery.* London: Folio Society, 2006. Exhaustive history of the monastic movement and its powerful influence, including extensive discussion of the Rule of Benedict. More than 100 illustrations.

Cels, Mark. *Life in a Medieval Monastery.* New York: Crabtree Publishing, 2004. Although written for a young audience, this book is a good place to begin a study of monastic life.

Clark, James G., ed. *The Religious Orders in Pre-Reformation England.* New York: Boydell Press, 2002. Collection of essays by eminent scholars on a variety of topics concerning monasticism's contributions and problems.

Eckenstein, Linda. *Women under Monasticism.* New York: Russell and Russell, 1963. A history of convent life from c. 500 to the end of the Middle Ages.

Greene, J. Patrick. *Medieval Monasteries.* London: Continuum International Publishing, 2005. Concerns mainly English and Irish monasteries and archaeological work being done at the sites. Bibliography and glossary included.

Gregory I. *Dialogos: Second Dialogue (Life of St. Benedict).* http://www.fordham .edu/halsall/basis/g1-benedict1.html. Although not written until fifty years after Benedict's death, this biography is a valuable source of information about him and his work.

Gregory I. *Dialogos: Second Dialogue (Life of St. Scholastica).* http://www.fordham .edu/halsall/basis/g1-schol1.html. Gregory also wrote about Benedict's sister in his *Dialogos.*

Gregory I. *The Life of St. Benedict: Text and Commentary.* Commentary by Alebart De Vogue. Trans. by Hilary Costello and Eoin De-Bhaldraithe. Petersham, MA: Saint Bede's Publications, 1993. Printed text of the entire biography.

Lawrence, C. H. *Medieval Monasticism: Forms of Religious Life in Western Europe in the Middle Ages* (3rd ed.). New York: Longman, 2000. Thorough examination of medieval monasteries, including role of women in monastic life. Begins with Egyptian monasteries of third century and goes through late middle ages.

Ludovicus, Milis. *Angelic Monks and Earthly Men: Monasticism and Its Meaning in Medieval Society.* Rochester, NY: Boydell Press, 1992. Evaluation of the place of monasticism in the Middle Ages, especially on the lives of ordinary individuals.

Sherrow, Victoria. *The Way People Live–Life in a Medieval Monastery.* Chicago: Lucent Books, 2000. Sherrow includes both a brief history of monasticism and an exploration of the everyday life of monks. Filled with interesting facts, illustrations, and quotations from primary sources.

Snyder, James, Luttikhuizen, Henry, and Verkerk, Dorothy. *Art of the Middle Ages,* 2nd ed. Upper Saddle River, NJ: Pearson, 2006. Includes Islamic, Western, and Byzantine art and the relationship of each to religion. More than 700 color and black-and-white illustrations.

Venarde, Bruce L. *Women's Monasticism and Medieval Society: Nunneries in France and England, 890–1215.* Ithaca: Cornell University Press, 1997. Chronological study of the pattern and extent of the establishment of nunneries, providing evidence that convents were much more universal than previously thought.

Warland, Rainer. *Monasteries and Monastic Orders: 2000 Years of Christian Art and Culture.* Konigswinter, Germany: Ullman, 2008. A combination of history, art, and biography that contains more than 700 color illustrations.

World Wide Web

The Abbey of Monte Cassino. http://www.officine.it/montecassino/main_e.htm. The Web site of the Abbey includes historical information and a virtual tour.

Medieval Illuminated Manuscripts. http://www.artsmia.org/education/teacher-resources/pnt-fivefacts.cfm?v=36. This site, produced by the Minneapolis Institute of Art, provides information about the creation of illuminated manuscripts and digitized examples.

Medieval Illuminated Manuscripts. http://www.kb.nl/manuscripts/. The National Library of the Netherlands has digitalized its vast collection of illuminated manuscripts and has hundreds of beautiful examples.

Medieval Manuscripts. https://ludos.leeds.ac.uk/R?func=search-simple&local_base=gen01-medmss. A collection of over 600 digitalized images of medieval-illuminated manuscripts and texts in Middle English produced by Leeds University.

The Order of Saint Benedict. www.osb.org. Maintained by Benedictine monks, this Web site not only contains information on the order today, but has extensive historical information and several translations of the *Rule.*

Multimedia Sources

The Medieval Manuscript: Art and Function. 2003. DVD. Films for the Arts and Humanities. 30 minutes. Describes the process and materials used in producing illuminated manuscripts.

Medieval Manuscripts. 1986. DVD. 30 minutes. Films Media Group. Describes materials used and how texts were illuminated in scriptoria.

The Middle Ages: Volume 19. 1989. Annenberg/CPB Project. Examines the emerging new social order of the early Middle Ages, consisting of the nobles, peasants, and clergy and how each class contributed to the social order.

The Monk. 2002. Schlessinger Media. 23 minutes. Part of the series *Life in the Middle Ages.* Shows how monks spent their time, how monasteries were organized, and how one became a monk.

Monks: The Keepers of Knowledge. 2004. Films for the Humanities. 53 minutes. Explores the lives of monks and the development of monasteries as centers of learning.

The Rule of St. Benedict Library: CD-ROM Edition (PC) Primary and Secondary Sources. Scott Rains, ed. Liturgical Press. Contains translations of Benedict's *Rule* and related documents.

The World Inscribed: The Illuminated Manuscript. 1996. DVD. Films Media Group. 24 minutes. Provides a brief history of the production of illuminated manuscripts from the fifth century until the development of the printing press.

10. Hagia Sophia Rebuilt and the Beginning of Byzantium Architecture (532–537)

Hagia Sophia, or the Church of Holy Wisdom, is one of the world's most spectacular churches, representing not only great beauty, but also masterful engineering. Byzantine emperor Justinian I ordered the reconstruction after the original church on the site was destroyed during the Nika Revolt. In only five years, workmen completed Hagia Sophia, incorporating many techniques of what became known as Byzantine architecture. The building stands in the modern city of Istanbul and has been a site of worship for Eastern and Roman Catholic Christians and for Muslims. Today, Hagia Sophia is a museum and one of Turkey's most-visited tourist sites. The building's dome and minarets make it also the most recognizable structure in Istanbul's skyline.

Only forty days after the original church was destroyed, Justinian's architects, Anthemius of Tralles and Isidorus of Miletus, began construction on Hagia Sophia. Justinian spared no expense on this monument to Christianity and himself. The massive structure, 260 × 270 feet, with a dome rising 210 feet above the floor with a diameter of 110 feet, presented challenges for its architects, especially since they did not have steel. The dome itself contains forty arched windows admitting light to the interior. Four supports for the dome are approximately 118 square yards at the base. The main dome is also supported by surrounding, smaller domes, giving the vast interior an even more open atmosphere. The nave is 135 feet wide, more than twice the width of the aisles, which measure 62 feet. During the time when Hagia Sophia served as the mother church for Eastern Catholicism, there were more than 80 priests and myriad deacons, lectors, and other officials employed. Hagia Sophia remained the largest church built for over a thousand years, until St. Peter's Basilica was constructed in Rome.

The interior was designed to demonstrate Justinian's wealth and power and that of the Byzantine Empire. Estimates suggest that more than 30 million tiny gold mosaic tiles were used throughout the structure. From floor to ceiling, the interior is covered with mosaics interspersed with red, green, and yellow marble and columns of purple porphyry. Ornate carvings, friezes, and capitals decorate the entire structure. Hagia Sophia set the standard for Byzantine churches as long as the empire stood.

When the Turks conquered Constantinople in 1453, Hagia Sophia was converted to a mosque. Muslims plastered over and painted many of the interior mosaics, most of which have been cleaned and restored. Four minarets at the outer corners of Hagia Sophia were added during its time as a mosque.

TERM PAPER SUGGESTIONS

1. Like that of other cultures, Byzantine art and architecture convey the society's essential beliefs—religious, social and political. Using Hagia Sophia for examples, discuss how this is true for Byzantium.

2. Compare the descriptions of Hagia Sophia written by Paul the Silentiary and Procopius. What aspects are emphasized by each writer? Are the descriptions more about the building, its function and meaning, or more about its architecture? How is the architecture of Hagia Sophia revolutionary in terms of its planning and spatial organization? How is the construction revolutionary in terms of building technology?

3. Study the mosaics found within Hagia Sophia. How are they deliberate statements of imperial authority and power?

4. What characteristics of Byzantine architecture have influenced later architects? Where do you see evidence of these influences?

5. Discuss the building of Hagia Sophia and similar structures from the point of view of the masons and master builders of the age. What issues did they face? What choices of materials and methods were available?

6. Discuss the development and implementation of the cross-dome in Byzantine architecture.

ALTERNATIVE TERM PAPER SUGGESTIONS

1. Discuss Byzantine architectural elements in a multimedia presentation focusing on three classic examples of churches: Sts. Sergius and Bacchus in Constantinople; Hagia Sophia, also in Constantinople; and St. Vitale in Ravenna, Italy.

2. Build a scale model of the dome of Hagia Sophia showing how the architects were able to support such a large, open space.

Primary Sources

Mango, Cyril. *The Art of the Byzantine Empire, 312–1453: Sources and Documents.* Toronto: University of Toronto Press, 1986. Mango has selected valuable primary source documents on the Byzantine Empire.

Paul the Silentiary: *Description of Hagia Sophia from Descriptio S. Sophia.* At *Medieval Sourcebook,* http://www.fordham.edu/halsall/sbook1c.html #Buildings. An English translation of Paul's contemporary description of Hagia Sophia.

Procopios. " *On the Great Church, [Hagia Sophia]"* from *De Aedificis. Medieval Sourcebook,* http://www.fordham.edu/halsall/source/procop-deaed1 .html. An English translation of Procopios' contemporary description of Justinian's newly rebuilt church.

Simocatta, Theophylactus. *Historiae.* Trans. by Michael and Mary Whitby. Oxford: Oxford University Press, 1986. English translation of Simocatta's late sixth-century history of Byzantium.

Secondary Sources

Krautheimer, Richard, and Curcic, Slobodan. *Early Christian and Byzantine Architecture,* Harmondsworth: Penguin Books, 1989. Contains introductory chapters with an overview of medieval architecture and four chapters specifically dealing with Justinian's buildings, including Hagia Sophia. Considered a classic resource.

Lowden, John. *Early Christian and Byzantine Architecture.* London: Phaidon, 1998. Includes a history of Byzantine art up until the mid-15th century. Extensive coverage of Hagia Sophia and Ravenna, Byzantine influences throughout the West, and the influence of religion on architecture. Numerous photographs.

Mango, Cyril. *Byzantium. The Empire of New Rome.* New York: Phoenix Press, 1980. Mango has organized this exhaustive resource into three broad sections: aspects of Byzantine life, the conceptual world of Byzantium, and the legacy.

Mango, Cyril, ed. *The Oxford History of Byzantium.* Oxford: Oxford University Press, 2002. Contains twelve essays written by leading Byzantine scholars, plus nine "special features" on topics such as the city of Constantinople, monasticism, and commerce.

Mathews, Thomas. *The Clash of the Gods: A Reinterpretation of Early Christian Art,* revised ed. Princeton: Princeton University Press, 1999. This book has interesting chapter titles such as "The Chariot and the Donkey" and "The Intimate Icon," which examine the conflict between pagan and Christian images. Packed with illustrations and photographs.

World Wide Web

The Byzantine Architecture Project. http://www.princeton.edu/~asce/const_95/const .html. Maintained by the architectural department at Princeton University, the site is filled with information and illustrations.

The Dumbarton Oaks Research Library and Collection, an Institute of Harvard University. http://www.doaks.org/. Dumbarton Oaks sponsors research on Byzantine culture and history and makes many research articles and other resources available on line. Choose the library link from the home-page to access more than 500,000 images related to Byzantium. Choose the publications link for articles.

Explore Byzantium. http://byzantium.seashell.net.nz/index.php. Contains articles, maps, and a timeline, as well as images of Hagia Sophia.

The Glory of Byzantium. http://www.metmuseum.org/explore/Byzantium/ byzhome.html. Online, interactive exhibit hosted by the Metropolitan Museum of Art. Includes images, a timeline, and articles.

Multimedia Sources

The Byzantines. Vol. IV of *Engineering an Empire.* 2006. DVD. A&E Home Video. 50 minutes. Host Peter Weller. Discusses the rise of Byzantium and the eastern empire from the standpoint of their greatest engineering achievements.

Byzantium ~ The Lost Dream. 1997. DVD. TLC/Discovery Channel production. Two-disc set; 209 minutes. Hosted by historian John Romer. Includes a visual tour of Hagia Sophia.

*Wonders Sacred and Mysterious.*1993. DVD. Pleasantville, N.Y.: Reader's Digest Home Entertainment. 68 minutes. Discusses many sacred buildings throughout the world, including Hagia Sophia.

11. First Toltec Empire (c. 550)

Before the arrival of Europeans in the 16th century, the history of the Toltec civilization in what is now Mexico relies primarily on archeological evidence, and scholars remain uncertain about many facts. The Toltecs are considered the first civilization in Mesoamerica, but scholars disagree about whether the term "empire" applies. Seemingly, there were two periods of Toltec preeminence; the first occurring during the third–seventh centuries and the second beginning around 850 and lasting until the Toltec disappearance around 1100.

At approximately the same time that Rome was gaining its great empire, the Toltec empire was rising. Sometime after 100 BCE, the Pyramid of the Sun, the third largest pyramid in the world, was erected. Around 200 CE, the great temple of Quetzalcoatl was constructed in the city of Teotihuacan, the "place where the gods were born." This image of the plumed serpent plays prominently in Toltec and later mythology. Murals in the city give evidence to the Toltec ability as warriors. They were more interested in capturing prisoners than in gaining territory, however, and their prisoners were sacrificed— some historians believe by the thousands—to appease the gods. Remains of human sacrifice have been discovered in each of the corners in the temple of Quetzalcoatl.

Teotihuacan's twelve square miles were filled with pyramids and palaces. At its height in the sixth century, the city was larger in both population and size than Rome. Beautiful paintings, many using brilliant red, adorned the walls of buildings. The Toltec nation traded throughout Mesoamerica; artifacts have been discovered throughout Mexico, in the southwest United States, and south in Guatemala. The Toltecs had a sophisticated knowledge of astronomy, and the city of Teotihuacan is carefully aligned with the planets.

By 700, the Toltecs had abandoned the city. Scholars have advanced various explanations for this, such as overpopulation and the exhaustion of natural resources. Whether they left as a group or gradually also remains unanswered. Archeological evidence reveals that a great fire destroyed the city about fifty years after it was abandoned, but, again, the cause is uncertain. In the 20th century and continuing today, parts of the city have been unearthed from the debris deposited by fire and time. About thirty miles north of Mexico City, Teotihuacan is one of Mexico's favorite tourist sites.

The Toltecs began building another capital city, Tula, around 850. By 1050, the Toltec written history begins when their existence is recorded in the Aztec codices and Mayan records. Around 1250, the last Toltecs in Tula were conquered by the Chichimec and their civilization vanished.

TERM PAPER SUGGESTIONS

1. How did the Toltecs use their knowledge of astronomy to determine the lay-out of the city of Teotihuacan?
2. What influences did Toltec culture have on later Mesoamerican cultures?
3. Evaluate the achievements of Toltec culture in art, science, and medicine.
4. Review explanations for the disappearance of the Toltec culture. Which is most viable? Why?
5. Compare the cities of Rome and Teotihuacan at their heights.
6. As in other cultures, the great buildings of the Toltecs reflect the society's spir-itual and political values. Discuss how this is true in the city of Teotihuacan.

ALTERNATIVE TERM PAPER SUGGESTIONS

1. Using images from the books and the Internet, create a multimedia presentation of the art and architecture of Teotihuacan.
2. Create a model of the city of Teotihuacan.

Primary Sources

The Toltecs did not have a system of writing. The earliest historical records about them are the Aztec codices, two sources of which follow:

Briehorst, John. *History and Mythology of the Aztecs: The Codex Chimalpopoca.* Tuscon: University of Arizona Press, 1998. A complete translation of the codex with commentary.

Keber, Eloise Quinones. *Codex Telleriano-Remensis: Ritual, Divination, and History in a Pictorial Aztec Manuscript.* Austin: University of Texas Press, 1995. A full-color photographic reproduction of the entire codex, with commentary from early Spanish explorers, an English translation, and commentary.

Secondary Sources

Adams, Richard, and McLeod, Murdo, eds. *The Cambridge History of the Native Peoples of the Americas.* Cambridge: Cambridge University Press, 2000. Part I contains eleven essays about the earliest Mesoamerican peoples, including the Toltecs.

Carrasco, David, Jones, Lindsay, and Sessions, Scott, eds.. *Mesoamerica's Classic Heritage: From Teotihuacan to the Aztecs.* Boulder: University Press of Colorado, 2000. Collection of scholarly essays arguing the impact of Toltec culture on later civilizations.

Fine Arts Museum of San Francisco. *Feathered Serpents and Flowering Trees: Reconstructing the Murals of Teotihuacan.* Seattle: University of Washington Press, 1988. Illustrations of the Toltec murals and discussion of how they are being restored.

Pasztory, Esther. *Teotihuacan: An Experiment in Living.* Norman: University of Oklahoma Press, 1997. Discussion of the Toltec civilization as interpreted through its art and artifacts.

Sugiyoma, Saburo. *Human Sacrifice, Militarism, and Rulership: Materialization of State Ideology at the Feathered Serpent Pyramid, Teotihuacan.* Cambridge: Cambridge University Press, 2005. Archeological evidence, interpretations of symbols, and discussion of Toltec methods of construction, including the measurement system.

World Wide Web

Dumbarton Oaks Research Library and Collection. http://www.doaks.org/. Dumbarton Oaks is a Harvard University Research institute devoted in part to preColumbian studies. A large collection of scholarly papers on many topics is available online. It also provides a searchable database with translations of the surviving Mayan codices.

Foundation for the Advancement of Mesoamerican Studies. http://www.famsi.org/. Drawings, photos, texts, videos, and other resources are accessible from this site. Available in both English and Spanish.

Mesoamerican Civilizations and Cultures. http://www.anthroarcheart.org/precolum.htm#TEOTIHUACAN. This is a stock photographic site, but it has a number of excellent photographs of the city and its buildings. Other Mesoamerican sites are pictured also.

Teotihuacan: City of the Gods. http://archaeology.la.asu.edu/teo/. Maintained by the Department of Archaeology at Arizona State University, this informative site offers photos, video clips, maps, articles, and a chronology of Teotihuacan.

Multimedia Sources

Global Treasures: Teotihuacan Mexico. 2007. DVD. TravelVideoStore.com. 10 minutes. Brief visual tour of the city.

Living Stones in Mesoamerica. 2003. DVD. Princeton, NJ: Films for the Humanities. 27 minutes. Filmed in the city of Teotihuacan, the video discusses archeological discoveries that aid understanding of the ancient people of Mesoamerica.

Teotihuacan: City of the Gods. 2004. DVD. Educational Video Network. 18 minutes. Visual tour of the city.

12. Gregory of Tours Writes *Historia Francorum* (c. 575–594)

French Bishop and later saint, Gregory of Tours (c. 538–594) was the author of the ten-volume *Historia Francorum (History of the Franks),* one of the most valuable resources available on the sixth century. Gregory also wrote extensively on church history and the lives of saints and produced a liturgical guide for determining the hours for prayers from the position of stars.

Gregory was the son of an important political family in the Arverni region of southern France. Given the name Georgius Florentius, he adopted his maternal grandfather's name when he became bishop of Tours. As a young man, Gregory received an education in both religious and secular subjects. He first came to Tours and the shrine of St. Martin to seek a cure for an illness. In 573, he was selected bishop of the See.

Merovingian disputes divided sixth-century France into three regions warring among themselves. The city of Tours came under attack and changed hands frequently. Gregory's immense popularity with the people of the region enabled him to remain in office under various rulers and to influence politics.

Historia Francorum reveals not only the political turmoil of the sixth century, but is a lively discussion of social custom, daily life, and personalities. As with many medieval histories, it begins with the creation of the world. The first volume ends with the conquest of Gaul by the Franks in 397. Book II deals with the reign of Clovis, founder of the Frankish empire. The ten volumes together provide a remarkable resource on the history of early France. Gregory admitted his Latin grammar was sometimes poor, but this does not make his work any less important. He was meticulous in historical detail and provides the only historical substantiation of an event mentioned in the English epic *Beowulf*: a battle in 520 between the Franks and the Scandinavians.

TERM PAPER SUGGESTIONS

1. Contemporary historiography recognizes that history has often been subjective and has justified the abuse of power and continuation of the status quo. Discuss the ways in which Gregory's telling of history privileges the stories of supporters of the Catholic faith and ignores or treats others less favorably.

2. Research Gregory's relationship with the ruthless ruler Chilperic. Were Gregory's actions justified? Were they ethical? Were his actions beneficial for the people of his region or did they encourage Chilperic's brutality?

3. Discuss Gregory's use of the supernatural, strange events, and superstition in his writing. How do you account for so many of these occurrences in historical writing?

4. What are the strengths of *Historia Francorum* as a work of history? How does the work enhance our understanding of the time between the fall of the Roman Empire and the rise of the nation of France?

ALTERNATIVE TERM PAPER SUGGESTIONS

1. Using a translated version of Gregory's discussions with Chilperic, plan and present a dialogue between these two powerful men. Be sure to highlight the most significant points of disagreement between the two.

2. Consider the perspective Gregory had on history as a powerful church official in the Middle Ages. Assume you have attained the position of bishop of a large See today. Choose three or four major events that have occurred during your own lifetime. Write a history of those events from a point of view and in a writing style similar to Gregory's.

Primary Sources

Episodes of Medieval Warfare from the History of the Franks by Gregory of Tours. Trans. by O. M. Dalton. Oxford, 1927. http://www.deremilitari.org/resources/sources/tours.htm. Web versions of portions of the Dalton translation are listed below.

Gregory of Tours. *History of the Franks: Books I–X*. http://www.thelatinlibrary.com/gregorytours.html. The book has also been digitalized in the original Latin.

Gregory of Tours. *History of the Franks: Books I–X. Medieval Sourcebook*. http://www.fordham.edu halsall/basis/gregory-hist.html#pref1.

Gregory of Tours. *History of the Franks: Books I–X*. Trans. O.M. Dalton. (2 vols.) Oxford: Clarendon Press, 1927. A well-respected translation that includes extensive commentary and criticism in the introduction.

Gregory of Tours. *History of the Franks: Books I–X, Selections*. Trans. with notes by Ernest Brehaut. New York: Octagon Books, 1973. (Originally printed 1916). Not a complete translation, but contains Brehaut's extensive notes. Because these notes were written so long ago, students should be aware that modern historians may not agree with all of Brehaut's premises.

The Medieval Sourcebook. http://www.fordham.edu/halsall/source/gregory-mirac
.html#merit. In addition to *History of the Franks,* this site provides translations of selections from Gregory's *Eight Books of Miracles.* Murray,
Alexander Callander, ed. *Gregory of Tours: The Merovingians Readings in
Medieval Civilizations & Cultures.* Peterborough, Ontario: Broadview
Press, 2005. Murray provides selected translated passages from Books II
to X and insightful comments on Gregory and his times.

Secondary Sources

Brown, Peter Robert Lamont. "The Study of Elites in Late Antiquity."
Arethusa, Fall 2000, *33,* 3, pp. 32–346. Brown's article is especially
interesting because of his discussion of the relationship between the
powerful and the powerless and how that influenced early history. He
gives considerable attention to Gregory of Tours and his impact on
sixth-century history.

Goffart, Walter. *The Narrators of Barbarian History (A.D. 55–800): Jordanes,
Gregory of Tours, Bede, and Paul the Deacon.* Princeton: Princeton University Press, 1988. Goffart, a senior researcher at Yale, places these four
historians in the context of their times. His commentary makes generous
use of quotations from the works of these men.

Heinzelmann, Martin. *Gregory of Tours: History and Society in the Sixth Century.* Trans. by Christopher Carrol. Cambridge: Cambridge University
Press, 2006. This translation from the German makes Heinzelmann's
interpretations of Gregory's work available in English for the first time.
Heinzelemann argues that Gregory was not a mere reporter of the
events of his day; his work is a highly complex treatise on politics and
theology predicated on his belief in a society where church and state
are equal.

James, Edward. *The Origins of France: From Clovis to the Capetians, 500–1000.*
London: Palgrave Macmillan, 1989. James devotes the first half of the
book to the political and social institutions of sixth-century Gaul, providing a context and framework for understanding Gregory's work.

World Wide Web

Liber Gentium: Medieval Biography. http://www.medievalhistory.net/liber.htm.
Contains essays, timeline, images, and translations, including some work
by Gregory of Tours.

Muhlberger, Steve. *A Visual Tour through Late Antiquity with an Emphasis on
Gaul and the Time of Gregory of Tours.* http://historymedren.about.com/
gi/dynamic/offsite.htm?site=http://www.nipissingu.ca/department/

history/muhlberger/4505/show.htm. The images were compiled by Professor Muhlberger for his medieval history students and help place Gregory in context of his time.

Multimedia Sources

Barbarians II: The Franks. 2006. History Channel. DVD. Segments are available at http://www.history.com/media.do. The video gives a succinct picture of the Franks who conquered Gaul and their first kings. It does not extend until Gregory's time but is helpful in building a background for the rulers he discusses in his *History of the Franks.*

The End of Rome, the Birth of Europe. 2002. Films Media Group. 52 minutes. Part of the video series *The Wandering Tribes of Europe,* this video covers sixth-century kingdoms of the Ostrogoths, the Merovingians, and the Anglo-Saxons.

13. Reunification of China: Sui and Tang Dynasties (581–907)

After the Yellow Turban Rebellion in 184, China went through a period of fragmentation into various political units that, in 420, developed into the Northern and Southern Kingdoms. In 581, the Northern prime minister *(Chengxiang)* Yang Jian took control of part of the south and named himself Emperor Wen, beginning the Sui Dynasty. Eight years later, Wen's forces defeated the remaining Southern opposition and reunited the nation. This reunification under the Sui Dynasty began an era of achievements profoundly affecting the future of the Chinese nation.

At peace after decades of civil strife, China's economic progress was immediate. Farming acreage increased and the system of Junti or equal division of land boosted agricultural production. At first, a system of tax moderation also improved the general economy. Emperor Wen ordered the construction of the Grand Canal, the longest man-made canal in the world, to increase interaction between North and South. The Sui emperors undertook rebuilding of the Great Wall and the capital, Louyang.

At the beginning of the Sui Dynasty, political corruption was rampant throughout the nation. Appointments to importance positions were almost always the result of nepotism. Wen reinstituted the system of three departments and six ministries begun after the Han Dynasty and continued by dynasties that followed the Sui. This administrative organization, which lasted more than 1,000 years, divided the authority formerly held by the prime minister among various departments and restricted the power of military generals, thereby actually increasing the authority of the emperor.

In addition to reinstituting this centralized administrative system, in 606 the Sui Dynasty returned to using examinations to determine qualifications for civil service. The Chinese examinations were based on study of the writings of Confuscianism, which had been reestablished as the national religion. Even the poorest citizens were able to take the examination, and passing the various stages meant that one's social status increased.

In spite of these social and political achievements, the second Sui emperor, Wen's son Yang, was not able to preserve his rule. As money ran out for building programs, he required both men and women to work part of the year for the emperor. He also began to tax the population more heavily to pay for expensive military campaigns to conquer Vietnam and Korea. In 613, the first of several rebellions broke out. In 618, a rebel leader, Liyuan bribed one of the emperor's aides to murder him and named himself emperor, ending the 37-year rule of the Sui.

The new dynasty, the Tang, ruled from 618–907 and continued many of the policies of its predecessor, but also forged new models of governing. The Tang family claimed descent from the Daoist priest Laozi, who was highly revered among the Chinese. Seeking to solidify the unity of the nation, Tang emperors periodically called local officials and priests to the capital for consultation. In addition, the civil service examination continued to grow in prestige, attracting intelligent, ambitious men to the capital and spreading literacy throughout more of the countryside. Literature and the arts flourished under the Tang. Together, the Sui and Tang dynasties created a sense of Chinese nationalism and unity.

TERM PAPER SUGGESTIONS

1. Discuss the effects of Confucianism, Taoism, and Buddhism upon the arts and architecture of early China.
2. Explore the contents of the Chinese civil service examinations. Evaluate the validity of these as measures of one's ability to serve the government.

3. In what ways did the teachings of Confucius influence politics and government in Sui and Tang China?

4. To what extent were literacy and education in China key factors in the development of its major traditions?

5. What was the effect of epidemic diseases in China between the third and tenth centuries?

6. The Tang dynasty ruled China for almost 300 years. Analyze the reasons for its fall in 907.

7. What was the position of women during the Sui and Tang dynasties? Consider the Princess Pingyang and Empress Wu Zetian in particular. Were women such as they the rule or the exceptions?

8. Discuss how the establishment of the Three Departments and Six Ministries worked to increase the emperor's power.

ALTERNATIVE TERM PAPER SUGGESTIONS

1. Construct a model of the Great Canal showing how the Chinese were able to dig the channel and support the walls.

2. With a partner, create and perform a dialect between a follower of Confucius and a Buddhist monk in China. What are the major concerns each has about the other's faith? What areas of consensus exist?

Primary Sources

Confucius. *The Analects. Exploring Ancient World Cultures.* http://eawc.evansville
.edu/anthology/analects.htm. Translation of influential teachings of Confucius used in civil service examinations in the Sui and Tang dynasties.

Confucius. "The Doctrine of the Mean," in *The Chinese Classics.* Trans. by James Legge. New York: Hurd & Houghton, 1870, pp. 124–146. http://www
.shsu.edu/~his_ncp/Confu.html. Although Confucius lived in the sixth century BCE, his teachings such as presented here were revered during the Sui and Tang dynasties.

Sun-tzu, The Art of War; The Oldest Military Treatise in the World. Trans. by Lionel Giles. London: Luzac and Company, 1910. http://www.shsu
.edu/~his_ncp/SunTzu. html. Gives insight into Chinese war strategy.

Secondary Sources

Benn, Charles. *China's Golden Age: Everyday Life in the Tang Dynasty.* New York: Oxford University Press, 2004. Vivid descriptions of all aspects of Chinese life, including marriage, crime, nobility, and farming. Includes several translations from primary sources.

Gascoigne, Bamber. *The Dynasties of China: A History.* New York: Carroll & Graf, 2003. History of the eight Chinese dynasties from the Shang to the Qing. Includes illustrations, maps, and extensive notes.

Gerent, Jacques, Foster, J. R., and Hartman, Charles. *A History of Chinese Civilization.* Oxford: Oxford University Press, 1982. Thorough history of the Chinese from antiquity to the 20th century. Several chapters on the medieval period.

Hucker, Charles. *China's Imperial Past: An Introduction to Chinese History and Culture.* Stanford: Stanford University Press, 1975. Extensive coverage of Chinese history. Includes five chapters on the early empire.

Wright, Arthur F. *The Sui Dynasty: the Unification of China, A.D. 581–617.* New York: Knopf, 1978. A classic study of the Sui dynasty and its influence on Chinese history.

Xiong, Victor Cunrui. *Emperor Yang of the Sui Dynasty: His Life, Times, And Legacy* (Suny Series in Chinese Philosophy And Culture). Albany: State University of New York Press, 2006. Tables, appendices, a chronology and notes accompany this biography of Emperor Yang.

World Wide Web

Ebrey, Patricia Buckley. *A Visual Sourcebook of Chinese Civilization.* http://depts.washington.edu/chinaciv/. An extensive collection of images from ancient Chinese history through the 21st century; brief commentary, and, in some cases, a bibliography for further reading.

Internet East Asian History Sourcebook. http://www.fordham.edu/halsall/eastasia/eastasiabook.html. Provides many links to primary documents, images, and other Web resources for the study of Asian history.

Multimedia Sources

The Ancient Chinese. 1998. Video. 100% Educational Videos. 24 minutes. Provides brief descriptions of ancient dynasties and their accomplishments.

Chinese Art and Architecture. 1987. Video. Alarion Press. 102 minutes. Five brief programs, the second of which concerns the art of the Tang dynasty.

Kung-Yuan, Lo. *Chinese Poems of the Tang and Sung Dynasties: Read by Lo Kung-Yuan in Northern Chinese, Peking Dialect.* CD Recording. 2004. Smithsonian Folkways Recordings. A digitalized version of the 1963 recording of ancient poetry by Chinese artist King-Yuan. In Chinese.

Medieval Times in China and Beyond. 2008. http://teachingforthinking
.com/med_chinamain.html. DVD. 25 minutes. Contains segments on
China, Japan, and India with accompanying music and art from the
period.

14. St. Augustine Leads Christian Mission to Britain (597)

By the time Rome fell around 410, much of the Empire had been
Christianized. In the British Isles, many monasteries, abbeys, and
churches constructed by the Romans continued to function after Rome
withdrew. Over time, Britain's Christians, separated from the Latin
church, developed different practices, even assimilating some Celtic
pagan traditions into their worship.

Pope Gregory I (Gregory the Great, r. 590–604) understood the threats
to the church at the beginning of his reign: the Visigoths with whom
Spanish bishops had aligned themselves, Arianism in Gaul and other parts
of the West, the Byzantine emperor in the West, and Celtic Christianity in
Britain. The Irish monasteries, some of which had been founded by
St. Patrick in the fifth century, were flourishing as centers of learning and
were initiating successful missionary efforts in northern Britain. Gregory
feared that the growing influence of the Celtic church might lead to a
schism with Roman Christians. When he received a castigating letter from
Columba, a leader in the Irish Church, Gregory decided he must try to
bring the Celtic Christians under Roman authority.

The pope commissioned forty monks under the leadership of Augustine
to go to England and begin the conversion of the heathen population. He
directed them to start at the southern city of Kent, for he knew that
although Ethelbert, king of Kent, was a pagan, he was married to the
Christian queen Bertha.

In 597, Augustine landed in Kent and, at the queen's request, was
granted a meeting with the king. Ethelbert gave Augustine the small
church of St. Martin, which stands to this day, as the center of his work
and gave permission for the monks to preach their message to the people.
Thus began the conversion of England to Roman Catholicism.

Eventually, Augustine convinced King Ethelbert to be baptized, and the
king ordered many of his people to also be converted. The missionary
work soon outgrew St. Martin's, and Christ's Church, the predecessor of

Canterbury Cathedral, was constructed on the site and became the center of the English church. Augustine also founded the abbey of St. Peter and St. Paul nearby. In 601, Augustine was named the first Archibishop of Canterbury. That position still holds primacy over the Anglican Church.

Canterbury Cathedral has undergone major building programs three times in its history. More important than the construction of this center of British faith, Augustine helped stabilize society in the Middle Ages by reestablishing the ties between England and the continent.

TERM PAPER SUGGESTIONS

1. Pope Gregory I was a major force in the development of the church during the Middle Ages. There are three main areas of achievement for which he was responsible. Gregory reinforced the power of the papacy, established a new relationship between the church and the monarchy, and used monastic missionaries such as St. Augustine to increase the church's authority. Research one of these and discuss how his actions influenced the course of Catholicism and society.

2. Research the growth of Christianity in Ireland from the time of St. Patrick until the seventh century Synod of Whitby.

3. Discuss the relationship between church and state in the sixth and seventh centuries.

4. What effects did the Christian church have on the literature of the Anglo-Saxon period?

5. St. Augustine and the monks who came to England with him were Benedictines. Discuss how they applied the *Rule of Benedict* to their lives in Britain.

6. How did (and does) Canterbury Cathedral reflect the theology of the Anglo-Saxon church?

7. Discuss the development of illuminated manuscripts in Britain. How do they compare to those produced on the continent?

ALTERNATIVE TERM PAPER SUGGESTIONS

1. Build a model of Canterbury Cathedral in its Saxon, Gothic, or Norman stage.

2. Create a multimedia presentation showing the Saxon, Gothic, and Norman elements of the interior and exterior of Canterbury Cathedral.

3. English historian Bede reported that before Augustine reached England, he turned back and asked the pope to release him from his commission. Recreate the conversation that might have occurred between Augustine and Pope Gregory about the mission to England.

Primary Sources

Unless URL is listed, resources can be accessed through *The Medieval Sourcebook,* http://www.fordham.edu/halsall/sbook.html:

Bede. *Gregory the Great,* from the *Ecclesiastical History.*

Bede (673–735). *Ecclesiastical History: The Conversion of England.*

Gregory I. *The Book of Pastoral Rule* in *Nicene and Post-Nicene Fathers, Series II, Vol. XII.* http://ccel.churchdocs.org/fathers2/npnf212/npnf2321 .htm#.

Gregory I. *Letter to Abbot Mellitus,* c. 600.

Gregory I. *Selected Letters.* Collected in *Nicene and Post-Nicene Fathers, Series II, Vol. XIII.* http://ccel.churchdocs.org/fathers2/npnf213/toc.htm.

Gregory I the Great. *The Book of Pastoral Rule,* excerpts, c. 590.

Gregory I the Great. *Letters Showing Papal Activity.*

Gregory I the Great. *Moralia in Iob: Discussion of His Own Mind* (d. 604), from the draft translation by James O'Donnell (at the University of Pennslvania).

Gregory I the Great. *The Papal Estates,* c. 600.

Paulus Diaconus (*Paul the Deacon): Pope Gregory the Great and the Lombards,* c. 593.

Secondary Sources

Blair, John. *The Church in Anglo-Saxon Society.* Oxford: Oxford University Press, 2006. Comprehensive study of the interrelationship between the early English church and society. Extensive use of primary sources.

Cavill, Steve. *Anglo-Saxon Christianity.* Zondervan Press, 1999. Along with other topics, this short volume explores the expressions of Christianity found in Anglo-Saxon works of literature.

Cutts, Edward L. *Augustine of Canterbury.* Becker Press, 2008. Republication of an out-of-print volume about Augustine.

Evans, G. R. *The Thought of Gregory the Great.* Cambridge: Cambridge University Press, 1988. Helps explain the missionary zeal of Gregory that led to Augustine's mission to England.

Gameson, Richard. *St. Augustine and the Conversion of England.* Gloustershire: Alan Sutton Publishing, 2000. Discusses the historical, social, and artistic implications of the Anglo-Saxon conversion.

Green, Michael. *Augustine of Canterbury.* London: Janus Publishing Company, 1997. Supports the story of Augustine's life and work with documentation from primary sources.

Maclear, G. F. *S. Augustine's Canterbury: Its Rise, Ruin, and Restoration*. Baltimore: Kessinger Publishing Company, 2007. Reprint of out-of-print volume.

Markus, R. A. *Gregory the Great and his World*. Cambridge: Cambridge University Press, 1997. Well-researched examination of Gregory's work and how he influenced both secular and religious society.

Mayr-Harting, Henry. *The Coming of Christianity to Anglo-Saxon England*. Oxford: Oxford University Press, 2006. Discusses the influences on the development of the English church and the church's influence on society.

Robertson, J. C. *Sketches of Church History, from AD 33 to the Reformation*. New York: Edwin S. Gorham, 1904. Digitalized version available from Classic Christian Ethereal Library (ccel.org). Chapter 2 concerns Augustine's mission to England.

Schaff, Phillip. *History of the Christian Church, Volume IV: Mediaeval Christianity. A.D. 590–1073*. Oak Harbor, WA: Logos Research Systems, 1997. A facsimile reproduction of Schaff's 1910 publication. Digitalized version available from Classic Christian Ethereal Library (ccel.org).

World Wide Web

The Cathedrals of Britain. http://www.bbc.co.uk/history/. Part of the *British History* site maintained by the BBC; contains many links to informative articles and to picture galleries; has interactive features.

Cathedrals in England A–Z: A gazetteer of medieval cathedrals in England. http://www.britainexpress.com/Where_to_go_in_Britain/Cathedrals/ Cathedrals1.htm. A commercial site; lists all Britain's cathedrals and provides links to their individual Web sites.

Vess, Dr. Deborah. *St. Augustine's Abbey: A Brief History and Virtual Tour*. http://www.faculty.de.gcsu.edu/~dvess/ids/medieval/augustine/augustine .shtml#conflict. Discussion of Augustine's work in England, images, and links to additional information.

Multimedia Sources

Beowulf & the Anglo-Saxons. 2007. Rykon. Approximately 50 minutes. Investigates the relationship between the epic poem and the religious thought of Anglo-Saxon society.

Gothic Cathedrals of Europe. No date. Films Media Group. Interactive CD-ROM with more than 2000 photos, 35 cathedral histories, and articles.

The Lindisfarne Gospels: A Masterpiece of Anglo-Saxon Book Painting. 1995. DVD. Films Media Group. 35 minutes. Explores the creation of the Lindisfarne text and explains the process of making and decorating illuminated manuscripts.

15. Buddhism Becomes Japan's State Religion (c. 607)

The medieval Japanese people intermingled religious traditions, but until the seventh century primarily practiced the Shinto and Tao faiths. In the fifth century, the Chinese writing system, Chinese texts and thought were introduced to Japan. A century later, in 539, a Korean monarch seeking an alliance sent a gift of a statue of Buddha and some *sutra* (sacred writings) to Japan. Despite the initial opposition from Shinto priests, the new faith spread quickly, primarily through acceptance of Buddhism by members of the royal court.

The most influential proponent of Buddhism was the prince regent, Prince Shotuku. In 607, he began construction of one of Japan's oldest temple complexes, Horyuji, in the Asuka region. Shotuku also built other temples and monasteries and wrote commentaries on the *sutras*. Although Buddhism is an ancient religion, its teachings were considered progressive for the time. For example, each temple complex provided tangible means for the faithful to demonstrate compassion through the dispensaries for sick humans and animals and shelters for the sick, aged, and orphaned.

Prince Shotuku's most lasting impact on the acceptance of Buddhism was his introduction of a new constitution based on Buddhist principles—in effect making it the state religion. For centuries, the laws of the land and Buddhist teachings were identified with one another. In the 13th century, Shinto replaced Buddism as the official religion. However, the principles of the Buddist faith revolutionized Japanese art, literature, music, and architecture as well as politics.

TERM PAPER SUGGESTIONS

1. As in other cultures, the sacred buildings of Japan reflect the essential beliefs of the culture. Using the temple of Horyuji as an example, explain how the structure embodies the beliefs of Buddhism.

2. Prince Shotuku instituted a policy of "cultural borrowing" in Japan. Research this policy and its effects on Japanese society.

3. Describe and analyze the connections and/or tensions between state and religion in medieval Japan.

4. Compare the life of a medieval Buddhist monk or nun in Japan with that of a Christian monk in the West.

5. How are the ideals of Buddhism reflected in the art of medieval Japan?

6. Explore how the aristocracy adhered to Buddhist principles in their everyday lives.

7. How did the geographic situation of Japan influence its economic, social, and religious development in the Middle Ages?

8. Compare the Buddhist constitution initiated by Prince Shotuku to a Western document expressing the principles of governing, such as *Magna Carta*.

ALTERNATIVE TERM PAPER SUGGESTIONS

1. Create a multimedia presentation showing how medieval Japanese art reflected the religious beliefs of the culture. Add medieval court music *(gagaku)*.

2. Create a dramatic monologue in the persona of Prince Shotuku and deliver it to the class.

Primary Sources

"The Birth of Prince Shotuku." http://www.wsu.edu:8080/~dee/ANCJAPAN/ SHOTOKU.HTM. An English translation from the *Nihongi,* a medieval history of Japan.

De Bary, William Theodore, et al., eds. *Sources of Japanese Tradition, Volume I: From Earliest Times to 1600.* New York: Columbia University Press, 2001. An extensive collection of primary documents from history, politics, literature, and private writing.

Diaries of Court Ladies of Old Japan. Trans. by Annie Shepley Omori and Kochi Doi. Boston: Houghton Mifflin, 1920. Digitalized book made available by The Celebration of Women Writers at http://web.archive.org/web/ 19990420204049. The diaries offer an authentic picture of the lives of women of the aristocracy and often reveal the religious beliefs of the time.

The Japanese Constitution of Prince Shotuku. http://www.wsu.edu:8080/ ~dee/ANCJAPAN/CONST.HTM. A modern English translation.

Lu, David John. *Japan: A Documentary History.* New York: M.E. Sharpe, 2005. A collection of primary Japanese historical documents with annotations and comments written by Lu.

Secondary Sources

Deal, William E. *Handbook to Life in Medieval and Early Modern Japan.* Oxford: Oxford University Press, 2005. Maps, tables, charts, illustrations, and a lengthy bibliography make this a valuable resource, although its main focus is the later medieval period.

Mason, R. H. P., and Craiger, J. G. *A. History of Japan: Revised Edition.* Melbourne, Australia: Charles E. Tuttle Company, 1997. Covers Japanese history from premedieval times to the occupation of the 20th century.

Najita, Tetsuo. *Japan: The Intellectual Foundations of Modern Japanese Politics.* Chicago: University of Chicago Press, 1974. Traces influences of medieval politics on the modern nation.

World Wide Web

East Asian History. http://www.east-asian-history.net/. This informative site is maintained by the East Asian Studies Department at Pennsylvania State University.

Institute for Medieval Japanese Studies. http://www.medievaljapan.org/. The Web site provides general information about medieval Japan and is constantly adding material. Some resources are available for purchase, including some about Buddhist convents.

Internet East Asian History Sourcebook. http://www.fordham.edu/halsall/eastasia/eastasiabook.html. Provides many links to primary documents, images, and other Web resources for the study of Asian history.

Multimedia Sources

Buddha in the Land of the Kami (7th–12th Centuries). 1989. Part One of the DVD series *Japan Past and Present.* Films Media Group. 50 minutes. Discussion of how Buddhism and the traditional religious beliefs were integrated in Japan.

The Eastern Empires. 2006. DVD. Kultur Video. 50 minutes. Part of the series *The Story of Civilization.* Concerns both China and Japan and how they developed empires.

16. Muhammad and the Beginning of Islam (622)

The powerful force of Islam that rose in the Arabic world in the seventh century began with one individual, Muhammad al-Amin (c. 570–632). Born into a family of merchants in Mecca, Muhammad was orphaned at an early age and taken in by an uncle. He spent some years managing caravans for the widow Khadija, many years his senior, whom he eventually married. Muhammad traveled throughout the Arabian Peninsula with caravans and must have dealt with both Jews and Christians. Seeking answers to questions of faith, Muhammad frequently withdrew to a cave near Mecca to meditate and seek guidance.

When Muhammad was forty, he experienced a vision of the archangel Gabriel who proclaimed him a prophet. Subsequent experiences with Gabriel convinced Muhammad to share his prophetic vision with others. His first converts were his wife and his cousin Ali, and he was soon reciting the messages of Gabriel—messages that eventually became the Koran *(Qur'an)*—in public gatherings. Muhammad attracted large numbers of followers, in part because he advocated social change and the distrust of political and religious leaders. In 622, Muhammad was forced to flee Mecca and seek refuge in Medina. This event became known as the Hegira (*hirjah* "flight") and marks the beginning of the Islamic calendar.

Muhammad solidified his following in Medina and raised an army to fight Mecca. In 630, Mecca surrendered to Muhammad and the nation of Islam began. Muhammad died in 632 and his follower Abu Bakr became the first caliph or successor of Muhammad. The faith he had founded spread rapidly throughout the Arabian Peninsula and beyond.

Islam was able to unite the warlike people of Arabia under a single banner of faith and religious authority. The assaults on the Byzantine Empire by Islam were able to drive the Eastern and Western Roman Empires further apart. Essentially, Islam divided the world into three civilizations: the Byzantine, the European, and the Islamic; these three were to dictate the history of the remainder of the Middle Ages.

TERM PAPER SUGGESTIONS

1. How was Islam a decisive factor in the success of the Arabic invasions of the Mediterranean during the seventh century?

2. Describe the process by which the *Qur'an* came into being. Compare and contrast the Muslim view of the nature and origin of the *Qur'an* to Jewish and Christian views of the Bible.

3. Describe the various meanings of the concept of *jihad* (holy war)and its significance for the growth of Islam.

4. Islam spread more rapidly than any other major world religion. Trace its expansion during the 100 years after Mohammed's death. What aspects of the religion made it appealing? How was the cultural climate conducive to the rapid expansion of Islam?

5. After Muhammad died, what were the challenges faced by *dar al-Islam* (an area under Islamic rule or domination) and how were they resolved within the first century of Islam's existence?

6. How did the growth of the realm of Islam contribute to agricultural, commercial, and urban development?

ALTERNATIVE TERM PAPER SUGGESTIONS

1. Create a multimedia presentation tracing the expansion of Islam in the first century after Muhammad's death. Include information about Islamic architecture, especially the Dome of the Rock in Jerusalem.

2. The Islamic world was much more advanced in science, mathematics, and learning than the Western world during the Middle Ages. Create a multimedia presentation concerning the advances that were made in these areas by Islamic scholars and their influence on later cultures.

Primary Sources

Ibn Ishaq. Selections from *The Life of Muhammad.* http://www.fordham.edu/halsall/source/muhammadi-sira.html. An English translation of excerpts from a biography written about a century after Muhammad's death.

The Koran (Qu'ran). www.islamicity.com provides English and more than twenty other language translations of Islamic scripture. The ElectronicText Center of the University of Virginia (http://etext.virginia.edu/koran.html) also makes an English translation available.

Muhammad. Selections from *The Sunnah (The Traditions of Muhammad).* http://www.fordham.edu/halsall/source/sunnah-horne.html.

Secondary Sources

Berkey, Jonathan P. *The Formation of Islam: Religion and Society in the Near East, 600–1800.* Cambridge: Cambridge University Press, 2002. Scholarly treatment of the history of Islam.

Graham, Mark. *How Islam Created the Modern World.* Beltsville, MD: Amana Publications, 2006. Traces the Islamic contributions to science, medicine, mathematics, and social institutions.

Gunther, Sebastian, ed. *Ideas, Images, and Methods of Portrayal: Insights into Classical Arabic Literature and Islam.* The Netherlands: Brill Academic Publishers, 2005. Sixteen essays by various scholars along with an introduction by the editor and several indices to aid in finding information.

Kennedy, Hugh. *The Great Arab Conquests: How the Spread of Islam Changed the World We Live In.* Philadelphia: De Capo Press, 2007. Kennedy writes of the time from Muhammad's call for the establishment of an Islamic state until the eighth century, as Islam spread from Spain to Constantinople.

Lewis, Daniel Levering. *God's Crucible: Islam and the Making of Europe, 570–1215.* New York: W.W. Norton, 2008. Very readable and informative resource. Includes maps, illustrations, and an extensive bibliography.

World Wide Web

Internet Islamic History Sourcebook. http://www.fordham.edu/halsall/islam/. An extensive list of primary and secondary resource links.

Internet Sacred Texts. http://www.sacred-texts.com/isl/. This site provides English translations of many Islamic religious texts.

Islam and the Global Muslim eCommunity. Islamicity.com. A wealth of information about present-day Islam, the site also includes historical information and digitalized texts.

The Islamic World to 1600. http://www.ucalgary.ca/applied_history/tutor/islam/index2.html. This thorough resource on early Islam includes history, art, architecture, the caliphates, images, and tutorials.

Multimedia Sources

Arts of Islam. 1989. Video. Educational Dimensions, 29 minutes. Historical look at Islamic art and culture.

Islam. Video. 1998. DVD. Schlessinger Media. 50 minutes. Discusses history of Islam and its contributions to world culture.

Islam: History, Society, and Civilization. 2004. DVD. Discovery Channel School. 52 minutes. Program is divided into four parts: history and teachings, Suleiman, the Crusades, and Afghanistan.

Shiites, Followers of Ali. 1984. Video. Insight Media. 27 minutes. Discusses the formation of two major sects of Islam and their practices.

17. Byzantium Conquers Persia (627)

For centuries, Byzantium, the Eastern Roman Empire, and the Persian Empire had struggled with one another over their borders. The Byzantine Emperor Justinian (r. 527–565) successfully concentrated his military efforts on regaining Roman territory in the West that had been captured by

Germanic tribes. In order to lessen the Persian threat, he began paying the Persians to maintain "endless peace." Both these endeavors were expensive.

Emperors who followed Justinian either continued to pay the tribute or fought against the Persians. During the reign of Maurice I (r. 582–602), the Persian king Hormisdas (r. 579–590) was killed and his throne usurped. The legitimate heir fled to Constantinople to seek Maurice's help, which he gave. An interval of peace ensued, allowing both empires a period of respite. However, other forces such as the Avars and Slavs were threatening Byzantium. A series of bad decisions by Maurice led to a revolt by his army that ended in his death and replacement by Phocas (r. 602–610).

Phocas turned out to be a brutal tyrant who lost a great deal of Byzantine territory and again inflamed the Persians. In 609, Heraclius the Elder, the capable governor of Byzantine Africa, began a revolt. Under the naval leadership of his son, Heraclius the Younger, Constantinople was captured and Phocas was executed. The city immediately made the younger man its emperor, and he reigned from 610–641.

Under Heraclius, Byzantium mounted a miraculous effort to save the empire and Christianity. Since the treasury was exhausted, the people of the empire voluntarily brought forth their valuables to raise funds for an army. Heraclius himself took the lead in the fighting. When the Slavs and Avars were repulsed, Heraclius turned his efforts toward Persia. He used his naval power to protect Constantinople and to gain coastal territory. Then, Heraclius led his army deep into Persian territory. In 627, the Byzantine forces defeated the last Persian armies near Nineveh, thereby quelling the Persian threat for good. Heraclius returned to Constantinople a hero, but his peace was to be short-lived. The growing armies of Islam would soon attack Persia, and then Byzantine territory in 634. The ultimate effect of the prolonged fighting in which both empires had engaged was their vulnerability to the forces of Islam.

TERM PAPER SUGGESTIONS

1. Evaluate the effectiveness of the Byzantine practice of organizing its military into "themes."
2. Analyze the economic and social problems faced by Byzantium in the seventh century.
3. Analyze the economic, political, and military status of Persia on the eve of the victory of Heraclius at Nineveh.
4. How did the military policies of Maurice weaken the Byzantine Empire?

5. What innovations in military warfare did Byzantium develop during the sixth through eighth centuries? How did these innovations affect the outcome of battles?

6. Choose one of the descriptions of Byzantine warfare from primary sources and compare it to a modern history of the same event.

ALTERNATIVE TERM PAPER SUGGESTIONS

1. Prepare a speech that Heraclius might deliver as he passes judgment on the emperor Phocas. Be sure to consider the promise at the beginning of his reign and how he had not lived up to that promise.

2. Prepare a multimedia presentation showing how the seventh-century city of Constantinople was able to defend itself against attack.

Primary Sources

Charles, R. H. *The Chronicle of John, Bishop of Nikiu: Translated from Zotenberg's Ethiopic Text,* 1916. http://www.tertullian.org/fathers/nikiu2_chronicle .htm. Translation includes information about Phocas and Heraclius.

Malalas, John. "Byzantine Warfare in the Sixth Century," Excerpts from the *Chronicles* of Malalas. http://www.deremilitari.org/resources/sources/malalas.htm. This account of Malalas' *Chronicles* covers warfare from prehistoric times until his day. He used eyewitness accounts for much of the information about sixth-century Byzantium.

Simocatta, Theophylactus. *Historiae.* Trans. by Michael and Mary Whitby. Oxford: Oxford University Press, 1986. English translation of Simocatta's late sixth-century history of Byzantium. Includes extensive information about Maurice.

Strategos, Antiochus. *The Sack of Jerusalem.* http://www.fordham.edu/halsall/ sbook1c.html#After%20Justinian. An account of the Persian capture of Jerusalem in 614. Strategos makes Byzantine antiSemitism evident in his writing.

Theophanes Confessor. "The Campaigns of Emperor Herakleios," excerpts from the *Chronicle* of Theophanes Confessor. http://www.deremilitari.org/ resources/sources/theophanes.htm. This work includes a contemporary description of the battle at Nineveh.

Secondary Sources

Gregory, Timothy. *A History of Byzantium.* Malden, MA: Blackwell Publishing, 2005. Gregory calls the sixth and seventh century the "Dark Ages" of Byzantium and devotes a large amount of space to this period.

Haldon, John. *Byzantium at War.* Oxford, UK: Osprey Publishing, 2002. Extensive discussion of warfare in the Byzantine Empire, including specifics about military strategies.

Haldon, John. *Byzantium in the Seventh Century. The Transformation of a Culture.* London: Routledge, 1999. Haldon looks at topics such as the Byzantine attitude toward war and the organization of the army. Contains appendices with helpful information about the actual operation of campaigns.

Mango, Cyril, ed. *The Oxford History of Byzantium.* Oxford: Oxford University Press, 2002. A collection of entries by Byzantine scholars.

McCotter, Stephen. "'The Nation which Forgets Its Defenders Will Itself Be Forgotten': Emperor Maurice and the Persians." *De Re Militari: The Society for Medieval Military History.* 2003. http://www.deremilitari .org/resourcesarticles/mccotter2.htm. Detailed discussion about the conflict between Byzantium and Persia during Maurice's reign.

McCotter, Stephen. "The Strategy and Tactics of Siege Warfare in the Early Byzantine Period from Constantine to Heraclius." *Golden Horn: Journal of Byzantium* (4) 1996. Also online at http://www.deremilitari.org/ resources/articles.htm.

Threadgold, Warren. *A History of the Byzantine State and Society.* Stanford: Stanford University Press, 1997. Includes a chapter devoted to the war against Persia.

World Wide Web

De Re Militari: The Society for Medieval Military History. http://www.deremilitari .org/. Maintained by an international association of scholars, the site offers articles on many aspects of medieval warfare, links to other sites, a bibliography, and book reviews.

Dumbarton Oaks Research Library and Collection. http://www.doaks.org/. Dumbarton Oaks is a Harvard University Research institute devoted in part to Byzantine studies. A large collection of scholarly papers on many topics is available.

Explore Byzantium. http://byzantium.seashell.net.nz/index.php. Extensive site with articles, timeline, images, and maps. Includes information concerning warfare.

The Tertullian Project. http://www.tertullian.org/. This site is primarily devoted to the works of Tertullian, but continues to add primary sources from other writers. Follow the link to additional church fathers.

Multimedia Sources

Byzantium and the Holy Roman Empire: Christianity in the 7th and 8th Centuries. 1999. DVD. Films Media Group. 48 minutes. Two parts; the first of which deals with the threats of Persia and Islam to Byzantium.

Engineering an Empire: The Byzantines. 2006. DVD. The History Channel. Approximately 45 minutes. Follows the rise of Byzantine power until the Turks captured Constantinople.

18. Xuanzang's Pilgrimage across Central Asia to India (629–645)

In the early Chinese Tang period, Buddhism had spread through much of the nation. However, several sects with conflicting practices had emerged. Xuanzang (Hsuan-tsang), who had been a Buddhist monk since age thirteen, continually sought deeper understanding of the teachings of Buddha and was troubled by rival teachings. In 629, he began a 16-year journey to the centers of Buddhist learning throughout Asia and India. He remained at some monasteries for extended periods of study, but traveled approximately 10,000 miles on his pilgrimage.

Returning to China with more than 600 scrolls of sacred writing, Xuanzang began the arduous task of translation. He also wrote *Records of the Western Regions (Da tang xi yu ji)*, the story of his pilgrimage and what he learned in his travels. Xuanzang's work made more Buddhist teachings available throughout China and increased the number of converts. During the decades immediately following his pilgrimage, nobles sponsored the construction of many important temples and monasteries, including Da Ci'en Temple, where Xuanzang served as abbot.

Records of the Western Regions broadened knowledge of the Asian continent, particularly India, and opened the way for increased commerce and diplomatic relations. Xuanzang's objective and detailed observations included information on climate, geography, literature, people, language, and customs, as well as facts about Buddhism and other religions in the places he visited. The title *Sanzang,* or eminent monk, was added to Xuanzang's name, and at his death in 664, the emperor Gaozang honored him by cancelling audiences for three days.

In the last years of the Tang dynasty, the number of Buddhist followers decreased among both commoners and nobility. In the 16th century, a popular mythological novel based on Xuanzang's pilgrimage, *The Journey to the West* by Wu Cheng'en, reintroduced Xuanzang's story to the Chinese.

TERM PAPER SUGGESTIONS

1. What was the importance of Xuanzang's journey to Chinese technology?
2. What was the importance of Xuanzang's journey to Chinese literature?
3. What was the effect of Xuanzang's journey on the spread of Buddhism in China?
4. Compare the life a Chinese Buddhist monk to that of a Christian monk in the West in the seventh century.
5. Select one of the Buddhist temples built in seventh-century China. How does the structure of the temple embody the principle beliefs of the worshippers?

ALTERNATIVE TERM PAPER SUGGESTIONS

1. Create a map of Xuanzang's 16-year pilgrimage to India and back to China. Highlight places where he spent time and their importance in his mission to better understand Buddhism.
2. Study the construction of seventh-century Buddhist temples and monasteries. Create a multimedia presentation of their significant features and the construction techniques that were employed by the builders.

Primary Sources

Devahuti, D., ed. *The Unknown Hsuan-Tsang.* Oxford: Oxford University Press, 2001. A collection of rare Xuanzang works, with extensive notes and commentary. A list of the work and translations completed by Xuanzang is provided.

Xuanzang (Hiuen Tsiang). Excerpts from *Buddhist Records of the Western World, Vol. I.* Trans. by Samuel Beal. London: Kegan Paul, Trench, Tabner, 1906. http://www.mssu.edu/projectsouthasia/HISTORY/PRIMARYDOCS/FOREIGN_VIEWS/CHINESE/XuanZang/BookIII.htm.

Xuanzang. *The Great Tang Dynasty Record of the Western Regions.* Trans. by Li Rongxi. Berkeley: Numata Center for Buddhist Translation & Research, 1997. Complete translation of the work of Xuanzang.

Secondary Sources

Chappell, David. W., ed. *Buddhist and Taoist Practice in Medieval Chinese Society.* Honolulu: University of Hawaii Press, 1987. Discusses the spread and practice of Buddism and Taoism throughout China.

Cheng'en, Wu. *The Monkey and the Monk: An Abridgment of The Journey to the West*. Trans. Anthony C. Yu. Chicago: University of Chicago Press, 2006. This is a retelling of the story of Xuanzang's journey in an allegorical form.

Sen, Tansen. "In Search of Longevity and Good Karma: Chinese Diplomatic Missions to Middle India in the Seventh Century." *Journal of World History* 12.1 (Spring 2001). Discusses the significance of Xuanzang's and other Tang missions to India and how the missions advanced diplomacy, Chinese learning, and technology.

Wriggins, Sally. *The Silk Road Journey with Xuanzang*. Boulder, CO: Westview Press, 2003. A biography of Xuanzang, concentrating on his 16-year journey along the Silk Road. The last chapter discusses the legacy of Xuanzang in history.

World Wide Web

Asia for Educators. http://afe.easia.columbia.edu/. An extensive site designed for teachers, but also making a great deal of information available for students on ancient and modern China. Material is added frequently.

China. http://hua.umf.maine.edu/China/tang.html. Maintained through the University of Maine, this Web site provides an extremely thorough bibliography on all topics Chinese, including the age of the Tang Dynasty.

China Institute in America. http://www.chinainstitute.org/index.cfm. Home page for the China Institute; provides a variety of information and links to other resources.

Routledge Encyclopedia of Philosophy Online. http://www.rep.routledge.com/LOGIN? sessionid=5a1e978cf5ce24c5ec06485e05fcc699&authstatuscode=400. Excellent resource for information about Buddhist and other philosophies. Requires a subscription, but has a free trial and is available through some libraries.

Multimedia Sources

Overview of Chinese History. 1991. Video. National Video Communications. 29 minutes. Includes a segment on the Tang dynasty.

Well-known Cultural Literates of China: Xuanzang/Yue Fei. 2007. DVD. Qilu Audio and Video Press. 50 minutes. In Chinese with English subtitles; two parts, about the title individuals.

19. First Seige of Constantinople (c. 671–c. 678)

After defeating the Persian Empire in 627, the Byzantine Empire, centered in Constantinople, enjoyed a period of relative peace. Regions of the empire remote from the capital, however, continued to be assaulted by Muslims, Avars, Slavs and other groups eager to share in the wealth and power of Byzantium, and within ten years of Emperor Heraclius's (r. 610–641) recapture of Jerusalem, Constantinople was lost to the Muslims. Syria, Palestine, Mesopotamia, and Egypt fell to Muslim forces in the mid-seventh century, and Byzantium was forced to draw back, restructure, and stabilize its new borders. By doing so, it was able to successfully defend itself for some time.

One of the greatest threats to the empire was the naval assault mounted by Muslims against the capital city itself beginning around 671. Constantinople was one of the world's greatest seaports and the primary center of trade between the East and West. One of the best fortified cities in the world and well prepared for siege warfare, it proved to be impregnable. In addition, the Byzantines were superior sailors and had developed a powerful new incendiary weapon called Greek fire that proved effective against troops, ships, and weaponry.

Historians disagree about the exact dates and extent of the siege, but it was a costly effort for both parties in terms of the number of deaths and the cost of military equipment. The Muslim naval forces were destroyed, but the Byzantines were unable to protect all their territory. The first siege of Constantinople demonstrated the strength that remained in Byzantium and served as a unifying force among the populace. The city was also able to repulse a land and sea attack by Muslims in the late eighth century.

TERM PAPER SUGGESTIONS

1. Discuss both the geography and the man-made defenses that made it possible for Constantinople to resist the siege by Muslim forces.
2. Even while the capital city was under siege, Byzantine forces met Muslims in major sea battles. Research these battles and discuss the naval strategies used by both sides.
3. What was Greek fire? In which battles was it most effective? Why?

4. Research trade and commerce between the East and West in the seventh and eighth centuries. Why was Constantinople so important to trade?

5. Research the costs in manpower and material of the siege. What did each side gain from the war? What did each side lose? Eventually the Muslims withdrew from Constantinople, but would you say Byzantium won the war?

ALTERNATIVE TERM PAPER SUGGESTIONS

1. Create a multimedia presentation with a chronology of the major battles of the war between Muslim and Byzantine forces between 671 and 678. Use maps to show the locations of the battles and include details about the outcomes.

2. Assume the persona of a citizen of Constantinople in 671 such as a mother, a soldier, a merchant, or a priest. Create a journal recording what happens to your city during the next seven years. Include news you receive about the status of the siege.

Primary Sources

Geanakoplos, Deno John, ed. *Byzantium: Church, Society, and Civilization Seen through Contemporary Eyes.* Chicago: University of Chicago Press, 1986. A remarkable collection of excerpts from medieval documents, topically arranged.

Theophanes Confessor. "The Campaigns of Emperor Herakleios," in the *Chronicle of Theophanes Confessor.* http://www.deremilitari.org/resources/sources/theophanes.htm.Includes a discussion of siege warfare.

Secondary Sources

Gregory, Timothy. *A History of Byzantium.* Malden, MA: Blackwell Publishing, 2005. Gregory calls the sixth and seventh century the "Dark Ages" of Byzantium and devotes a large amount of space to this period.

Haldon, John. *Byzantium at War.* Oxford: Osprey Publishing, 2002. Extensive discussion of warfare in the Byzantine Empire, including specific information about military strategies.

Haldon, John. *Byzantium in the Seventh Century. The Transformation of a Culture.* London: Routledge, 1999. Haldon looks at topics such as the Byzantine attitude toward war and the organization of the army. Contains appendices with helpful information about the actual operation of campaigns.

Mango, Cyril, ed. *The Oxford History of Byzantium.* Oxford: Oxford University Press, 2002. A collection of entries by Byzantine scholars.

Oikonomides, Nicolas, ed. *Byzantium at War.* Athens: Institute for Byzantine Studies, 1997. Contains 14 scholarly essays, some in French or Greek. Three of the English essays are particularly helpful with research on seventh-century Byzantium.

Threadgold, Warren. *A History of the Byzantine State and Society.* Stanford: Stanford University Press, 1977. Excellent information on the political and military developments of the seventh century.

World Wide Web

De Re Militari: The Society for Medieval Military History. http://www.deremilitari .org/. Maintained by an international association of scholars, the site offers articles on many aspects of medieval warfare, links to other sites, a bibliography, and book reviews.

Dumbarton Oaks Research Library and Collection. http://www.doaks.org/. Dumbarton Oaks is a Harvard University Research Institute devoted in part to Byzantine studies. A large collection of scholarly papers on many topics is available online.

Multimedia Sources

Byzantium and the Holy Roman Empire: Christianity in the 7th and 8th Centuries. 1999. DVD. Films Media Group. 48 minutes. Two parts; the first of which deals with the threats of Persia and Islam to Byzantium.

Engineering an Empire: The Byzantines. 2006. DVD. The History Channel. Approximately 45 minutes. Follows the rise of Byzantine power until the Turks captured Constantinople.

Siege Machines. DVD. Part of the *Modern Marvels* series. History Channel Production. 50 minutes. Although the production does not deal specifically with the first siege of Constantinople, it provides understanding of how siege weapons were used.

20. Moorish Conquest of Spain (711)

In the century following Mohammad's death, Islamic armies conquered much of Northern Africa and the Near East. They then turned their attention to Europe. In 711, the Muslim general Tariq ibn-Ziyad and an army of 10,000 crossed the Strait of Gibraltar from Northern Africa and invaded the Iberian Peninsula. The army landed at a promontory that was given his name *Djabal Tarik* (Tarik's Mountain; known today as the Rock of Gibraltar). Easily defeating the army of the Visigoths under King Roderick (r. 710–711), Tariq ordered the prisoners to be divided into two groups. He had one group cut to pieces and boiled; the second group was released with orders to tell the rest of Spain about the Moors (from the Greek *maures,* dark). Tariq then quickly pressed his advantage north to the city of Toledo. Within a month, the Islamic army had control of a large amount of Iberian territory.

The governor of North Africa, Musa ibn Nusayr, a representative of the first Islamic dynasty, the Umayyad, brought an additional 18,000 troops to Iberia, and together the two armies conquered the east of Spain, Portugal, Basque, and as far north as the Pyrenees. Thousands of Moors emigrated to Al-Andalus (Iberia) following the conquest. Musa returned to his capital in Damascus, as did Tariq. Musa's son married Roderick's widow and named himself governor of the new Islamic province. His unpopular rule was short-lived, however, with his own men rebelling and beheading him. His head was shipped back to Damascus. The Moorish advance into France was stopped in 732 by the army of the Frankish ruler Charles Martel, but the Moors ruled Spain for another 800 years. There were periodic uprisings by the inhabitants of the territory, but no serious threats to Moorish rule.

In 750, a Syrian prince, Abd-er-Rahman, became governor of Al-Andalus. A ruthless ruler, he declared the territory autonomous and named himself emir (ruler). He raised an army of 40,000 and easily defeated his opposition.

During the Moorish occupation, Spain became a center for learning and for advancement in the arts and sciences. Islamic historians carefully recorded the events of the period, and scholars in other fields translated the writings from the Greeks and Romans into Arabic and Spanish. The religions of Christianity, Judaism, and Islam coexisted with remarkable tolerance during the early years of Moorish rule. Intermarriage was common, and it was possible for one to advance his or her position in society. In the 9th century, Al-Andalus declared itself a fully independent Islamic state with its own caliph and a capital city in Cordoba. The Umayyad dynasty in Spain ended in 1086.

TERM PAPER SUGGESTIONS

1. How did the Muslim government of Spain differentiate between the community of believers and the people of the Book (those who had received the holy scripture)? How did it deal with polytheists?

2. What was the effect on trade after Spain came under Moorish rule?

3. Assess the position of Jews in the culture of Moorish Spain.

4. Between c. 750–1200, Spain was considered the most advanced nation in the field of science. Why was this so? What improvements in scientific fields occurred in Spain during these times?

5. How do you account for the relative peace among the three major religious groups during the first centuries of the Moorish rule in Spain?

6. *Civilized* is a relative term. What is your definition of *civilized,* and based on your definition, was Spain more or less civilized after the Moorish invasion? Why?

7. Analyze the Islamic influences on Spanish art and architecture.

ALTERNATIVE TERM PAPER SUGGESTIONS

1. Create a multimedia presentation reflecting the art and architecture of Moorish Spain. Include music as well as the visual arts.

2. Create a dialogue among representatives of each of the faiths of Islam, Christianity, and Judaism about their rights and responsibilities in the early years of Moorish Spain.

Primary Sources

Al Maggari: *Tarik's Address to His Soldiers,* 711, from *The Breath of Perfumes.* http://www.fordham.edu/halsall/islam/islamsbook.html. Translated on *Medieval Sourcebook.*

Anonymous. *The Battle of Tours, 732.* http://www.fordham.edu/halsall/. Translated on *Medieval Sourcebook.*

Constable, Olivia Remie, ed. *Medieval Iberia: Readings from Christian, Muslim, and Jewish Sources.* Philadelphia: University of Pennsylvania Press, 1997. Contains translations of excerpts and entire documents on religious, political, and social issues in Moorish Spain.

http://www.fordham.edu/halsall/source/sunnah-horne.html. Translation includes an account of the first Muslim violence against Spanish Jews.

Ibn Abd-el-Hakem: *The Islamic Conquest of Spain.* http://www.fordham.edu/halsall/islam/islamsbook.html. Translated on *Medieval Sourcebook.*

Ibd Daud, Abraham. *On Samuel Ha-Nagid, Vizier of Granada, 993-d after 1056.* http://www.fordham.edu/halsall/source/ha-nagid.html. Translation of biography of a Jew who rose to a powerful position in Spain.

Secondary Sources

Fletcher, Richard. *Moorish Spain.* Berkeley: University of California Press, 1993. A brief and very readable introduction to Moorish history, culture, and politics.

Kennedy, Hugh. *Muslim Spain and Portugal: A Political History of al-Andalus*. Essex, UK: Pearson Education Unlimited, 1997. Divides the history of Moorish Spain into eleven periods for discussion. Includes a number of maps.

Lane-Poole, Stanley. *The Story of the Moors in Spain*. Baltimore: Kessinger Publishing, 2007. This is a facsimile reproduction of Lane-Poole's standard history of the Moors, first published in 1886.

Lowney, Chris. *A Vanished World: Muslims, Christians, and Jews in Medieval Spain*. Oxford: Oxford University Press, 2006. Lowney concentrates on the cooperation and antagonism among the three major religions in medieval Spain.

Menocal, Maria Rosa. *The Ornament of the World: How Muslims, Jews and Christians Created a Culture of Tolerance in Medieval Spain*. Boston: Little, Brown, and Company, 2002. Discusses relationships among the three major religions in Spain and the advances in art, literature, and science between 836 and the late 13th century.

Reilly, Bernard F. *The Medieval Spains*. Cambridge: Cambridge University Press, 1993. History of Spain from its invasion by the Visogoths to the defeat of the Moors in the 15th century.

Watt , W. Montgomery, and Cachia, Pierre. *A History of Islamic Spain*. Edinburg: Edinburg University Press, 2007 (1965). Comprehensive history of Islamic Spain and its influence on European culture.

World Wide Web

The Islamic World to 1600. http://www.ucalgary.ca/applied_history/tutor/islam/index2.html. Maintained by the Applied History Research Group of the University of Calgary, this site provides information on periods, individuals, and the arts in Moorish Spain. Has an extensive bibliography of print and online resources.

Library of Iberian Resources on Line. http://libro.uca.edu/. Makes available a wide collection of recent, out-of-print resources on Spain between the fifth and seventeenth centuries.

Multimedia Sources

The Alhambra. 1989. Spanish Ministry of Culture. 30 minutes. A tour of the building and grounds of the famed Spanish castle with a discussion of its construction and purposes.

Christians, Jews, and Muslims in Medieval Spain. 1979. Films Media Group. 33 minutes. Traces 300 years of interactions among the three major religious groups in Moorish Spain.

Cities of Light: The Rise and Fall of Islamic Spain. 2007. DVD. PBS Productions. 120 minutes. Filmed on location, uses reenactments and interviews with scholars to present the tolerant relationship among religions in the early years of the Islamic rule of Spain and the reasons the tolerance was destroyed.

Islamic Spain. 2004. CD. San Antonio, TX: Babbitt International Resources. 39 minutes. Covers the complete history of Moors in Spain, emphasizing their contributions to architecture, sciences, and language.

The Moorish South: Art in Muslim and Christian Spain from 711 to 1492. 2007. BBCW Production. 51 minutes. Art historian Andrew Graham-Dixon hosts this program about the art and architecture of the Moors. Tours of buildings and examination of artifacts and gardens.

The Moors: At the Height of the Empire. 2007. Insight Media. 50 minutes. Explores cultural developments, especially in art and architecture in Moorish Spain.

When the Moors Ruled Europe. 2007. Films Media Group. Two segments, 50–53 minutes each. Author Bettany Hughes focuses on the mutual influences of Christians and Muslims in the art and architecture of Moorish Spain.

21. Iconoclast Controversy (c. 730–843)

Iconoclast literally means "one who breaks images." The Church had used icons and images since its earliest days. Icons as a doctrinal issue arose repeatedly but did not cause a serious rift in the Christian church until the eighth century. In 724, Bishops Constantine of Nikoleia and Thomas of Claudiopolis of the Eastern church condemned the use of icons. The bishops were opposed by Patriarch Germanus I, but supported by Emperor Leo III (r. 717–741). The disagreement culminated with Leo removing the figure of Christ from the Chalke palace and pressuring Germanus to sign a decree banning icons and to resign as patriarch. The iconoclasts then destroyed a number of figures and icons in churches and monasteries.

This first period of iconoclasm lasted about 30 years. During this period, monks and church officials were the major opponents of Leo's policies. John Damascene, an official connected to the patriarch of Jerusalem, wrote three documents in defense of the use of images. From the Western church, Popes Gregory II and Gregory III wrote letters protesting, and the Roman synod of 731 voted to oppose the policy. Leo's son and heir to the throne, Constantine V (r. 741–775), tried to make the interdiction against icons official church doctrine. He wrote a lengthy treatise on the theological basis of iconoclasm and coerced the Byzantine episcopate general council into endorsing his arguments. A period of persecution of iconophiles followed, during which at least four monks were martyred.

The outrage over the persecutions led Pope Stephen III (r. 768–772) to hold a second Roman synod on the subject of icons in 769. A backlash of public opinion against the presecution by iconoclasts prompted the synod to reaffirm the theological basis for sacred icons. Many images were restored in the following years. A final conflict between the two groups arose in the first half of the 9th century but was again resolved in favor of the use of icons by the Second Council of Nicaea in 842.

Iconoclasts based their objections to images on the first commandment, which warns against idols. Most of those who were against icons were devout believers who were truly concerned that the icons would lead individuals to idolatry. Individuals supporting icons were just as genuine in their belief that they were an important element of worship. This prolonged and recurring doctrinal dispute further separated the Byzantine church from that of Rome and helped guarantee that the emperor would continue to be in the West.

SUGGESTED TERM PAPER TOPICS

1. On what principles or beliefs did iconoclasts base their arguments against holy images? What principles or beliefs were used by their opponents? Consider the theological arguments in favor of icons. How does the redecoration of the temple in Constantinople, Hagia Sophia, after iconoclasm incorporate these arguments?

2. Discuss the representations of the Byzantine empress during and after the Age of Iconoclasm.

3. What is the significance of the depiction of Jesus and Mary in visual art in the light of theological controversies of the iconoclastic period?

4. How did the iconoclast controversy affect the relationship between the Eastern and Western church?

5. Why is it important to study the church when studying the political and social history of Byzantium?

ALTERNATIVE TERM PAPER SUGGESTIONS

1. Create a multimedia presentation concerning the Byzantine icons. Use music from the period along with the images and information you include.

2. Prepare a debate between the two sides of the iconoclast controversy. Use the arguments presented by each side in the eighth and ninth centuries.

Primary Sources

"The *Apology* of Claudius of Turin." http://urban.hunter.cuny.edu/~thead/claudius .htm. Translation of 9th-century bishop's argument against the use of icons.

Mango, Cyril. *The Art of the Byzantine Empire, 312–1453: Sources and Documents.* Toronto: University of Toronto Press, 1986. Mango has selected valuable primary source documents on the Byzantine Empire to appear in this one book.

Statement from the Synod of Constantinople (753 AD) and Confession from the Council of Nicea (787 AD). http://www.iclnet.org/pub/resources/ christian-history.html#fathers. These documents represent opposing church views on iconoclasm.

St. John Damascene. *On Holy Images, Followed by Three Sermons on the Assumption.* Trans. by Mary H. Allies. London: Thomas Baker, 1898. http://www .archive.org/stream/stjohndamasceneo00alliuoft. Digitalized copy of John of Damascene's treatises in opposition to iconoclasm.

Secondary Sources

Besancon, Alain. *The Forbidden Image: An Intellectual History of Iconoclasm.* Trans. by Jane Marie Todd. Chicago: University of Chicago Press, 1994. A complete history of iconoclast arguments from earliest Christian times to the present day.

Eastmond, Anthony, James, Liz, and Cormack, Robin, eds. *Icon and Word: The Power of Images in Byzantium.* Burlington, VT: Ashgate Publishing, 2003. A collection of sixteen essays on Byzantine icons.

Mango, Cyril, ed. *The Oxford History of Byzantium.* Oxford: Oxford University Press, 2002. Contains twelve essays written by leading Byzantine scholars, plus nine "special features" including icon and iconoclasm.

Norwich, John Julius. *A Short History of Byzantium.* New York: Random House, 1999. Includes two chapters on the iconoclast controversy.

Peers, Glenn. *Subtle Angels: Representing Angels in Byzantium.* Berkley: University of California Press, 2001. Discussion of issues involving the images of angels during the iconoclastic controversy.

Schaff, Peter. *History of the Christian Church, Volume IV: Mediaeval Christianity. A.D. 590–1073.* New York: Charles Scribner & Sons, 1910. http://www .ccel.org/. Includes chapters on iconoclasm.

World Wide Web

Christian Classics Ethereal Library. http://www.ccel.org/. Contains digitalized copies of many writings by Christian scholars.

Dumbarton Oaks Research Library and Collection. http://www.doaks.org/. Dumbarton Oaks is a Harvard University Research institute devoted in part to Byzantine studies. A large collection of scholarly papers on many topics is available.

Multimedia Sources

Byzantium and the Holy Roman Empire: Christianity in the 7th and 8th Centuries. 1999. DVD. Films Media Group. 48 minutes. History of Christian church in Byzantium.

History of Orthodox Christianity. 1992. DVD. Vision Video. 90 minutes. Includes a segment on iconoclasm.

Introduction to the Eastern Catholic Churches. 2007. Twelve-minute streaming video produced by the Eparchy of Parma. Provides a history of the development of Byzantine Christianity. http://www.byzcath.org/Faith-and -Worship/Videos.htm.

Reflections of Glory: The Origins of Byzantine Art. 1982. Twenty-minute streaming video by the Byzantine Catholic Church in America. Discusses icons in Byzantine churches. http://www.byzcath.org/Faith-and-Worship/ Videos.htm.

Sacred Craft. 1997. DVD. Global Catholic Network. 75 minutes. Brendan McAnery discusses the theology and characteristics of Eastern empire iconography.

22. Bede Writes the *Ecclesiastical History* (735)

The most admired scholar of his time, Bede spent his entire life in and around the paired monasteries of Wearmouth and Jarrow in England. He entered Wearmouth when he was seven years old in 680 and was tutored by the renowned clerics Benedict Biscop and Ceolfred. Bede became a deacon at 18 and an ordained priest at 30.

Fluent in Latin, Greek, and English, Bede studied mathematics, astronomy, and music, as well as theology and philosophy. His writing on a myriad of topics helped create Jarrow's reputation as one of Europe's finest centers of learning. While Bede remained in Northumbria throughout his life, he actively engaged in scholarship with many of the learned who visited him there. His reputation was so great that he was referred to as "the Venerable Bede."

In 731, Bede completed his most ambitious and well-known work, *Ecclesiastical History of the English Church and People,* which earned him the title "father of English history." Significant because it is the first history of England written by a native Englishman, the *History* provides most of our information about Anglo-Saxon England. The Latin text is a product of its time, presenting history as the work of God in the lives of men and telling of miracles related to saints and kings. Bede, however, predated modern historians by using a narrative style, consulting multiple sources, using eye-witness accounts, reporting conflicting stories, and, most importantly, by meticulously recording the sources for his information. He even asked that later copies of his work keep these references intact. His work set the standard for historians throughout the Middle Ages and set the precedent for considering England as a single nation rather than separate kingdoms.

Among Bede's approximately forty works is extensive commentary on scripture and other theological works. His "Musica theoretica" and "De arte Metricâ" provide some of the earliest information available about the Gregorian chant. Bede's scholarship extended to the study of chronology, and in *De Temporum Ratione* (*On the Reckoning of Time,* 725), he introduced the practice of recording time from Christ's birth, which he used in his *Ecclesiastical History.*

TERM PAPER SUGGESTIONS

1. Why were so many children like Bede placed in medieval monasteries? What benefits did they, or their parents, receive from this?

2. How does Bede's work help prepare England for Alfred the Great's (r. 871–899) reign?

3. Discuss the method of calculating the calendar before Bede. Why were his innovations significant?

4. Some scholars suggest that Bede and his fellow monks at Jarrow began a period that reversed the intellectual decline of Western Europe, essentially bringing England and Europe out of the Dark Ages. Discuss the economic, political, and intellectual factors that contributed to this turnaround and evaluate whether Bede's work was really a significant contribution to this change.

5. One of the major themes of Bede's *Ecclesiastical History* is the unification of the English nation under one faith: Roman Catholicism. Using other primary

sources, including Anglo-Saxon literature, evaluate the soundness of this depiction.

6. Read Bede's *On the Reckoning of Time* and evaluate him as a scientist. Does he follow scientific methods? Are his conclusions scientific in nature?

ALTERNATIVE TERM PAPER SUGGESTIONS

1. Choose an event described by Bede and research it in other sources. Create a reenactment of the event in a manner of your choice, such as a dialogue, a radio drama, a news program, a video, or a play.

2. Choose a significant event from modern history and write about it, imitating Bede's style and adopting his world view.

3. Scholars from throughout Europe travelled to Jarrow to be instructed by Bede. Pretend you are able to make this journey to consult with Bede. Create the dialogue that might occur. Do not write an interview of Bede, but create a dialogue between two individuals well versed on a topic.

Primary Sources

Bede. *The Complete Works of Venerable Bede, 8 vols.* Trans. by Rev. J. A. Giles. London: Whittaker and Co., 1843. *The Online Library of Liberty.* http://oll .libertyfund.org/index.php?option=com_frontpage&Itemid=149.

Bede. *Ecclesiastical History of the English Church and People.* English translations are readily available. An online version of the 1907 translation and commentary by A. M. Sellar is available at the Christian Classic Ethereal Library, http://www.ccel.org/ccel/bede/history.i.html?highlight=bede#highlight.

Secondary Sources

Blair, Peter Hunter. *Roman Britain and Early England 55 B. C. to A. D. 871.* New York: W. W. Norton and Company, 1966. Chapter 10 is devoted to monasteries in Northumbria.

Blair, Peter Hunter, and Keynes, Simon. *An Introduction to Anglo-Saxon England.* 3rd ed. Cambridge: Cambridge University Press, 2003. After two chapters on the history of the age, Blair devotes the remaining chapters to social institutions: the church, the economy, the government, and letters.

Blair, Peter Hunter, and Lapidge, Michael. *The World of Bede.* Cambridge: Cambridge University Press, 1997 (reprint). A standard work on seventh-century England and the role of the church.

Evan, Gillian Rosemary. *Fifty Key Medieval Thinkers.* London: Routledge, 2002. Contains a chapter concerning each of 50 influential medieval intellectuals from all walks of life, including Bede.

Goffart, Walter. *The Narrators of Barbarian History (A.D. 550–800): Jordanes, Gregory of Tours, Bede, And Paul the Deacon.* Princeton: Princeton University Press, 1988. Goffart, a senior researcher at Yale, places these four historians in the context of their times. His commentary makes generous use of quotations from the works of these men.

Wright, J. Robert. *A Companion to Bede: A Reader's Commentary on the Ecclesiastical History of the English People.* Grand Rapids: Wm. B. Erdmans Publishing Company, 2008. Contains the complete *History* along with comments and informative appendices.

World Wide Web

BedeNet. http://bede.net/. An academic resource site devoted to the study of the Venerable Bede and his works.

The Internet Medieval Sourcebook. http://www.fordham.edu/halsall/. Provides translations of some of Bede's works, as well as other early English texts.

British History at Britannia Magazine. http://www.britannia.com/history/index.html. Links to articles on all ages of British history; includes images, articles, and chronologies of the early church. Also provides access to some primary documents, including excerpts from Bede.

Multimedia Sources

Living in the Past: Life in Anglo-Saxon Times. No date. DVD. Kultur Video. 50 minutes. Includes a segment on the *Ecclesiastical History.*

Memorable Leaders in Christian History: Bede (673–735). 2006. DVD. Vision Video. 56 minutes. Includes a companion PDF guide on the DVD.

23. Abbasid Dynasty (750–1258)

For 500 years the Abbasid Dynasty, so named because it claimed descent from Islamic founder Mohammed's uncle al-Abbas, ruled the Islamic world, except for the Iberian Peninsula. Around 718, the Abbasids began quietly opposing the ruling Umayyads with a propaganda war. The opposition grew to open revolt around 749 when Abu al-Abbas (r. 750–754) named himself the new caliph. At the Battle of the Zab in 750, the Abbasids defeated the Umayyad forces, capturing and killing the caliph Marwan II (r. 744–750) and later marching into the capital of Damascus. Al-Abbas lived up to the name he took—al-Saffah (the bloodthirsty)—by attempting to kill all surviving members of the Umayyad family.

Changes in governance were immediate. The Abbasids dismissed provincial governors, killing any who were popular enough to represent a threat, and installed their own administrators. A newly created position of the vizier oversaw the administration of government. When al-Abbas died in 754, his brother al-Mansur (r. 754–775) began a successful reign in the new capital city of Baghdad. During his rule, the caliphate grew in size and power. Al-Mansur and two of his successors, al-Rashid (r. 786–809) and al-Mamun (r. 813–833), were especially devoted to the expansion of education, science, the arts, and trade. One of the greatest intellectual achievements of the age was the translation of many Greek texts into Arabic, which sparked a renewed interest in learning. For instance, the recovered mathematical knowledge of the Greeks was further developed by Islamic mathematicians such as al-Biruni and Abu Nasr Mansur. Medical knowledge also increased rapidly. In the 9th century, Baghdad claimed to have more than 800 physicians.

By the end of the 9th century, however, Abbasid power was waning. The government had, like the Romans before them, employed large numbers of mercenaries for its armies, largely Turks who cared little for the people and their traditions. Territorial disputes broke out in various parts of the vast empire, leading eventually to the establishment of several local dynasties. In the mid-11th century, the caliphate was so weakened that it was an easy target for the invading Seljuk Turks. The Turks allowed the Abbasids to retain the title of caliph, but only in a religious, not political, sense.

TERM PAPER SUGGESTIONS

1. What were the achievements of the Abbasid dynasty in arts, architecture, and learning?
2. What was the position of women within the Golden Age of the Abbasid dynasty?
3. Assess the position of minorities during the Abbasid dynasty's rule.
4. What were the goals of Islamic expansion under the Ummayad Caliphate (650–750)? Were these the same goals the Abbasid Caliphate (750–1050) had? Did they use the same methods to achieve their goals? Which caliphate was more successful?
5. Evaluate the achievements of the Abbasid Caliphate as compared with those of Western Europe during the same time period.
6. Why did the Abbasid caliphs move the capital of the Islamic world from Damascus to Baghdad? What were the results of this move?

ALTERNATIVE TERM PAPER SUGGESTIONS

1. Prepare a multimedia presentation about medicine during the Abbasid caliphate. Include what the Muslims learned from the Greeks and their own discoveries.

2. What were the major disagreements between the Umayyads and the Abbasids? Prepare an oral presentation in a format of your choice that clarifies these disagreements.

Primary Sources

Al-Kirmani. *Al-Masabih fi ithbat al-imama.* Trans. by Paul E. Walker in *Master of the Age: An Islamic Treatise on the Necessity of the Immamate.* London: I. B. Tauris & Co., 2007. Walker translated this important Assabid text and places it in its historical context through his introduction and comments.

Avicenna. *The Metaphysics of the Shifa.* Trans. and annotated by Michael E. Marmura. Salt Lake City: Brigham Young University Press, 2004. A parallel English and Arabic text by a well-known Islamic physician of the 9th century.

Lamoreaux, John, ed. *Theodore Abu Qurrah.* Salt Lake City: Brigham University Press, 2006. Trans. and commentary on the work of the Christian Arab theologian Abu Qurrah. Influences from both Christian and Arabic culture are evident.

Secondary Sources

El-Hibri, Tayeb. *Reinterpreting Islamic Historiography: Harun al Rashid and the Narrative of the Abbasid Caliphate.* Cambridge: Cambridge University Press, 1999. Looks at the eighth and ninth century narratives of the Abbasid rulers from a literary/critical perspective, arguing that these accounts were cultural teaching devices more than historical documents.

Gutas, Dimitri. *Greek Thought, Arab Culture: The Graeco-Arabic Translation Movement in Baghdad and Early Abbasid Society.* London: Routledge, 1998. Traces the translation of the Greek scientific works into Arabic during the Abbasid Caliphate and discusses the significance of these translations.

Le Strange, Guy. *Baghdad during the Abbasid Caliphate.* London: Kessinger Publishing, 2004. A reprint of the 1900 publication by Le Strange, who used many primary sources to show how Baghdad changed during eight time periods and to discuss the great buildings of the Islamic capital city.

Le Strange, Guy. *The Lands of the Eastern Caliphate: Mesopotamia, Persia, and Central Asia from the Moslem Conquest to the Time of Timur.* London: Elibron Classics, 2006. A facsimile reprint of Le Strange's 1905 classic work on the Islamic world.

Sypeck, Jeff. *Becoming Charlemagne: Europe, Baghdad, and the Empires of A.D. 800.* New York: HarperCollins, 2007. This volume is divided into two sections on empires and emperor, and discusses each in the decade leading up to and following 800.

Young, M. J. L., Latham, J. D., and Serjeant, R. B., eds. *Religion, Learning and Science in the Abbasid Period.* Cambridge: Cambridge University Press, 1990. A collection of 29 essays about scholarship under the Abbasids.

World Wide Web

Internet Islamic History Sourcebook. http://www.fordham.edu/halsall/islam/islamsbook.html. Provides translated excerpts from documents written during the Abbasid caliphate, as well as links to other resources.

Islamic Medical Manuscripts at the National Library of Medicine. http://www.nlm.nih.gov/hmd/arabic/welcome.html. This site provides biographies of scientists and doctors, as well as links to images and locations of manuscripts. You will not be able to read translations here, but the site reveals the extent of medieval Islamic knowledge about medicine.

MuslimHeritage.com. http://www.muslimheritage.com. Hosted by the Foundation for Science Technology and Civilisation in Manchester, UK, this site provides a wealth of information on the contributions of the Islamic world to science, technology, medicine, and the arts. Contains numerous images and virtual tours.

Multimedia Sources

The Bridge: How Islam Saved Western Medicine. 1996. DVD. Films Media Group. 50 minutes. Examines how the medieval Islamic world preserved Greek and Roman knowledge and how that knowledge was passed on to the West.

Bringing to Life Muslim Heritage: A Video Documentary. 2005. BBC Production. 90 minutes. A history of the contributions of Muslim thinkers to the modern world. Clips are available at http://www.muslimheritage.com.

El Islam y la Resistencia Cristiana. 2004. DVD. Films for the Humanities and Sciences. 53 minutes. In Spanish with English subtitles. Discusses the Moorish contributions to culture on the Iberian Penisula.

Remembering the Language of History and Science: When the World Spoke Arabic. 2009. BBC. Three 60 minute segments trace the growth of science and technology in the medieval Islamic world.

The Secrets of the Human Body: Islam's Contributions to Medicine. 1999. DVD. Films Media Group. 27 minutes. Looks at the practice of medicine during the Abbasid caliphate and at the prominent medical practitioners such as Rhazes and Avicenna. Partially in French with subtitles in English.

24. Merovingian Dynasty Ends and Carolingian Dynasty Begins (751)

Although the kingdom consolidated by the first Merovingian king Clovis I (r. 481–511) was divided among his four sons and was reunited and divided several times during the Merovingian reign in what is now France, it remained basically intact until the mid-seventh century. Around this time, the Merovingian kings allowed their power to quietly slip into the hands of aristocratic families, and they became mere figure-heads. In 732 when Charles Martel, the mayor of the palace, and the real power behind the king, led the Frankish army against the Moors, he became, in effect, the nation's ruler. When King Theuderic IV (r. 721–737) died, Martel continued to rule until his own death. His two sons who became mayors of the palace at Martel's death, however, put another puppet monarch, Chelderic III (r.743–751), on the throne. One of Martel's sons, Carloman, retired from the mayoral position to become a monk, leaving the other, Pepin, to rule alone.

Pepin III (the Short) set about to consolidate his power and to enlist the support of the church. In 751, he had Chilperic deposed and had himself anointed as the new king, beginning the era of "Carolingian" rule. Pepin's investiture ceremony instituted the tradition of the church consecrating the king at his coronation. In 754, Pepin made it possible for his sons to succeed him on the throne, the oldest of whom was Charles, later to be called Charlemagne.

The Carolingians advocated ecclesiastical reform and maintained a close relationship with church officials. Pope Stephen visited Pepin in 754 with the result of mutual support being given—the Franks agreeing to support the papacy against the Lombards and the Pope agreeing to support Pepin's claim to the throne. In addition, Pepin required the use of the Roman liturgy throughout the kingdom's churches. The Carolingians also instituted administrative changes in the government, including the practice of issuing capitularies, or instructions from the king, oaths of fidelity made by free men to the king, and a reform of the European monetary system.

TERM PAPER SUGGESTIONS

1. Discuss the Carolingian reform of the monetary system instituted by Pepin the Short. What advantages did this system have over the old one? What were some of the results of the change?

2. Discuss what is meant by the term *Carolingian Renaissance.* What did it attempt to do? Who were the leading participants in this renaissance? What were its effects?

3. Describe the conditions of religious minorities under Carolingian rule.

4. How did the office of mayor of the palace develop? What were the duties of the mayor? Was the position more beneficial to the ruler or to the people?

5. How did the actions of Charles Martel and Pepin the Short prepare the way for Charlemagne to become Holy Roman Emperor?

6. Consider the role of the king in the early days of Carolingian rule. Why didn't Charles Martel oust Theuderic IV? Why didn't he claim the title after Theuderic's death? Why did his sons install a puppet king?

7. What was the *Donation of Constantine?* What was its purpose? What effect did it have?

ALTERNATIVE TERM PAPER SUGGESTIONS

1. Create a series of maps showing how the Frankish kingdom was divided and united under different rulers between 511 and 800.

2. Create a dialogue between two of the following concerning the *Donation of Constantine:* Pepin the Short, Pope Stephen II, a monk charged with creating the document, or Lorenzo Valla (a Renaissance scholar who proved the document was a forgery). Include a discussion of the long-term effects of the document.

Primary Sources

Annals of Fulda: 9th Century Histories. Trans. by Timothy Reuter. Manchester: Manchester University Press, 1992. Historical writings from several authors covering the years from Louis the Pompous to the accession of Louis the Child in 900.

Dutton, Paul Edward, ed. *Carolingian Civilization: A Reader.* Peterborough, ON: Broadview Press, 2004. A collection of English translations of documents from the Carolingian dynasty.

Regino of Prum. "On the Breakdown of the Carolingian Empire" in Julius Kirshner, and Karl F. Morrison, eds. *University of Chicago Readings in Western Civilization: 4, Medieval Europe.* Chicago: University of Chicago Press, 1986. A contemporary account of the last kings of the Carolingian dynasty and the first Capetians.

Secondary Sources

Bachrach, Bernard. *Early Carolingian Warfare: Prelude to Empire.* Philadelphia: University of Pennsylvania Press, 2001. Discusses how the military exploits of Charles Martel and Pepin the Short prepared the way for Charlemagne to become Holy Roman Emperor.

Geary, Patrick J. *Before France and Germany: The Creation and Transformation of the Merovingian World.* 1988. Follows the history of the western provinces from the end of the Roman Empire through the collapse of the Merovingian dynasty.

Jasper, Detley, and Fuhrmann, Horst. *Papal Letters in the Middle Ages.* Washington, DC: Catholic University Press, 2001. Contains a detailed discussion of the *Donation of Constantine.*

Riche, Pierre. *The Carolingians: A Family Who Forged Europe.* Trans. by Michael Idomir Allen. Philadelphia: University of Pennsylvania Press, 1993. Discusses not only the Carolingian monarchs but their complex relationships with other noble families and the church.

Sypeck, Jeff. *Becoming Charlemagne: Europe, Baghdad, and the Empires of A.D. 800.* 2007. This volume is divided into two sections, empires and emperor, and discusses each in the decade leading up to and following 800.

Wormald, Patrick, and Nelson, Janet A., Eds. *Lay Intellectuals in the Carolingian World.* Cambridge: Cambridge University Press, 2007. A series of essays on the developing role of the secular scholar in the Carolingian Renaissance.

World Wide Web

Carolingian Canon Law Project. http://www.rch.uky.edu/CCL/. Part of the Collaboratory for Research for Computing in Humanities at the University of Kentucky, this site has digitalized images of Carolingian documents and links to translations and other helpful sites.

The Medieval Sourcebook. http://www.fordham.edu/halsall/source. Provides translated excerpts from documents written during Carolingian dynasty.

Multimedia Sources

La Bataille de Poitiers: 733. No date. DVD. Films Media Group. 55 minutes. Describes the battle between the forces of Charles Martel and the Moors of Spain. Available in French and in English.

Water and Baptism. 2006. Audio recording. L'empreinte Digitale. Anne-Marie Deschamps conducts the Ensemble Venance fortunat in performances of medieval music, including two Carolingian chants.

25. Battle of Roncevaux Pass (778)

The Battle of Roncevaux (Roncesvalles) Pass is less significant for its military outcome than it is for the legend it inspired. In 768, Charles, later to be called Charlemagne (r. 768–814), inherited part of his father's lands. When his brother Carloman died in 771, Charles became ruler of the Frankish Empire. To increase his holdings, he engaged in military campaigns against neighboring lands, including a series of invasions of Spanish territory beginning in 778.

Plans for the first expedition called for Charlemagne's forces to be divided into two armies. One, led by the emperor himself, was to enter Spain through the Pyrenees, capture Pamplona and then proceed northward to meet the other army. This part of the offensive went well until the troops reached the city of Zaragoza, which refused to yield to the invaders. Realizing the costs of a prolonged siege and having received word that Saxony was in revolt, Charlemagne negotiated a settlement with the city's mayor, al-Ansari. In return for a large amount of gold and some prisoners, the Frankish forces would withdraw from what was then called the Upper March of Al-Andalus (northern Spain).

Charlemagne's army then turned homeward and marched back to Pamploma. Here, Charlemagne ordered the city's walls torn down. This action, and Charlemagne's harsh treatment of the Basque people, aroused their hostility toward him. In mid-August of 778, when his army reached the Pyrenees and was travelling through the Roncevaux Pass, the rearguard was attacked by a large number of Basque guerillas. The surprise of the attack and Basque knowledge of the terrain gave them the advantage. While the remainder of Charlemagne's army continued to safety, the rearguard was annihilated, the baggage trains plundered, and the Zaragoza gold recaptured. The battle was only a minor setback, costing Charlemagne goods and men, but little else. Charlemagne soon returned to Al-Andulas and by 795 had created the Spanish March, a province of his realm with Barcelona as its capital.

The Battle of Roncevaux is remembered primarily through the legends it inspired. Roland, the prefect of Brittany, was among the many soldiers killed in the battle. Only one historical reference to Roland exists. Charlemagne's biographer, Einhard, mentions his name, identifies his position, and records him among those killed at Roncevaux. However, Roland became a folk hero who inspired the 11th-century epic tale and first example of the *chanson de geste* (songs of great deeds), a popular medieval French literary genre.

The Song of Roland (La Chanson de Roland) portrays Roland as Charlemagne's nephew and possessor of the sword Durandal and the horn Olifant. Most significantly, this battle became a symbol of the conflict between Christians and the infidel, since it is not Basque Christians but 100,000 Muslim soldiers who attack Charlemagne's Christian forces in the song. Legends concerning Charlemagne were propagated in many forms after his death and throughout the remainder of the Middle Ages. Those concerning Roland are among the best known and most widely dispersed.

TERM PAPER SUGGESTIONS

1. Research the history of the Battle of Roncevaux and compare the facts to the representation in *The Song of Roland.* What do these sources tell us about the writing of history?

2. Compare two translations of *The Song of Roland* from different time periods. What changes have occurred? Why do you think these changes were made?

3. Research the body of legends that grew up around Charlemagne. Why were these legends significant to the French? Why did the legends spread beyond the Frankish kingdom?

4. Why was *The Song of Roland* so popular in the Middle Ages? What does it reveal about the values of society? About the warrior ethic?

5. Compare Roland in the French tales to Roland as he was translated into other cultures, for example, to Orlando in Italy.

6. In what ways did *The Song of Roland* and the other French tales that grew from it influence a sense of nationalism? What is the significant ethnosymbolism of the tales?

7. Analyze the position of women in the *chanson de geste.*

8. How did medieval romance literature such as *The Song of Roland* relate to the Crusades?

9. How is aristocratic life characterized in the romances of the Middle Ages?

ALTERNATIVE TERM PAPER SUGGESTIONS

1. Create a multimedia presentation concerning the representation of Carolingian legends in the art of the Middle Ages. What do the images reveal about the values of the Carolingians?

2. Perform selections from *chanson de gestes* . Choose excerpts that illustrate what you consider to be the most significant characteristics of this form of literature. Use music from the age as well.

Primary Sources

Anonymous. *The Song of Roland.* Trans. by Glyn S. Burgess. New York: Penguin Classics, 1990. One of many available translations.

Brault, Gerad J. *Song of Roland: An Analytical Edition.* Philadelphia: University of Philadelphia Press, 1970. Complete translation and a standard critical resource on the legend of Roland.

Dutton, Paul Edward, ed. *Carolingian Civilization: A Reader.* Peterborough, ON: Broadview Press, 2004. A collection of English translations of documents from the Carolingian dynasty.

Einhard. *The Life of Charlemagne.* Trans. by Sidney Painter. Ann Arbor: Ann Arbor Paperbacks, 1960. English translation of a contemporary biography written by Charlemagne's friend. Other translations are available.

Secondary Sources

Baldwin, John W. *Aristocratic Life in Medieval France: The Romances of Jean Renart and Gerbert de Montreuil, 1190–1230.* Baltimore: Johns Hopkins University Press, 2000. Details of life as presented in the romances and comparisons to historical personages and their way of life.

Burland, Margaret Jewett. *Strange Words: Retelling and Reception in the Medieval Roland Textual Tradition.* Notre Dame: University of Notre Dame, 2007. Discusses the historical basis for the Roland legends and compares four versions of the tale.

Krueger, Roberta L. *The Cambridge Companion to Medieval Literature.* Cambridge: Cambridge University Press, 2000. A collection of scholarly essays on the development of literature in the Middle Ages; several essays concern the romance.

McKittrick, Rosamond, ed. *Carolingian Culture: Emulation and Innovation.*
Cambridge: Cambridge University Press, 1994. A collection of 11 essays
about Carolingian literature, history, politics, and the arts.

Wilson, Derek. *Charlemagne.* New York: Random House, 2006. Wilson divides
his discussion of Charlemagne into three sections: the man, the emperor,
and the myth. Provides a genealogy of the Carolingians, a timeline, and
bibliography.

World Wide Web

The Medieval Sourcebook. http://www.fordham.edu/halsall/source. Provides translated excerpts from documents written during the Carolingian dynasty.

The Society for Medieval Military History. http://www.deremilitari.org/. Includes
articles, books, and links to information about all aspects of medieval
warfare, including that during the Carolingian period.

The Voice of the Shuttle. http://vos.ucsb.edu/index.asp. This site serves as a clearing house for humanities research on the Web. Provides an easy-to-use
search feature.

Multimedia Sources

The Age of Charlemagne. 1989. DVD. Annenberg. Part 18 of *The Western Tradition*
video series. 30 minutes. Discusses Charlemagne's efforts to create a new
empire in the West.

The Song of Roland. 2005. DVD. Films Media Group. 73 minutes. Presents an
abridged version of the story using images from the Middle Ages and
later. Features commentaries from historians and critics that acknowledge the inaccuracies but point to the significance of the work.

26. Vikings Invade England (793)

Vikings were the people of Northern Europe, primarily from the region
that today comprises the nations of Norway, Finland, Sweden, and
Denmark. They were the same people who invaded England in the Anglo-
Saxon age and who became the Normans of northwest France. Excellent
sailors, they had long engaged in trade with kingdoms to the south and
knew how to navigate around those lands. They also raided other settlements by sea if their needs weren't met through trade. Most of these raids
were sack-and-run attacks. Their longboats could transport as many as fifty

soldiers and were shallow enough to travel up many rivers to attack inland. Vikings raided both the British Isles and the European continent.

By the beginning of the eighth century, the north countries experienced a population growth that changed the Viking war strategies. Although many invaders returned to their homelands, others began to settle along the coastal areas of the lands they invaded. The settlements became their homes and served as staging points for forays deeper inland.

Further raids and settlements had a significant influence on the course of medieval history. The *Anglo-Saxon Chronicles* records that in 793 the church at Lindesfarne off the coast of England was destroyed in a Viking raid. However, most historians think that by this time the Vikings were already firmly established on the islands of Orkney and Shetland.

TERM PAPER SUGGESTIONS

1. Read the *Saga of Harald Hardrade* (the last Viking king). What was the impact of the Vikings on the medieval world as suggested in this work?
2. What political and social circumstances in the British Isles made them vulnerable to invasion and conquest by the Vikings?
3. Read and compare two of the Norse sagas.
4. What archetypes are found in the literature of the Vikings? Discuss how these reflect the values of the culture that produced them.
5. Research the Oseberg and Sutton Hoo ships. What can we learn about the culture from the artifacts on these ships?
6. Argue for the proposition that the Vikings were skilled and sophisticated artists and artisans who appreciated beauty as well as functionality.

ALTERNATIVE TERM PAPER SUGGESTIONS

1. Research the Scandinavian motifs that were adopted in the art, ornamentation, and clothing of the Anglo-Saxon and Norman people. Present your findings in a multimedia format.
2. Construct a model of a Viking ship. Explain how its design fit its function.
3. Prepare an oral presentation concerning the contributions of the Vikings to European history.

Primary Sources

The Anglo-Saxon Chronicles. A record of English history kept by monks for more than 300 years. A variety of translations are available in print and online.

The Saga of Harald Hardrade. Part I and Part II. Medieval and Classical Library. http.//www.omacl.org/Heimskringla/hardrade1.html. Translation of the saga of the last major Viking king.

The Story of the Volsungs. Online Medieval and Classical Library. http.//www .omacl.org/Volsunga/introduction.html. Another of the most famous Norse sagas.

Secondary Sources

Blair, Peter Hunter, and Keyes, Simon. *An Introduction to Anglo-Saxon England.* 3rd ed. Cambridge: Cambridge University Press, 2003. Chapter 2 is a discussion of the Vikings in England.

Forte, Angelo, Oram, Richard, and Pendersen, Frederik. *Viking Empires.* Cambridge: Cambridge University Press, 2005. This thorough history includes a great deal of information on Vikings in England, Ireland, and Scotland.

Jones, Gwyn. *A History of the Vikings.* Oxford: Oxford University Press, 2001 (1968). Has four sections: prior to 700, kingdoms to the close of the 10th century; the movement overseas, and the end of the Viking era.

Logan, F. Donal. *The Vikings in History.* 3rd ed. New York: Routledge, 2005. One of the best resources on the Vikings; uses historical, literary, and archeological evidence to examine their role in medieval Europe.

Richards, Julian D. *The Vikings: A Very Short Introduction.* Oxford: Oxford University Press, 2005. A good place to start research on the Vikings; provides a general overview, plus a chapter on the English invasions.

Rosedahl, Else. *The Vikings: Revised Edition.* London: Penguin Books, 1998. Probes Viking history life in Scandinavia and the motivations for and effects of their expansion into Europe.

Stenton, Frank M. *Anglo-Saxon England.* Oxford: Oxford University Press, 2001 (1943). One of the most thorough histories of Anglo-Saxon England available. Has an extensive chapter (VIII) on the age of Alfred, including the Viking raids and settlement.

Story, Johanna. *Carolingian Connections: Anglo-Saxon England and Carolingian Francia, c. 750–870.* Burlington, VT: Ashgate, 2003. Discusses the political, social, and personal connections between the two states during the century when Vikings were raiding England and France.

World Wide Web

Northvegr Foundation. http://www.northvegr.org/main.php. An extensive collection of texts and resources, including *The Anglo-Saxon Chronicles* and many early Scandinavian works.

The Viking Society for Northern Research. http://www.le.ac.uk/ee/viking/
index.html. The Viking Society's Web page provides links to a variety of
resources, as well as articles that can be accessed from the site.

The Vikings: 780–1100. http://www.metmuseum.org/toah/hd/vikg/hd_vikg
.htm. Metropolitan Museum of Art Web site contains essays and examples of various types of medieval art.

Multimedia Sources

Viking Ships. 2003. DVD. The History Channel. 50 minutes. Examines the
design of the ships that carried Vikings throughout Europe.

Vikings. 2000. DVD. Arts and Entertainment Network. 50 minutes. Tells the story
of Viking invasions throughout Europe through reenactments, visiting
archeological sites, and interviews with scholars.

Vikings: Fury from the North. 2001. DVD. The History Channel. 50 minutes. Goes
beyond the story of invasions to look at the achievements of the Vikings in
other areas. Reenactments, interviews with scholars, archeological evidence.

27. Charlemagne Becomes Holy Roman Emperor (800)

In 768, the Frankish king Pepin III (r. 751–768) divided his kingdom
between his two sons, Charles (r. 768–814) and Carloman (r. 768–771).
The strained relationship between the brothers ended with Carloman's
death. Carloman's widow and sons went to the court of the Lombards,
enemies of Pepin and the pope. Charles (Charlemagne) mounted an invasion of Lombard territory and defeated them in 774. The king, the king's
brother, and Carloman's family were captured and denied any right to
recapture their lands. Charlemagne endorsed the spurious Donation of
Constantine, giving the pope dominion over Rome and most of Italy.

At that point, Charlemagne continued his military conquests of parts of
Spain, Brittany, Saxony, and Bavaria. In 787, he forced his cousin Tassilo to
surrender. When Tassilo enlisted aid from the Avars and continued to revolt,
he was condemned to death—a sentence Charlemagne later revoked, allowing the entire family to enter monasteries. This latter action was uncharac-
teristic of Charlemagne. In fact, he once had 4,000 killed to punish rebels.

Charlemagne believed he was building a new Roman Empire in the
West. After restoring Pope Leo III to power in Rome in 800, the pope
acknowledged Charlemagne's position by crowning him Holy Roman

Emperor. This coronation set a precedent for the relationship between pope and king that was to continue through most of the Middle Ages. In addition, the Byzantine Empire was unhappy with the decision, since it removed the throne from their territory. It was not until 814 that Byzantium formally accepted Charlemagne's position.

Charlemagne's military exploits continued throughout his life, but he is also credited with major reforms in the administration of government, in religion, and in education, continuing the work of his father in a movement that became known as the Carolingian Renaissance. Charlemagne could not write, but he knew Latin and Greek as well as French. He encouraged a reform in script for easier reading, which resulted in the clear style known as the Carolingian minuscule. Along with other scholars, the learned English monk Alcuin came to Charlemagne's court at Aachen where he headed the palace school and oversaw the copying of many manuscripts. Both Alcuin and Charlemagne were interested in ecclesiastic reform, and under them the liturgy was revised. Charlemagne built churches and monasteries and introduced the singing of royal lauds—liturgical songs that praised the king and linked him with God and the church.

The governmental reforms of Charlemagne included general conventions of aristocrats and ecclesiastic leaders, the use of *missi dominici* (representatives sent by the lord) to make his intentions known throughout the kingdom, and the continuation of his father's requirement of an oath of fealty from free men. These oaths of fealty, and the land grants that usually accompanied them, were the beginnings of the feudal system in Europe. In addition, Charlemagne's army was composed of large numbers of cavalrymen who had also sworn their loyalty to the king and their lords. Charlemagne's army and his devotion to establishing a Christian empire set the stage for the institution of knighthood.

Charlemagne ruled for forty-six years. This fact alone may account for the stability established by the Carolingians. In 814, Charlemagne died and was interred in the octagonal chapel he had constructed at Aachen. Only one of his sons survived him to become the next emperor, Louis I the Pious.

SUGGESTED TERM PAPER TOPICS

1. Discuss the accomplishments of Charlemagne. How did he unify such a large area militarily? What cultural and administrative means did he use to maintain control over such a diverse area?

2. What was the legacy of the Carolingian Renaissance?

3. What problems with succession arose after the death of Charlemagne? How did these problems lead to the Treaty of Verdun? What implications did the treaty have for later generations?

4. Discuss how Charlemagne was able to transform the Frankish kingdom into the successor of the Roman Empire.

5. How did Charlemagne interpret the responsibilities, legacy, and rights that went with the title Holy Roman Emperor?

6. Analyze the contributions the monk Alcuin made to the Carolingian Renaissance.

7. Charles has been given the title "the Great" (*magne*). What were the conditions of greatness at this time in history? Assess Charlemagne's greatness in terms of his own time and our own time.

8. What are the political and religious implications of a western king receiving the title Holy Roman Emperor?

9. Compare the Salic Law of the early Frankish kingdom to Charlemagne's Capitularies.

ALTERNATIVE TERM PAPER SUGGESTIONS

1. Create a multimedia presentation detailing the major battles and conquests of Charlemagne.

2. Create a multimedia presentation about the representations of Charlemagne in art and literature. What qualities are emphasized in these representations?

3. Prepare a story for presentation that retells the legends about Charlemagne. Use your best storytelling skills in your performance.

Primary Sources

Capitulary of Charlemagne Issued in the Year 802: Concerning the Fealty to be Promised to the Lord Emperor. Avalon Project: http://avalon.law .yale.edu/medieval/capitula.asp.

Dhuoda. *Handbook for William: A Carolingian Woman's Counsel for Her Son.* Trans. by Carol Neel. Washington, DC: Catholic University of America Press, 1999. A 9th-century woman separated from her son by war writes to him, advising him on living a good and just existence. Includes notes and commentary.

Dutton, Paul Edward, ed. *Carolingian Civilization: A Reader.* Peterborough, ON: Broadview Press, 2004. A collection of English translations of documents from the Carolingian dynasty.

Einhard. *The Life of Charlemagne.* Trans. by Sidney Painter. Ann Arbor: Ann Arbor Paperbacks, 1960. English translation of a contemporary biography written by Charlemagne's friend. Other translations are available.

Einhard, and Notker the Stammerer. *Two Lives of Charlemagne.* Trans. by David Ganz. London: Penguin Classics, 2008. Ganz has translated two biographies of Charlemagne in one volume, the second of which was written about fifty years after Charlemagne's death.

Secondary Sources

Becher, Matthias. *Charlemagne.* Trans. by David Bachrach. New Haven, CT: Yale University Press, 2003. Traces Charlemagne's rise to power, his military actions, and the contributions he made to the culture of the French kingdom.

Hodges, Richard. *Mohammed, Charlemagne and the Origins of Europe.* Ithaca: Cornell University Press, 1983. An integration of archeological evidence and historic resources to trace Islamic and European developments with many illustrations.

McKittrick, Rosamond, ed. *Carolingian Culture: Emulation and Innovation.* Cambridge: Cambridge University Press, 1994. A collection of eleven essays about Carolingian literature, history, politics, and the arts.

McKitterick, Rosamond. *Charlemagne: The Formation of a European Identity.* Cambridge: Cambridge University Press, 2008. Traces narrative and historical images of Charlemagne through a wide variety of primary sources.

Riche, Pierre. *Daily Life in the World of Charlemagne.* Trans. by Jo Ann McNamara. Philadelphia: University of Pennsylvania Press, 1978. Topics include life in palaces, cities, and rural communities; travel, geography and language.

Sypeck, Jeff. *Becoming Charlemagne: Europe, Baghdad, and the Empires of A.D. 800.* New York: HarperCollins, 2007. This volume is divided into two sections, empires and emperors, and discusses each in the decade leading up to and following 800.

Verhulst, Adriaan. *Carolingian Economy.* Cambridge: Cambridge University Press, 2002. Thorough overview of agriculture and commerce in 9th- and 10th-century France.

Whiting, Jim. *The Life & Times of Charlemagne.* Hockessin, DE: Mitchell Lane Publishers, 2005. A brief and easy-to-read biography. A good place to start learning about Charlemagne and his empire.

Wilson, Derek. *Charlemagne.* New York: Random House, 2006. Wilson divides his discussion of Charlemagne into three sections: the man, the emperor, and the myth. Provides a genealogy of the Carolingians, a timeline, and bibliography.

Wormald, Patrick, and Nelson, Janet A., eds. *Lay Intellectuals in the Carolingian World.* Cambridge: Cambridge University Press, 2007. Series of essays on the developing role of the secular scholar in the Carolingian Renaissance.

World Wide Web

Carolingian Canon Law Project. http://www.rch.uky.edu/CCL/. Part of the Collaboratory for Research for Computing in Humanities at the University of Kentucky, this site has digitalized images of Carolingian documents and links to translations and other helpful sites.

The Internet Medieval Sourcebook. http://www.fordham.edu/halsall/sbook1h.html. Features a large section of primary documents of the Carolingians in translation.

Multimedia

The Age of Charlemagne. 1989. DVD. Part 18 of *The Western Tradition* video series produced by Annenberg. 30 minutes. Traces Charlemagne's efforts to establish a new Roman Empire in the West.

Charlemagne. 1994. Five videotapes. Acorn Media. 300 minutes. Commercially produced dramatization of the life of Charlemagne.

Charlemagne: Holy Barbarian. 2008. DVD. Phoenix Learning Group. 26 minutes. Story of Charlemagne's Saxon offensive.

Charlemagne and the Holy Roman Empire. 1989. Films Media Group. 31 minutes. Brief overview of Charlemagne's life; segments on court life and military exploits. Also recounts the hardships of ordinary people during Carolingian rule.

28. Angkor Kingdom Founded (c. 802–1369)

Deep in the jungles of what is now Cambodia, one of the most remarkable architectural structures in the world lies in ruin, evidence of the once great civilization that built it. The Khmer kingdom was founded by Jayavarman II (r. 802–850) when he took back part of the kingdom of Chenla from the Southeast Asian kingdom of Sri Vihaya and united it with other territory. Revered as a god-king, Jayavarman undertook a building program that founded the city of Angkor and began constructing shrines to honor Hindu gods. Successive kings added to the temples and shrines in the city. When

King Yasovarman I (r. 889–900) came to power, he moved the capital city to Angkor and called it Yasodharapura. From the late 9th through the 12th century, the Khmer kingdom grew steadily, taking land from Viet Nam, Thailand, and what was then called Champa, present-day India.

In the 13th century, powerful new kingdoms arose in Thailand that threatened Khmer. After repeated attacks by the Thais, the Khmer abandoned the beautiful city of Angkor around 1430 and withdrew to Phnom Penh. They returned to Angkor for a brief period in the mid-16th century, but later abandoned the site. Angkor was overtaken by jungle and rediscovered by the French in the 1860s. Today, it is the site of archeological research and restoration efforts.

At its zenith, the city of Angkor was one of the largest cities in the world, covering more than 39 square miles and filled with temples and shrines. Angkor Wat is the most magnificent of the surviving structures and the largest temple in the world. Constructed by Suryavarman II (r. 1113–1150), the complex measures about 2,800 by 3,300 feet and honors the king as an incarnation of Vishnu. Concentric walled courtyards surround five towers decorated with various symbols of Vishnu legends.

TERM PAPER SUGGESTIONS

1. What do we learn about the values and beliefs of the Khmer people from the city of Angkor?
2. What value do the Cambodian people place on Angkor today? Why is the city significant to them? How is their sense of nationalism tied to the city?
3. Read Zhou Daguan's travelogue, *A Record of Cambodia*. What was the contemporary opinion of the Khmer civilization as represented in this work?
4. Consider the construction of Angkor Wat. What materials were used? What building techniques? What do these things tell us about the Khmer people?

ALTERNATIVE TERM PAPER SUGGESTIONS

1. Create a model of the city of Angkor. Prepare an oral presentation discussing how the city plan reflects Hindu cosmology.
2. Create a multimedia presentation concerning the art and architecture of the Khmer empire. Use medieval Cambodian music in the presentation.

Primary Sources

Falser, Michael S. *The Pre-Angkorian Temple of Preah Ko: A Sourcebook of the History, Construction and Ornamentation of the Preah Ko Style.*

Bangkok: White Lotus Press, 2006. Includes some primary documents and some translations.

Koller, John M., and Koller, Patricia, eds. *Sourcebook in Asian Philosophy.* Upper Saddle River, NJ: Prentice Hall, 1991. Includes English translations of many of the basic philosophical texts from Asia.

Zhou Daguan. *A Record of Cambodia: Its Land and Its People.* Trans. by Paul Harris. Chiang Mai, Thailand: Silkworm Books, 2007. Written in 1296 by a Chinese envoy, this is the only outside description of Angkor when it was inhabited.

Secondary Sources

Aasen, Clarence. *Architecture of Siam: A Cultural History Interpretation.* Oxford: Oxford University Press, 1998. Comprehensive history of Siamese architecture, with two chapters on the medieval period.

Chandler, David. *A History of Cambodia,* 4th ed. Boulder, CO: Westview Press, 2007. Chapters 3 and 4 deal with the medieval history of Angkor.

Church, Peter. *A Short History of South-East Asia.* Singapore: John Wiley & Sons, 2005. Each chapter is short, but informative; includes Cambodia.

Glover, Ian, ed. *Southeast Asia: From Prehistory to History.* London: Routledge, 2004. Fourteen scholarly essays on many aspects of Southeast Asian history. Includes essays on Angkor.

Inden, Ronald, Ali, Daud, and Walters, Jonathan S. *Querying the Medieval: Texts and the History of Practices in South Asia.* Oxford: Oxford University Press, 2000. Scholarly discussion of the difficulties of historians when using ancient texts and artifacts.

Laur, Jean. *Angkor: An Illustrated Guide to the Monuments.* Rome: Arthaud, 2002. Beautifully illustrated guide to the architecture and landscapes of Cambodia.

Tully, John. *A Short History of Cambodia: From Empire to Survival.* Crow's Nest, AU: Allen & Unwin, 2005. Begins with a description of the land and people; contains detailed chapter on Angkor.

World Wide Web

Angkor Tourism. http://www.cambodian/angkor/. Although this is a tourism site, it is valuable for the photographs of many of the architectural monuments that still exist in Cambodia. Provides brief, historical information with each photo.

APSARA: Authority for the Protection and Management of Angkor and the Region of Siem Reap. http://www.autoriteapsara.org/en/apsara.html. This is a site created and maintained by the Cambodian government in cooperation with the UNESCO effort to protect World Heritage Sites. Contains a great deal of historical information, as well as updates on efforts to protect and restore archeological treasures.

World's Most Endangered Sites. http://www.history.com/classroom/unesco/. Part of the History Channel's Save Our History campaign, this site provides information about the ancient city of Angkor and the efforts to save it. A study guide and other links are available.

Multimedia Sources

Angkor Wat: Eighth Wonder of the World. 2004. DVD. The History Channel. 50 minutes. Host Zay Harding takes the audience on a trek through the Cambodian jungle to the site of the ancient temple of Angkor Wat to discuss its construction and why it might have been abandoned.

Journey into Buddhism: Prajna Earth. 2006. DVD. PBS Production. 85 minutes. Although it visits other sacred sites, the video is primarily about Angkor and Angkor Wat. Beautiful cinematography.

Lost Spirits of Cambodia. 1996. DVD. The History Channel. 50 minutes. Interviews with archeologists and historians and onsite filming reveal the ancient 75-mile square city of Angkor.

29. *Anglo-Saxon Chronicle* (800–1154)

The *Anglo-Saxon Chronicle* is the first history written in English, and the first European history written in the language of the people. Since earlier histories had been written primarily in Latin, the language used makes the work noteworthy. However, this is not the only significance to this work that took over 300 years to complete. The *Chronicle* is the work of many monks in several monasteries throughout England who kept a year-by-year account of the most significant events of the day. The *Chronicle* is also the foremost resource for the history of England during these centuries. The records begin with the conversion of England to Christianity, but the information about events before 800 was taken from Latin sources. There are seven versions of the *Chronicle,* listing the same events for the most part, but having some variations.

Although there is no written evidence, many scholars believe that King Alfred the Great ordered this systematic record of events be written. The work did begin about the time he became king, and the events during his reign are meticulously recorded. However, the recording continued long after Alfred's death. Most of the work is in prose, but several poems, such as "The Battle of Brunanburh," are included. The years after the Norman Conquest (1066) provide a picture of its effect on England.

Linguists also value the *Chronicle* for the information it provides about the changing English language, especially the Middle English that was developing in the decades after the Norman Conquest.

TERM PAPER SUGGESTIONS

1. Examine the contents of the *Anglo-Saxon Chronicle.* What parts do rumor, superstition, and legend play in this history?

2. Compare two or more of the *Chronicle* manuscripts. Examine the mix of local and national concerns in the *Chronicle.* How do you account for this?

3. Is the *Chronicle* history as we know it? Evaluate the information contained in the manuscript on the basis of accuracy, bias, and completeness.

4. Compare Bede's *Ecclesiastical History* to the *Chronicle,* evaluating their usefulness and importance as histories.

5. What do we learn about the values of the Anglo-Saxon culture from the *Chronicle?*

ALTERNATIVE TERM PAPER SUGGESTIONS

1. Using only information from the *Chronicle,* prepare a speech about one of the kings of England.

2. For many years when the *Chronicle* was being kept, the entries are very short. Using news magazines from the past year, develop your own *Chronicle.* You are limited to 1,000 words to record the significant events of the year.

Primary Sources

Anglo-Saxon Chronicle. Online Medieval and Classical Library. http://omacl.org/ Anglo/.

The Annales Cambriae (The Annals of Wales) 447–954. Numerous translations available. Overlapping for a century and a half, these histories record some of the same events listed in the *Chronicle.*

Asser, Bishop of Sherborn. *The Life of King Alfred.* Numerous translations available. Written in the 9th century when the *Chronicle* was being written.

Crossley-Holland, Kevin. *The Anglo-Saxon World: An Anthology.* Oxford: Oxford University Press, 1999 (reissue). Anthology of many Anglo-Saxon works, including excerpts from the *Chronicle, Beowulf,* riddles, and legal documents.

William of Malmesbury. *Chronicle of the Kings of England: The Anglo-Saxon Kings.* c. 1140. Numerous translations available. History of English kings written after the *Chronicle,* but relying on it and other previous sources.

Secondary Sources

Arnold, C. J. *An Archaeology of the Early Anglo-Saxon Kingdoms,* 2nd ed. London: Routledge, 1997. Using evidence from archeology, Arnold reconstructs life as the Anglo-Saxons lived it.

Campbell, James, John, Eric, and Wormald, Patrick. *The Anglo-Saxons.* New York: Penguin, 1991. Ten chapters, one by each of the three authors, cover Britain from the end of the Roman occupation to the Battle of Hastings.

Clemoes, Peter, et al., eds. *Anglo-Saxon England,* Vol. 1–28. Cambridge: Cambridge University Press, 2008. Paperback publications of the periodical *Anglo-Saxon England.* Original publication dates vary. Each volume includes a collection of essays by scholars on all areas of Anglo-Saxon life.

Hindley, Geoffrey. *A Brief History of the Anglo-Saxons: The Beginnings of the English Nation.* Philadelphia: Running Press, 2006. Hindley focuses on the influences of the Germanic invaders on the English character and nation.

Lapridge, Michael. *The Anglo-Saxon Library.* Oxford: Oxford University Press, 2006. An examination of the growth and importance of libraries in Anglo-Saxon England.

Mitchell, Bruce. *An Invitation of Old English and Anglo-Saxon England.* Malden, MA: Blackwell Publishers, 1995. An introduction to the Anglo-Saxon language through its literature and historical context.

Sheppard, Alice. *Families of the King: Writing Identity in the Anglo-Saxon Chronicle.* Toronto: University of Toronto Press, 2004. Sheppard analyzes how the *Chronicle* constructed the identities of English kings.

Stenton, Frank M. *Anglo-Saxon England.* Oxford: Oxford University Press, 2001. This reissue of Stenton's original 1943 work offers over 600 pages of comprehensive history of the period. The author draws heavily on primary sources and early historians.

World Wide Web

BBC History. http://www.bbc.co.uk/history/. The Ancient History section has articles, images, interactive content, and a timeline for Anglo-Saxon England.

Britannia History. http://www.britannia.com/history/index.html. An abundance of information, links, and images. Complete online translation of the *Chronicle* and other primary documents.

The British History Club. http://www.britishhistoryclub.com/index.html. Large number of resources available at this site, including online translations of both the *Chronicle* and *The Annales Cambriae.*

Multimedia Sources

Birth of a Language. 2003. DVD. Films Media Group. 52 minutes. The story of how the Anglo-Saxon language endured despite numerous invasions. One segment discusses Alfred the Great's determination to preserve the English language.

Life in Anglo-Saxon Times. 2006. DVD. Kultur Video. 50 minutes. Includes a segment on the *Chronicle.*

30. Institution of Knighthood Established (c. 800)

Nothing epitomizes the Middle Ages in popular conception more than the image of the knight in armor. Yet, following a single thread of history to find the beginning of knighthood is complex because kingship, the papacy, knighthood, feudalism, and the Crusades are all woven into a fine-textured fabric. When Pepin III (r. 751–768) and his son Charlemagne (r. 768–814), Frankish kings, were anointed by Popes Zacharias and Leo, respectively, in return for Lombard land and the promise of protection, they were laying the ground for knighthood to grow. Pepin had also required oaths of fealty from his barons, a practice his son continued.

Charlemagne's greatest military weapon was his well-trained and well-armed cavalry, which required armor and the finest horses and were expensive troops to maintain. He also extended his empire to the point that he needed administrators to help govern far provinces. To manage both problems, Charlemagne allotted fiefs (estates) to nobles to administrate. Receiving a fiefdom required loyalty oaths to the king, as well as the promise of a supply of troops when the king needed them. Since few kingdoms in the 9th century were safe from attacks by Vikings, Muslims, or neighboring invaders, lords found it necessary to fortify their central holdings. These fortifications often grew into the castles of medieval Europe. If the lord remained loyal to the king, these fortifications were of immense benefit in defending the countryside because they provided headquarters for trained, armed troops who were ready whenever the king needed them. The lords also controlled economic power since they possessed the land and means of agricultural production, thereby giving rise to manors and the feudal system. Knights were of necessity from the wealthy class since they were required to provide their own mounts and equipment.

The institution of knighthood developed throughout the 9th and 10th centuries and became even more important with the Crusades that began in the 11th century. Knights now became not only soldiers, but soldiers for God. Orders of knighthood, such as the Templars and the Hospitallers, recruited members throughout Europe and became wealthy and powerful in their own right. The code of chivalry developed as part of knighthood as well and significantly influenced the literature of the age and the idea of romantic or courtly love.

Although knighthood continued into the Renaissance, by the end of the Hundred Years War (1337–1453), the soldier knight was less important. More nobility were declining to become knights and were hiring mercenaries to meet their obligations to the king. Military strategy depended less on the heavily armed mounted cavalry and more on the foot soldier. Developments in weaponry, such as the canon, also lessened the need for knights in battle. However, the jousting tournaments that had begun in the 10th century continued to be popular entertainment throughout the medieval period.

TERM PAPER SUGGESTIONS

1. Between 800 and 1500 the equipment of knighthood underwent many changes. Trace the technological developments in the manufacture of armor and arms for knights during this period.

2. Tournaments developed as a byproduct of knighthood, but they in turn influenced the role of knights. How did tournaments affect the image and the reality of being a knight?

3. Research the economic costs and rewards of becoming a knight.

4. Although knights were considered Christian soldiers of God in the Crusades, they committed many atrocities in their fighting. Why do you think this occurred and how were knights able to reconcile their actions with the ideals of Christianity?

5. Research one of the major orders of knight such as the Hospitallers, Templars, or Teutonic knights. In what ways did the order maintain the concept of

knighthood in general? How did the order set itself apart? Why was the order eventually disbanded?

6. Compare an account of being a knight, written by an actual knight, with one of the medieval romances.

7. By the 10th century, most knights were required to go through a series of training stages before they could officially become a knight. Research this process and discuss why you think it developed. Why was it not enough to swear one's allegiance to the king and be willing to fight for him?

8. The code of chivalry was a complex set of expectations. What inherent characteristics of the code made it unrealistic? Do you think knights were ever able to achieve the goals of chivalry? Why?

9. According to the code of chivalry, what was the position of women? What social implications did chivalry have for women in the Middle Ages? What were later effects of chivalry for women?

ALTERNATIVE TERM PAPER SUGGESTIONS

1. Build a model of a typical tournament site. Explain the manner in which a typical tournament was operated.

2. Create a multimedia presentation on the evolution of the knight's armor and weapons.

3. Adopt the persona of one of the well-known knights from the Middle Ages. Prepare a performance telling about the life the knight lived. Use primary sources as much as possible.

4. Create an interactive, hyperlink glossary concerning the terminology of knighthood, including the clothing, armor, and tools used.

Primary Sources

Charny, Geoffrey. *A Knight's Own Book of Chivalry.* Philadelphia: University of Pennsylvania Press, 2005. Translation of Charny's 14th-century manual for chivalry.

"Letters of Crusaders." *The Hanover Historical Texts Project.* http://history.hanover.edu/project.html#ma. Twelve letters from Crusaders are available in translation. More are being added.

Lull, Ramon. *The Book of Knighthood and Chivalry.* Trans. by Brian R. Price. Highland Village, TX: Chivalry Bookshelf, 2001. Written in the 14th century, this is a guidebook to how to be a knight. Also included in this translation is the anonymous text from the same time, *The Orders of Chivalry.*

Kaueper, Richard, and Kennedy, Elspeth. *The Book of Chivalry of Geoffroi de Charny: Text, Context, and Translation.* Philadelphia: University of Pennsylvania Press, 1996. Kaueper provides a discussion of the context and the value of French knight de Charny's 14th-century work; Kennedy translated and annotated the text.

Shaw, Margaret R. B., ed. *Chronicles of the Crusades.* London: Penguin Books, 1963. Includes translations of two of the best-known first-person accounts of the Crusades, Jean de Joinville's *The Life of St. Louis* and Geffroy de Villehardouin's *The Conquest of Constantinople.*

Ross, James Bruce, and McLaughlin, Mary Martin, eds. *The Portable Medieval Reader.* New York: Penguin Books, 1977. A collection of many translations of primary documents with a section on knighthood.

Secondary Sources

Baker, Alan. *The Knight.* Hoboken, NJ: John Wiley & Sons, 2003. This very brief book gives an informative introduction to the reality of knighthood.

Barnhouse, Rebecca. *The Book of the Knight of the Tower: Manners for Young Medieval Women.* London: Palgrave Macmillan, 2006. Barnhouse retells the stories written by a nobleman in the late 1300s to educate his daughters. She combines these with commentary on the life of the upper class in the Middle Ages.

Bouchard, Constance Brittain. *Strong of Body, Brave and Noble: Chivalry and Society in Medieval France.* Ithaca: Cornell University Press, 1998. Examines the relationships of knights to their families, the peasants, the church, and their lords. Pays particular attention to the attitude of the knight toward women.

Dressler, Rachel. *Of Armor and Men in Medieval England: The Chivalric Rhetoric of Three English Knights' Effigies.* Burlington, VT: Ashgate, 2004. Historian Dressler examines the commemorative figures of prominent English knights from three social classes and analyzes what can be understood about the values of knighthood.

Duby, Georges. *William Marshall: The Flower of Chivalry.* New York: Random House, 1985. Trans. by Richard Howard. French scholar Duby tells the story of one of the greatest knights in Christendom, examining historical data and legend.

Gies, Francis. *The Knight in History.* New York: Harper & Row, 1984. Gies discusses three major periods of knighthood: the brutal knight of the 9th and 10th centuries, the age of chivalry in the next three centuries, and the demise of knights during the Hundred Years War.

Kaeuper, Richard W. *Chivalry and Violence in Medieval Europe.* Oxford: Oxford University Press, 1999. Discusses the obligations of knights to the church and to their lords, and contrasts the knights of romance to reality.

Kaeuper, Richard W. *Holy Warriors: The Religious Ideology of Chivalry.* Philadelphia: University of Pennsylvania Press, 2009. Examines the assimilation of religious ideas into the chivalric code in order to sanction the violence associated with being a knight.

Oakeshott, R. Ewart, and Oakeshott, Ewart R. *The Knight and His Horse,* 2nd ed. Chester Springs, PA: Dufour Editions, 1998. Discussion of the reality of warfare on horseback. Extensive glossary.

World Wide Web

De Re Militari: The Society for Medieval Military History. http://www.deremilitari .org/. Maintained by an international association of scholars, the site offers articles on many aspects of medieval warfare, links to other sites, a bibliography, and book reviews.

Mulberger, Steve, ed. *Deeds of Arms: A Collection of Accounts of Formal Deeds of Arms of the Fourteenth Century.* http://www.nipissingu.ca/department/ history/muhlberger/chroniqu/texts/deedsch.htm. A wide collection of primary source translations concerning knights and tournaments of the 14th century.

Works of Art: Arms and Armor. http://www.metmuseum.org/Works_Of_Art/ department.asp?dep=4. The Metropolitan Museum of Art's online exhibit of medieval arms and armor. Includes informational text.

Multimedia

The Knight. 2002. DVD. Schlessinger Video. Part of the *Life in the Middle Ages* series. 23 minutes. Produced especially for schools. Focuses on the role of the knight in medieval society.

Knights and Armor. 1994. DVD. The History Channel. 100 minutes. Reenactments of the life of medieval knight William Marshall, with a discussion of the history of arms and armor.

The Knights Templar. 2002. DVD. PBS. 120 minutes. Tells the story of the monk/knights Templar from their rise to power until their condemnation as heretics.

The Middle Ages: The Feudal Order. 1989. The Annenberg/CPB Project. Discusses the stabilizing effect of the feudal system. This video series is available on demand to registered (free) users. http://www.learner.org/resources/ series58.html.

31. Feudal System is Established in Europe (c. 825)

Feudalism was the political and social system that dominated most of Europe in the 9th through 15th centuries and developed in conjunction with the continual warfare of the age. Beginning with Charles Martel, mayor of the palace at the end of the Merovingian dynasty, the ruler needed soldiers, especially trained cavalrymen, for his military ventures. He began a system of *benefices*, later known as fiefs, whereby individuals (vassals) were given land in return for military service or soldiers. The land could be held as long as the vassal maintained his loyalty and service to the ruler, thus each gained from the transaction. Land holding meant power, both economic, since the chief means of gaining wealth was through agricultural production, and political, since vassals had under their control the vast majority of the peasant population.

The fiefs were held, not owned, by the vassals, who later became known as lords or barons. But as time passed, it became more difficult for rulers to dislodge the children of the lords, and many fiefs were inherited. In order to protect their lands, lords built fortifications on them which evolved into the medieval castle. The fortifications and castles were also beneficial to rulers because they provided storehouses of military supplies, housed trained soldiers, and were often built in advantageous places. Lords were able to create smaller manors within their own demesne (domain), allowing knights to hold a portion of the property the king had given the lord. This caused some problems because a knight might take an oath of loyalty to two lords to gain two manors; therefore, the custom of naming a liege lord arose. The knight would personally serve his liege, but provide a soldier for his second lord. In England, William the Conqueror prohibited this practice, requiring the lord and all his subvassals to swear allegiance directly to the king.

From the Carolingians in France, feudalism spread to Germany and other continental kingdoms and reached its height in the 11th through 13th centuries. The Norman invasion of William the Conqueror brought the feudal system to Britain. Although feudalism began out of military necessity, it did not disappear when knights on horseback became less important on the battle front. At first, substitute soldiers were sent by the lords instead of them serving themselves, and the cavalry was soon composed primarily of mercenary soldiers. Then, new weaponry and large numbers of foot soldiers, especially archers, superseded the knights. However, the pattern of land holding that was a part of the feudal system outlasted knighthood and influenced the social and economic structure of Europe for centuries. Perhaps the greatest legacy of feudalism is the wonderful medieval castles that still exist throughout Europe and the British Isles.

The term feudalism was not familiar to the individuals who actually lived on a manor; it was not used to describe this social system until the Renaissance. Feudalism has also been used to describe the social systems in medieval India, China, and Japan, and each has elements in common with Western feudalism, but there are also significant differences in the systems.

TERM PAPER SUGGESTIONS

1. Today we look at feudalism and manorialism in a negative light. It has been argued, however, that they were necessary developments in medieval civilization. Explain why these institutions appeared, what the benefits were to society, and why they disappeared.

2. Describe the operation of the medieval manor as an economic and social unit. What did it produce? What were the relationships among the people living on the manor and the lord? What duties and rights did each have?

3. Compare at least two primary sources on feudal manors with secondary sources. Do the generalizations in the secondary sources distort the reality of life on a manor?

4. Explain the function of a manor and its role in feudalism.

5. Compare the feudal system in Europe with similar systems in Japan, China, or India. Do you think feudalism should be used to describe these countries' economic and social systems?

6. How did the feudal manor encourage the rise of a middle class in the late Middle Ages?

7. It has been said that the English (and American) system of constitutional government has its roots in the feudal system's contract theory of government. Do you agree with this statement? Why or why not?

8. Choose a famous medieval castle about which a great deal is known. How does the castle's structure reflect the times in which it was built and the people who inhabited it? Remember that most castles are the products of generations, rather than a single individual.

9. How did the feudal system affect social class positions in Europe? How did the church fit into the feudal system?

ALTERNATIVE TERM PAPER FORMATS

1. Create a model of a typical medieval manor and explain how this model of land management worked.

2. Using illustrations, drawings, and photographs, trace the development of the medieval castle from its beginning as a small fortification to the structures we recognize as castles.

3. You are the reeve or manager of a medieval manor and would like to find a job on another manor. Write a letter of application and prepare a resume that reflects your training and skills. Keep the resume to no more than two pages, but do not omit any important skills. (One of your skills is that you are literate!)

Primary Sources

Anonymous. *The Dialogue between Master and Disciple: On Laborers.* C. 1000 http://www.fordham.edu/halsall/sbook.html. Translated discussion of the lives of common laborers.

Amt, Emilie, ed. *Women's Lives in Medieval Europe: A Sourcebook.* New York: Routledge, 1993. Extensive collection of documents about and by women of the Middle Ages, including a section on women's working life.

Evergates, Theodore, ed. *Feudal Society in Medieval France, Documents from the County of Champagne.* Philadelphia: University of Pennsylvania Press, 1993. Approximately 200 documents from medieval Champagne, illustrating the legal and economic life of feudal society.

Gebhard, Bishop of Constance. *Allocation of Serfs to Crafts,* 990. http://www .fordham.edu/halsall/source/990serfcrafts.html. Bishop Gebhard writes that serfs should be taught crafts that would be to their and the estate's advantage.

Munro, Dana Carlton, ed. "Documents Illustrative of Feudalism" in *Translations and Reprints from the Original Sources of European History.* Philadelphia: Department of History of the University of Pennsylvania, 1902. http:// www.shsu.edu/~his_ncp/Feudal1.html. Provides resources on a variety of aspects of feudal life.

Secondary Sources

Arnold, Benjamin. *Power and Property in Medieval Germany: Economic and Social Change c.900–1300.* Oxford: Oxford University Press, 2004. Arnold explores the power of the German monarch as the largest landowner in the nation, the relationships between the king and lords and between lords and serfs, and what those relationships meant for the social and economic lives of each.

Backman, Clifford R. *The Worlds of Medieval Europe.* Oxford: Oxford University Press, 2003. Contains a chapter on the rise of feudalism.

Gies, Francis, and Gies, Joseph. *Life in a Medieval Village.* New York: Harper Perennial, 1991. Using primary sources and the evidence of archeology, this book paints a picture of the lives of peasants in the medieval village of Elton in England.

Hamerow, Helena. *Early Medieval Settlements: The Archaeology of Rural Communities in North-West Europe 400–900.* Oxford: Oxford University Press, 2003. Contains chapters on agriculture, the development of rural trade, and the social conditions of rural Europe.

Hilton, Rodney H. *Class Conflict and the Crisis of Feudalism: Essays in Medieval Social History.* Ronceverte, WV: Hambledon Press, 1985. Views feudalism from Marxist perspective.

Stephenson, Carl. *Mediaeval Feudalism.* New York: Cornell University Press, 1942. This highly-respected book is a classic in medieval studies.

White, Lynn. *Medieval Technology and Social Change.* Oxford: Oxford University Press, 1964. Examines the effects of technology on the feudal system.

White, Stephen. *Re-Thinking Kinship and Feudalism in Early Medieval Europe.* Burlington, VT: Ashgate Publishing, 2005. Collection of essays by White on the feudal order up until the 17th century.

World Wide Web

British History Online. http://www.british-history.ac.uk/Default.aspx. Extensive collection of documents from British history.

The Internet Medieval Sourcebook. http://www.fordham.edu/halsall/sbook.html. Contains many translated documents on feudal law and the economics of a feudal society.

Middle Ages. http://www.learner.org/interactives/middleages/. An interactive Web site produced by the Annenburg Foundation. A good introduction to the age with a great deal of information about feudalism.

Multimedia Sources

The Middle Ages: The Feudal Order. 1989. The Annenberg/CPB Project. Discusses the stabilizing effect of the feudal system. This video series is available on demand to registered (free) users. http://www.learner.org/resources/series58.html.

Europe in the Middle Ages: The Feudal Society. 1989. DVD. Films Media Group.
36 minutes. Brief overview of operation of feudal society.

32. Saracens Begin Invasion of the Mediterranean (825)

The term Saracen was often used by Europeans to refer to any follower of Islam, especially during the Crusades. However, there is a distinction to be made between two large groups of Muslims. Those who crossed the Strait of Gibraltar from Africa to conquer the Iberian Peninsula were Berbers and Moors; Saracens were Muslims from the eastern Muslim lands, such as the former Persian Empire and Arabian Peninsula. As early as 800, Saracen pirates were raiding ships and coastal cities in the Mediterranean. In 805, Constantine, the imperial patrician of the island of Sicily, negotiated a 10-year treaty with Emir Ibrahim I Ibn al-Aghlab of Ifriqiya to prevent his ships from raiding, but this did not stop the raiding from other Muslim territories.

In 825, efforts to take Mediterranean territory began in earnest. Saracens captured the island of Crete and used settlements there as a base for raids on other Greek islands. Two years later, Muslim forces began the conquest of southern Sicily and Sardinia. They defeated the Byzantine army at Mazara and laid siege to Syracuse. The Saracens gained enough land by 832 that they appointed Abu Fihr Muhammad as the governor of Sicily, but several Byzantine strongholds remained. When new governor Abbas ibn Fadl was appointed in 851, he began a fierce campaign to conquer the remaining Byzantine lands. In the winter of 859, he captured the city of Castrogiovanni, killing all the Christian men in the city and selling the women and children as slaves. Yet, it was not until 901 that the Saracens finally were able to capture the remaining Byzantine territory on Sicily.

Meanwhile, using Sicily and Crete as bases, the Saracens had been able to raid other coastal areas throughout the Mediterranean. They attacked Marseilles and started to settle in what is now southern Italy in 832. Muslims penetrated Italy as far as Rome by 846, the same year in which they took the islands of Corsica and Sardinia and destroyed the Venetian fleet. Malta fell to the Saracens in 869, and in 882 Islamic forces took the city of Agropoli, a well-fortified stronghold that gave them an advantage on the Tyrrhenian Sea. They were able to capture

Reggio Calabria on the Italian mainland in 901. The population of Sicily grew rapidly as more territory was captured, and Muslims immigrated to other coastal areas of the Mediterranean. The conquered Sicilians who did not convert lived as *dhimmi,* or people of the book, a recognized minority. Saracens began land reform and increased agricultural production through improved irrigation. In the 10th century, Palermo, the Saracen capital, was the largest city in Italy with a population of almost 300,000. By the end of the 10th century, Muslims were in control of most of the land surrounding the Mediterranean Sea.

TERM PAPER SUGGESTIONS

1. Compare the training, equipment, and skills of a Saracen faris (soldier) to that of a European knight.
2. Research the advances in land distribution and agricultural production introduced to Sicily during the 10th century. How did these changes benefit the general population?
3. What was the position of the people of the book under Islamic rule? What rights and privileges did they have? What limitations were placed on them?
4. What were the effects of the Saracen conquest of Sicily and other coastal areas on the arts and culture of the Mediterranean?
5. Compare trade between the East and West before the 9th century and after the Muslims took control of the Mediterranean.
5. How did the Mediterranean being in Muslim hands affect the cultural and scientific progress of Europe?

ALTERNATIVE TERM PAPER SUGGESTIONS

1. Create a display of maps tracing the progress of Saracen or Arab control of Mediterranean lands. Indicate strategic holdings for control of the sea.
2. Create a multimedia presentation showing the influences of Muslim conquests on the art and architecture of the Mediterranean area.
3. Assume the persona of one of the *dhimmi* living in 10th-century Palermo. Create a performance piece telling what life in the city is like.

Primary Sources

Ahimaaz ben Paltiel. *The Chronicle of Ahimaaz.* Trans. by Marcus Salzman. Brooklyn, NY: AMS Press, 1966. Covers the history of Jewish settlements in Southern Italy during the years 850–1054.

Hawqal, Ibn. *Oriental Geography of Ebn Haukal, An Arabian Traveller of the Tenth Century.* Athens, Greece: Aristide D. Caratzas, 1985. An English translation of the work describing Sicily in the 10th century.

Jansen, Katherine L., Drell, Joanna, and Andrews, Francis, eds. *Medieval Italy: Tests in Translation.* Philadelphia: University of Pennsylvania Press, 2009. Includes translations of Hebrew, Latin, Greek, and Arabic documents written between 1000 and 1400, from southern Italy and Sicily.

Latham, J. D. *Saracen Archery: An English Version and Exposition of a Mameluke Work on Archery (ca. A.D. 1368).* London: Holland Press, 1970. A classic translation of a work attributed to Arab writer Taybughaā.

Secondary Sources

Ali, Syed Ameer. *A Short History of the Saracens: Being a Concise Account of the Rise and Decline of the Saracenic Power, and of the Economic, Social and Intellectual Development . . . and the Expulsion of the Moors from Spain.* Bel Aire, CA: Elibron Classics, 2005. Fascimile reprint of 1899 publication. Contains information on many Muslim figures.

Calkin, Siobhain Bly. *Saracens and the Making of English Identity: The Auchinleck Manuscript.* New York: Routledge, 2005. By examining a number of texts, the author discusses how depictions of Muslims in England during the High Middle Ages influenced the English self-image.

Freeman, Edward Augustus. *The History and Conquests of the Saracens: Six Lectures Delivered before the Edinburgh Philosophical Institution.* Bel Aire, CA: Elibron Classics, 2005. Reprint of an 1856 classic series of lectures, two of which are about the Saracens in the 9th and 10th centuries.

Lewis, Bernard. *The Muslim Discovery of Europe.* New York: W. W. Norton & Co., 2001. Using Islamic primary sources and scholarship, Lewis examines events of the Middle Ages from the Muslim perspective.

Nichol, David. *Saracen Faris: A.D.1050–1250.* Oxford: Osprey Press, 1994. Discussion of the training of the Saracen mounted cavalry and their importance to Muslim victories. Heavily illustrated.

Tolan, John V. *Saracens.* New York: Columbia University Press, 2002. Thorough history of the Saracens from the seventh to the 13th century. Concentrates on the attitudes of Christians toward Muslims.

World Wide Web

De Re Militari: The Society for Medieval Military History. http://www.deremilitari .org/. Maintained by an international association of scholars, the site offers articles on many aspects of medieval warfare, translations of primary sources, links to other sites, a bibliography, and book reviews.

IslamiCity. www.islamicity.com. This Web site is operated by HADI, a nonprofit corporation dedicated to peace and understanding. Current and historic information about the Muslim world is available.

Museum with no Frontiers. http://www.discoverislamicart.org/home.php. Internationally sponsored site with virtual exhibits and information about Islamic art.

Multimedia Sources

Islam: Empire of Faith. 2001. DVD. PBS Production. Three hours. Traces the history of Islam for 1,000 years using reenactments, interviews, and visits to historic sites. Companion Web site: http://www.pbs.org/empires/islam/.

Islam: 600–1200. 1985. DVD. Landmark Media. 26 minutes. Discusses rise of Islam to its powerful presence in the Middle Ages.

33. Developments in Mathematics (c. 840)

The science of mathematics dates back to ancient China, India, and Greece. Roman scholars were familiar with the writings of some of the ancient mathematicians. However, when barbarians conquered the Western Roman Empire, this mathematical knowledge was lost to the West. From the fifth century on, the Byzantine Eastern Empire continued to preserve the texts of earlier mathematicians and to add to the body of knowledge. For example, Boethius, descended from a noble Roman family, was educated in Greece, and wrote a mathematics text around 510. One of the innovative architects of the Emperor Justinian, who reconstructed Hagia Sophia, Anthemius of Tralles, was also a geometry professor in Constantinople. India continued scholarship in mathematics as well, becoming the first to use decimals around 594 and using zero and negative numbers around 630.

When Islamic armies conquered cities such as Alexandria, they gained possession of ancient texts on medicine, astronomy, and mathematics. Their scholars valued these resources and around 810 founded the House of Wisdom in Baghdad where large numbers of the texts were translated into Arabic, moving the Islamic countries far ahead of those in the West. Muslim intellectuals began to study mathematics in earnest and augmented the existing knowledge. In the early 9th century, mathematician, geographer, and astronomer Al-Khwarizmi wrote a number of treatises including *Hisab al-jabr w'al-muqabala (Calculation by Completion and Balancing),* in which the word *algebra* is used for the first time. His name is the source for the term *algorithm.*

Almost all advancements in mathematics developed in India or in the Islamic nations for the next two hundred years. In the mid-9th century, Thabit ibn Qurra introduced a number of concepts to mathematics, including integral calculus, theorems in spherical trigonometry, analytic geometry, and nonEuclidean geometry. Fifty years later, Abu Kamil wrote *Book on Algebra,* using algebra to solve geometric problems. And within two more decades, around 970, Abu'l-Wafa wrote books on geometry and introduced the tangent function.

When the Islamic armies conquered the Iberian Peninsula in the 8th century and moved through the Mediterranean in the 9th century, the mathematical knowledge they possessed began to be disseminated in the West. Yet it was not until the mid-11th century, however, that Europeans began to study and write about mathematics. The work of Muslims in mathematics has often been undervalued for the enormous contribution it made to human knowledge.

TERM PAPER SUGGESTIONS

1. Evaluate the role that religion played in the advancement or in the hindrance of the sciences in the Islamic or the Christian culture of the 9th through 11th centuries.

2. Some historians have suggested that medieval scientists, including mathematicians, were concerned with practical applications rather than theoretical suppositions. Do you agree or disagree with this statement? What evidence supports your opinion?

3. Between the 8th and 11th centuries, mathematics was almost unknown in Western Europe. Discuss both the institutions and the individuals who were most responsible for the survival of the rudiments of science and mathematics during this period.

4. Choose a mathematical concept introduced during the Middle Ages. What led the mathematician to develop this concept? What developments were necessary before this step could be taken? What questions was the mathematician trying to answer? What is the significance of the concept to later developments in mathematics?

5. How did mathematical advancements of the Middle Ages prepare the way for the developments of the Renaissance, including world exploration?

6. How did the use of the Roman system of numbers inhibit the advancement of mathematics?

7. In spite of the enormous advantage Islam culture had in the Middle Ages in the sciences, why did the West surpass Islamic in scientific advancement?

8. Compare the developments in Arabic science and mathematics with those in China between the 8th and 14th centuries.

ALTERNATIVE TERM PAPER SUGGESTIONS

1. Choose a significant mathematical discovery of the Middle Ages. Prepare a presentation for the class in which you explain this discovery, demonstrate its use, and discuss its significance to modern mathematics.

2. Using primary sources and historical information, investigate a problem based in the Middle Ages. Apply mathematical processes to solve the problem. Examples might include how to construct a specific tall building so that it would be supported, or planning the number of acres of various crops needed to sustain a manor with a certain number of people throughout a year.

Primary Sources

Al-Khwarizmi. *The Book of Algebra.* Trans. by Frederic Rosen. Islamabad: Pakistan Hijra Council, 1989. Translation of a foundational mathematical text.

Fauvel, John, and Gray, Jeremy, eds. *The History of Mathematics: A Reader.* New York: Macmillian, 1996. A varied collection of translations from early mathematicians, including Islamic and medieval European writers.

Katz, Victor, et al., eds. *The Mathematics of Eqypt, Mesopotamia, China, India, and Islam: A Sourcebook.* Princeton: University of Princeton Press, 2007. Includes translations of the work of mathematicians from the five cultures mentioned in the title.

Pisano, Leonardo. *The Liber Abaci (Book of Calculation).* Fibonacci was Pisano's Latin name. Laurence Sigler translated the work as *Fibonacci's Liber Abaci,* published in New York by Springer-Verlag in 2002.

Secondary Sources

Bergrren, J. L. *Episodes in the Mathematics of Medieval Islam.* New York: Springer-Verlag, 1986. This text is a history of mathematics, an explanation of concepts, and an exercise book.

Gulberg, Jan. *Mathematics from the Birth of Numbers.* New York: W. W. Norton Company, 1997. Comprehensive overview of math history. Includes illustrations, cartoons, and example problems.

Lindberg, David C. *The Beginnings of Western Science: The European Scientific Tradition in Philosophical, Religious, and Institutional Context, 600 B.C. to A.D. 1450.* Chicago: University of Chicago Press, 1992. Traces the history of science from its beginnings in Egypt and Mesopotamia to the Middle Ages.

Struik, Dirk J. *A Concise History of Mathematics.* Mineola, New York: Dover Publications, 1987. Includes a chapter on mathematics in medieval Europe.

World Wide Web

The MacTutor History of Mathematics. http://www-groups.dcs.st-and.ac.uk/~history/. Maintained by the School of Mathematics and Statistics at the University of St. Andrews, Scotland, this site has biographies of hundreds of mathematicians, lists of resources, and links to other websites.

The Math Forum@Drexel. http://mathforum.org/. Web site with a variety of resources and links for teachers and students, including a section on famous historical math problems (http://mathforum.org/isaac/mathhist .html). Some resources require membership to access.

Searce, Carolyn. "Adelard's Questions and Ockham's Razor: Connections between Medieval Philosophy and Modern Science: A Discovery Guide." November 2008. http://www.csa.com/discoveryguides/discoveryguides -main.php.

Multimedia Sources

Culture and Math: How Numbers Have Shaped Civilization. 2006. Series of eight DVDs. Discovery Channel. 28–31 minutes. Includes segments on the Moors, Arabs, and Greeks.

Early History of Mathematics. 1991. DVD. Project Mathematics. Traces landmark developments in mathematics from ancient times to the 17th century. Available in several languages.

Engineering the Impossible. 2007. DVD. National Geographic. 150 minutes. Discusses the mathematical engineering necessary to create the Coliseum in Rome, the Great Pyramids, and Chartres Cathedral.

The Genius of the East: Mathematics During the Middle Ages. 2008. DVD. Films Media Group. 60 minutes. Marcus du Sautoy leads viewers through the mathematical achievements of China, the Islamic world, and the late medieval period.

Math and Culture: The Moors of Spain. 2006. Streaming video. Discovery Learning United Streaming. 23 minutes. Discusses how the Islamic moors were able to use mathematics to determine the appropriate times for prayer.

34. Scotland's Kingdoms Unite (843)

The land to the north of the Roman barrier between England and Scotland, Hadrian's Wall, in Great Britain was inhabited by people the Romans called the Picts because of their habit of painting themselves before battle. Later the Irish (called Scots) settled in the western part of the territory. Britons, Angles, and Vikings also established their own small states in what would become known as Scotland. Intermarriage among the tribes would sometimes lead to two tribes accepting a single king for a time. In the early 9th century, Alpin led the Scots in successful battles against the Picts and the Vikings; however, he did not gain sovereignty over either tribe. The Picts mounted an offensive against the Scots, captured Alpin, and displayed his severed head in their camp.

Alpin's chosen heir was his son Cinaeth (Kenneth) MacAlpin, who took up the war with the Picts. The Pictish king Eagan had been killed by the Vikings, and no one had ascended to the throne. When Kenneth was able to occupy several of the Picts' most valuable strongholds, they accepted him as their king. In 843 at Moot Hill in Scone, the sacred center of Pictish lands, Kenneth was enthroned on the Stone of Scone as ruler of the united Picts and Scots in Alba. Legend purports that the Stone of Scone is the pillow upon which the Biblical Jacob rested his head and dreamed of angels going to and from heaven. The Stone connected the king to the church and indicated his rule had the approval of God. Although Kenneth I did not conquer any of the other tribes in Alba, in the following decades these tribes were absorbed, and the MacAlpin dynasty ruled the independent kingdom of Scotland for two centuries.

Kenneth I's reign (843–858) was still plagued with fighting, especially among the nobles. At his coronation banquet at Scone, Kenneth murdered the seven earls from Dalriada whom he feared might challenge his claim to the Scottish throne. This act of murder became known as MacAlpin's Treason. Kenneth selected Dunkeld in Perthshire as the capital during his 17-year reign. His younger brother Donald I succeeded him to the throne.

Scotland remained independent until 1603 when James VI of Scotland became James I of the United Kingdom of England, Scotland, and Wales.

TERM PAPER SUGGESTIONS

1. Scotland had few natural resources and was a poor nation. How were the Scots able to survive and build a sound economy?
2. Compare the Scottish tanistry system of determining kings with the ways kings were selected in other European nations. What effects did tanistry have on the stability of the Scottish government?
3. Medieval Gaelic is still spoken by many Scots. How do you explain the fact that the language has continued so long in a nation whose official language is English?
4. Discuss the effects of the arrival of the Christian church in Scotland. How was the development of the church different in Scotland from its development in other parts of the British Isles?
5. The social structure of medieval Scotland was less rigid than that in many areas of Europe. Discuss the position of the common man or woman. What was the relationship between ordinary citizens and the king? How were the political traditions of the nation shaped by this relationship?
6. Macbeth was an early king of Scotland. Compare the history of his life and reign with the story Shakespeare tells in his tragedy. How do you account for the differences?

ALTERNATIVE TERM PAPER SUGGESTIONS

1. Learn some basic characteristics of the Gaelic language—sounds, words, letter combinations. Teach your classmates to read a few lines of Gaelic.
2. The bagpipes of Scotland are more than just an instrument. What was the importance of the instrument and music to the culture and unity of Scotland?

Primary Sources

Calise, J. M. P., ed. *Pictish Sourcebook: Documents of Medieval Legend and Dark Age History.* Westport, CT: Greenwood Publishing, 2002. Collection of translations of some of the earliest documents and regnal lists from Scotland.

Chronicon Scotorum. http://www.ucc.ie/celt/published/T100016/. Translation of an annual listing of events, primarily in Ireland, composed from 353–1150.

Skene, W. F., ed. *Chronicles of the Picts, Chronicles of the Scots, And Other Early Memorials of Scottish History.* Whitefish, MT: Kessinger Publishing,

2007. A facsimile reproduction of Skene's 1867 collection of early documents including the Annals of Tighernac, one of the first Scottish histories.

Secondary Sources

Barrell, A. D. M. *Medieval Scotland.* Cambridge: Cambridge University Press, 2002. An introductory text on Scottish history.

Keith, Stringer, and Grant, Alexander, eds. *Medieval Scotland.* New York: Columbia University Press, 1998. Thirteen essays from historians on the formation of the Scottish nation.

Laing, Lloyd. *The Picts and the Scots.* Gloucestershire: Sutton Publishing, 2002. This short volume describes the culture of the Picts and Scots, their everyday lives, and their art through the lens of recent archaeological material.

MacKenzie, Agnes Mure. *The Foundations of Scotland.* Edinburgh: Barton Press, 2007. Discusses the major tribes who settled Scotland, the medieval unification and the reigns of kings through 1287.

MacQuarrie, Alan. *Medieval Scotland: Kingship and Nation.* Stroud, UK: Sutton Publishing, 2004. Examines Scottish history from the Roman invasion until the time of James I. Includes both social and political history.

Magnusson, Magnus. *Scotland: The Story of a Nation.* New York: Harper Collins Publishers, 2000. A complete history of Scotland from the Roman occupation until James VI.

Smyth, Alfred. *Warlords and Holy Men: Scotland 80–1000 AD.* Edinburgh: Edinburgh University Press, 1989. Smyth includes chapters on the Britons, Picts, Vikings, Christianity, and early kings.

Woolf, Alex. *From Pictland to Alba: Scotland, 789–1070.* Edinburgh: Edinburgh University Press, 2007. Discusses the events and the process that transformed the splintered factions of Scotland into a nation.

World Wide Web

ElectricScotland.com. Maintained by the Scottish Studies Foundation, the site has valuable digitalized books, many pictures, and links to other resources. Articles may not be as useful since they can be submitted by the public.

In Search of Scotland. http://www.bbc.co.uk/history/scottishhistory/independence/features_independence_arbroath.shtml. An interactive Web site produced by the BBC. Includes timelines, articles, games, images, online debates, and short videos. Covers from the Dark Ages to modern Scotland.

Multimedia Sources

The Guid Scots Tongue. 1986. DVD. Films Media Group. 59 minutes. Studies the influences on the Scottish language and how it traveled through the world influencing other speakers. Visits places where the Gaelic tongue is still used.

Scottish Legends. 1995. DVD. Kultur Films. 50 minutes. Explores legends that have grown around real people as well as familiar stories such as the legend of the spider, the ghost of the field of Flodden, and others.

35. Mayan Empire Declines (c. 850)

At its zenith, the Mayan Empire encompassed much of Central America, including the modern countries of Guatemala, Belize, El Salvador, Honduras, and part of Mexico. By far the most advanced medieval culture in Mesoamerica, the Maya developed the only known written language in the ancient Americas, were skilled astronomers and architects, and autonomously developed the mathematical concept of zero. Mayan ruins indicate that they began building large structures around 1000 BCE, but the golden age of Mayan culture flourished between 300 and 900 CE.

During this classical period, the Mayans built a number of large city-states, including Tikal, Chichen Itza, Palenque, and Uxmal. As the city-states developed, they engaged in both trade and warfare with one another. In the later days of the empire, the warfare was curbed and relegated to a more ceremonial role. Although terrain dictated the structure of cities, some common characteristics were present, including large pyramid temples and splendid palaces for the rulers. Buildings are also laid out in what is called E-groups because of the resemblance to the letter *E*: a large pyramid temple on the western side of the city facing three smaller pyramids. Although the exact function of this arrangement remains a mystery, the buildings are aligned with the sun during equinoxes and solstices. Ball courts are also found in the cities where teams engaged in deadly sport. Some cities grew to be quite large; Tikal, then known as Mutul, covers approximately 52 square miles. More than 4,000 structures have been identified by archeologists working in Tikal, which is a national park in Guatemala today.

A distinct social class system appeared in Mayan culture during the classical period, with clear divisions between royalty and commoner. Kings of city-states, who also functioned as chief priests, were part of the hereditary ruling class. Mayan religion was polytheistic and sometimes practiced human sacrifice.

Sometime around 850, a complex social structure and cities of the empire began to devolve. A number of theories for this have been proposed, including renewed warfare, drought, and famine resulting from the overuse of cropland and increasing populations. Around 1200, some small city-states resurrected themselves, but the Mayan culture the Europeans found in the 16th century was much diminished from what it had once been. Although the Spanish conducted a vigorous war against them, Native Americans of Mayan heritage still live in parts of Central America and have preserved much of their native language. Many of the texts written by the Maya were destroyed under the orders of the Spanish Bishop Diego de Landa in the 16th century.

TERM PAPER SUGGESTIONS

1. Compare the astronomical knowledge of the Maya with that of Western Europe in the 9th century.

2. Research agricultural methods. Compare them to those of Western Europe in the same period.

3. Research the ball courts found in Mayan cities. What was their function? How did the competitions held here reflect the Mayan understanding of the universe?

4. Although the Mayan culture was sustained primarily by agriculture, trade was a significant part of the economy. Research this aspect of the Mayan Empire and discuss its impact on the culture.

5. Compare the religious beliefs and practices of the Maya with those of another Mesoamerican culture.

6. Explore the characteristics of the Mayan system of writing. What other written language systems are similar? Who was literate in the Mayan culture and for what purposes was writing used?

ALTERNATIVE TERM PAPER FORMATS

1. Research the developments of textiles and clothing during the Mayan Empire's classical age. Create a display of their techniques of weaving, embroidery, and construction. Pay particular attention to the symbolic elements of the textiles.

2. Research the art and architecture of the Mayan Empire. Create a multimedia presentation detailing their construction materials and techniques and the methods and purposes of the decorative arts.

3. Mayans developed an extremely accurate calendar. Reproduce the calendar in a large format and prepare an oral presentation explaining how it was used by the Maya and the significance of the dates to the culture.

4. Mayas used a base 20 numerical system. Design a PowerPoint presentation explaining this system and giving examples of its usage.

Primary Sources

Book of Chilam Balam of Chumayel. Trans. by Ralph L. Roys. Washington DC; Carnegie Institution, 1933. http://www.sacred-texts.com/nam/maya/index .htm. Although some parts of this text were not written until after the Spanish began their conquest of Central America, other sections date from a much earlier time.

Popul Vuh: The Definitive Edition of the Mayan Book of the Dawn of Life and the Glories of. Trans. by Dennis Tedlock. New York: Touchstone, 1996. Translation with introduction of ancient Mayan religious text.

Secondary Sources

Coe, Michael D. *The Maya,* 7th ed. London: Thames & Hudson, 2005. Follows many aspects of Mayan civilization from its earliest days to today.

Demarest, Arthur. *Ancient Maya: The Rise and Fall of a Rainforest Civilization.* Cambridge: Cambridge University Press, 2004. Using recent archeological evidence, Demarest considers the ecological implications of and on Mayan culture.

Freidel, David, and Schele, Linda. *A Forest of Kings: The Untold Story of the Ancient Maya.* New York: Morrow, 1990. Looks at Mayan culture through the archeological research at the sites of six major cities.

Hassig, Ross. *War and Society in Ancient Mesoamerica.* Berkeley: University of California Press, 1992. Study of the importance of warfare to the Mayan and Aztec cultures.

McKillop, Heather. *The Ancient Maya: New Perspectives.* New York: W. W. Norton Co., 2006. A comprehensive discussion of all aspects of Mayan civilization. Includes a glossary, chronology, and lengthy bibliography.

Miller, Mary Ellen. *Mayan Art and Architecture.* London: Thames & Hudson, 1999. Filled with illustrations, this volume explores Mayan artistic creations from hand-held objects to large pyramid temples.

Sharer, Robert, Traxler, Lao, and Morley, Sylvanus Grisley. *The Ancient Maya,* 6th ed. California: Stanford University Press, 2006. Sharer and Traxler revised and added to Morley's classic 1946 study of the Maya.

World Wide Web

Altar Q and Copan. http://www.peabody.harvard.edu/Copan/default.html. A special project of the Peabody Museum at Harvard, this site includes brief online videos and an article on the Mayan culture.

Archaeology: A Publication of the American Archaeological Institute. http://www.archaeology.org/. Search feature leads to many articles from *Archaelogy Magazine.*

Dumbarton Oaks Research Library and Collection. http://www.doaks.org/. Dumbarton Oaks is a Harvard University Research institute devoted in part to preColumbian studies. A large collection of scholarly papers on many topics is available. Site also provides a searchable database with translations of the surviving Mayan codices.

Foundation for the Advancement of Mesoamerican Studies. http://www.famsi.org/. Drawings, photos, texts, videos, and other resources are accessible from this site. Available in both English and Spanish.

Multimedia Sources

The Ancient Maya: Tools of Astronomy. 2006. DVD. The History Channel. 50 minutes. Examines Mayan use of the sun to plan cities and their development of the calendar.

Chichen Itza: At the Mouth of the Well. 2001. DVD. Films Media Group. 27 minutes. Tours one of the best examples of Mayan civilization. Archeological evidence and computer recreations.

Culture and Math: The Maya. 2006. DVD. Discovery Channel. 30 minutes. Discusses Mayan calendar calculations, explains the number system, and provides digital effects examples.

In Search of History: The Maya. 2008. DVD. The History Channel. 50 minutes. Archeologist Alberto Ruz, who has made significant Mayan discoveries, hosts this tour of Mayan ruins.

Living Stones in Mesoamerica. 2003. DVD. Films for the Humanities and Sciences. Tour of archeological sites in Mesoamerica and look at what they tell us about the early inhabitants.

Lost Civilizations: The Maya. 2002. DVD. Time-Life/Ventura. 50 minutes. Uses reconstructions, location filming, interviews, and digital effects to explore the Mayan civilization.

Lost Kingdoms of the Maya. 1993. Video. National Geographic. 60 minutes. Presents reenactments of rituals in Mayan locations.

The Lost King of the Maya. 2001. DVD. PBS. 60 minutes. Explores the existence of the legendary founder of the Mayan civilization, Yax Kiuk Mois, through archeological and written evidence.

The Mayans. 1996. DVD. Films Media Group. 47 minutes. Discusses the advancements of the Mayan civilization, their practices, and their art.

36. Founding of Kievan Rus' (858)

Viking tribes known as the Varangians raided and eventually settled in Eastern Europe during the 9th century. They gained a large foothold in the land between the Dneiper and Volga Rivers, which is largely modern Ukraine. The two rivers functioned as strategic trade routes between the East and West and also gave the Varangians military advantages. Under the leadership of their first ruler, the semilegendary Rurik (r. c. 862–879), the Varangians captured the towns of Kiev and Novgorod and much of the surrounding territory. Rurik fortified the towns and he and his descendants turned them into thriving cities of government and trade. The Varangians became known as the Rus, the origin of the word Russia, and the medieval kingdom was known as the Kievan Rus'. Under Rurik's successor Oleg (r. 879–912), Kiev became the capital city.

The Slavic tribes who inhabited the area were conquered during the century after the Varangians arrival, who frequently executed the local leaders and destroyed the villages. Much of the population was nomadic, engaging in agriculture and forestry until the land was depleted, and then moving on. When Grand Prince Vladimir I (r. 978–1015) inherited the throne, he made major revisions to the social fabric of Rus', including the landholding system. To stabilize his kingdom, he hired Varangian mercenaries to patrol the borders. Vladimir also promoted the expansion of cities, which were well-fortified and could withstand sieges. Cities became centers of craftsmanship, with glassblowers, jewelers, metalworkers, and other artisans plying their trades and advancing commerce in the kingdom. A Christian himself, Vladimir instituted the Christian faith as the state religion. Although it was some time before the Slavs were converted, this action established close ties between the Rus' and Byzantine Church, especially since many Byzantine monks and scholars were invited to Rus' to found churches and schools. The Russian feudal system was introduced by Vladimir when he inaugurated the concept of land ownership. Rewarding his supporters with large tracts of land, Vladimir limited the peasants' nomadic movements. They became joined to the land, working it for the owner who now assumed greater power over them.

By the time Vladimir's son Yaroslav the Wise (r. 1019–1054) assumed power, Kievan Rus was a well-established and relatively prosperous nation enjoying an era of peace. Yaroslav devoted much of his energy to building cathedrals and other great buildings. The *Russkaia Pravda,* the first Russian law code, was written by Yaroslav. After his death, Russian unification began to fragment, and over the next century the resulting principalities developed rivalries with one another. When the Mongols invaded Rus' in 1236, the individual principalities were easily subjugated and dominated by the Mongols for more than two hundred years.

TERM PAPER SUGGESTIONS

1. How was Byzantine church art adapted for political and religious purposes in Rus' Kiev?

2. Analyze the *Russkaia Pravda* (Russian Justice) and compare this law code to Germanic law in the Salic Law, or to Roman Law in the Justinian Code.

3. Compare the feudal systems of Kievan Rus' and that of Western Europe.

4. Compare the invading Varangians with the Slavic tribes that inhabited Russia. What characteristics facilitated or impeded their assimilation?

5. When it began, the Russian church acknowledged the Byzantine primate as its leader and aligned itself with Greek Orthodox teachings. Later, however, the Russian church began to disconnect from the Greek church and establish its own leadership and doctrine. What were the causes of this split? How is the Russian Orthodox Church different from the Greek Orthodox?

6. What characteristics of the medieval Russian state and character influenced the later developments in Russian politics and culture?

ALTERNATIVE TERM PAPER FORMATS

1. Design a multimedia presentation on the Cyrillic alphabet and teach your classmates how to write a few words using the alphabet.

2. Prepare a multimedia presentation about medieval Russian art and architecture. How was this art influenced by Byzantine art? How did it depart from the Byzantine traditions? Pay particular attention to Russian iconography.

3. Design an interactive map pinpointing significant places in medieval Russian history hyperlinked to reliable information about these places and people connected with them.

Primary Sources

Dmytryshyn, Basil, ed. *Medieval Russia: A Source Book, 900–1700.* 2nd ed. New York: Holt, Rinehart and Winston, 1973. Translations of partial and complete documents written by Russians, as well as travelers and observers who visited Russia. Includes selections of *The Primary Chronicles.*

Kaiser, Daniel H. and Marker, Gary, eds. *Reinterpreting Russian History: Readings 860–1860s.* Oxford: Oxford University Press, 1994. Translations of early personal and public documents and literature from Russian history.

Nestor. *The Primary Chronicle.* Trans. by Samuel Hazzard Cross and Olgerd P. Sherbowitz-Wetzor. Cambridge, MS: The Mediaeval Academy of America, 1953. Compiled in the early 12th century from earlier Slavic, Rus, and Byzantine chronicles, oral sources, and annals, *The Primary Chronicles* is considered the most reliable source of information on Rus' Kiev from 850 to 1100.

Secondary Sources

Duke, Paul. *A History of Russia: Medieval, Modern, Contemporary, c.882–1996,* 3rd ed. Durham: Duke University Press, 1998. Part one consists of three chapters on medieval Russia.

Franklin, Simon, and Shepard, Jonathan. *The Emergence of Rus 750–1200.* White Plains, NY: Addison Wesley Publishing Company, 1996. Discusses the rise of government, culture, and the church in early Russia.

Heyman, Neil M. *Russian History.* New York: McGraw-Hill, 1993. First three chapters deal with the history of early Kiev.

Moss, Walter G. *A History of Russia, Vol. 1: To 1917.* London: Anthem Press, 2005. Early chapters discuss the politics, religion, culture, and cities of medieval Russia.

Vernadsky, George. *Kievan Russia.* New Haven: Yale University Press, 1973. This volume relies heavily on primary sources and remains one of the best sources on medieval Russia.

World Wide Web

Introduction to Russian Culture. http://www.und.edu/dept/lang/russian/162/culture.html. Lists links to Russian studies resources.

Medieval and Early Modern Russia and Ukraine. http://faculty.washington.edu/dwaugh/rus/ruspg1.html. Site authored by Daniel C. Waugh of the University of Washington. Includes translations of documents by Waugh and links to other sites with translations and images from Kievan Rus'.

Multimedia Sources

The Face of Russia. 1998. DVD. PBS. 3-part series, 50 minutes each. Russian art, architecture, music, and cinema are the subjects of this cultural history going from the founding of Kievan Rus' to the 12th century. Companion Web site: http://www.pbs.org/weta/faceofrussia/intro.html.

Alexander Nevsky. 1938. DVD. Directed by famed Russian Sergei Eisenstein. 112 minutes. Historical fiction about the Russian 12th-century hero and saint.

37. Macedonian Dynasty in Byzantium (867–1059)

Basil I (r. 867–886), a descendant of peasants who were Macedonian Armenians and Slavs, served in the Byzantine court of Michael III (r. 842–867). In 866, Basil helped Michael murder Bardas, his uncle and chief minister. Michael rewarded Basil by naming him coemperor. A year later, fearing he was losing favor with Michael, Basil had him assassinated and proclaimed himself sole emperor of Byzantium. Basil's taking of the throne marked the beginning of the Macedonian Dynasty in Byzantium, which was to last for almost two centuries and is sometimes called the "golden age" of Byzantium.

Basil and his successors regained and expanded their territory and greatly increased the wealth of the empire. Basil pushed the Byzantine border with the Abbasid caliphate eastward and captured important areas of Italy. His reign also saw the Greek church become more independent of Rome and the Bulgarian church come under the administration of the Greek rather than Roman church. Along with his son and successor Leo VI, Basil codified the tangle of Byzantine laws in the *Basilica.* Although a capable ruler in many ways, he could also be tyrannical and cruel. In 886, a hunting accident caused a fever that led to his death.

The zenith of Byzantine power and influence came during the reign of Basil II, the Bulgar Slayer (r. 976–1025) and great-grandson of Basil I. At the age of two, Basil II was named coemperor with his brother Constantine. The empire was ruled by Nicephorus Phocas and later by John Tzimisces, both of whom married Basil's mother. When Tzimisces died in 976, Basil ascended to the throne, but the eunuch Chamberlain Basil had immense power in the empire. A few years later, Basil forced the eunuch from power, confiscated all his wealth, and from that point on was sole ruler. His early reign was troubled by revolts led by two of his generals, but these were eventually quelled. Basil led his troops into battle against Bulgaria in 986 but suffered a humiliating defeat. In 1014, he met the Bulgarians for a second time and earned his soubriquet in a cruel display of power. After capturing an estimated 14,000 Bulgarian soldiers, Basil divided them into groups of 100. Ninety-nine men in each group were blinded and the one-hundredth was left with his sight to lead the others home.

During Basil II's reign, the capital city of Constantinople was a cosmopolitan center of trade with a population of around three-quarters of a million people, making it the largest city in the West. Jews, Muslims, Christians, Balkans, Asiatics, and Europeans lived together within the bustling metropolis. In art and architecture the period is called the Macedonian renaissance because of the revival of neoclassical Byzantine styles. Libraries, monasteries, and churches were built throughout the empire, and Byzantium was the world center of culture. Monasteries in cities funded hospitals, orphanages, and homes for the poor. In the country, monasteries also functioned as agricultural industries. Literature flourished, manuscripts were copied and translated, encyclopedias were written, and there was a rekindling of interest in science, mathematics, and astronomy.

Basil II was the last emperor of the Macedonian line, but the dynasty is said to have lasted until 1059 when Isaac I died and Byzantium was being invaded by the Turkish Empire.

TERM PAPER SUGGESTIONS

1. How did Byzantine emperors of the Macedonian era view their imperial offices? What relationship did they have with the nobility? With the lower classes? What was their position in the church? What was the extent of their power?

2. One of the most unusual reigns in Byzantine history is that of the sisters Zoe and Theodora who ruled jointly for a short time in 1042. Theodora regained the throne from 1054–1055. Research how these two women came to power, what the reaction to their rule was, and why they had such a brief reign. What does their sovereignty say about the position of women in Byzantium?

3. Research the work of the monasteries in Macedonian Byzantium. Compare the social role they developed to that of earlier monasteries.

4. Although they fought numerous wars, the Macedonian dynasty excelled in the art of diplomacy. Research the diplomatic efforts of the emperors and the effects these efforts had on the power and status of Byzantium.

5. The Byzantine emperors used both ceremony and images to bolster the impression of a strong empire. Research the verbal and visual images of the rulers and how they employed various ceremonies as propaganda.

6. Compare the illuminated manuscripts produced during the Macedonian dynasty with those produced in the West during the same time period.

7. Military power is often crucial to imperial power, but that was particularly true in Byzantium. Research the connection between the emperor's power and his relationship to his army.

ALTERNATIVE TERM PAPER FORMATS

1. Assume the persona of the one of 140 Bulgarians who was not blinded by Basil II. Create a dramatic monologue retelling what happened after you were captured and about your journey home. Include the route you took and the specific hardships you and the other men faced.

2. Create a series of maps showing the extent of the early Byzantine Empire, the extent at the beginning of the Macedonian Dynasty, and the end of the Macedonian Dynasty. Explain how the possession of certain strategic locations helped the empire increase or maintain its power.

Primary Sources

Geanakoplos, Deno John, ed. *Byzantium: Church, Society, and Civilization Seen through Contemporary Eyes.* Chicago: University of Chicago Press, 1986. Extensive collection of translations representing legal and governmental documents, histories, and personal papers covering 1,000 years of Byzantine history. Arranged both chronologically and by topic.

Mango, Cyril, ed. *The Art of the Byzantine Empire 312–1453: Sources and Documents.* Toronto: University of Toronto Press, 1986. Translations of medieval documents concerning the art of Byzantium.

Porphyrogenitus, Constantine. *Constantine Porphyrogenitus: De Administrando Imperio.* G. Moravcsik, ed. Compilation of documents from the 10th century written by Emperor Constantine Prophyrogenitus.

Siegecraft: Two Tenth-Century Instructional Manuals by Heron of Byzantium. Trans. by Dennis F. Sullivan. Washington, DC: Dumbarton Oaks, 2000. http://doaks.org/publications/doaks_online_publications/Siegecraft.pdf. Introduction to both works, comments, and a side-by-side presentation of the Greek text and English translation.

Secondary Sources

Dagron, Gilbert. *Emperor and Priest: The Imperial Office in Byzantium*. Trans. by Jean Birrell. Cambridge: Cambridge University Press, 2007. Meticulous research into the nature of the Byzantine kingship. Includes a chapter on Basil the Macedonian.

Holmes, Catherine. *Basil II and the Governance of Empire (976–1025)*. Oxford: Oxford University Press, 2006. A discussion of the style and substance of the rule of Basil II; includes translations of two contemporary works of John Skylitzes.

Jeffreys, Elizabeth. *Byzantine Style, Religion and Civilization: In Honour of Sir Steven Runciman*. Cambridge: Cambridge University Press, 2006. A collection of 22 essays on many aspects of Byzantine culture; includes an essay on Basil II and on images and art in the 9th century.

Laiou, Angeliki E., and Morrison, Cecile. *The Byzantine Economy*. Cambridge: Cambridge University Press, 2007. A chronologically arranged study of economics in Byzantium, this book also compares the Eastern and Western medieval economies.

Muldoon, James. *Empire and Order: The Concept of Empire, 800–1800*. London: Palgrave, 1999. Includes thorough discussion of the relationship between the medieval church and empires and the powers assumed by empires.

Runciman, Steven. *The Emperor Romanus Lecapenus and his Reign: A Study of Tenth-Century Byzantium*. Cambridge: Cambridge University Press, 1988. A biography and detailed study of the rule of Romanus.

Tobias, Norman. *Basil I, Founder of the Macedonian Dynasty: A Study of the Political and Military History of the Byzantine Empire in the Ninth Century*. Lewiston, NY: Edwin Mellen Press, 2007. Thorough examination of the life and reign of Basil I.

World Wide Web

Brownworth, Lars. *12 Byzantine Rulers: The History of the Byzantine Empire Podcast*. A series of 12 podcasts by Brownworth covering twelve significant emperors of Byzantium, including Basil II.

The Byzantine Studies Page. http://www.fordham.edu/halsall/byzantium/. Articles, translations, and links to other sources.

Dumbarton Oaks Research Library and Collection. http://www.doaks.org/. Dumbarton Oaks is a Harvard University Research institute devoted in part to Byzantine studies. A large collection of scholarly papers on many topics is available online.

History of Macedonia. http://www.historyofmacedonia.org/. Web site devoted to Macedonian history from ancient times until today. Many links to articles, exhibitions, and book reviews. Includes section on Byzantine rulers.

Multimedia Sources

Byzantium: The Lost Empire. 1997. Koch Vision, The Discovery Channel. Two 50-minute videos. Volume 1 tells of the growth of the Byzantine Empire through the late 1400s; volume 2 discusses the empire's fall.

Byzantium ~ The Lost Dream. 1997. TLC/Discovery Channel production. Two-disc set. 209 minutes. Hosted by historian John Romer, program follows the rise and fall of the empire.

38. Beginning of a Unified England (871)

When Alfred (r. 871–899) became king of Wessex, England was divided into four small kingdoms—Wessex, Northumbria, Mercia, and East Anglia—which were often in conflict with one another. While still a teenager, Alfred made two trips to Rome, but he had little formal schooling. As the fourth son of King Ethelwulf and Queen Osburth, it seemed unlikely that he would become king. Yet, after Ethelwulf's death, each of his four sons ruled Wessex, with Alfred assuming the throne at age 22. The only English king to receive the sobriquet "the Great," Alfred began the process of uniting the nation under one monarch, a process completed by his grandson Athelstan.

Alfred's dream of a united England influenced many aspects of his life and reign. He married a Mercian princess, Elswitha, which by all accounts seems to have been a happy marriage, but which also gave him some claim to Mercia. The king emphasized the need for his people to be literate, and he set up schools where young freemen could learn English and, if they wished, Latin. He himself studied Latin with his biographer Asser and translated a number of Latin works into English so they would be accessible to a wider audience. Alfred is also credited with having the *Anglo-Saxon Chronicle* kept, along with the preservation of many earlier works. While Latin remained the language of the church, in Alfred's time English began to unite the various groups living throughout the country. The church, too, became a unifying force under Alfred's leadership. A devout Christian himself, Alfred supported the work of the church. He sustained close contact with the Celtic peoples on the fringes of his border, encouraging them to adopt Christianity. Part of Alfred's terms of peace with the Danes was that their leaders be baptized, he himself serving as sponsor for their chief Guthrum.

The Danes were the predominant threat to the unity of Alfred's kingdom throughout his reign. A half century before Alfred's birth, the Vikings began their raids on England, and by the time he became king of Wessex, they had made major inroads in the other three English kingdoms. Alfred and the Danes fought a number of battles during the first seven years of his reign without much success for either side. Alfred probably paid tribute during these years to keep down the number of attacks. Then, in late 877, the Danes began an offensive that actually drove Alfred into hiding. He was able, however, to organize an army that defeated the Danes at the battle of Ethandune in 878. Alfred gave the Danes the right to continue to live in the eastern part of the island, which became known as the Danelaw. The newly Christianized Danish chiefs accepted Alfred as their overlord, setting the precendent of homage to the English king, even though Danish fighting continued through the coming years,

In order to further defend the country, Alfred organized a system of military service whereby every man spent part of the year in military training and part of the year engaged in agriculture. He is also considered "the father of the British navy," since he constructed a fleet of ships of his own design to protect the coast. Fortifications at strategic landings for foreign invasions were also strengthened. Perhaps Alfred's most enduring legacy to English unity was his codification of the laws of Wessex and Mercia into a system that served as the basis of English law until the Norman Conquest in 1066.

TERM PAPER SUGGESTIONS

1. During the early period of Anglo-Saxon England, to what extent was Britain isolated from the Continent? What was the relationship between Britain and Europe? How was English culture shaped by this relationship?

2. Alfred called himself "King of the Anglo-Saxons." Why did he choose this title? What was the significance of the title to his efforts to unify England? To what extent was he able to unify the nation?

3. Alfred and Cnut were among the kings who were considered successful rulers. In contrast, Æthelred is almost universally seen as an unsuccessful king. Why? What were the causes of his failure and the reasons for the success of other kings? Was it something about the men, or did the circumstances of their reigns dictate their success or failure? Choose other Anglo-Saxon kings for the discussion if you prefer.

4. Both Alfred and Charles are called "Great." Read the contemporary biographies of the men by Asser and Einhard and compare the qualities that were viewed as great in each man.

5. How did Alfred shape the English legal system? Were his laws influenced more by Roman law or Saxon law? What rights did commoners gain under Alfred's rule?

6. What were Alfred's influences on language, learning, and history? What were the long-term consequences of his influence?

7. Study the political, diplomatic, and military policies of Alfred. What were the effects of his policies on the stability and growth of England?

8. The invasions by Danish Vikings were one of the most troublesome issues with which Alfred had to deal. Discuss his attitude toward the Danes and how he was able to keep their invasions from destroying his kingdom.

9. It has been said that Alfred the Great saved the English language. Do you agree or disagree with this statement? Present a well-researched case for your position.

10. Discuss how Alfred was able to strengthen the church in England. How did a stronger church help to unify the nation?

ALTERNATIVE TERM PAPER FORMATS

1. A number of legends have arisen about Alfred the Great. Research these legends and prepare a storytelling presentation about them. Discuss why these legends were important to the historical personage of Alfred. What do the legends say about the man?

2. Alfred himself designed the ships for his navy. Study his designs and create a large drawing of one of the ships. Annotate the drawing with information about how Alfred's ships were different from most ships of his time.

Primary Sources

Alfred, King of England. *The Whole Works of King Alfred the Great: With Preliminary Essays, Illustrative of the History, Arts, and Manners of the Ninth Century.* New York: AMS Press, 1969. Translations of the writing of Alfred with additional commentary.

The Anglo-Saxon Chronicle. A number of modern English translations of these early records of English history are available in print. A Web-based reproduction is available at http://omacl.org/Anglo/. The text was originally produced under orders from Alfred the Great around 890. Additions were made at various locations throughout England until about the time of the Norman invasion.

Anglo-Saxon Law—Extracts From Early Laws of the English. Part of the Yale School of Law's Avalon Project. http://avalon.law.yale.edu/medieval/saxlaw.asp. Translations of historic and contemporary documents of law.

Anonymous. *Alfred the Great: Asser's Life of King Alfred & Other Contemporary Sources.* Trans. by Simon Keys. London: Penguin Group, 1983. Contains the text of Asser's *Life* plus other documents. Includes an introduction, analysis of sources, maps, and genealogical information.

Secondary Sources

Abels, Richard. *Alfred the Great: War, Culture and Kingship in Anglo-Saxon England.* Harlow, UK: Pearson Educational, 1998. Begins with discussion of Wessex and the context of Alfred's kingship, including his father's and brothers' reigns before him. Analysis of Alfred's entire reign.

Duckett, Eleanor Shipley. *Alfred the Great and His England.* Chicago: University of Chicago Press, 1958. Reconstructs the times of his reign and the man who ruled as "the great" king of Anglo-Saxon England.

Harding, Alan. *Medieval Law and the Foundations of the State.* Oxford: Oxford University Press, 2002. Chapter 2 concerns Frankish and Anglo-Saxon ideas of justice.

Horspool, David. *King Alfred: Burnt Cakes and Other Legends.* Cambridge: Harvard University Press, 2006. Retellings of the Alfred legends with discussion of their significance.

Peddie, John. *Alfred: Warrior King.* Thrupp, UK: Sutton, 1999. Focuses on Alfred as a successful leader in conflicts with the Danish Vikings.

Pollard, Justin. *Alfred the Great: The Man Who Made England.* London: John Murray, 2007. Analytical biography of Alfred and his accomplishments.

Pratt, David. *The Political Thought of King Alfred the Great.* Cambridge: Cambridge University Press, 2007. Extensive analysis of the political and religious decisions made by Alfred and his relationships to his people, his lords, and his bishops.

Reuter, Timothy, ed. *Alfred the Great: Papers from the 11th-Centenary Conferences.* Aldershot, UK: Ashgate, 2003. A collection of 21 essays on King Alfred, his life, kingship, and reputation. The first is by the eminent scholar James Campbell.

Smyth, Alfred P. *King Alfred the Great.* Oxford: Oxford University Press, 1996. Includes extensive biographical information, discussion of the myths concerning Alfred, and examination of legal documents and how Alfred governed.

World Wide Web

BBC History. http://www.bbc.co.uk/history/. The Ancient History section has articles, images, interactive content, and a timeline for Anglo-Saxon England.

The British History Club. http://www.britishhistoryclub.com/index.html. Many resources are available at this site. Includes a section on monarchs.

The Medieval Internet Sourcebook: Selected Sources: England. http://www.fordham.edu/halsall/sbook1n.html#Anglo-Saxon%20Britain. A number of documents from Alfred's time are translated at this site.

Multimedia Sources

Great Kings of England: Alfred the Great. 1994. DVD. Kultur Video. 50 minutes. Part of series *The Great Kings of England.* Biography and analysis of Alfred's contributions to culture.

Kings and Queens of England: The Anglo-Saxons to Elizabeth I. 1993. Films Media Group. 52 minutes. Brief stories of English monarchs until 1603.

39. Fatimid Dynasty (909–1171)

Fatimid Muslims rose to power in North Africa, first in Tunisia, Algeria, and Libya. From ports in these countries, the Fatimid fleet staged attacks on the Mediterranean islands, then chiefly under Islamic control. The Fatimids were supporters of the Shi'ite Islamic tradition, putting them in opposition to the ruling caliphs, the Sunni Abbasids. Their name derives from Fatima, Mohammed's daughter and wife of Ali, from whom the leaders claimed descent. In 969, under the fourth caliph, Moezz, the Fatimids moved into Egypt, founded the city of Cairo, which became a powerful center of commerce, and made it their capital. The kingdom continued to expand into Syria and Palestine. The caliphs considered themselves equal to the caliphs in Baghdad and also took the title of *imam,* seeing themselves as both spiritual and secular leaders. With the exception of al-Hakim (r. 996–1021), the caliphs followed the practice of tolerance, and the different religious groups lived together peacefully.

Under the Fatimids, Egypt's economy and culture flourished. The fertile Nile Valley was already a source of agricultural wealth. Egyptian textiles from linen, wool, and silk were sought throughout the Mediterranean. Islamic ceramics and other arts were also highly valued. Fatimids controlled many of the busiest ports along the East-West trade routes and became skilled ship builders. The Shi'ite dynasty erected some of the most beautiful and famous mosques in North Africa, including Al-Azhar in the center of Cairo. The mosques were centers for learning as well as for worship, and Al-Azhar has the distinction of being the oldest university in the world. Lectures began there in 975, and today, the mosque is surrounded by a modern university that includes schools of medicine, science, and languages.

The Fatimid army, like those of many other Islamic dynasties, consisted of mercenary soldiers from outside the nation they ruled. During the caliphate of al-Mustansir (r.1036–1094), Turkish troops rebelled and looted the palace in Cairo, carrying away jewels, art, and countless manuscripts. Mustansir was able to regain control of his caliphate, but when he died in 1094, the army, and soon the kingdom, broke into factions. In 1171, Ayyubid general Al-Nasir Yusuf, better known as Saladin, replaced the last Fatimid caliph and named himself sultan of Egypt where he ruled from 1175–1193.

TERM PAPER SUGGESTIONS

1. Compare the Islamic mosques built in Egypt under the Fatimids with those in other Islamic countries.

2. During the Fatimid period, Egypt became a center or trade and shipbuilding. What innovations in shipbuilding were introduced? How did these improve the transport of goods?

3. In what ways did the Fatimid government regulate, promote, and control the production of textiles in its territory?

4. Explain how the persecution practiced under the caliph al-Hakim helped set in motion the Crusades of the 11th century.

5. Analyze the governmental structure employed by the Fatimid dynasty. What was the relationship between the caliph, sultans, and princes in the kingdom? How did the Fatimid rulers establish law in their empire? What part did meritocracy play in the Fatimid government?

6. What was the position of women under the Fatimid dynasty?

7. How did the Fatimid caliphs utilize ceremony and procession as tools of governance?

ALTERNATIVE TERM PAPER SUGGESTIONS

1. Create a multimedia presentation about the arts and crafts of Fatimid Egypt.

2. Study the Fatimid weaving and/or embroidery methods. Create a piece of weaving or an embroidered piece using these techniques. Explain the processes you used.

3. Ancient Cairo was a planned city. Create a representation of how the Islamic city was conceived and explain the principles that were used. Was the city designed to reflect religious beliefs, to promote commerce, or for other reasons?

Primary Sources

El Daly, Okasha. *Egyptology: The Missing Millennium: Ancient Egypt in Medieval Arabic Writings.* Walnut Creek, CA: Left Coast Press, 2005. Discusses and provides translated excerpts from a large number of medieval sources on Egypt.

Sheikh, Samira, Kassam, K., and Landolt, H., eds. *An Anthology of Ismaili Literature: A Shi'i Vision of Islam.* London: Institute for Ismaili Studies, 2008. Contains English translations of many works by Shi'i scholars, beginning with those of the Fatimid dynasty.

Secondary Sources

Bierman, Irene A. *Writing Signs: The Fatimid Public Text.* Berkeley: University of California Press, 1998. Bierman examines the inscriptions on buildings and textiles from Fatimid Egypt to explore the ways in which rulers transmitted their ideologies to their people.

Bloom, Jonathan. *Arts of the City Victorious: Islamic Art and Architecture in Fatimid North Africa and Egypt.* New Haven: Yale University Press, 2007. This is the first full-length book on the arts of the Fatimid dynasty. The introductory chapter places Fatimid art in the context of the larger Islamic tradition and then moves to discussions of ceramics, calligraphy, textiles, architecture, and other artist creations.

Hopkins, T. C. F. *Empires, Wars, and Battles: The Middle East from Antiquity to the Rise of the New World.* New York: Forge Books, 2007. Includes a lengthy chapter on medieval Egypt.

Jankowski, James. *Egypt: A Short History.* Oxford: Oneworld Publications, 2000. Professor Jankowski's book contains a good introduction to the Fatimid Dynasty in his chapter on Islamic Egypt.

Lindsay, James E. *Daily Life in the Medieval Islamic World.* Cambridge, MA: Hackett Publishing, 2008. Thorough reference; includes chapters on worship, war, and cities. Extensive appendices with additional material.

World Wide Web

Eternal Egypt. http://www.eternalegypt.org/EternalEgyptWebsiteWeb. A fascinating site with articles, video segments, animations, images, and virtual tours from 5,000 years of Egyptian history, including the Fatimid era.

MuslimHeritage.com. http://www.muslimheritage.com. Searchable Web site produced by the Foundation for Science Technology and Civilisation. Articles, images, timelines, and maps.

Petrie Museum of Egyptian Archaeology. http://www.petrie.ud.ac.uk/index2 .html. Lists the caliphs for the 877 years of Islamic rule in Egypt. Provides access to thousands of images, part of which are from the Islamic period.

40. Monastery at Cluny is Founded (909)

Since the founding of Western monasticism by St. Benedict in 529, most Roman Catholic monasteries followed his Rule. The monasteries were generally under the authority of their own abbot who had some obligations to the bishop, but there was little in the way of central administration. Individual monasteries often interpreted the Rule in different ways, and not all monks were faithful in observing the strict admonitions to work, study, and pray. St. Benedict of Aniane, realizing that monasticism had changed a great deal since the original Rule was imposed, revised the first St. Benedict's work in 817. The modified instructions recognized the work of monks as intercessors with God for the laity and their work in the political and educational spheres. In 909, a new monastery was founded at Cluny that would wield great power for centuries, and although Benedictine in name, would make significant changes in the monastic life.

William the Pious, count of Auvergne and duke of Aquitaine, endowed Cluny and freed it from all obligations other than that of continual prayer for his family. Cluny would have no higher authority except the pope. No longer was a monk to perform manual labor on a self-sufficient agricultural enterprise; the monk's work was to engage in *laus perennis,* perpetual prayer. Cluny developed a beautiful and extensive liturgy and began the custom of chanting or singing the mass and prayers by choirs. The devout in the 10th century believed that intercession was necessary to achieve grace, thus the endless prayers of Cluny were sought through additional gifts of land and the hiring of benefices.

Cluny also instituted a major change in the administration of monasteries. With Cluny as the center, priories sprang up throughout Europe with priors who served as deputies for the abbot of Cluny. Once a year, the priors met at Cluny to report and consider administrative matters.

The abbot also made frequent inspection visits to the priories. When, in 1016, the pope decreed that the privileges of Cluny extended to its priories, there was increased incentive to join the Clunaic organization. The close association of the priories to the monastery and the popularity of pilgrimages allowed for the exchange of knowledge, which enhanced learning throughout Europe.

The vast wealth at the disposal of Cluny made an extensive building campaign possible. The third and final church constructed on the grounds was the largest building in Europe until St. Peter's Basilica was rebuilt in the 16th century. Cluny is also said to be the source of the *truce of God* movement that eventually led to the code of chivalry. Odilo, abbot from 994–1048, first wrote about the *truga dei,* (truce of God) in 1017 in an effort to encourage restraint and Christian conduct in the professional soldier. Warriors promised to refrain from military action between noon on Saturday and Monday morning and during holy seasons.

At its zenith in the early 12th century, Cluny was the center of an organization of an estimated 10,000 monks throughout Europe. Previously, the selection of abbots had been influenced by nobles who endowed monasteries in order to secure positions for relatives. Cluny instituted the means of an orderly succession of abbots from among its own highly educated and worthy monks , thus ensuring the continuation of effective leadership. Although free from obligations to the secular world, the Clunaics did not rebuff patronage. In fact, they cultivated a close relationship with royalty and were largely responsible for the idea of a theocratic monarchy in Europe. Cluny's influence is also evident in the fact that four popes were former abbots: Gregory VII, Urban II, Paschal II, and Urban V.

TERM PAPER SUGGESTIONS

1. How did the changing relationship between clergy and laity reflect the social changes occurring in other aspects of medieval life? How did the increasing piety of laity influence the reforms at Cluny?

2. What was the business model used by Cluny? Explore the economic influence Cluny had on France and other parts of Europe as a result of its business management and its vast accumulation of money and property.

3. Research the truce of God. How did it spread after 1017? How effective was it in making a gentler warrior?

4. It has been said that Cluny was responsible for the Christianization of Europe that characterized the later Middle Ages. To what extent do you agree with this assessment?

5. Discuss the influence of one of the abbots of Cluny in both the secular and religious life of his time.

ALTERNATIVE TERM PAPER SUGGESTIONS

1. Create a graphic representation of the business management model used by Cluny. How were the priories tied financially to Cluny, and how was Cluny tied to the larger church in Rome? Be sure to indicate some of the specific priories in your representation.

2. Cluny was known for the beauty of its liturgy. Research this topic and prepare a class presentation that incorporates music to demonstrate the Clunaic liturgical reform.

Primary Sources

"Foundation Charter of Cluny." http://www.fordham.edu/halsall/source/chart-cluny .html. Translation.

Guibert of Nogent. *The Autobiography of Guibert of Nogent, Abbot of Nogent-sous-Coucy.* Trans. by C. C. Swinton Bland. New York: E.P. Dutton,1925. Written in 1125, Guibert's autobiography provides insight into the life of a clergyman in the 12th century.

"The Peace of God" and "The Truce of God." Trans. in Emerson Lavender and Norman Sheffe, eds. *A Sourcebook for Ancient and Medieval History.* New York: McGraw-Hill, 1964. These two documents, proclaimed in 989 and 1027, respectively, show the influence of the church in keeping peace.

Secondary Sources

Bennett, Judith M., and Hollister, C. Warren. *Medieval Europe: A Short History.* Boston: McGraw-Hill, 2006. Chapter 8, "New Paths to God," concerns the changes in monasteries and the church in the 11th through 13th centuries.

Bruce, Scott G. *Silence and Sign Language in Medieval Monasticism: The Cluniac Tradition, c.900–1200.* Cambridge: Cambridge University Press, 2007. Explores the use of regulation of speech as a form of asceticism and renunciation of worldly concerns. Includes a lexicon of Cluniac signs.

Burton, Janet. *Monastic and Religious Orders in Britain, 1000–1300.* Cambridge: Cambridge University Press, 1994. Explores the daily life of the monastery, the reform movement, and the political and social influences of monasticism in Britain.

Harding, Alan. *Medieval Law and the Foundations of the State.* Oxford: Oxford University Press, 2002. Chapter 3, "The Spread of the Organized Peace," concerns the efforts of the Peace of God and Truce of God movements.

Marquardt, Janet T. *From Martyr to Monument: The Abbey of Cluny as Cultural Patrimony.* Cambridge: Cambridge Scholars Publishing, 2008. A chronologically arranged picture of Cluny from its beginning with emphasis on its reconstruction in the 20th century.

Rosenwein, Barbara H. *To Be the Neighbor of Saint Peter: The Social Meaning of Cluny's Property, 909–1049.* Ithaca: Cornell University Press, 1989. Using computerized databases, the author examines the history of property donations to Cluny, analyzes the motives of the donors, and discusses the way the property was used by the monastery.

Wishart, Alfred Wesley. *A Short History of Monks and Monasteries.* Charleston, SC: BiblioBazaar, 2006. Chapter 4 concerns the reform monasteries of the 10th–12th centuries.

World Wide Web

"Monasticism in Medieval Christianity." http://www.metmuseum.org/toah/. Part of the Heilbrunn Timeline of Art History on the Metropolitan Museum of Art Web site. Includes essays and images.

"Romanesque Art and Architecture in France." http://www.romanes.com/. Although the site is in French, images of medieval monasteries are easy to find.

Multimedia Sources

Cluny: A Light in the Night. 1995. BBC. DVD. 53 minutes. Discusses the power of the Cluniac order and its relationship to the papacy, the development of chivalry, the increase in pilgrimages to monasteries, and economic growth related to monasticism.

The Dark Ages and the Millennium: Christianity in the 9th and 10th Centuries. 1999. LWT/Bravo co-production. Part of the series *Two Thousand Years: The History of Christianity.* DVD. 96 minutes. The second part of the program places the work of Cluny in the context of social and political events of the 10th century.

Monks: Keepers of Knowledge. 2004. DVD. Films for the Humanities and Sciences. 53 minutes. Examines the work of monasteries in preserving and expanding knowledge as well as in spiritual matters.

41. The Ottonian Dynasty (919–1024)

In the century following the death of Charlemagne, his Carolingian empire had splintered into a host of independent states. Those in the western part of the empire remained nominally affiliated to the king of France, while the eastern states leaned towards German leaders. In 919, Henry I, the Fowler (r. 919–936), began solidifying his power and strengthening the kingdom of Saxony for his son Otto I (r. 936–973). The Ottonian dynasty (also called the Saxon dynasty), named for three of the five emperors, reestablished the Holy Roman Empire (although the term was not applied until later) in the West and built the foundation for the nation of Germany. Beginning with Henry, the Ottonians followed the practice of naming their successors, endeavoring to make the monarchy hereditary.

Otto I assembled a powerful army that enabled him and his descendants to keep German dukes from gaining autonomy, despite a series of rebellions throughout the period, several of which were led by members of his own family. Otto's strong alliance with the church also helped curtail the power of the dukes.

Otto I and his son Otto II (r. 961–983) expanded their territory into Italy and the Byzantine Empire. In 951, Otto I received a request for help from the widow Queen Adelaide of what is now Italy. The new Italian king, Berengar II (r. 950–963), had imprisoned Adelaide until she agreed to marry him. Otto invaded the northern Italian peninsula, which had no organized defense, and easily defeated the Italian king. Otto then married Adelaide himself and immediately proclaimed himself "King of the Lombards," but did little to establish governance in northern Italy. When a rebellion broke out in Italy in 955, Otto quickly brought it to an end.

A few years later, in 962, the pope appealed to Otto for help against Berengar, who had retained power in most of Italy. Again, Berengar was quickly defeated, and Otto insisted that Pope John XII crown him as Holy Roman Emperor, thus transferring the title to German kings, where it remained until the 19th century. Yet, almost as soon as the pope placed the crown on Otto's head, he began to regret his decision to give the king such power, for Otto proceeded to march into Rome, convene the bishops, and install a pope more to his liking, Leo VIII. The new Roman Emperor also confiscated papal property, except for that nearest to Rome.

Just as when Charlemagne was crowned emperor, Byzantium was displeased with the fact that there was a Western emperor. In order to appease the Eastern empire, Otto arranged for his son to marry Theophano, daughter of the Byzantine emperor. By the end of Otto I's reign, he had assured the ascension of his own son to the throne, quelled much of the dissatisfaction among the German dukes, established ties with Byzantium, forged a strong alliance with the church, and built a strong bureaucracy for the Ottonian dynasty. For all this, he earned the designation Otto the Great.

TERM PAPER SUGGESTIONS

1. Discuss the idea of kingship as it evolved in Germany during the Ottonian period. What was the source of the king's authority? What was his relationship to the church? To the nobles in his kingdom? To his people?

2. What part did noble women play in the advancement of culture during the Ottonian dynasty?

3. Ottonian culture was influenced by Byzantium, Late Antiquity (fourth and fifth centuries), and the Carolingians. Discuss how these influences are observable in the art and architecture of the age.

4. When Otto I united the German duchies, he put the resulting nation under his law. Discuss the nature of the Ottonian legal system and the modifications made during this age. Are there elements of Ottonian law that have influenced modern justice?

5. When Otto II died, his son Otto III was only three years old. During his childhood, his mother Theophano and grandmother Adelaide acted as regents for the kingdom. Research the rule of these two women and compare it to that of the Ottonian emperors.

ALTERNATIVE TERM PAPER SUGGESTIONS

1. With a partner, prepare a dialogue between Otto I and Pope John XII concerning whether Otto should receive the title of Holy Roman Emperor. Include the pope's change of heart after the coronation and Otto's reaction.

2. Create a series of maps depicting the Ottonian dynasty's territorial expansion and the extent of the Holy Roman Empire.

Primary Sources

Gervase of Tilbury. *Otia Imperialia*. Trans. and ed. by S. E. Banks and J. W. Binns. Oxford: Oxford University Press, 2002. Written for Otto IV, this volume is an entertaining account mixing science, folklore, and theology.

Ludiprand of Cremona. *The Complete Works*. Ed. and trans. by Paolo Squatriti. Washington, DC: Catholic University of America Press, 2007. Includes Ludiprand's biography of Otto I and his description of his mission to the court at Constantinople.

Ottonian Germany: The Chronicon of Thietmar of Merseburg. Trans. and ed. by David A. Warner. Manchester, UK: Manchester University Press, 2001. Concerns the 10th and 11th centuries. Bishop and historian Thietmar discusses everything from politics, to dress, to historic events.

Pullan, Brian. *Sources for the History of Medieval Europe: From the Mid-eighth to the Mid-thirteenth Century*. New York: Barnes & Noble, 1966. Volume includes a chapter on the Ottonians and Salians, containing translations of several contemporary documents, including the monk Widukind's description of Otto's coronation.

Widukind of Corvey. *Res gestae saxonicae (The Deeds of the Saxons)*. Book three is translated in Claude J. Dolan. *Widukind, the Monk of Corvey Relating the Deeds of the Saxons : Historical Survey and Translation of Book III*. Sine Nomine: Sine Imprimo, 1957.

Secondary Sources

Bowlus, Charles R. *The Battle of Lechfeld and Its Aftermath, August 955: The End of the Age of Migrations in the Latin West*. Surrey, UK: Ashgate Publishing, 2006. Thorough analysis of the Battle of Lechfeld and the effect it had on German security and on incursions from nomads into the West. Uses primary sources such as Thietmar's *Chronicle*.

Davids, Adelbert, ed. *The Empress Theophano: Byzantium and the West at the Turn of the First Millennium*. Cambridge: Cambridge University Press, 1995. Seventeen scholarly essays on Theophano and her influence and on women's lives in general in Ottonian Germany.

Fichtenau; Heinrich. *Living in the Tenth Century: Mentalities and Social Orders*. Trans. by Patrick Geary. Chicago: University of Chicago Press, 1991. Discusses the importance of a hierarchy in the 10th century in church, government, and in the day-to-day lives of individuals. Examines life in rural, urban, and monastic settings.

Mayr-Harting, Henry. *Church and Cosmos in Early Ottonian Germany: The View from Cologne.* Oxford: Oxford University Press, 2008. The Archbishop of Cologne, Bruno, was the brother of Otto I. Mayr-Harting uses a contemporary biography of Bruno, Boethius's *Arithmetic,* and other contemporary works to portray the complexity of the relationship between church and state.

World Wide Web

Ottonian Art. http://www.metmuseum.org/toah/. Part of the Heilbrunn Timeline of Art History on the Metropolitan Museum of Art Web site. Includes essays and images.

Multimedia Sources

Germany. 2005. DVD. New Dimension Video. 30 minutes. The first portion of the film uses maps to show how the towns and duchies of early Germany grew into a nation and became the Holy Roman Empire. The last part is about modern Germany.

The Holy Roman Empire. 2002. DVD. Schlessinger Media. 30 minutes. Introduction to the entire span of the Holy Roman Empire. Helps to put the Ottonian dynasty in context of the long history of Roman emperors.

42. Islamic Medical Knowledge and Its Transfer to the West (c. 925)

When the Roman Empire fell to the barbarians, many manuscripts written in Greek and Latin were lost, including medical texts such as those written by Hippocrates and Galen. Even the manuscripts preserved in the Byzantine Empire were lost to the West for centuries. Muslim expansion during the seventh through 10th centuries gave Islamic scholars access to many earlier works found in Byzantine and Egyptian libraries. There then followed an intense period of preservation through translation of learned texts into Arabic, which remained inaccessible to most of the West. In addition, Islamic scholars such as Rhazes and Avicenna created new medical texts based on their studies of the body and disease. Medical practice in Europe was primarily based on a few fragments of ancient works, folklore, and astronomy. As trade increased with the East and with Islamic caliphates, including those on the Iberian Peninsula, and as Europe began to reestablish itself in the Mediterranean in the 8th and 9th centuries, more medical texts became available. From the 10th century on, the West would make significant progress in medicine, chiefly as a result of the transfer of Islamic learning.

Among the influential Islamic physicians, the Persian Abu Bakr Muhammad ibn Zakariyya al-Razi (Rhazes) is known for nearly 250 works, including his 10-book (chapter) *Al' Mansuri* (c. 925). This work is a complete catalog of medical knowledge and was used as a text in medical schools until after the Renaissance. In addition, Rhazes wrote one of the earliest clinical descriptions of measles and smallpox, based on symptoms he saw in the patients he treated. Another work, *Secret of Secrets,* is a systematic manual for creating pharmaceuticals. Rhazes is also responsible for creating a number of tools for the pharmacy, such as the mortar and pestle, phials, and beakers.

The physician Ibn Sina (Avicenna) wrote more than 100 books, including *The Canon of Medicine,* a compendium of diseases listing their causes, symptoms, and treatments. This volume, too, was used in medical schools long after Avicenna's death, along with his works about the functions of major organs. Other significant physicians of the Middle Ages include Ibn Nafis, who was the first to describe how blood is transported to the lungs to absorb oxygen, and Maimonides, the Jewish physician of Saladin.

Latin translations of the great works of Islamic and ancient physicians provided Europe with the foundations and practices that evolved into modern medicine. Constantine the African, a teacher at the medical university in Salerno, is credited with much of this transfer of knowledge. He translated 37 medical books from Arabic into Latin before his death in 1087. The knowledge of all medieval physicians was to be tested in the 14th century as the bubonic plague swept through the world.

TERM PAPER SUGGESTIONS

1. Explain the appeal that Galenic-Hippocratic (pagan) medicine had for medieval (Christian) medicine.

2. How did medieval patients and practitioners view medical authorities of the past? Explain any differences in attitude.

3. How important were developments in art and technology to the history of medicine?

4. Explain the importance of religion in healthcare in the Middle Ages.

5. How did women's medical care compare with men's? How does it explain the attitude of male physicians?

6. What is meant today by "medicine," "health," "disease," "illness," "cure"? Were the same meanings understood by medieval cultures?

7. What was the relationship between "magic," "medicine," and "religion" in the medieval period?

8. What kinds of treatments and medicines could the sick receive in the Middle Ages? Can you explain the logic behind any of them?

9. Alchemy, chemistry, and the apothecary were significant parts of the practice of medicine in the Middle Ages. Research the medical advances made through alchemy and discuss the position of the apothecary within the field of health care.

10. Choose a disease or illness common in both medieval and modern times. Compare the medical knowledge about it and the treatment of the problem in the two ages.

ALTERNATIVE TERM PAPER SUGGESTIONS

1. Herbal remedies were common in the Middle Ages. Prepare a visual and oral presentation explaining the uses of plants and herbs in healing.

2. Prepare a multimedia presentation that analyzes the artistic representations of illness, disease, and physicians in paintings, mosaics, and illuminated manuscripts. What do these representations tell us about medieval medicine?

Primary Sources

Avicenna. *The Canon of Medicine.* Birmingham, AL: The Classics of Medicine Library, 1984. Contains translations of the five major books of Avicenna on the human body and general treatments, the pharmacology of herbs, the pathology of organs, symptoms, and the pharmacopoeia.

Avicenna. *The Metaphysics of the Healing.* Salt Lake City: Brigham Young University, 2005. Trans. by Michael E. Marmura. Avicenna's philosophy of medicine.

Gervase of Tilbury. *Otia Imperialia.* Trans. and ed. by S. E. Banks and J. W. Binns. Oxford: Oxford University Press, 2002. Written for Otto IV as a medical text, this book mixes science, folklore, and theology.

Hildegarde of Bingen. *Hildegard von Bingen's Physica: The Complete English Translation of Her Classic Work on Health and Healing.* Trans. from the Latin by Patricia Throop. Rochester, VT: Healing Arts, 1998. Hildegard was a 14th-century nun, well known for her skills as a physician. This is one of her many books.

Rhazes. The Spiritual Physic of Rhazes. Trans. By Arthur J. Arberry. London: John Murray, 1950. http://oll.libertyfund.org/?option=com_staticxt&staticfile

=show.php%3Ftitle=1791&Itemid=27. This work deals with the relationship of human spirituality and psychology to healing.

The Trotula: An English Translation of the Medieval Compendium of Women's Medicine. Trans. by Monica H. Greene. Philadelphia: University of Pennsylvania Press, 2002. A discussion of women's diseases and their treatment; one of the first sources to regard women as physically different from men.

Secondary Sources

French, Roger. *Medicine before Science: The Business of Medicine from the Middle Ages to the Enlightenment.* Cambridge: Cambridge University Press, 2003. An introduction to the university as a training ground for physicians. Examines the traditional medicine relying on natural philosophy and how it informed medical practice.

García-Ballester, Luis, French, Roger, Arrizabalaga, Jon, and Cunningham, Andrew, eds. *Practical Medicine from Salerno to the Black Death.* Oxford: Oxford University Press, 1994. Eleven essays by medieval medical scholars on the application of medical knowledge.

Pormann, Peter, and Savage-Smith, Emilie. *Medieval Islamic Medicine.* Washington: Georgetown University Press, 2007. Black and white illustrations, extensive lists of sources, detailed account of Islamic medicine in the Middle Ages. Discusses the transfer of medical knowledge to the West.

Shatzmiller, Joseph. *Jews, Medicine and Medieval Society.* Berkeley: University of California Press, 1994. Examines the paradox of medieval attitudes towards Jewish physicians and medicine. While Jews were prohibited from most professions, many became highly respected and influential physicians.

Siraisi, Nancy G. *Medieval and Early Renaissance Medicine: An Introduction to Knowledge and Practice.* Chicago: University of Chicago Press, 1990. Explores the knowledge and technical skills of physicians in the Middle Ages.

Ullmann, Manfred. *Islamic Medicine.* Edinburgh: Edinburgh University Press, 1997. Exacting description of what Islamic scholars understood about medicine in the Middle Ages.

World Wide Web

Muslim Heritage.com. http://www.muslimheritage.com/Default.aspx. This searchable Web site has hundreds of pages of information about Muslim contributions to culture. Also features a timeline and topical lists.

Islamic Medical Manuscripts at the National Library of Medicine. http://www.nlm.nih.gov/hmd/arabic/welcome.html. Biographies, glossary, and historical accounts in addition to images of the manuscripts in the National Library.

Multimedia Sources

The Bridge: How Islam Saved Western Medicine. 1996. DVD. Films Media Group. 50 minutes. Examines how the medieval Islamic world preserved Greek and Roman knowledge and how that knowledge was passed on to the West.

The Secrets of the Human Body: Islam's Contributions to Medicine. 1999. DVD. Films Media Group. 27 minutes. Looks at the practice of medicine during the Abbasid Caliphate and at prominent medical practitioners such as Rhazes and Avicenna. Partially in French with subtitles in English.

Ulema and Philosophers: Faith vs. Reason in Islamic Arabia. 1999. DVD. Films Media Group. 26 minutes. Looking at prominent *ulema* (doctors of law) and philosophers, this film examines their conflicts over Islamic law codes.

43. Muslim Invasions of India (980–1194)

Within a few years of the founding of Islam (622), Arab forces had made inroads into the Sindh area of India (now Pakistan) and installed their own ruler. For nearly 300 years, India was not subject to further invasions. However, people along the trade routes were exposed to the Islamic faith and a small number converted. At the end of the 10th century, the Afghan general Mahmud of Ghazni began a series of aggressive raids in northern India. Although he primarily sought India's riches, he persuaded his army that they should slaughter the Hindu "infidels" in the name of Islam. Mahmud's forces sacked Delhi and destroyed parts of the Shiva temple. Some historians believe Mahmud forced conversions of large numbers of Hindus, but if he did so, as soon as he left, they returned to Hinduism. After 17 raids, Mahmud annexed the Punjab region to his kingdom. The sultans Qutb ud-din Aibak and Ala un-din Khilji, and other Islamic leaders, staged further invasions and established Delhi as the capital. By the end of the 12th century, almost all of India was under Islamic rule.

During the Islamic sultanate, a number of Hindus converted to Islam so that by the 13th century there was a significant minority of Muslims among the population. Rather than occurring because of mass conversions, conversion was more likely the result of the exorbitant *jizya,* or tax on all nonMuslims. Intermarriage, trade relationships, the caste system, and attraction to the faith resulted in more conversions. Islamic rulers allowed most local Hindu rulers to remain in their positions as long as they enforced the Qur'an (the Islamic holy text) and sharia (Islamic law). Arabs in India transported new inventions to the West via the trade routes: paper, printing, gunpowder, the compass, and tea all passed from China to the West by way of India. Hindu numerals, now called Arabic numerals, were relayed along the trade routes as well.

In the 13th century, the Mamluk Turks under Iltutmish conquered Delhi and most of India and maintained their rule there until the 16th century. Several areas of India still have strong Islamic populations today.

TERM PAPER SUGGESTIONS

1. Compare the primary beliefs of Islam and Hinduism. Are the religions compatible, thus making it likely that Hindus converted easily? Do you believe that forced conversions are more likely?

2. Research the Sharia laws concerning business and trade. Why would these laws have been conducive to world trade?

3. Islamic rulers enhanced economic development in India by establishing *karkhanas,* small factories specializing in a particular product. Discuss the effects of *karkhanas* on India's culture, society, and economy.

4. Discuss the influences of Islam on Indian art and architecture.

ALTERNATIVE TERM PAPER SUGGESTIONS

1. The Taj Mahal, one of the world's most magnificent buildings, was built by one of India's Islamic rulers. Create a multimedia presentation about the Taj Mahal. Incorporate music from the period.

2. Create a multimedia presentation on the art and architecture of Islamic India.

Primary Sources

Alberuni, Muhammad ibn Ahmad. *Alberuni's India: An Account of the Religion, Philosophy, Literature, Geography, Chronology, Astronomy, Customs, Law and Astrology of India about A.D. 1030.* Vol. I and II. Trans. by Edward C. Sachau. London: Kegan Paul, Trench, Trubner & Co., 1910. Alberuni was one of Islamic India's chief scholars. This translation of his work is available from Columbia University Libraries E-Books. http://www.columbia.edu/cu/web/digital/collections.

Gettleman, Marvin E., and Schaar, Stuart, eds. *The Middle East and Islamic World Reader.* New York: Grove Press, 2003. Contains a wide range of Islamic documents from the Qur'an to modern day. Arranged chronologically.

Secondary Sources

Ahmad, Aziz. *Studies in Islamic Culture in the Indian Environment.* Oxford: Oxford University Press, 1999. Traces the history of Islamic settlement in India, examines why the faith was able to establish itself there, and why the Islamic and Hindu cultures have integrated little with one another.

Eaton, Richard M. *India's Islamic Traditions: 711–1750.* Oxford: Oxford University Press, 2003. Contains 17 scholarly essays on many aspects of Islam in India.

Husain, Wahed. *Administration of Justice During the Muslim Rule in India— With a History of the Origin of the Islamic Legal Institutions.* Calcutta: Husain Press, 2007 (1937). Discusses the court system, the powers of judges, the sources of their authority, and the application of law in India.

Jackson, Peter. *The Delhi Sultanate: A Political and Military History.* Cambridge: Cambridge University Press, 2003. Looks at India's Islamic rulers and their policies during the 13th century.

Khanna, Meenakshi, ed. *Cultural History of Medieval India.* New Delhi: Social Science Press, 2007. A collection of scholarly essays on India in the Middle Ages.

Kulke, Hermann. *A History of India,* 4th ed. New York: Routledge, 2004. Comprehensive history, includes two chapters on medieval India.

Sharif, Ja'far. *Islam in India or the Qanun-I-Islam: The Customs of the Musalmans of India, Comprising a Full and Exact Account of Their Various Rites and Ceremonies from the Moment of Birth to the Hour of Death.* Trans. G. A. Herklots and William Crooke. New Delhi, India: Atlantic Publishers and Distributors, 1999. Reprint of the 1921 classic study of Islam in India.

World Wide Web

Know India. http://india.gov.in/knowindia.php. This is the national portal of India sponsored by the government and containing a number of pages on many aspects of Indian life and culture, including its history.

Manas: India and its Neighbors. http: //www.sscnet.ucla.edu/southasia/History/mainhist.html. Web site maintained by Vinay Lal, assistant professor of history at UCLA. Contains articles, images, and other resources on Indian culture and history.

Multimedia Sources

Islamic Art: India and the Middle East. 2007. DVD. Films Media Group. 60 minutes. Art critic Waldemar Januszczak leads viewers through many of Islam's most impressive monuments including the Taj Mahal and the Great Mosque in Damascus. He also discusses the mosaics that have survived the centuries.

Journeys into Islamic India. 2004. DVD. Films Media Group. 50 minutes. Examines the Islamic heritage of India by visiting Muslim historic sites and by talking to Muslims living in India today.

44. Capetian Dynasty (987–1328)

The French royal line known as the Capetians takes its name from its founder, Hugh Capet, who was chosen king in 987. After the death of Charlemagne in 814, his empire was divided and reunited in many different forms until it was, at the end of the 10th century, only a collection of duchies. The dukes and counts who had once sworn fealty to the king in return for lands had claimed the lands as their own and passed them on to members of their own families. These noblemen still swore loyalty to the king, but they, rather than the king, held the real power. In fact, at the death of the last Carolingian ruler, Louis V (r. 986–987), the king only controlled a very small territory called "Ile de France" in the middle of the country, and even here, it was his advisors who wielded authority.

On June 5, 987, Hugh Capet was crowned king of France, having been chosen, as was the custom, by the nobles and clergy of the kingdom. He became king at one of the lowest points of royal power in French history, and little changed during the first four Capetian reigns. For the most part, the Capetians gave aid when it was advantageous and made decisions that would win friends for them. The greatest achievements of the period were perpetuating the idea of a united France, where the king maintained sovereignty over the nobles and church, and continuing to propagate the legend of the royal touch. The early Capetians realized they did not have the military strength to increase their territory, and they did not have the possibility of adding lands through marriages because of consanguinity laws and their close ties to other royal lines. Capetian fortunes turned in the 12th century under King Louis VI (r. 1108–1137). Louis granted charters to towns within the lands of dukes and bishops, asserting his authority to do so. He destroyed castles of some of the lords and replaced them with his own. His biographer, Abbot Suger of St. Denis, created an impeccable pedigree connecting Louis to Charlemagne and touting him as the champion for St. Denis, the patron saint of France. Louis judiciously worked to strengthen the ties of the crown and the dukes in the kingdom by uniting them against common threats. Aquitaine was the one principality that had not fully recognized the supremacy of the king; however, the duchy came in line when Louis's son Louis VII (r. 1137–1180) married the duke of Aquitaine's daughter Eleanor. They were divorced and Eleanor later married the Duke of Normandy and king of England, Henry II. Louis VII's third marriage was to Adela of Champagne, solidifying ties with that duchy. Louis supported the land claims of Henry and Eleanor's children in Normandy and Aquitaine and upheld the rights of vassals, lessening Henry's power on the continent.

By the time Louis VII died and his son Philip Augustus (r. 1180–1199) became king, most of the nation of France was firmly united under the monarch and turned to Paris for leadership.

TERM PAPER SUGGESTIONS

1. Discuss the ways in which the Capetian relationship to the church facilitated the monarch's growth in power.

2. After Charlemagne, why did the French monarchy become so weak in comparison to some of its own vassal states, such as Normandy and Aquitaine? How did the Capetians work to overcome this weakness?

3. Discuss the importance to the Capetians of political marriages in the 12th century. What were they able to gain in the way of land, wealth, and power as a result of these marriages?

4. Evaluate the diplomatic skills of the Capetian monarchs. How were they able to obtain what they wanted without alienating those with whom they needed to work?

5. Study the charters of medieval towns. Compare the relationship outlined for a town and a monarch to that of a vassal and lord. Under what circumstances would a lord or king support a commune? Why would he suppress a commune or town?

ALTERNATIVE TERM PAPER SUGGESTIONS

1. Create a series of maps demonstrating the lands held by Hugh Capet when he became king and how Capetian territory expanded during the dynasty he founded.

2. Research Eleanor of Aquitaine's life. Create a dramatic monologue in which you assume her persona and tell your life story to the class.

Primary Sources

Guibert of Nogent. "Life of His Mother," from Guibert of Nogent. *The Autobiography of Guibert of Nogent, Abbot of Nogent-sous-Coucy.* In Emilie Amt, ed., *Women's Lives in Medieval Europe: A Sourcebook.* New York: Routledge, 1993. Guibert devotes a portion of his autobiography to an account of his mother's life.

Kowaleski, MaryAnne, ed. *Medieval Towns: A Reader.* Toronto: UTP Higher Education, 2008. Offers a wide selection of translations dealing with the establishment of and life in medieval towns.

Odo of Cluny. *Count Gerald of Aurillac, A Late Ninth-Century French Magnate.* Odo, the abbot of Cluny, wrote this biography of St. Gerald in 930. Excerpts are found in Archibald R. Lewis, ed., *The High Middle Ages: 814–1300.* Englewood Cliffs, NJ: Prentice-Hall, 1970.

Regino of Prum. "On the Breakdown of the Carolingian Empire," in Julius Kirshner and Karl F. Morrison, eds., *University of Chicago Readings in Western Civilization: 4, Medieval Europe.* Chicago: University of Chicago Press, 1986. A contemporary account of the last kings of the Carolingian dynasty and the first Capetians.

"The Rise of Capetian France." http://www.fordham.edu/halsall/sbook1m.html. This section of the Medieval Sourcebook has several primary documents available.

"The Rise of Towns." http://www.fordham.edu/halsall/sbook1m.html. This is one of the larger sections of the Medieval Sourcebook and contains a number of town charters.

Secondary Sources

Bull, Marcus, ed. *France in the Central Middle Ages: 900–1200.* Oxford: Oxford University Press, 2002. Contains six chapters by medieval scholars on such topics as the political culture and the church after 900.

Duby, George. *France in the Middle Ages: 987–1460, From Hugh Capet to Joan of Arc.* Oxford, UK: Wiley-Blackwell, 1993. Contains three sections: "The Inheritance," which discusses the land and people of the Frankish empire; "Lordship," which discusses the village, castle, and church; and "Origins of State and Nation," which discusses the development of France under the Capetians.

Dunbabin, Jean. *France in the Making: 843–1180.* Oxford: Oxford University Press, 2000. Divides the Capetian era into three periods and discusses the sources, political life, aristocratic life, and principalities of each period.

Fawtier, Robert. *The Capetian Kings of France: Monarchy and Nation, 987–1328.* London: Macmillan, 1964. Traces the growth of national unity in France.

Harding, Alan. *Medieval Law and the Foundations of the State.* Oxford: Oxford University Press, 2002. Chapter 5 compares the judicial systems of France and England in the 11th century.

McLean, Simon. *Kingship and Politics in the Late Ninth Century: Charles the Fat and the End of the Carolingian Empire.* Cambridge: Cambridge University Press, 2003. Deals with the nature of kingship as visualized and implemented by the late Carolingians.

Nolan, Kathleen D., ed. *Capetian Women.* London: Palgrave Macmillan, A series of 12 essays examining the role of royal women in Capetian France through contemporary accounts, including women's endowments to churches and monasteries and commissions for manuscripts and sculptures.

World Wide Web

Bibliothèque Nationale de France. http://www.bnf.fr/default.htm. This site is available in French, English, and Spanish. Images, virtual tours, and information.

Creating French Culture: Treasures from Bibliotheque Nationale de France. http://www.loc.gov/exhibits/bnf/. This Library of Congress online exhibit includes essays and images from medieval France as well as later periods.

"France, 1000–1400 A.D." http://www.metmuseum.org/toah/. Part of the Heilbrunn Timeline of Art History on the Metropolitan Museum of Art Web site. Includes essays and images.

45. Rise of the Textile Industry in Europe (c. 1000)

The manufacture of textiles was the first industrial development in medieval Europe. Individuals had been making fabric for their own use for centuries, but not until the Middle Ages did textiles become an economic commodity and a means of increasing one's wealth. Linen, wool, and hemp were the primary raw products for textiles since they could be produced indigenously. Yet, even in the centuries after the fall of Rome, trade ships carried silk and cotton.

With the expansion of overland trade routes to the East and sea lanes throughout the Mediterranean and European waters, the demand for textiles increased. Fabric was such an important part of commerce that the land routes traveled by caravans were known as the Silk Road. Nobles, who were growing wealthy from their manorial lands, sought beautiful fabrics not only for their clothing, but also to decorate their homes. Woven rugs from the East and decorative tapestries adorned the walls and floors of manor houses and castles and helped to keep the interiors warmer.

The economy at all levels benefited from the production of textiles. At first, most textiles were manufactured by the wives and daughters of farmers and sheep herders who produced the raw materials. These fabrics were sold in local markets, and some were purchased by merchant traders. Soon, the families could not keep up with the growing demand— demand that created additional opportunities for wealth. Merchants now bought the raw materials directly from farmers and sold them to dyers and weavers in towns and cities. The dyers and weavers then sold their fabrics to traders who either marketed them locally or transported them to foreign ports and centers of trade. By the 12th century, a significant part of Europe's economy was based on the textile trade.

Textile manufacturing became more specialized, leading to the establishment of guilds. Cities or regions gained reputations for the quality of their products. English wool generally garnered the highest price because of its superior quality, but before the Hundred Years' War, most was shipped to Flanders for weaving. Woolen cloth woven in Flanders was the most desired, whereas Sicily became noted for its tapestries.

For centuries, women were the spinners, weavers, embroiderers, and garment makers. When it became profitable to trade in textiles, men entered the manufacture at all levels. Work in textiles remained one of the few medieval professions considered suitable for women. Contemporary art often depicts women at spinning wheels or looms or engaged in needlework. Chaucer's wife from Bath was a weaver by trade and made fabrics that "rivaled those of Ipres and Ghent."

The textiles manufactured for personal consumption supported the economies of many nations and created political bonds among rulers. For example, Flanders, dependent on raw wool from England for its manufacture of cloth, supported England in its wars against France.

TERM PAPER SUGGESTIONS

1. Dyeing fabric was a highly developed art in medieval Europe. Master dyers developed their own techniques and materials for creating deep, beautiful colors and carefully guarded their secrets. Research the use of color in medieval textiles. Why were some colors prized? What methods did dyers employ to create these colors?

2. Choose one of the major medieval textile manufacturing regions. Explore the factors that favored the success of the industry and the economic impact textiles had on the region.

3. Research sumptuary laws of medieval Europe. What was the purpose of these laws? Who did they affect? How were they enforced?

4. What technological advances were made in the manufacture of textiles between the 11th and 15th centuries? How did the changes and inventions affect the locations of manufacturing centers?

5. Wool was one of the first commodities to be regulated by trade laws. What were some of these laws and why were they important to trade? What precedents did they set?

6. In the 13th century, communes of women called Beguines formed and often supported themselves by weaving. What was the significance of the Beguine communities to social attitudes and women's rights?

7. Research the cost of raw products and finished textiles from the 11th to 15th centuries. What do the changes in prices indicate about the economic conditions of Europe?

8. How did the growth of the textile industry directly impact the rise of the middle class in medieval Europe?

ALTERNATIVE TERM PAPER SUGGESTIONS

1. Study the weaving techniques of the Middle Ages. Create a small loom and demonstrate how certain weaves or fabrics were created.

2. The tapestries of the Middle Ages are legendary for their beauty and intricacy. They are not only textiles, but works of art. Create a multimedia presentation on medieval tapestries, showing how the styles and techniques developed over time.

Primary Sources

Amt, Emilie, ed. *Women's Lives in Medieval Europe: A Sourcebook.* New York: Routledge, 1993. Contains translations of medieval documents on many topics, including weaving, wool work, tapestries, and embroidery.

The Medieval Internet Sourcebook: Selected Sources: Economic Life. http://www .fordham.edu/halsall/sbook1n. This section of the Medieval Sourcebook has primary documents concerning guilds, prices, and laws for the textile industry.

Secondary Sources

Dyer, Christopher. *Making a Living in the Middle Ages: The People of Britain, 850–1520.* New Haven: Yale University Press, 2002. Discusses economic changes in medieval England, including the growth in industry and the rise of towns.

Koslin, Desiree G., and Snyder, Janet, eds. *Encountering Medieval Textiles and Dress: Objects, Texts, Images.* New York : Palgrave Macmillan, 2002. Collection of scholarly essays on topics such as the rise of English textiles, sumptuary laws, and clothing fashion.

Owen-Crocker, Gale, and Netherton, Robin, eds. *Medieval Clothing and Textiles.* Vol.1–5. Suffolk, UK: Boydell Press, 2006–2008. Each volume contains an edited collection of essays on textiles in the Middle Ages.

Mazzaoui, Maureen Fennell. *The Italian Cotton Industry in the Later Middle Ages, 1100–1600.* Cambridge: Cambridge University Press, 1981. Studies the rise of textile production in Italy and its effects on the larger economy.

Power, Eileen Edna. *The Wool Trade in English Medieval History: Being the Ford Lectures.* London: Oxford University Press, 1941. This landmark series of lectures concentrates on the changes in the wool industry after the Norman invasion.

World Wide Web

Center for Textile Research. http://ctr.hum.ku.dk/intro/. An institute of the University of Copenhagen, the CTR site provides information about textile history and archaeology.

Elizabethan Costume Page. http://www.elizabethancostume.net/. Although this site is primarily concerned with the 16th century, it also has articles about medieval textiles and clothing construction.

Historic Needlework Resources. http://medieval.webcon.net.au/index.html. Divided into three broad categories: location, period, and techniques, this Web site is an excellent resource for all needlework topics.

Medieval Economics (1998). http://www.geocities.com/elangoc/medieval/medieval.html. This site provides discussions of money and trade, medieval professions, commodities, and guilds, in addition to an extensive bibliography and links to other Web sites.

Multimedia Sources

Chinese Silk. 2004. DVD. Insight Media. 30 minutes. Explores the history of silk production in China and its importance in trade. Examines silks from several dynasties.

The Lady and the Unicorn: Making Sense of the Senses. 1997. DVD. Films Media Group. 32 minutes. Examines the symbolism and history of the set of six medieval tapestries known as The Lady and the Unicorn.

46. Kingdom of Ghana (c. 1000)

Ancient Ghana is different from the modern country of Ghana, located some 400 miles away from the medieval kingdom. Although there had been an agricultural society in the area of ancient Ghana for centuries, medieval international trade established Ghana as a powerful kingdom. The first of the subSaharan kingdoms to arise in West Africa, Mali and Songhai later arose in the same area.

Ghana's first entry into commerce was in the profitable salt trade. The people grew more on their fertile land than they needed, and they were able to trade grain for salt. In addition, traders placed a high value on Ghana's superior ironwork. Ironwork gave the people of Ghana better weapons than their neighbors had, allowing them to conquer surrounding territory and control trade routes. Although Ghana did not produce gold itself, by the 10th century the nation controlled the Senegal River, the most travelled trade route for gold. Muslim traders also brought the Islamic faith to Ghana, and cities in the kingdom had sizable Muslim populations.

By the 11th century, Ghana was ruled by the Sefawa dynasty from the dual cities of Kumbi Saleh. Kumbi was the royal city, containing the king's castle and the houses of his noble attendants. Saleh was the city of commerce. Islamic chronicler Al-Bakri recorded stories he heard from travelers about Ghana and other areas of Africa in *The Book of Roads and Kingdoms.* He reported that great ceremony accompanied the king in public appearances where he dressed in luxurious robes and gold ornaments. The king set taxes, to be paid in gold or slaves, and dispensed justice by serving as judge in disputes and criminal cases. He was succeeded on the throne by one of his sister's sons.

Around 1050, Ghana launched an attack on the Berbers to the north and captured the important trade center of Audaghost. At the height of its power, however, fortune began to turn for Ghana. Gold was discovered in areas that did not require shipment through Ghana, and traders established alternate routes to avoid the king's taxes. Early in the 12th century, a series of rebellions among the people weakened the king's power. Later, Berbers from the north and Sosso from the south took over more and more of Ghana's land, so that by 1300 the kingdom had ceased to exist.

TERM PAPER SUGGESTIONS

1. What were the roles of Christianity and Islam in the development of the empire of Ghana?

2. What was the significance of the kingdom of Ghana to world history? Why was control of trade across the Sahara so important?

3. What were the major causes for the kingdom of Ghana's eventual decline?

4. What were the effects of the influx of African gold on the economies of Islamic and European states in the Middle Ages?

ALTERNATIVE TERM PAPER FORMATS

1. Create a series of hyperlinked maps showing the prominent trade routes through Africa in the 10th through 15th centuries. Indicate what goods were generally transported on the routes.

2. After reading from the primary sources on the culture of Ghana, create a monologue in which you assume the persona of an Arab traveler visiting the kingdom. Describe what you find there.

Primary Sources

Al-Bakri. *The Book of Routes and Realms.* http://www.bu.edu/africa/outreach/materials/handouts/k_o_ghana.html and http://web.archive.org/web/20010210035839/http://www.humanities.ccny.cuny.edu/history/reader/ghana.htm. Translations of short segments from Al-Bakri.

Levtzion, Nehemia, and Hopkins, J. F. P., eds. *Corpus of Early Arabic Sources for West African History.* Cambridge: Cambridge University Press, 1981. A collection of translations of what Islamic scholars wrote about West Africa between the 9th and 15th centuries.

Levtzion, Nehemia, and Spaulding, Jay, eds. *Medieval West Africa: Views from Arab Scholars and Merchants.* Princeton, NJ: Marcus Weiner Publishers, 2003. Contains many documents on Ghana in the 11th century and after.

Secondary Sources

Akyeampong, Emmanuel Kwaku, ed. *Themes in West Africa's History.* 2006. This collection of essays includes works on ancient kingdoms as well as today's countries. Religion, government, economics, and languages are discussed.

Lewicki, Tadeuz. *West African Food in the Middle Ages, According to Arabic Sources.* Cambridge: Cambridge University Press, 1974. By consulting primary documents from medieval writers, Lewicki has produced a study of the diet of the people of West Africa.

Maquet, Jacques. *Civilizations of Black Africa.* Oxford: Oxford University Press, 1972. In a section called "Civilization of Cities," Maquet discusses the rise of important cities related to the gold trade.

McKissack, Patricia, and McKissack, Frederick. *The Royal Kingdoms of Ghana, Mali, and Songhay: Life in Medieval Africa.* New York: Henry Holt and

Co., 1995. Written for middle school students, the book provides a good overview of the three kingdoms. Includes two chapters on Ghana prior to 1700.

Quigley, Mary. *Ancient West African Kingdoms: Ghana, Mali, and Songhai.* Portsmouth, NH: Heinemann, 2002. Discusses the political, social, and economic facets of the three kingdoms.

World Wide Web

Department of Arts of Africa, Oceania, and the Americas. "The Empires of the Western Sudan: Ghana Empire." In *Heilbrunn Timeline of Art History.* New York: The Metropolitan Museum of Art, 2000. http://www.metmuseum .org/toah/hd/ghan/hd_ghan.htm. Six related essays and images.

The History of Africa. http://www.bbc.co.uk/worldservice/specials/1624_story _of_africa/. Produced by BBC World Service, this site has information on the complete history of Africa and includes the West African kingdoms.

Multimedia Sources

African Art. 2003. DVD. Films Media Group. 23 minutes. Examines the art tradition of subSaharan Africa, with artifacts such as masks, clothing, sculpture, and ornaments.

Ancient Africa. 1998. DVD. Schlessinger Media. 23 minutes. Provides a very brief overview of the major kingdoms of ancient Africa.

Forts and Castles of Ghana. 2003. DVD. Image Entertainment. 84 minutes. A tour of structures built in the ancient kingdom of Ghana and during the height of the slave trade.

Sub-Saharan Cultures. 2003. DVD. Schlessinger Media. 39 minutes. Visits the Gold Coast and areas where the ancient kingdom of Ghana arose. Not a history video, but valuable for the context it provides.

47. Persecution of Jews (c. 1050)

After the fall of the Roman Empire, Jews living in Palestine were faced with the same uncertainties as individuals living in the remainder of the former Roman lands. The administrative and protective powers Rome had executed were gone, barbarian forces roamed the land, and the stability of life was destroyed. In Rome, Jews had sometimes been able to become citizens, and many had dispersed throughout the Empire, as did other citizens. Under some emperors, however, Jews faced restrictions and persecution. The fifth and sixth centuries saw Jews, as well as many other groups, searching for new homes and safety. Because Judaism is a communal faith, groups of Jews settled together in towns throughout Europe and Africa. Each community was dominated by elite merchant families who had often intermarried with aristocratic rabbinic families. The majority of the population remained in the working class, performing labor for the elite or for Christians or Muslims. Some Jews did very well in this period of great migration. They were educated, possessed craftsmanship that was valued, and were able to lend money.

Because monarchies often found themselves in need of large sums of money, they found the Jews useful. Frankish kings in the Carolingian period placed Jews under their protection. William the Conqueror did the same in England after 1066. When Christians and Arabs were at war in the early Middle Ages, Jews were able to traverse political boundaries and keep commerce moving. Another advantage Jewish merchants possessed was a greater literacy than many of the kings they served. Jews generally faced exorbitant taxes from the monarchy, but they paid them, since their livelihoods depended on the protection of the monarchs. Even though the church repeatedly and vehemently condemned the Jews, encouraged popular distrust of them, and passed laws constricting their rights, monarchs needed the Jews, and persecution did not begin in earnest until the 11th century.

By the middle of the 11th century, economic circumstances were changing. Trade routes were more established, and banking had entered the economic picture. Christian and Islamic merchants could serve the same functions as Jews. Kings no longer needed the Jews. In fact, decrees throughout Europe and Africa took more and more rights away from Jews. Various areas proclaimed they could not join guilds, enter professions, attend university, own land, write wills, intermarry, enter a church, or hold a government position. By the mid-15th century, most Jews were required to wear some type of badge on their clothing so everyone who saw them could identify them. A number of countries expelled Jews from their lands and confiscated Jewish property.

Passage of these laws usually occurred at the instigation of church officials. Stripping Jews of their human rights did not satisfy the church, however. From the mid-11th century on, violence against Jews spread throughout the world. The church circulated pamphlets and documents charging that Jews tortured children and drank their blood. When children were killed, either through murder or by accident, Jews were often blamed, which lead to massacres or public executions of innocent people. Another prevalent rumor put forth by the church was that Jews desecrated the Host, the bread of communion. Church officials even commissioned paintings showing Jews (depicted as ugly, deformed people) stabbing the Host with weapons or table knives or needles. Sermons and church texts also kept the population aroused against Jews.

The year 1189 saw England turn against its Jewish residents. When a deputation of Jewish citizens came to Westminster to present coronation gifts to Richard the Lionhearted (r. 1189–1199), they were turned away, mocked, stoned, and chased to their homes. The mob set the straw roofs of the houses on fire. When the king learned what had happened, he had three of the rioters executed and issued an order that the Jews were not to be harmed in England or in his French lands. Almost as soon as Richard left to join the Crusades, however, the violence began again. An angry mob attacked Benedict of York's home and killed his wife and children. They continued to set fire to homes, and the Jewish citizens sought refuge in the castle of Clifford's Tower. This did not stop the mob. Knowing they were going to die, many Jews chose to take their own lives. Others died when the tower was set on fire, and those that survived the fire were massacred. At least 150 men, women, and children died that day. Incidents like this were repeated throughout Europe and the Holy Land into the Renaissance.

TERM PAPER SUGGESTIONS

1. Trace the growing animosity toward Jews from the Christian church in the early Middle Ages. What arguments did church officials make to arouse hatred of Jews? What "evidence" did the church supply?

2. St. Augustine of Hippo, a theologian in the fifth century, believed that Jews were important because they were the essential witnesses to the truth of Christianity. Given this understanding by some church fathers, expulsion of Jews was a serious matter. Why do you think this expulsion happened? Look at the places that expelled Jews and when they did so. Why did it happen in these places? Was expulsion a theological act or a political act?

3. How have medieval, negative representations of Jews influenced the anti-Semitism of later generations?

4. Jews were excluded from most professions except medicine. Why would Christians set aside their negative feelings for Jews and allow them to treat their illnesses? What social and economic forces allowed Jewish doctors to survive?

5. Some Jews converted to the Christian or Islamic faith. Determine whether this was a significant enough number to decrease the Jewish population. What reasons might they have had for conversion? How were they treated after their conversions?

6. It has been said that more killings have been committed in the name of God than for any other reason. Evaluate this statement in light of what you discover about the Middle Ages.

7. Compare contemporary Christian and Islamic documents concerning the Jews. How reliable are the pictures they present?

ALTERNATIVE TERM PAPER SUGGESTIONS

1. Create a multimedia presentation outlining the contributions of Jews to science, philosophy, and culture during the Middle Ages.

2. Create a multimedia presentation showing the incidents of Jews expelled, tortured, or massacred during the Middle Ages.

3. Select a country and assume the persona of a Jew living there during the 11th or 12th century. Write a series of diary entries about the events you are witnessing in your country.

Primary Sources

Guibert of Nogent. *The Autobiography of Guibert of Nogent, Abbot of Nogent-sous-Coucy.* Trans. by C. C. Swinton Bland. New York: 1925. Written in 1125, Guibert's autobiography provides insight into the attitude of Christians toward Jews and Muslims.

The Jewish History Internet Sourcebook. http://www.fordham.edu/halsall/jewish/jewishsbook.html. Like the next source, this site is hosted by Fordham University. Many primary documents are available here, including a section from the Middle Ages.

Marcus, Jacob Rader, and Saperstein, Marc, eds. *The Jew in the Medieval World: A Sourcebook, 315–1791.* Translations of a variety of laws, proclamations, and commentary concerning Jews in the Middle Ages and beyond.

Medieval and Renaissance Studies: Primary Sources. http://apps.carleton.edu/curricular/mars/Translations/primary_sources/. This Web site, maintained by Carleton College, includes translations of three treatises written by the monk Agobard of Lyon condemning the Jews.

The Medieval Internet Sourcebook: Selected Sources: Medieval Jewish Life. http://www.fordham.edu/halsall/sbook1n. This section of the Medieval Sourcebook has an extensive collection of primary documents concerning medieval Jews.

Secondary Sources

Baumgarten, Elisheva. *Mothers and Children: Jewish Family Life in Medieval Europe.* Princeton, NJ: Princeton University Press, 2007. Contains chapters on birth, circumcision and other birth rituals, the feeding and care of infants, and parental values.

Chazan, Robert. *European Jewry and the First Crusade.* Berkeley: University of California Press, 1987. Detailed analysis of the events leading up to the violence against Jews in the Rhineland as Crusaders made their way to Jerusalem.

Chazan, Robert. *God, Humanity, and History: The Hebrew First Crusade Narratives.* Berkeley: University of California Press, 2000. Textual analysis of the three surviving narratives of the Jewish experience during the First Crusade. Also compares these with earlier narratives of Hebrew history.

Chazan, Robert. *The Jews of Medieval Western Christendom, 1000–1500.* Cambridge: Cambridge University Press, 2007. This text considers Jewish life in the various areas where they settled and were an influence during the Middle Ages.

Katz, Jacob. *Exclusiveness and Tolerance: Studies in Jewish-Gentile Relations in Medieval and Modern Times.* Oxford: Oxford University Press, 1961. A classic study of the attitudes of Jews toward Christians and vice versa in medieval Europe.

Rubin, Miri. *Gentile Tales: The Narrative Assault on Late Medieval Jews.* Philadelphia: University of Pennsylvania Press, 2004. Rubin includes translations of primary documents and analyzes the intent and affect of these denunciations.

Shatzmiller, Joseph. *Jews, Medicine, and Medieval Society.* Berkeley: University of California Press, 1995. Shatzmiller examines the nature of the doctor-patient relationship when the Jews were doctors and the patients Christians who distrusted Jews.

Steinberg, Theodore. *Jews and Judaism in the Middle Ages.* Westport, CT: Greenwood Publishing, 2007. Presents both Jewish history from the Middle Ages and a history of Jewish thought. Studies everyday life, persecution, and the scientific and creative achievements of medieval Jews.

Trachtenberg, Joshua, and Saperstein, Marc. *The Devil and the Jews: The Medieval Conception of the Jew and Its Relation to Modern Anti-Semitism.* Philadelphia: Jewish Publication Society, 2002. Chapter titles are indicative of common medieval representations of Jews by others: Demon, Sorcerer, and Heretic. Authors connect these images to later attitudes toward Jews.

World Wide Web

The Jewish History Resource Center. http://www.dinur.org/1.html?rsID=219. Maintained by the Dinur Center for Research in Jewish History at the Hebrew University of Jerusalem, this site has a wealth of information, primary source documents, publications, translations, and timelines on Jewish history from ancient to modern times.

Teaching Heritage: Civilization and the Jews .http://www.thirteen.org/edonline/teachingheritage/. This is a companion Web site for the DVD series listed next. Extensive collection of resources, lesson plans, articles, short videos on demand, multimedia presentations.

Multimedia Sources

Heritage: Civilization and the Jews: The Crucible of Europe. 2003. DVD series. PBS. 9 hour-series; approximately 75 minutes each. This program deals with Europe during the Middle Ages.

Jewish Communities in the Middle Ages. 1994. Video. Ergo Media. 30 minutes. Discusses the Jewish presence in Spain and in Ashkenaz on the banks of the Rhine and Danube Rivers.

48. Guilds are Established (c. 1050)

Guilds were professional and economic organizations first formed around 1050. Both merchant and craft guilds served to safeguard and advance special interests. Merchant guilds established monopolies in local markets and helped stabilize the economic system. Guilds strictly regulated trading by foreigners within the community, imposed uniform pricing policies, and worked to maintain fair trade practices for their members.

Craft guilds were concerned with the training and licensing of artisans. Master craftsmen who were experts or who operated their own shops constituted the voting membership of the guilds. Journeymen who had learned the trade but were still employed by craftsmen comprised the second layer of guild membership. Guilds carefully controlled the terms of apprenticeship and the quality of workmanship. The organizations were thus able to limit competition, establish prices, wages, and control working conditions.

Guild members represented a rising and often wealthy middle class that developed during the late Middle Ages. In some cities and towns, guilds were closely allied to government, even to being appointed to positions within the political structure. The power of guilds reached its height in the late 14th century. Around this time, merchants began buying the raw products themselves, setting up their own production facilities, and hiring craftsmen as wage laborers. Guilds were no longer in control of either their members working conditions and wages or the quality of products that were produced.

TERM PAPER SUGGESTIONS

1. Discuss the influence guilds had on the transformation of the early medieval economy based on barter, to the mid and late medieval economy based on money.

2. Discuss the reasons for the decline of guilds from the late 14th century on.

3. Study the representation of the five tradesmen and their cook in Geoffrey Chaucer's classic *The Canterbury Tales*. Consider not only their descriptions in the Prologue, but also other references in the narrative. Compare Chaucer's depiction to information found in other historical sources. How closely do the men Chaucer created epitomize the values and social positions of actual guildsmen?

4. Guilds were formed primarily to protect the interests of their own members, yet their existence also protected workers and consumers and provided many social services. Research this aspect of the work of guilds.

5. Choose one of the major crafts of the Middle Ages (book industry, leather, textiles, building trades, metal work, victuallers) and research its development and influence. You may want to choose a specific industry from these broad categories; for instance, choosing weavers from the textile category or bakers from the victuallers category.

6. Research the role of women in guilds and in industry of the Middle Ages.

ALTERNATIVE TERM PAPER SUGGESTIONS

1. Assume you were able to form a guild with the same powers to control production, prices, wages, quality, and membership for a modern profession. Design the rules you would establish for the guild.

2. Create a graphic representation of the relationships among a group of guilds within a single city (e.g. Paris in the 11th century) or within one of the major medieval craft groups (e.g., textile guilds). Prepare an oral presentation that explains your representation.

Primary Sources

"Apprenticeship Agreements: To a Barber, 1248." http://www.fordham.edu/halsall/source/1248apprentice-barber.html. This brief document is typical of the contracts between master craftsmen and those who wished to be trained in the profession.

Book of the Eparch (Eparchikon Biblion). http://homepage.mac.com/paulstephenson/trans.html. Partial translation. This is a collection of 10th-century guild regulations from Constantinople.

"Guild Regulations for the Shearers of Arras." In C. Warren Hollister, et al., eds. *Medieval Europe: A Short Sourcebook.* New York: Alfred A. Knopf, 1982. A good example of the guild regulations that might be found for a number of medieval trade associations.

"Two Apprenticeship Agreements for Weavers, c. 1250 [Arras and Marseilles]." http://www.fordham.edu/halsall/source/1250weaversapp.html. Translation of French apprentice agreements are typical, but also show that differences in terms were common.

The Medieval Sourcebook. http://www.fordham.edu/halsall/sbook1j.html#Roots%20of%20the%20Commercial%20Revolution. A section of The Medival Sourcebook entitled "Bourgeois Institutions: Gilds" has translations of a large number of documents related to guilds.

Smith, Joshua Toulmin. *English gilds: the original ordinances of more than one hundred early English gilds: together with The olde Usages of the cite of Wynchestre; the Ordinances of Worcester; the Office of the Mayor of Bristol; and the Costomary of the Manor of Tettenhall-Regis: from manuscripts of the fourteenth and fifteenth centuries.* London: Published for the Early English Text Society by the Oxford University Press, 1870 (reprinted 1963). *The Middle English Compendium.* http://quod.lib.umich.edu/c/cme/. Smith collected and published the charters of over 100 early guilds in England.

Secondary Sources

Epstein, Stephen. *Wage Labor and Guilds in Medieval Europe.* Durham: University of North Carolina Press, 1995. The five chapters in this book present a history of guilds, beginning with guilds in Roman society as forerunners of medieval guilds and ending with the weakening of guilds in the 14th century.

Howell, Martha C. *Women, Production, and Patriarchy in Late Medieval Cities: Women in Culture and Society Series.* Chicago: University of Chicago Press, 1990. Howell's study discusses the roles of women in the shifting economies of the late Middle Ages as production moved from being concentrated in the family to a capitalistic owner/worker system. The book concentrates primarily on the cities of Leiden, Cologne, Frankfurt, and Douai.

Lopez, Robert C. *The Commercial Revolution of the Middle Ages, 950–1350.* Cambridge: Cambridge University Press, 1976. Lopez offers an in-depth analysis of the shift from an agricultural economy to a commercial economy during the Middle Ages. Chapters 4 ("The Uneven Diffusion of Commercialization") and 5 ("Between Craft and Industry") are especially helpful in understanding the importance of guilds.

Murray, James M. *Bruges, Cradle of Capitalism, 1280–1390.* Cambridge: Cambridge University Press, 2005. Murray presents a case study of how one European city transformed itself from a medieval city with a barter economy into an early capitalist center of trade. There are chapters on the wool, cloth, and gold guilds and on the roles of women in the city's economy.

World Wide Web

Medieval Economics. http://www.geocities.com/elangoc/medieval/medieval.html. This site provides discussions of money and trade, medieval professions, commodities, and guilds, in addition to an extensive bibliography and links to other Web sites.

Guilds. http://medievaleurope.mrdonn.org/guilds.html. A brief overview of guilds with several helpful links.

Florilegium Urbanum. http://the-orb.net/encyclop/culture/towns/florilegium/flor00.html. Features English translations of primary source medieval documents on urban life. The "Economy" section contains documents concerning guilds.

Multimedia Sources

Bankers, Builders, and New Beginnings, part of the series *Europe in the Middle Ages: A Way Out of Darkness.* 2004. Films Media Group, 53 minutes. Depicts the creation of medieval urban centers of trade and commerce.

Guilds and Trades. No date. VHS. Phoenix Learning Company. 30 minutes. Filmed in European locations, the video shows how trade was conducted in the medieval world. Discusses both merchant and craft guilds.

49. Norman Conquest of England (1066)

The people who became known as Normans descended from Vikings (Northmen) who conquered the Normandy area of France in the 9th and 10th centuries. They intermarried with the local population, accepted Christianity, and adopted the native French language, but they did not abandon their desire for expansion. In 1016, Norman troops sailed to what is now Italy, ostensibly to help local nobles fight against Byzantine rule and capture land for themselves. The invasions continued until mid century when Normans controlled the island of Sicily and a large part of the Italian peninsula.

In France, Duke Robert (r. 1026–1035) had become one of the most powerful of the regional lords. Before departing on a pilgrimage to the Holy Land, Robert made his barons swear they would accept his illegitimate son William, then a child, as duke if he did not return. Robert died on the pilgrimage, and the next 12 years were characterized by internal struggles for the throne that included attempts on William's life. When William put down his cousin's rebellion in 1046–1047, he gained control of his inheritance.

William I (r. 1035–1087) then began to expand his kingdom by taking Maine and Brittany, and when he married Matilda of Flanders, he increased his influence to the east. When the half French king of England, Edward the Confessor, died in 1066, William and his lords invaded England. The one major battle of the conquest was the Battle of Hastings on October 14, 1066, where William soundly defeated the English army led by Harold I (r. 1066). On Christmas Day, 1066, William I received the English crown from the Archbishop of Canterbury in Westminster Abbey. The invasion brought changes to England in government, social structure, culture, and language.

TERM PAPER SUGGESTIONS

1. Between the reigns of Alfred the Great and William the Conqueror, what circumstances, influences, or ideals unified Anglo-Saxon England? What conditions were more divisive than unifying? Was England more or less united after William's conquest?

2. Although it seems that William conquered England at the Battle of Hastings, his victory was more difficult than a single battle. What difficulties did the Normans face as they gained control of the nation? What circumstances were in William's favor? Did William of Normandy have a right to the throne of England? Was his invasion a step to obtain his rightful property or was he a usurper of the English throne?

3. How did the Norman Conquest impact the church in England?

4. How much change did William's laws bring to the legal system and the administration of justice in England? What is evident from the laws about the relationships between the Norman and Saxon populations?

5. One of the most famous artifacts from the period of William's reign is the Bayeux Tapestry, which isn't a tapestry at all, but an embroidered piece.

Research the Battle of Hastings as presented in the Bayeux Tapestry and compare it to one or more textual histories of the battle. In what ways could one say that the tapestry presents a Norman version of events? Specifically, how does the tapestry attempt to support William's claim to the English throne?

6. What developments in the English language occurred after the Norman Invasion? What were the causes and effects of these changes? Why do you think English prevailed in the end?

7. Compare the political systems William established in England and in Normandy.

ALTERNATIVE TERM PAPER SUGGESTIONS

1. Assume the persona of William the Conqueror. Write and present a speech directed to your troops as you prepare to cross the Channel to defeat the English king. What can you promise those who are loyal? Why is this something they should want to do?

2. With a partner, prepare cases for William and for Harold having rightful claims to the throne of England. Present your debate to the class in the persona of the two men.

3. Compare the architecture of Anglo-Saxon England to that of Norman England in the years following the invasion. Do this in a multimedia format and include music from the period.

Primary Sources

Anderson, Roberta, ed. *Medieval Worlds: A Sourcebook.* London: Routledge, 2003. A wide variety of documents from the personal, religious, and political worlds; arranged topically.

Guy, Bishop of Amiens. *Carmen de Hastingae Proelio.* Trans. by Frank Barlow. Oxford: Oxford University Press, 1999. This is one of the earliest accounts of the Battle of Hastings, written by the uncle of one of William's vassal lords. Each document is accompanied by commentary.

Morillo, Stephen. *The Battle of Hastings: Sources and Interpretations.* Suffolk, UK: Boydell Press, 1996. Extensive collection of primary accounts of Hastings in one resource; includes the Bayeux Tapestry.

Vitalis, Orderic. *Ecclesiastical History.* Written between 1114 and 1141, this is a detailed history of the Normans and their society. Oxford University Press published a series of five volumes trans. by Marjorie Chibnall between 1973 and 1993.

William of Poitiers. *Gesta Guillelmi.* Trans. and ed. by R. H. C. Davis and Marjorie Chibnall. Oxford: Oxford University Press, 1998. Has both

Latin and English on facing pages. Provides introduction and commentary throughout.

Secondary Sources

Barlow, Frank. *The Feudal Kingdom of England, 1042–1216,* 5th ed. Essex, UK: Longman, 1999. Considers the social and political cultures of England before, during, and after the Norman Conquest, putting the Conquest in context of the total history of England.

Bennett, Matthew. *Campaigns of the Norman Conquest.* Oxford: Osprey Publishing, 2001. A full history of the Norman Conquest during the five years it took William to quell all opposition, including effects on government, church, peasants, and language.

Bloch, Howard R. *A Needle in the Right Hand of God: The Norman Conquest of 1066 and the Making and Meaning of the Bayeux Tapestry.* New York: Random House, 2006. Examines the Bayeux Tapestry as a work of art and history and considers its meaning and importance to Norman kingship in England.

Christo, Daniell. *From Norman Conquest to Magna Carta: England 1066–1215.* London: Routledge, 2003. Contains chapters on government, court life, people and families, and the church.

Clanchy, Michael T. *England and Its Rulers, 1066–1272: With an Epilogue on Edward I (1272–1307).* Blackwell Publishers, 1998. Considers the reigns of the English kings in the context of England's rising importance in medieval Europe.

Dahmus, Joseph Henry. *Seven Decisive Battles of the Middle Ages.* Chicago: Nelson-Hall, 1983. Describes seven battles and their importance, including Crecy and Hastings.

Garnett, George. *Conquered England: Kingship, Succession, and Tenure, 1066–1166.* Oxford: Oxford University Press, 2007. Beginning with a justification for the conquest, this volume follows Norman government through the reign of Henry II.

Harding, Alan. *Medieval Law and the Foundations of the State.* Oxford: Oxford University Press, 2002. Chapter 5 compares the judicial systems of France and England in the 11th century.

World Wide Web

The Medieval Sourcebook. http://www.fordham.edu/halsall/sbook1n.html. The section on Norman England provides a number of documents from the reigns of William I and II, Henry I, and Stephen I.

Sources of British History. http://www.britannia.com/history/. Provides timelines, articles, biographies, and translations of a number of primary documents, including the laws of William the Conqueror.

Additional Resources for Medieval England. http://www.luminarium.org/medlit/ medresource.htm. This page has a very extensive list of links on many topics related to medieval England.

The Bayeux Tapestry. http://www.hastings1066.com/. Includes high-resolution images of the entire tapestry and translation of the words. Also has information on its creation.

Britain's Bayeux at the Museum of Reading. http://www.bayeuxtapestry.org.uk/. Images of the entire tapestry, articles about its history, interactive sections, additional resources.

British Battles. http://britishbattles.com/. Beginning with the Battle of Hastings, this site has an overview, detailed information, images, and battle maps for some of Britain's most important battles.

De Re Militari: The Society for Medieval Military History. http://www.deremilitari .org/. Includes articles on all aspects of medieval military operations, including the Battle of Hastings. Provides an extensive bibliography of related materials. Also has some primary sources.

Multimedia Sources

The Conquerors: William the Conqueror. 2005. DVD. The History Channel. 46 minutes. Produced as part of a series on the world's conquerors, this video begins with the facts of William's childhood and follows the events of his life. Dramatizations and reenactments, especially of the Battle of Hastings, are well done.

The History of Warfare: The Battle of Hastings 1066—Tapestry of a Battle. 2007. DVD. Allegro Studios. 55 minutes. Has reenactments, dramatized primary accounts, period images, and discussions with scholars.

Norman Conquest. 2008. DVD. CreateSpace Studio. 49 minutes. Dramatizations of eye-witness accounts, reenactments, period images, commentary by medieval scholars.

The Normans: The Complete Epic Saga. 2008. DVD set. Kultur Films. 152 minutes. This 3-part series tells the story of the Normans using new archeological evidence, visuals, and commentary from scholars.

William, the Conqueror. 2006. DVD. Kultur Films. 50 minutes. Biography and examination of William as a warrior, politician, statesman and architect of a new dynasty.

50. Investiture Controversy (1075–1122)

Medieval Christian kings, who felt they ruled by God's authority, maintained the right to appoint or invest bishops within their own lands. As the papacy gained more power in the 11th century, the church voiced objections to simony, the buying and selling of ecclesiastical offices. Bishops and archbishops frequently came from among the king's friends and relatives, and many did not have theological training. Monarchs preferred to keep the power of lay investiture. A stalemate between Pope Gregory VII (r. 1073–1085) and Holy Roman Emperor Henry IV (r. 1056–1105) brought the issue to the surface.

In his zeal for reform, Gregory condemned lay investiture of bishops in *Dictatus papae,* which clearly said that all people owed allegiance to the pope. The pope, he wrote was to be judged by God alone, and the pope had the authority to depose kings. This papal supremacy over the monarchy was contradictory to European practice. No monarch had ever allowed the pope to interfere in the internal affairs of his kingdom, and Henry had no intention of doing so now. The emperor promptly proceeded to back his own candidate for the bishopric of Milan ahead of Gregory's choice. Angry words led to Henry declaring that the pope was deposed and the pope excommunicating Henry. In the winter of 1077, Henry traveled over the Alps to Canossa to ask the pope's forgiveness, primarily because his German princes had asked him to do so. Legend says that Gregory made the king wait for three days in the snow before he would grant him audience. Henry received forgiveness, but the reconciliation was short-lived.

Henry had been humiliated, and the pope refused to compromise on his reforms. The controversy engendered a great number of pamphlets on both sides. And when Gregory again excommunicated the king, he made the German princes so angry that they and Henry began a campaign to replace the pope. In 1081, Henry invaded Italy, and appointed Clement III pope (antipope). When Italian forces joined Henry in 1084, Gregory was forced to flee Rome. He died in exile the next year.

The investiture controversy continued to plague popes and kings until an agreement was reached at the Concordant of Worms in 1122. Neither

Gregory nor Henry saw the issue resolved, but their actions changed the relationship between church and state forever.

TERM PAPER SUGGESTIONS

1. In the investiture controversy, was the Holy Roman Emperor Henry VI trying to exert too much power over the church, or was Pope Gregory VII trying to exert too much power over the secular government?

2. The papacy of Gregory VII has often been referred to as the Gregorian Reform or Gregorian Revolution. Do either of these terms fit? Did the religious and social changes have positive or negative results for the church as a whole?

3. England had its own conflict with the pope over lay investiture, but it lasted only four years (1103–1107). Why was the conflict much shorter in England? How did the English outcome impact the conflict in Germany?

4. How did the investiture controversy influence the development of nations in Europe? How did it change papal power?

ALTERNATIVE TERM PAPER SUGGESTIONS

1. What was the disagreement all about between Pope Gregory VII and Emperor Henry IV? Present a debate between these two men illustrating the point of view of each. Use quotations from primary documents in your presentation.

2. Pope Gregory VII is not only known for the investiture controversy, but also for liturgical reform, including the Gregorian chant. In an oral presentation, explain what the Gregorian chant is. Share examples from recordings and explain why you think the chants remain popular.

Primary Sources

Arnulf of Milan. *The Book of Recent Deeds.* Trans. by W. L. North from the edition of Claudia Zey, *MGH Scriptores Rerum Germanicrum 67.* Hannover: Hahnsche Buchhandlung, 1994. http://www.acad.carleton.edu/curricular/MARS/Arnulf.pdf. Concerns German kings and church authorities, written by an 11th-century contemporary.

The Avalon Project of Yale Law School. http://avalon.law.yale.edu/subject_menus/investm.asp. "Documents Relating to the War of the Investitures." A series of documents in chronological order from the beginning of the controversy to the papal dictate after the Concordant of Worms.

Gregory VII. *The Correspondence of Pope Gregory VII.* Ed. and trans. by Ephraim Emerton. New York: Columbia University Press, 1990. Gregory was a copious letter writer. Emerton has selected and edited some of his most significant epistles.

Healy, Patrick. *The Chronicle of Hugh of Flavigny: Reform and the Investiture Contest in the Late Eleventh Century.* Burlington, VT: Ashgate Publishing, 2006. Includes a translation of *The Chronicle,* along with extensive commentary on its context and significance.

Kirshner, Julius, and Morrison, Karl F., eds. *University of Chicago Readings in Western Civilization: 4, Medieval Europe.* Chicago: University of Chicago Press, 1986. Chapter 2, "The Investiture Conflict," contains more than 60 pages of translations of documents dealing with the topic.

Robinson, Ian, ed. *The Papal Reform of the Eleventh Century: Lives of Pope Leo IX and Pope Gregory VII.* Manchester: Manchester University Press, 2004. Book includes translations of five of the earliest works about Gregory and Leo.

Secondary Sources

Blumenthal, Uta-Renate. *The Investiture Controversy: Church and Monarchy from the Ninth to the Twelfth Century.* Philadelphia: University of Pennsylvania Press, 1991. Using numerous primary sources, the volume traces and analyzes the investiture arguments.

Cowdrey, H. E. J. *Pope Gregory VII, 1073–1085.* Oxford: Oxford University Press, 1998. Includes a biography and discussion of Gregory, along with a number of primary documents.

Miller, Maureen C. *Power and the Holy in the Age of the Investiture Conflict: A Brief History with Documents.* London: Palgrave Macmillan, 2004. Along with an introductory essay and comments, the volume also provides a wide range of primary documents that put the investiture controversy in social and political context.

Robinson, I. S. *Henry IV of Germany 1056–1106.* Cambridge: Cambridge University Press, 1999. This is the first biography of Henry IV in English. Robinson discusses the difficulties Henry faced in preserving the rights of the monarchy, particularly against the church.

Tellenbach, Gerd. *Church, State and Christian Society at the Time of the Investiture Contest.* New York: ACLS Humanities E-book, 2008. A facsimile reproduction of Tellenbach's classic 1940 study.

World Wide Web

The Bishops of Rome, the Popes; the Patriarchs of Constantinople, Alexandria, Antioch, Jerusalem, Armenia, and the East; Archbishops of Canterbury and Prince Archbishops of Mainz, Trier, Cologne, and Salzburg. http://www.friesian

.com/popes.htm. An abundance of information about church authorities: articles, chronological lists, diagrams, and maps.

The Medieval Sourcebook. http://www.fordham.edu/halsall/sbook1l.html. The section entitled "Empire and Papacy" offers a large collection of primary documents on the investiture controversy.

Multimedia Sources

"The Investiture Controversy," part seven of *Popes and the Papacy.* 2006. DVD or audio CD. The Teaching Company. Twenty-four 30-minute lectures in entire set. DVD includes images, charts, maps, etc.

Out of the Dark Ages: A Tale of Four German Emperors. 1996. Video. Films for the Humanities and Sciences. 50 minutes. Includes a segment on Emperor Henry IV.

51. Domesday Book is Compiled (1086)

William the Conqueror commissioned the Domesday Book in 1085, and it was completed the next year. This fact indicates the administrative ability of William and his officials. In an orderly manner, the task of inventorying all the property in England as it existed before the Norman invasion and as it existed in 1086 was conducted. Each locality provided a list of landowners, their property, tenants, livestock, and resources, such as water and timber. Property values were assessed using a formula based on preNorman and present worth. When completed, the results were summarized in two enormous volumes that provided the government valuable information for taxation. In addition, the record proved invaluable to courts in disputes over property.

Domesday Book stands alone as a detailed record of medieval life. Royal officials verified the information they received through hundreds of inquests with local juries, where individuals took sworn oaths to tell the truth. No other country approached this kind of detailed record for centuries.

TERM PAPER SUGGESTIONS

1. What circumstances in England made possible such a monumental task as compiling the Domesday Book? What characteristics of the government made it possible?

2. How adequate a picture of rural England do you think the Domesday Book provides? Why?

3. How is the compilation of the Domesday Book related to the legal system established in Norman England?

4. What can we learn about the continuity and the change between Anglo-Saxon and Norman England from the Domesday Book?

5. Why were cities such as London and Winchester not surveyed in the Domesday Book?

ALTERNATIVE TERM PAPER SUGGESTIONS

1. Create a large map showing the castles that William built throughout England. What conclusions can you make about the placement of these castles?

2. Chose one manor inventoried in the Domesday Book. Read the inventory and draw a representation of the manor as it is described.

Primary Sources

Anderson, Roberta, ed. *Medieval Worlds: A Sourcebook.* London: Routledge, 2003. A wide variety of documents from the personal, religious, and political worlds; arranged topically.

Domesday Book: A Complete Translation. Trans. by G. Martin and Ann Williams. New York: Penguin Classics, 2004.

Henry of Huntingdon. *The History of the English People 1000–1154.* Trans. by Dianna Greenway. Oxford: Oxford University Press, 2009. Contemporary historian Henry of Huntingdon tells an exciting story of life in England before, during, and after the Norman Conquest.

William of Poitiers. *Gesta Guillelmi. (The Deeds of William).* Trans. and ed. by R. H. C. Davis and Marjorie Chibnall. London: Oxford University Press, 1998. This history of William's reign has both Latin and English on facing pages. Provides introduction and commentary throughout.

Secondary Sources

Erskine, R. W. H., and Williams, Ann. *The Story of Domesday Book.* Phillimore & Co., 2003. Contains interpretive essays by leading scholars on the Domesday Book.

Fleming, Robin. *Domesday Book and the Law: Society and Legal Custom in Early Medieval England.* Cambridge: Cambridge University Press, 2003. Discusses the impact of the Domesday Book in relation to such legal practices as the inquest, selection of jurors, legal disputes, and written evidence. Also contains translations of the "Little Domesday Book" and the "Exchequer Domesday Book."

Galbraith, Vivian H. *Domesday Book: Its Place in Administrative History.* Oxford: Oxford University Press, 1975. Considers the effects of the Domesday Book on future governmental and administrative practices.

Maitland, Fredrick William. *Domesday Book and Beyond—Three Essays in the Early History of England.* New York: Adamant Media, 2005. Fascimile reproduction of the 1897 book. Essay 1 discusses the plan and contents of the Book itself. Essay 2 is about England before the Norman Conquest, and Essay 3 discusses the significance of the *hide,* a unit of land measure.

Planche, J. R. *The Conqueror and His Companions.* London: Tinsley Brothers, 1874. Complete text online at http://genealogy.patp.us/conq/default.aspx. Lists many of the Norman lords who came to England with William and gives information about each.

World Wide Web

Domesday: Britain's Finest Treasure. http://www.nationalarchives.gov.uk/domesday/default.htm. Produced by Britain's National Archives, this extensive resource allows searches for places in Britain in the Domesday Book, has interactive features, and provides information about 11th-century Britain in a section called "The Domesday World."

The Domesday Book Online. http://www.domesdaybook.co.uk/. Contains a great deal of information including some of book's contents, lists of towns, counties, and landholders, information about how the book was compiled, and links to other helpful sites.

Multimedia Sources

Great Kings of England: William the Conqueror. 2000. DVD. Kultur Studios. 50 minutes. Biography with emphasis on the Norman Conquest.

Norman Conquest. 2008. DVD. CreateSpace Studio. 49 minutes. Dramatizations of eye-witness accounts, reenactments, period images, commentary by medieval scholars. Includes a segment on the Domesday Book.

52. First Crusade (1096–1099)

Christians under Rome had been mainly pacifist. But as early as the fifth century, the shedding of blood for Christ was being justified by church fathers such as St. Augustine. When Islam rose as powerful religion, the Christian church became more militaristic. Between the seventh and

11th centuries, Christians and Muslims had battled one another throughout the Western world, as much for territory as for souls. Pope Gregory VII (r. 1073–1085) openly supported the Spanish nobles who were trying to drive the Muslims out of Iberia and would have liked to drive the Muslims out of the Mediterranean, but he was too involved in the investiture controversy to turn his full attention there. Seluk Turks killed the Byzantine emperor at the Battle of Manzikert in 1071, and his successor, Alexius Comnenus, appealed to the West for aid against the Turkish forces, opening a door for Western interference. When the Muslims in Jerusalem closed the city to both Christian and Jewish pilgrims, Pope Urban II had everything he needed to convince Christians to join a Crusade.

On November 27, 1095, at the Council of Clermont, Urban II issued his call for all Christians to fight the enemies in the East, saying it was Christ's command that they do so and promising that all who did so would receive forgiveness for their sins. Word of Urban's appeal spread quickly and within a few months more than 5,000 crusaders set out on a land route through Germany and the Balkans for Constantinople. No ruling monarchs joined them, but a large number of lesser nobles and princes made the journey. With their militaristic and religious fervor at a high point, the Crusaders wreaked havoc on the lands through which they passed, massacred Jews, and robbed and abused the Balkan people. When they arrived in Constantinople, Alexius Comnenus transported the crusaders across the Mediterranean as quickly as possible.

The Crusaders pressed on and were able to capture the cities of Antioch and Jerusalem, slaughtering the Moslem and Jewish people living there, and for a while established the small Latin Kingdom of Jerusalem. Little else resulted from this contact between Christian and Moslem. Seven more crusades followed in the next two centuries, with varying degrees of success.

TERM PAPER SUGGESTIONS

1. Considering the state of affairs in the West, discuss what motives, other than religious ones, that Pope Urban II might have had for encouraging the first Crusade. Did the Crusade achieve his goals? Why or why not?

2. Compare the Holy War called for by Pope Urban II to medieval Islamic calls for *jihad.* Are the purposes the same? The methods?

3. In the fourth century, St. Augustine wrote about the idea of "a just war," a concept debated throughout the Middle Ages and even today by scholars from all religions. What constitutes a just war? Was the first Crusade a just war?

4. Analyze the rhetorical construction of Pope Urban's speech at Clermont. How did he plan the speech so it would have the desired effect?

5. Discuss the "people's crusade" that organized itself and went to Constantinople. Why did this happen? What is the significance of this popular reaction to Urban? What were the results? How much of this crusade was Urban responsible for?

6. What factors in the Moslem world at the time of the First Crusade contributed to the victory of the crusaders in capturing Jerusalem?

7. Pope Urban's call for the First Crusade had the stated purpose of recapturing the Holy Land from the infidels. What other political and social outcomes did Urban expect to gain from the Crusades?

8. When the Latin Kingdoms were established in the East after the First Crusade, how did the Frankish rulers treat fellow Christians who were already living there, but whose faith was different from their own? What reasons can you give for the rulers' means of dealing with this type of religious difference?

ALTERNATIVE TERM PAPER SUGGESTIONS

1. Pope Urban's speech at Clermont is a model of clear, effective, persuasive writing. Prepare a dramatic reenactment of the delivery of this speech. Introduce the speech with some background and end with a short discussion of the effects.

2. Create a large map of the route the first crusaders took to Jerusalem. Label significant events of the Crusade along the route, including the numbers of individuals who were killed by the army along the way.

2. Design a board game based on the Crusades. You may use events from the later Crusades, not just the First Crusade.

Primary Sources

Albert of Aachen. *Albert of Aachen: Historia Ierosolimitana, History of the Journey to Jerusalem.* Trans. and ed. by Susan B. Edgington. Oxford: Oxford University Press, 2007. Albert himself did not travel to

Jerusalem, but he based his accounts of the first Crusade on interviews and eye-witness accounts.

Gabrieli, Fanncesco, ed. *Arab Historians of the Crusades.* London: Routledge & Kegan Paul, 1969. Includes translations from the works of seventeen Arab historians on the Crusades.

Gilbert of Nogent. *The Deeds of God Through the Franks.* Trans. by Robert Levine. http://www.bu.edu/english/levine/guibprol.htm. Gilbert's memoir is better known than this book on the First Crusade, which was not translated into English until the end of the 20th century.

Gilo of Paris. The *Historia Vie Hierosolimitane* of Gilo of Paris and a second, anonymous author. Ed. by C. W. Grocock and J. E. Siberry. Oxford: Oxford University Press, 1997. Gilo, not among the Crusaders himself, collected stories from those who were for this history. This edition has Latin and English texts on facing pages.

Munro, Dana Carleton, ed. "Letters of the Crusades Written from the Holy Land," in *Translations and Reprints from the Original Sources of European History,* Vol. I. Philadelphia: Department of History of the University of Pennsylvania, 1900, pp. 1–40. http: //www.shsu.edu/~his_ncp/Cruslet .html.

Peters, Edward, ed. *Christian Society and the Crusades, 1198–1229: Sources in Translation including "The Capture of Damietta" by Oliver of Paderborn.* Philadelphia: University of Pennsylvania Press, 1971. Translations of texts written either by Crusaders or about the wars.

Peters, Edward, ed. *The First Crusade: "The Chronicle of Fulcher of Chartres" and Other Source Materials,* 2nd ed. Philadelphia: University of Pennsylvania Press, 1998. Fulcher was one of the Crusaders on the first trip to the Holy Land.

Robert the Monk. *Robert the Monk's History of the First Crusade: Historia Iherosolimitana* Ed. and trans. by Carol Sweetenham. Burlington, VT: Ashgate Publishing, 2006. Includes the text of Robert's history in translation, along with commentary and notes.

Secondary Sources

Asbridge, Thomas. *The First Crusade: A New History: The Roots of Conflict between Christianity and Islam.* Oxford: Oxford University Press, 2004. Asbridge begins with Pope Urban's call to war and tells the story of the first crusade and its aftermath. Illustrations and a list identifying individuals involved.

Chazan, Robert. *In the Year 1096: The First Crusade and the Jews.* New York: Jewish Publications Society, 1996. Studies the origins of the antiSemitic massacres of the Crusades and places them within the context of Jewish history.

Highland, Ann. *The Medieval Warhorse from Byzantium to the Crusades.* Conshohocken, PA: Combined Books, 1996. Discusses ways horses were employed in medieval warfare and their importance in battle, particularly in the Crusades.

Kaeuper, Richard W. *Holy Warriors: The Religious Ideology of Chivalry.* Philadelphia: University of Pennsylvania Press, 2009. Examines the assimilation of Christian ideology into the code of chivalry in order to justify the violence of the Crusades.

Maalouf, Amin. *The Crusades through Arab Eyes.* New York: Schocken Books, 1989. The author uses contemporary chronicles and eye-witness accounts to probe the Arab point of view during the Crusades.

MacEvitt, Christopher. *The Crusades and the Christian World of the East: Rough Tolerance.* Philadelphia: University of Pennsylvania Press, 2007. Tells the story of the interactions among the Frankish Crusaders who ruled the Latin Kingdoms in the East and the Christians who were living there but who practiced a different form of faith.

Madden, Thomas, ed. *The Crusades: The Essential Readings.* London: Wiley-Blackwell, 2002. A collection of twelve recent essays on the character, purpose, and impact of the Crusades.

Mayer, Hans Eberhard. *The Crusades,* 2nd ed. Trans. by John Gillingham. Oxford: Oxford University Press, 1988. A comprehensive history of all the medieval Crusades. Excellent introduction to the topic.

Riley-Smith, Jonathan. *The First Crusade and the Idea of Crusading.* Philadelphia: University of Pennsylvania Press, 1986. Using a wide array of contemporary documents, Riley-Smith traces the medieval attitudes toward the Crusades.

World Wide Web

Crusades-Encyclopedia. http://www.crusades-encyclopedia.com/. A portal that links to an astonishing amount of information on the Crusades; primary sources, encyclopedia articles, secondary sources, women in the Crusades, and bibliographies.

De Re Militari: The Society for Medieval Military History. http://www.deremilitari .org/. Includes articles on all aspects of medieval military operations, including the Crusades. Provides extensive bibliography of related materials. Also has some primary sources.

Multimedia Sources

Crusades. 2007. DVD. The Military Channel. 60 minutes. Noted archeologist leads viewers through the dig site at Acre, the site of a decisive battle in which the Saracens took the city that had been held by Christians for over a century.

The Crusades. 2003. DVD. Insight Media. 51 minutes. Archeologists and historians discuss recent evidence of the military strategies used in the Crusades; features discussions of Richard the Lionhearted and Saladin.

The Crusades: Crescent and the Cross. 2005. DVD. A&E Entertainment. 180 minutes. Uses reenactments, interviews with scholars, maps, time-lines, and period images to tell the story of the first three Crusades.

The Crusades: The Holy Wars. 2007. DVD. Kultur Media. 50 minutes. Uses reconstructions and animation to retell the story of the Crusades.

In Search of History: The Knights Templar. 2005. DVD. The History Channel. 50 minutes. Tells the story of the knights who formed for the purpose of protecting travelers to the Holy Land and how they became more than protectors.

In the Name of Christ. 2004. DVD. Films Media Group. 30 minutes. Draws parallels between the East and West, focusing on the martyrdom of both sides.

53. The Cistercian Order and Reform of Monasteries (1098)

The 11th century witnessed an increasing devotion to the church among the laity in Europe. In some cases, the new piety was a result of fears over the world ending in 1000; in others, it was the result of the laity having been educated by monks. As the church became more involved in the everyday world, the calls for a return to apostolic simplicity grew louder and reached a point of crisis. The population was well aware that the pope, bishops, and even Clunaic monks lived in luxury, or at least what seemed luxury to the ordinary person. Scandals at all levels of the church were also well known. Now, as the laity became more pious, often far exceeding the clergy in their faithfulness, the clergy were in danger of losing their distinction in the world. Respect for the clergy could only be maintained if there was an increase in the devotion and morality of the clergy themselves.

Dissatisfied with the church's leadership in faith, a number of monks sought ways to find the simplicity and return to the spiritual ideal. This led to the formation of several new orders during the 11th and 12th centuries, the most influential of which was the Cistercians. Robert of Molesme founded the order at Citreaux in 1098 with the intention of returning to the Benedictine tradition. Cistercians dressed in white robes that distinguished them from the Benedictines and earned the name "white monks." A devout Englishman, Stephen Harding, joined Citreaux and became a leader. Other important thinkers, such as St. Bernard, soon joined the monastery. The new monastery adopted the economic model of self-sufficiency advocated by Benedict, and all monks engaged in manual labor. They introduced new methods of cultivation and began raising sheep to produce wool for the textile industry; Cistercians also built mills and did ironwork. By the year 1150, there were 350 Cistercian abbeys spread throughout Europe. Most of the abbeys are built in isolated areas, which suited both the monks who wanted to withdraw from society and the wealthy who could bestow less valuable properties and still reap the spiritual benefits of giving.

The Cistercian abbeys were joined together in a tighter federation than that of the Clunaics, which gave them a substantial voice in the church. However, Cluny was not happy with the criticism, implied and open, that it received from the Cistercians. In the 1130s, a bitter debate began between St. Bernard, abbot at the daughter abbey of Clairvaux, and Peter the Venerable, the abbot of Cluny. In spite of the high ideals on which it was founded, the Cistercian order, like that of Cluny, became involved in the world. By the 13th century, Cisterian monks had developed a reputation for being hard businessmen, and their abbots had become money lenders to nobles and large landowners. However, the Cistercian movement paved the way for a number of other, smaller ascetic orders founded in the 12th century.

TERM PAPER SUGGESTIONS

1. Compare the life of a monk at a Cistercian abbey with that of a monk at a Clunaic abbey.

2. How does the architecture of the Cistercian abbeys reflect the values and purposes of the order?

3. Discuss the relationship between the Cistercian order and the Christian orders of knights, such as the Templars.

4. How did the Cistercians advance agriculture in the 12th century?

5. It has been said that the Cistercians were victims of their own success, that they grew too fast, and did not have the leadership needed to face the challenges. Is this a valid assessment of the Cistercian movement?

6. Discuss the economic influence of medieval monasteries. Did monasteries pave the way for capitalism? You may discuss orders other than the Cistercians.

7. Evaluate the debate between the Cistercians and the Clunaics. Which side had the more valid argument?

ALTERNATIVE TERM PAPER SUGGESTIONS

1. Using a detailed description of one of the Cistercian abbeys, build a model of that community.

2. Prepare a multimedia presentation about Cistercian architecture. Include music from the order to accompany the presentation.

Primary Sources

Bernard, of Clairvaux, Saint. *On Loving God*. Christian Classics Ethereal Library, http://www.ccel.org/ccel/bernard/loving_god.html. St. Bernard is perhaps the best known of the Cistercian monks and a prolific writer.

Bernard, of Clairvaux, Saint. *Bernard of Clairvaux: Selected Works*. New York: Harper Collins, 2005. Contains a variety of Bernard's works, including spiritual writings, sermons, and letters.

Charta Caritatis (Charter of Charity). http://www.osb.org/cist/charta.html. The document framed by Abbot Stephen Harding and the monks at the abbey of Citreaux to delineate the organization of Cistercian abbeys.

Matarasso, Pauline M., ed. *The Cistercian World: Monastic Writings of the Twelfth Century*. London: Penguin Classics, 1993. Translations of many genres, including sermons, meditations, letters, biography, prayers and exemplum.

Secondary Sources

Berman, Constance Hoffman. *The Cistercian Evolution: The Invention of a Religious Order in Twelfth-Century Europe*. Philadelphia: University of Pennsylvania Press, 2000.

Ekeland, Robert B., et al. *Sacred Trust: The Medieval Church as an Economic Firm*. Oxford: Oxford University Press, 1996. Emphasizes the church's role in industrial production and manipulation of supply and demand.

Evan, Gillian Rosemary. *Fifty Key Medieval Thinkers.* London: Routledge, 2002. Contains a chapter concerning each of 50 influential medieval intellectuals from all walks of life, including St. Bernard of Clairvaux.

Leroux-Dhuys, Jean-Francois, and Gaud, Henri. *Cistercian Abbeys: History and Architecture.* Paris: h. f. ullmann, 2008. Part I deals with the history of the Cistercian order, and Part II provides information and images of more than 60 abbeys.

Robinson, David et al. *The Cistercian Abbeys of Britain.* London: Batsford, 1998. Contains chapters about the history of the order and its architecture. Includes photos, descriptions, and individual histories of 86 Cistercian abbeys in Britain.

Stercal, Claudio. *Stephen Harding: A Biographical Sketch and Texts.* Trans. by Martha F. Kreig. Collegeville, MN: Cistercian Publications, 2008. Contains biography of Harding compiled from contemporary sources and translations of five of Harding's works.

World Wide Web

The Cistercian Order in Yorkshire. http://cistercians.shef.ac.uk/. An extensive and informative site with historical articles about the order, images, videos, and details of the five abbeys in Yorkshire. Also has a list of British Cistercian abbeys with brief descriptions of each.

Rete Vitae Religiosae Mediaevalis Studia Conectens. http://www.vita-religiosa.de/. This site is maintained by The Research Center for the Comparative History of Religious Orders and provided links to many websites dealing with medieval studies. Available in English, German, French, and Italian.

Multimedia Sources

Cistercian Monks of Stift Heiligenkreuz. *Chant Music for Paradise.* 2008. Audio CD. Universal. Two-CD set with over 50 selections of Gregorian and Cistercian chants, psalms, and liturgical pieces.

The Medieval Monastery. 1979. DVD. University of Toronto: Information Commons. 23 minutes. Filmed at seven medieval monasteries, the film explores the daily lives of monks.

The Monk. 2002. Schlessinger Media. 23 minutes. Part of the series *Life in the Middle Ages.* Shows how monks spent their time, how monasteries were organized, and how one became a monk.

54. Banking Industry Begins in Europe (c. 1100)

Systematic trade across large expanses of land was carried out throughout the Islamic world in the 9th and 10th centuries. Needing a means of transferring payments, Arabs developed a sophisticated banking structure centered in the capital of Baghdad. The European economy was based primarily on subsistence agriculture until the 11th century, and there was no financial establishment in the West, where most money exchange and lending had been performed by Jews. However, heightened antiSemitism, which developed in the 11th and 12th centuries, caused many Jews to be expelled, have their property confiscated, or be killed. At the same time, international trade was flourishing. In addition, the Crusaders needed funds as they traveled from one country to another.

One of the first banking concerns in Europe was the Knights Templar organization. Formed with the purpose of protecting pilgrims who journeyed to the Holy Land, the Templars expanded their duties to include first caring for the goods of travelers, then to accepting money deposits, and finally to transferring and lending money. Eventually, the wealth of the Templars led to conflicts with the monarchy and the order was destroyed.

The cities of Florence and Genoa in Italy and Bourges in France, important centers of trade, became international banking centers in the 13th century. Banking families such as the Bardi, Peruzzi, and Medici gained political power as well as wealth. Medieval banks were institutions for the wealthy. They dealt in funds for the rising merchant class, for the church, and for the nobility. In the late 14th and early 15th century, a series of economic setbacks caused a number of banks to fail.

TERM PAPER SUGGESTIONS

1. Research the minting of money in the Middle Ages. What were some of the problems that occurred with the use of coins? In what ways did the banking system alleviate some of these issues?

2. How were the issues of profit and personal wealth viewed by the medieval church? What was the church's view of money lending? How true was the church to its teachings?

3. How did the banking industry contribute to the growth of a middle class?

4. Research one of the large banking families of Florence in northern Italy. What accounted for the success of this business? Why did the business collapse? How did the family's success reflect or challenge the prevailing economic conditions?

5. What was the relationship between banks and monarchies? How did banks influence political affairs?

ALTERNATIVE TERM PAPER SUGGESTIONS

1. Assume the persona of the last Templar grand master, Jacques de Molay. Prepare a final speech for your trial before the church inquisitor when he has pronounced your sentence. Be sure to include information about French king Philip the Fair's possible motives for charging you.

2. Prepare a multimedia presentation about the forms of exchange and currency used in Europe during the Middle Ages.

Primary Sources

Kirshner, Julius, and Morrison, Karl F., eds. *University of Chicago Readings in Western Civilization: 4, Medieval Europe.* Chicago: University of Chicago Press, 1986. The section entitled "Commerce Confronts the Usury Prohibition" contains several primary documents dealing with money and finance.

Lopez, Robert Sabatino, and Raymond, Irving W., eds. *Medieval Trade in the Mediterranean World.* New York: Columbia University Press, 1955. Varied collection of commercial documents including private documents, market charters, guild documents, and loan agreements. Includes extensive notes and commentary.

Secondary Sources

Hunt, Edwin S., and Murray, James. *A History of Business in Medieval Europe: 1200–1550.* Cambridge: Cambridge University Press, 1999. Thorough analysis of the commercial revolution of the 13th century. Has a chapter on the sources of capital in medieval Europe.

Postan, M. M. *Mediaeval Trade and Finance.* Cambridge: Cambridge University Press, 2002. A collection of essays by renowned scholar M. M. Postan that were originally published elsewhere but gathered in this one volume.

Spufford, Peter. *Money and Its Use in Medieval Europe.* Cambridge: Cambridge University Press, 1988. Looks at the economic and financial situation in Europe before, during, and after the commercial revolution of the 13th century. Has three informative appendices.

Weatherford, Jack. *The History of Money.* New York: Three Rivers Press, 1998. Thorough history of money with a chapter on medieval exchange, "Knights of Commerce."

Wood, Diana, ed. *Medieval Economic Thought.* Cambridge: Cambridge University Press, 2002. Using primary sources as varied as the works of poets, lawyers, and philosophers and legal and government documents, Wood provides a synthesis of the thinking about issues such as profit, private ownership, and usury.

World Wide Web

Medieval Economics. http://www.geocities.com/elangoc/medieval/medieval.html. This site provides discussions of money and trade, medieval professions, commodities, and guilds, in addition to an extensive bibliography and links to other Web sites.

The Medieval Sourcebook. http://www.fordham.edu/halsall/sbook1n.html. The section on Economic Life has a wealth of primary documents on trade, finance, and banking.

Multimedia Sources

Bankers, Builders, and New Beginnings. 2004. DVD. Films for the Humanities and Sciences. 53 minutes. Explores the growth of finance and commerce in the late Middle Ages from the point of view of an urban merchant. Some portions in other languages with English subtitles.

Decoding the Past: Templar Code, Parts I and II. 2007. DVD. The History Channel. Two 50-minute programs. Specialists in breaking codes examine the geometric forms carved in the Templar's prison and try to discover the truth behind the Templar legends.

The Knights Templar. DVD. 2000. BFS Entertainment. 120 minutes. Templar historian Malcolm Barber leads the audience through reenactments and interviews that explore the two centuries of Templar history, including their involvement in European banking.

The Knights Templar. 2005. DVD. The History Channel. 50 minutes. Filmed on location in Europe and Jerusalem, includes interviews with historians, period images, and primary source dramatizations.

Risky Business: Wealth-Building, 450 to 1497. 2000. DVD. BBC. 46 minutes. Part of the six-part series *The Road to Riches: The History of Wealth-Building.* Discusses the development of trade, commerce, and banking during the Middle Ages.

55. Gothic Architecture Introduced (c. 1136)

Visions of magnificent Gothic cathedrals are fixed in the modern imagination of the medieval world. Most of the world's Gothic cathedrals and churches were constructed during the 12th and 13th centuries and are in areas north of the Alps. By 1300 there were more than 80 cathedrals and 500 abbey churches built in the Gothic style. Technically, no matter how large the church is, it is not a cathedral unless it houses a bishop's throne or *cathedra*.

Gothic architecture originated in Saint Denis, Île-de-France, 1136, when the Abbot Suger decided to rebuild the Carolingian Church on a much grander scale. This architectural style, characterized by flying buttresses, ribbed vaults, and pointed arches, was not called *Gothic* until the 15th century, when architects began to return to classical styles. Interiors of Gothic churches inspire a feeling of soaring space and are flooded with multihued light from the many windows.

Cathedrals were engineering feats in the Middle Ages, and they took years to complete. Stone and wood sculptures adorned both the interiors and exteriors of the cathedrals. Stained glass for windows was designed not only for decoration but to educate the illiterate by teaching them the stories of the Bible and of saints. All this work created a great demand for stone masons, carpenters, glass workers, metal workers, and other artisans. In many cases, cathedrals were economic boons to localities; in others, their construction nearly bankrupted the diocese.

All design elements of Gothic cathedrals were selected to inspire faith and to draw people closer to God, and they remain among the most beautiful buildings in the world.

TERM PAPER SUGGESTIONS

1. How did the Gothic cathedrals of Europe embody the beliefs and ideals of the Christian faith which inspired their creation? What symbols were employed in the construction of the buildings?

2. What effect did the construction of Gothic cathedrals have on the economies of the towns in which they were built? What effect did the construction have on the rise of a middle class?

3. Analyze the collection of relics in cathedrals. Why were relics considered so important both spiritually and economically?

ALTERNATIVE TERM PAPER SUGGESTIONS

1. Writers sometimes write of the "geometry of Gothic cathedrals." What does this mean? Create a multimedia presentation that illustrates the concept of cathedral geometry.
2. Create a Web site with basic information about the history of Gothic cathedrals. Include a list of annotated links to additional Web information and to images of the cathedrals. Include medieval music and images of medieval art as well. Be sure that everything you include is public domain and that you cite your sources.

Primary Sources

Haseldine, Julian, ed. *The Letters of Peter of Celle.* Oxford: Oxford University Press, 2002. Peter was Bishop of Chartres Cathedral from 1181–1183. Most of the letters are from his years at Chartres.

Suger, Abbot of St. Denis. *Abbot Suger on the Abbey Church of St. Denis and Its Art Treasures.* Trans. by Erwin Panofsky and Gerda Panofsky-Soergel. Princeton: Princeton University Press, 1979. Translation of the writings of the founder of Gothic architecture from the Abbey of St. Denis.

Secondary Sources

Bony, Jean. *French Gothic Architecture of the Twelfth and Thirteenth Centuries.* Berkeley: University of California Press, 1983. One of the strengths of this book is its beautiful illustrations.

Clark, William W. *Medieval Cathedrals.* Westport, CT: Greenwood Publishing, 2005. Contains chapters on planning, construction, and religious importance of the medieval cathedral.

Fitchen, John. *The Construction of Gothic Cathedrals: A Study of Medieval Vault Erection.* Chicago: University of Chicago Press, 1997. Explains the steps involved in construction of cathedrals as deduced from medieval illustrations, manuscript illuminations, and the cathedrals.

Scott, Robert A. *The Gothic Enterprise: A Guide to Understanding the Medieval Cathedral.* Berkeley: University of California Press, 2006. Places Gothic cathedrals in the context of the time in which they were constructed; discusses construction, architectural details, and what the cathedrals meant to the church and community.

Simpson, Otto von. *The Gothic Cathedral: Origins of Gothic Architecture and the Medieval Conception of Order,* 3rd ed. New York: Pantheon Books, 1974. This is a classic study of Gothic cathedrals and still a valuable resource. Views cathedrals as manifestations of the 12th-century religious experience infused with the supernatural.

World Wide Web

British History: The Cathedrals of Britain. http://www.bbc.co.uk/history/british/ architecture_cathedral_01.shtml. Articles about the cathedrals, the craftsmen, and their architects; images; interactive content.

Chartres: Cathedral of Norte-Dame. http://images.library.pitt.edu./c/chartres. More than 3,000 images documenting the architecture, windows, and art work of Chartres.

Engines of Our Ingenuity. http://www.uh.edu/engines/. This is the archives for the National Public Radio program of the same name. Use the search feature to find several free downloads of programs on medieval architecture, cathedrals, and stone masonry.

West, George Herbert. *Gothic Architecture in England & France.* London: G. Bell & Sons, 1911. Online facsimile of book available through Questia.com.

Multimedia Sources

The Age of Gothic. 2007. DVD. Educational Film Services. 50 minutes. Overview of Gothic architecture using Chartres Cathedral to illustrate its beauty.

Cathedrals: Notre Dame to the National Cathedral. 2003. DVD. The History Channel. 48 minutes. Searches for the continuity in structure and spiritual support from cathedrals built over the last 900 years.

Chartres Cathedral–A Sacred Geometry. 2003. DVD. Janson Media. 60 minutes. Filmed at Chartres, introduces audiences to the use of sculpture and glass in cathedral construction through the marvels of Chartres.

Cities and Cathedrals of the Middle Ages. No date. Streaming video. Annenburg. Video 15 in a series of 25. Available online at learner.org. Individuals must register to view the videos, but there is no cost. Discusses how the cathedrals represented the spiritual and material values of the culture.

The Construction and Design of Gothic Medieval Cathedrals. 1998. Insight Media. 30 minutes. Traces the development of cathedral architecture and construction techniques.

Gothic Cathedrals of Europe. No date. Films Media Group. Interactive CD-ROM with more than 2000 photos, 35 cathedral histories, and articles.

The Jeweled City: The Cathedral of Chartres. 1995. DVD. BBC Production. 50 minutes. A narrated tour of the cathedral with a discussion of the political and social climate that created this masterpiece of Gothic architecture.

A White Garment of Churches–Romansque and Gothic. DVD. Annenburg. learner.org. Individuals must register to view the videos, but there is no cost. Part I discusses the Romansque cathedrals of the early Middle Ages, and Part II the Gothic architecture begun at St. Denis and Chartres Cathedral.

56. *The Alexiad* is Written by Anna Comnena (c. 1150)

The Alexiad, an account of the reign of Alexius I of Byzantium (r. 1078–1118), was written by his daughter, Anna Comnena. The work remains one of the best sources of 11th- and 12th-century Byzantine aristocratic life. Alexius, the second member of the Comnenus dynasty to rule in Constantinople, inherited a beleaguered kingdom. In 1071, at the disastrous Battle of Manzikert, Seluj Turks captured extensive Byzantine territory in Asia Minor. In addition, Normans were invading various sections of Byzantium, as were the Patzinak people from the east. It was Alexius I who made the decision to appeal to the Roman pope to send troops to fight the Turks, thereby opening the door for interference from the West in the affairs of the East. In spite of the damage done by the First Crusade, Alexius was able to regain some of his lost territory for a while. Near the end of his life, a conspiracy led by his wife, Empress Irene, and daughter Anna tried to have Anna's husband Nicephorus Bryennius named as the successor to Alexius, rather than his son John.

Anna had herself hoped to one day become empress, and she had been educated to fulfill that role. Her scheme to bypass her brother was discovered, and she spent the last years of her life in a convent. Nicephorus, who died a few years later, was a historian, and he inspired Anna to write. She continued Byzantine history from where Nicephorus stopped, the reign of Alexius I, a time she certainly knew well. Although she had plotted against her father's wishes, it is obvious from the *Alexiad* that she had great admiration for him. Anna also wrote extensively about the women in her family, especially her mother and grandmother, giving information about their lives found in no other sources. The *Alexiad* also includes extensive commentary on the Crusaders who passed through Constantinople in Anna's lifetime. Anna's skill as a writer as well as a historian creates an appealing text in the *Alexiad,* one of the masterpieces of medieval writing.

TERM PAPER SUGGESTIONS

1. Compare Anna Comnena's depiction of the Second Crusade to that of one or more Western authors.

2. An entry about Anna Comnena is in the 1907 edition of *The Catholic Encyclopedia* (available online). Compare this description of Anna's work to the history itself. Is the evaluation by the encyclopedia writer fair and accurate?

3. Consider the issues historians face as they try to present a factual report of events (i.e., tell the truth). Can that ever be accomplished? Compare the techniques of the historian in Anna Comnena's *Alexiad* to histories written earlier. Is she more or less biased in her presentation of the reign of an emperor than earlier writers had been?

4. Anna Comnena was a remarkable woman for her time: educated, strong, and talented. Would you also consider her a feminist? What evidence can you give to support your answer?

ALTERNATIVE TERM PAPER SUGGESTIONS

1. Assume the persona of Anna Comnena and tell the story of the Second Crusade into Byzantium from her point of view.

2. Construct a multimedia presentation using Anna Comnena's descriptions and images from the 11th century to show both the Crusaders who traveled through Constantinople and the people of Constantinople. Use the images to confirm or refute Comnena's appraisal.

Primary Sources

Comnena, Anna. *The Alexiad.* Trans. by E. R. A. Sewter. London: Penguin Classics, 2004. A complete translation of Comnena's classic work.

Thiebaux, Marcelle, ed. *The Writings of Medieval Women,* 2nd ed. Garland Library of Medieval Literature, 1994. Includes translations from more than thirty medieval women, including Anna Comnena.

Secondary Sources

Connor, Carolyn L. *Women of Byzantium.* New Haven: Yale University Press, 2004. History of women throughout the Middle Ages in Byzantium. Has a chapter on Anna Comnena and her world.

Edgington, Susan B., and Lambert, Sarah, eds. *Gendering the Crusades.* New York: Columbia University Press, 2002. Collection of scholarly essays on women in the era of the Crusades; includes an essay about Anna Comnena.

Gouma-Peterson, Thalia, ed. *Anna Komnene and Her Times.* London: Routledge, 2000. A series of critical essays on Anna Comnena's life and times and the effects of her work in her own time and on future literature.

Haldon, John, Jeffreys, Elizabeth, and Cormack, Robin. *The Oxford Handbook of Byzantine Studies.* New York: Oxford University Press, 2009. A compendium of articles by experts on all aspects of the Byzantine culture from the fifth through 15th centuries.

Highland, Ann. *The Medieval Warhorse from Byzantium to the Crusades.* Conshohocken, PA: Combined Books, 1996. Discusses ways horses were employed in medieval warfare and their importance in battle, particularly in the Crusades.

Kazhdan, A. P., and Epstein, Anne Wharton. *Change in the Byzantine Culture in the Eleventh and Twelfth Centuries.* Berkeley: University of California Press, 1990. The authors explore changes in Byzantium in the context of the larger world changes of these volatile centuries. A selection of primary documents is included.

Metropolitan Museum of Art. *The Glory of Byzantium: Art and Culture of the Middle Byzantine Era, A.D. 843–1261.* New York: Metropolitan Museum of Art, 1997. A companion book for a major exhibition on Byzantine art. Many pieces were on loan from world museums.

Norwich, John Julian. *A Short History of Byzantium.* New York: Alfred A. Knopf, 1997. Part III contains several chapters on the Byzantine rulers during Anna's lifetime.

World Wide Web

The Dumbarton Oaks Research Library and Collection, an Institute of Harvard University. *http://www.doaks.org/.* Dumbarton Oaks sponsors research on Byzantine culture and history and makes many research articles and other resources available online. Choose the library link from the homepage to access more than 500,000 images related to Byzantium. Choose the publications link for articles.

Explore Byzantium. http://www.byzantium.seashell.net.nz/. Timelines, biographies, maps, articles, and images about Byzantine history.

The Glory of Byzantium. http://www.metmuseum.org/explore/Byzantium/byzhome.html. Online, interactive exhibit hosted by the Metropolitan Museum of Art. Includes images, a timeline, and articles.

Multimedia Sources

The Crusades: Crescent and the Cross. 2005. DVD. A&E Entertainment. 180 minutes. Uses reenactments, interviews with scholars, maps, timelines, and period images to tell the story of the first three Crusades.

57. Hildegard of Bingen Writes *Scivias* (c. 1150)

The list of accomplishments for Hildegard of Bingen is lengthy: author, artist, naturalist, scientist, counselor, musician, abbess, visionary, and saint are some of her designations. One of the truly remarkable individuals of the Middle Ages, Hildegard was highly regarded during her own lifetime by a wide range of people. She was the 10th child of a noble family in Germany and was educated by nuns at a convent of Disenburg, which she eventually joined. In 1147, she took a group of nuns from Disenburg and formed a new convent at Bingen, where she became prioress. Hildegard had seen visions all her life, and when she reported these to her confessor Godfrey, he encouraged her to write about them. The resulting work, *Scivias (Know the Way)*, became immensely popular and spread her fame.

Hildegard was well known as a healer and she wrote two medical books: *Causae et curae (Causes and Cures)*, a treatise on the workings of the human body and a list of healing substances, and *Physica,* a series of meditations on the natural world. *Causes and Cures* was used in medical schools until well into the 15th century. Although women seldom spoke in public in the 12th century, Hildegard began a series of lecture tours, speaking to clergy and laity alike. Two other visionary books were completed before her death: *Liber vitae meritorum (The Book of Life's Merits)* and *Liber divinorum operum (The Book of God's Works).*

Hildegard did not confine her activity to the spiritual, but involved herself in the political world of her times. She was a prolific letter writer to people at all levels of society. She corresponded with the pope, archbishops, and kings on serious matters of the day. Her writing often took the unconventional point of view and still produced results. For instance, on one occasion, the diocese of Mainz had imposed an interdict on her convent because they had buried a man in their graveyard who had been excommunicated. Hildegard successfully argued her position and managed to get the interdict lifted. More than 300 of Hildegard's letters survive, providing insight into the spiritual and secular worlds of the 12th century.

In addition to her other talents, Hildegard was a skillful musician who made several innovations in music. She wrote a large number of choral songs, some of which blended church music with popular folksongs. And finally, Hildegard was a highly respected artist. The illuminations in her books are some of the finest from the Middle Ages. Scholars today say that all the illuminations were not completed by the same person but agree that Hildegard's influence is seen even in those she did not do herself. Part of that influence is the skillful weaving of subtle subtexts into the illustrations.

Hildegard died in 1179, leaving behind an extraordinary body of work, contributing greatly to the modern understanding of the medieval world.

TERM PAPER SUGGESTIONS

1. What is the significance of Hildegard of Bingen in the history of music? What was the purpose of music in the culture of her time? What polyphony, musical notation, genres, and forms were prevalent?

2. *Scivias* retells the visionary experiences of Hildegard, but it is also a work of religious philosophy. Analyze Hildegard's theories on the relationship among the soul, human will, the intellect, and human actions.

3. Hildegard was an artist herself, and she oversaw the creation of a number of illuminated manuscripts at Bingen. Select a few illuminations by Hildegard that you feel have the same theme. Analyze the images for the message she subtly conveys in them.

4. Where is there evidence that Hildegard von Bingen was not just a talented and strong woman, but actually a feminist, or at least subtly subversive to patriarchy?

5. Analyze some of the letters of Hildegard to determine her attitude toward individuals from different walks of life and from different classes. Was she a tolerant and accepting individual? Do you see evidence of personal biases?

6. Compare Hildegard's writing with that of a male member of the clergy from the same generation.

ALTERNATIVE TERM PAPER SUGGESTIONS

1. Hildegard was a writer, artist, and a musician. Create a multimedia presentation combining her words, images, and music.

2. Using letters written by Hildegard, create a readers' theater production about life in Europe during the 12th century.

Primary Sources

Hildegard of Bingen. *Correspondence.* New York: Oxford University Press, 1998. English translation reproduced electronically by NetLibrary.

Hildegard of Bingen. *The Letters of Hildegard of Bingen.* Vol. 1. Trans. by Joseph L. Baird and Radd K. Ehrman. Oxford: Oxford University Press, 1998. Contains 90 letters Hildegard addressed to bishops, archbishops, and popes.

Hildegard of Bingen. *The Letters of Hildegard of Bingen.* Vol. II. Trans. by Joseph L. Baird and Radd K. Ehrman. Oxford: Oxford University Press, 1998. Contains more than 100 letters Hildegard addressed to abbots, abbesses, and other clergy.

Hildegard of Bingen. *The Letters of Hildegard of Bingen.* Vol. III. Trans. by Joseph L. Baird and Radd K. Ehrman. Oxford: Oxford University Press, 1998. Contains more than 100 letters Hildegard addressed to nonclergy at all levels of society.

Larrington, Caro. *Women and Writing in Early and Medieval Europe.* London: Routledge, 1995. Translations spanning 1,000 years of women writing.

Thiebaux, Marcelle, ed. *The Writings of Medieval Women,* 2nd ed. New York: Garland Library of Medieval Literature, 1994. Includes translations from more than 30 medieval women, including Hildegard.

Secondary Sources

Classen, Albrecht. *The Power of a Woman's Voice in Medieval and Early Modern Literatures: New Approaches to German and European Women Writers and to Violence Against Women . . . of Medieval and Early Modern Culture.* Berlin: Hubert and Company, 2007. Two chapters deal with the work of Hildegard.

Dronke, Peter. *Women Writers of the Middle Ages: A Critical Study of Texts from Perpetua to Marguerite Porete.* Cambridge: University of Cambridge, 1984. Contains two chapters on Hildegard in addition to translations of excerpts of her work.

Evan, Gillian Rosemary. *Fifty Key Medieval Thinkers.* London: Routledge, 2002. Contains chapters on 50 influential medieval intellectuals from all walks of life, including Hildegard of Bingen.

Newman, Barbara, ed. *Voice of the Living Light: Hildegard of Bingen and Her World.* Berkeley: University of California Press, 1998. Collection of scholarly essays on the life and works of Hildegard. Looks at why the pope permitted her to write theological books, to preach openly, and to write on natural sciences.

Petroff, Elizabeth Alvilda. *Medieval Women's Visionary Literature.* New York: Oxford University Press, 1986. Includes translations from Hildegard's *Scivias* and an analysis.

World Wide Web

Feminae: Medieval Women and Gender Index. http://www.haverford.edu/library/reference/mschaus/mfi/mfi.html. Extensive bibliographic index of articles, resources, and journals on medieval women.

Hildegard of Bingen: A Working Group for the Promotion of the Tradition of Hildegard. http://hildegard.org. The site has links to a great deal of information about Hildegard and to the abbey at Bingen and other sites important in her life. Some information in German.

Monastic Matrix: A Scholarly Resource for the Study of Women's Religious Communities 400–1600 C.E. http://monasticmatrix.org/. Contains both primary and secondary sources, digitalized images, a list of monastic communities, and links to other Internet sites.

Multimedia Sources

A Feather on the Breath of God: Sequences and Hymns by Abbess Hildegard of Bingen. Sound recording. London: Hyperion, 1986. Christopher Page conducts Latin Gothic Voices in performance of eight of Hildegard of Bingen's hymns.

Hildegard von Bingen in Portrait. Video. England: Opus Arte, 2003. Two videos, 250 minutes. Includes a performance of Hildegard's musical composition *Ordo Vitutum,* a BBC dramatization of her life, and two other programs concerning her life and work.

Hildegard of Bingen. 2002. Insight Media. 49 minutes. Reenactments of Hildegard's life and a tour of the abbey she founded.

Music and Visions of Hildegard von Bingen. Sound recording. Arles: Harmonica Mundi France, 2004. Selections in Latin from Hildegard's musical compositions.

Pioneers of the Spirit. 2002. DVD. Vision Video. 55 minutes each. Set of seven disks, with the fourth one about Hildegard.

Symphonia Armonie Celestium Revelationum. Sound recording. Bloomington, IN: Focus, 1991. Recording of selected hymns, psalms, and other music by Hildegard performed by musicians of the Early Music Institute.

58. Suppression of Heretics (c. 1150–1480)

Heretics were nothing new in the Catholic Church in the 12th century, but the church's attention to their activities took on a different character around this time. Heresy is belief in a doctrine that is not in harmony with established church ideology. Even from its inception, the church faced conflict over interpretations of scripture and consistency of doctrine which led to the formation of statements such as the Apostle's Creed and the Nicene Creed. Groups with divergent ideas met to discuss and decide issues such as whether Christ had both divine and human natures (Council of Chalcedon, 451) and how to calculate the date of Easter (Synod of Whitby, 664). By 1150, however, the church had firmly established doctrine and believed in its own infallibility. Also by this time, Aristotle and philosophy had been reintroduced to the West and the 12th century renaissance was underway, both leading to old questions reasserting themselves and new questions being asked. Departure from sanctioned doctrine became more dangerous to church authority and required grave, direct action.

Another important reason for the rise in the persecution of heretics was the change that occurred in church administration in the 12th century. Civil law and canon law were codified during the 1100s. Civil law also provided a model of judge-centered procedures adopted in church courts. More and more clerics received training in law that emphasized royal and papal absolutism. From 1150 to 1300, almost every pope had been trained in canonical law. As a result, their emphasis was on the administrative and legal aspects of the papacy more than the theological and spiritual components.

Free-thinking individuals, such as the monk Peter Abelard, were sometimes charged with heresy, but were generally allowed to do penance and return to their lives. Only those who refused to recant were tortured or killed. However, around 1140, the church began to encourage the persecution of groups of dissenters. The Cathars, Waldensians, Lollards, Hussites, and other groups were subjected to all the fury and violence the church could muster against them, fully endorsed by the Fourth Lateran Council (1215) under Pope Innocent III, who promised those who exterminated heretics that they would receive all the indulgences and forgiveness granted to those who fought the infidels in the Holy Land. In 1233, Pope Gregory IX established the Papal Inquisition that authorized monks to conduct inquests into heresy. Pope Innocent IV later formally approved the use of torture in heresy trials. Monarchs adopted the persecution techniques of the church to confiscate land and property and to keep minorities from threatening their power.

TERM PAPER SUGGESTIONS

1. How did the growth of towns and cities influence the growth of religious sects that rebelled against orthodox church doctrine?

2. Compare two or more of the following groups that were considered heretical by the medieval church: Cathars (Albigensians), Waldensians, Lollards, or Hussites. What unorthodox beliefs did they hold? Why did the church consider them dangerous? How did the church misrepresent the beliefs of the sects?

3. Discuss the relationship between the growth of literacy and of medieval universities and the rise in unorthodox religious sects.

4. Examine the position of women in the Catharist movement. What was the medieval church's reaction to the Catharist attitude toward women?

5. Some of the Christian sects that formed in the Middle Ages translated the Bible into vernacular languages. Why did church authorities consider this to be heresy? How does this position establish a link between literacy and heresy? What social class was the most likely to be accused of such heresy?

ALTERNATIVE TERM PAPER SUGGESTIONS

1. Create a large graphic organizer or a multimedia presentation that compares the basic orthodox tenets of the Catholic faith in the Middle Ages to the doctrines of two or more of the major heretical sects.

2. Create a mock trial of a member of one of the major heretical sects of the Middle Ages. One person should be the clerical judge asking questions and another the defendant.

3. Assuming the persona of a member of one of the heretical sects, create a series of diary entries revealing your exposure and reactions to the new teachings, how local authorities react to the new sect, and how the group is persecuted.

Primary Sources

The Canons of the Fourth Lateran Council, 1215. The Medieval Sourcebook. http://www.fordham.edu/halsall/basis/lateran4.html. Full translation.

Edwards, Peter, ed. *Heresy and Authority in Medieval Europe.* Philadelphia: University of Pennsylvania Press, 1980. Includes secular and church documents related to heresy from the early days of the church up through the late 15th century.

Fudge, Thomas A., ed. *The Crusade Against Heretics in Bohemia, 1418–1437: Sources and Documents for the Hussite Crusades.* Burlington, VT: Ashgate Publishing, 2002. Collection of primary documents relating to the Hussites and their persecution.

Guidonis, Bernardua, Bishop of Lodeve. *The Inquisitor's Guide: A Manual on Heretics.* Welwyn, UK: Ravenhall, 2006. Bernardua served as Inquisitor of Toulouse against the Albigenses from 1307–1323.

Wakefield, Walter Leggett, and Evans, Austin Patterson, eds. *Heresies of the High Middle Ages.* New York: Columbia University Press, 1991. Translations of a large number of documents related to the prominent heresies by both their adherents and persecutors.

Secondary Sources

Ames, Christine Caldwell. *Righteous Persecution: Inquisition, Dominicans, and Christianity in the Middle Ages.* Philadelphia: University of Pennsylvania Press, 2008. Examines how members of a holy order, particularly the Dominicans, became involved in the persecution of heretics. Extensive bibliography.

Arnold, John H. *Inquisition and Power: Catharism and the Confessing Subject in Medieval Languedoc.* Philadelphia: University of Pennsylvania Press, 2001. Scholarly study of the transcripts of Inquisition trials of the Cathars, recorded by the church; looks at the nature of power revealed in those documents.

Audisio, Gabrielle. *The Waldensian Dissent: Persecution and Survival, c.1170–c.1570.* Trans. by Claire Davidson. Cambridge: Cambridge University Press, 1999. Traces the Waldensian sect from its inception in the 12th century through the 16th century.

Biller, Peter, and Hudson, Anne. *Heresy and Literacy, 1000–1530.* Cambridge: Cambridge University Press, 1996. This collection of essays explores the relationship between the rise of literacy and the growth of unorthodox sects.

Hunter, Ian, and Laursen, John Christian, eds. *Heresy in Transition: Transforming Ideas of Heresy in Medieval and Early Modern Europe.* Burlington, VT: Ashgate Publishing, 2005. A collection of essays on many aspects of medieval heretical sects.

Lambert, Malcom. *Medieval Heresy: Popular Movements from the Gregorian Reform to the Reformation.* Oxford: Blackwell Publishers, 1988. Chapters include such topics as the revival of heresy in the 11th century, the Cathars, the Waldensians, and the counterattack of Popes Innocent III and IV.

Lansing, Carol. *Power & Purity: Cathar Heresy in Medieval Italy.* Oxford: Oxford University Press, 1998. Lansing describes the Cathar life, political beliefs, religious beliefs, and how they came to be considered heretics.

Waugh, Scott L., and Diehl, Peter, eds. *Christendom and its Discontents: Exclusion, Persecution, and Rebellion, 1000–1500.* Cambridge: Cambridge University Press, 1996. A collection of essays on medieval heretics, on women accused of heresy, and on the persecution of non-Christian minorities.

World Wide Web

The Languedoc-Roussillon. http://www.midi-france.info/. A general information site about the Languedoc region of France. A number of articles and images from the medieval age are available, including information on Pope Innocent III, the Cathars, the Albigensian Crusade, and sites that were important in the crusade.

The Medieval Sourcebook. http://www.fordham.edu/halsall/sbook1s.html. The section called "High Medieval Church Life" contains a number of translated documents dealing with heresies.

Multimedia Sources

The Fires of Faith: Dissidents and the Church. 2000. DVD. BBC Production. 50 minutes. The video presents church reactions to conflicts of faith within the Christian community.

History's Mysteries: The Inquisition. 2005. DVD. The History Channel. 50 minutes. Traces the history of the crusade against heresy from Pope Gregory IX's establishment of the court of inquisition in 1231 to the end of the Middle Ages.

Kill Them All: Christian Crusaders Against Christian Heresy. 2006. DVD. Insight Media. 60 minutes. Tells the story of the Catholic Church's attempt to obliterate any variations in religious practice and belief during the Middle Ages.

59. Plantagenet Rule in England Begins (1154)

At the death of Henry I (r. 1100–1135), whose only son had died at a young age, English nobles revived the Germanic principle of the election of kings for two reasons: they did not want to accept Henry's daughter Matilda as their queen, and they were concerned about the growth of royal power. The barons chose Henry's nephew and the Conqueror's grandson, Stephen of Blois. Stephen I's reign from 1135–1154 was twenty years of internal turmoil involving fighting among English barons who were trying to increase their own power at the monarchy's expense. Stephen's reign also faced serious challenges from Matilda, who was actually able to capture Stephen and rule for a short time in 1141, and from Matilda's son Henry of Anjou. Under the Treaty of Westminster in 1153, Stephen agreed to name Henry his successor, which happened when Stephen died the next year. Thus Henry II (r. 1154–1189) became the first of the Plantagenet (Angevin) kings who were to rule until 1400. The name Plantagenet originated as a nickname for Geoffrey V of Anjou, Henry's grandfather, who had a fondness for wearing in his helmet a sprig of the common broom plant (*planta genista* in Latin). The name was not applied to the dynasty until 1448 when it was assumed by Richard of York. Henry II, as Duke of Normandy and Count of Anjou (source of the Angevin name), was already one of Europe's most powerful men, and his marriage to Eleanor of Aquitaine increased his holdings on the continent.

The Plantagenet era witnessed remarkable changes in England. Henry II came to power just at the right time for England to take advantage of the twelfth-century Renaissance, a period of intellectual and social growth. Laws were codified and the legal system reformed and stabilized, and an efficient administrative bureaucracy developed. Towns were emerging rapidly and altering the feudal relationship between lords and tenants. Aristotle's work became available to Western philosophers for the first time, influencing thinking in theology, education, government, and individual behavior. Universities, which removed higher learning from the monasteries and provided a more secular education, multiplied. Enormous changes occurred in the relationship between church and state. Wars were fought in the Holy Land and on the continent, but the system of *scutage,* paying the king to be released from the feudal duty of military service, changed the nature of the army. The Hundred Years War, the conquest of Wales, the development of Parliament, famine, the Magna Carta, and the Black Death all occurred during Plantagenet rule.

In the midst of these daunting cultural changes, the Plantagenets were able to maintain and strengthen their royal power until the abdication of Richard II (r. 1377–1399) resulting from Henry Bolingbrook's (Henry VI, r. 1399–1413) rebellion. Henry was a member of the House of Lancaster, which was related to the Plantagenets, but historians see his rise to the throne as the end of the Plantagenet dynasty.

TERM PAPER SUGGESTIONS

1. In spite of political and social turmoil, the Plantagenet kings were able to build a national monarchy. Explain how the kings of England were able to do this while the German monarchy fell apart. What kept England from falling into the feudal turmoil of the continental states?

2. Chose two of the Plantagenet kings and compare and contrast their theories and practices of kingship.

3. Compare the Justinian law accepted on the European continent with the Germanic law accepted in England. Why did the two systems develop in the 12th century? How did the systems influence the later governments of England and Europe?

4. Why were the English barons who had supported Stephen against the Plantagenets so eager to accept Henry II as their new king?

5. Henry II instituted a governmental accounting system and hired an exchequer. How did the system work? What were the exchequer's duties? How did the exchequer help to solidify royal power?

6. Under the Angevin (Plantagenet) monarchs, what was the source of conflict between the kings and the Church? What major conflicts occurred and how were they resolved? By the end of this period, which side was closest to achieving its goals?

7. Identify the legal and administrative arrangements of Henry II and explain why they have earned him the title, "father of common law."

ALTERNATIVE TERM PAPER SUGGESTIONS

1. Assume you are the emissary who must work out the marriage arrangements between Henry II and Eleanor of Aquitaine. Prepare the speeches you would give to each to convince them their marriage would be advantageous for both of them.

2. Create a multimedia presentation that could serve as a tutorial on the turmoil and triumphs of the Plantagenet kings. Include images of the rulers and other important people, art and architecture of the period, documents, quotations from primary sources, and music from the time.

Primary Sources

FitzNigel, Richard. *Dialogus de Scaccari and Constitutio Domus Regis (The Dialogue of the Exchequer and The Establishment of the Royal Household*. Trans. by Emilie Amt. Oxford: Oxford University Press, 2007. The two volumes in this translation give insight into the workings of the royal court during Henry II's reign. The first is a practical handbook for carrying out the work of tax collection and led to the recording of what became known as pipe rolls. The second describes the duties of and payments to the members of the royal household whose positions were to take care of the king's personal needs. Introductions and notes accompany each text.

Gerald of Wales. *The Journey Through Wales and The Description of Wales.* London: Penguin Classics. Trans. by Louis Thorpe, ed. by Betty Radice. Translations of the work of Gerald, Archdeacon of Brecon during the reign of Henry II, accompanied by an extensive introduction and commentary.

Henry of Huntingdon. *Henry, Archdeacon of Huntington: Historia Anglorum.* Trans. and ed. by Diana Greenway. New York: Oxford University Press, 2009. New facing-page translation of Henry's history and extensive notes.

John of Worcester. *The Chronicle of John of Worcester, Volume III: The Annals from 1067 to 1140 with The Gloucester Interpolations and The Continuation to 1141.* Edited with a facing-page translation by P. McGurk. Oxford: Oxford University Press, 1998. Although Worcester's *Chronicle* stops in the reign of Stephen, it provides valuable insight into the political and social condition of England shortly before Plantagenet rule began.

William of Newburgh. *William of Newburgh: The History of English Affairs, Books I and II.* Trans. by P. G. Walsh and M. J. Kennedy. Written at the close of the 12th century, William's history covers England from 1066–1198.

Secondary Sources

Aurell, Martin. *The Plantagenet Empire 1154–1224.* Trans. by David Crouch. Harlow, UK: Longman, 2007. Aurell's thorough history of the triumphs and failures of the Plantagenet dynasty translated into English.

Bartlett, Robert. *England under the Norman and Angevin Kings, 1075–1255.* Oxford: Clarendon Press, 2002. Bartlett considers the church, state, and common people in England during two centuries. Includes details of the everyday lives of each group.

Bingham, Caroline. *The Crowned Lions: The Early Plantagenet Kings.* Totowa, NJ: Rowman & Littlefield, 1978. Detailed study of Henry I, Richard I, and John.

Clancy, M. T. *England and Its Rulers, 1066–1272: With an Epilogue on Edward I (1272–1307).* Oxford: Blackwell Publishers, 1998. Covers topics such as the monarchs' relationships with European countries, the British Isles, the church, and the law.

Gillingham, John. *The Angevin Empire,* 2nd ed. Oxford: Oxford University Press, 2001. Considers the question of whether the distinct English and French territories ruled by the Angevin dynasty were really an empire.

Kennedy, Ruth, and Meecham-Jones, Simon, eds. *Writers of the Reign of Henry II: Twelve Essays.* New York: Palgrave Macmillan, 2006. A collection of literary essays about the chief writers of the early Plantagenet period.

Poole, Austin Lane. *From Domesday Book to Magna Carta 1087–1216.* Oxford: Oxford University Press, 1993. Using the two landmark documents of medieval England as end pieces, Poole discusses England as a feudal, rural state at the beginning of the period and charts its progress in social, political, and religious culture by 1216.

Prestwich, Michael. *Plantagenet England 1225–1360.* Oxford: Oxford University Press, 2007. Divided into three sections, Introductory, Politics and War, and Society and People, this book provided a comprehensive analysis of the events during the Plantagenet dynasty.

World Wide Web

British History: The Middle Ages. http://www.bbc.co.uk/history/british/middle_ages/. Maintained by the British Broadcasting Corporation, this site has articles about Plantagenet kings, images, a timeline, and articles by noted historians.

De Re Militari: The Society for Medieval Military History. http://www.deremilitari.org/. Includes articles on all aspects of medieval military operations, including Plantagenet battles on the continent, the Holy Land, and the British Isles. Provides extensive bibliography of related materials. Also has some primary sources.

English Monarchs. http://www.englishmonarchs.co.uk/. Includes biographies, family trees, images, and information about the reigns and influential individuals who were not monarchs.

Multimedia Sources

The History of Britain. 2002. DVD set. Arts and Entertainment Network. One-hour for each program. Set contains three programs about the Plantagenet period of English history: "Conquest!: (circa 1000–1087)," " Dynasty: (circa 1087–1216)," and "Nations: (circa 1216–1348)."

The Kings and Queens of England–The Middle Ages–1216 to 1471. 2005. DVD. Cromwell Productions. 50 minutes. Historical portraits of each of England's kings in the late Middle Ages.

The Kings and Queens of England–The Normans and the Angevins–1066 to 1216. 2005. DVD. Cromwell Productions. 50 minutes. Historical portraits of each of England's Angevin kings.

Medieval Realms: Britain from 1066–1500. No date. CD-ROM. Films for the Humanities and Sciences. Multimedia collection of original material from sources in the British Library; includes: literature, travel narratives, illuminated manuscripts, writs, charters, wills, music, maps, and deeds, along with images of buildings and artifacts.

60. Thomas Becket Becomes Archbishop of Canterbury (1162)

Thomas Becket, the son of an impoverished knight, joined the household of Theobald, archibishop of Canterbury, at the age of 24. Theobald sent Thomas to study canon law in France, and when he returned to England he made him archdeacon of Canterbury. A serious and conscientious young man when it came to his duties, Becket could also be extravagant and ostentatious. Theobald thought Thomas would be capable and at ease with court life, so he recommended him to Henry II as chancellor in the court. Theobald's hope that Becket would be a voice for the church in court did not occur, however. Becket took his responsibilities as chancellor just as gravely as he had his duties as archdeacon. He was Henry II's good friend and advisor, and he made recommendations that were in Henry's interests. Becket's skills as a diplomat, administrator, and advisor made him one of the most powerful and respected men in England. When Archbishop Theobald died, Henry seized the opportunity to appoint Becket to the position, hoping the new archbishop would advance his plans to weaken the church's power. Again, Becket surprised his mentor. As the leader of the church, Becket made decisions based on the church's interests. Henry intended to place clerics who had committed secular crimes under the authority of secular courts when he enacted the *Constitutions of Clarendon* in 1164. Becket was so strong in his opposition that he was forced to take flight to France. A few years later, Henry named his own son as the new archbishop of York, causing division in the church.

By 1170, Becket had returned to his duties at Canterbury, but was still an irritant to the King. At his court in Normandy, Henry pronounced one night that he would like to be rid of the troublesome bishop. Four of

Henry's knights took the statement as a directive from the king for action, crossed the English Channel, and assassinated Becket on December 29, 1170 as he was performing a mass in the cathedral.

Outrage at Becket's death was immediate and loud throughout Europe. Henry was forced to do public penance; Becket was canonized, and the church maintained its independence in judicial matters. Becket became even more renowned after his death as thousands of pilgrims, including those in Geoffrey Chaucer's *Canterbury Tales,* journeyed to Canterbury and his shrine, reputed to be a site where miracles occurred.

TERM PAPER SUGGESTIONS

1. Today, the disagreement between Becket and Henry II may not seem very important, but significant issues of power were at stake in this controversy. What was at issue for the church and the state? What was to be lost or won personally for each of these men?

2. How does the life of Becket indicate a radical shift in the feudal order of society? Was Becket a loyal and honorable servant of the king? What can be said about Becket's stand on other moral questions of his day?

3. Study *The Becket Leaves* and other primary source accounts of Becket's death. What is the image of Becket in these works? Are they an accurate representation of Becket the man? How did these works increase the image of Becket as a martyr?

4. Henry was a Norman king; Becket was a Saxon. How much do you think their disagreement was a result of their backgrounds and the way each group approached life? Was there an element of revenge in either man's motives?

ALTERNATIVE TERM PAPER SUGGESTIONS

1. With a partner, enact a debate between Henry II and Becket about the Constitutions of Clarendon and why Becket will not support Henry's actions.

2. Prepare at least a 30-minute dramatic presentation from one of the modern plays about Henry II and Becket. Choose either *Murder in the Cathedral* by T. S. Eliot or *Becket* by Jean Jean Anouilh.

Primary Sources

The Constitutions of Clarendon. The Avalon Project of Yale University. http://avalon.law.yale.edu/subject_menus/medieval.asp. Henry's edict placing clerics who committed crimes under civil law.

The Becket Leaves. Trans. by Janet Backhouse and Christopher de Hamil. London: British Library Publishing, 1988. This is a reprinting and translation of an anonymous manuscript completed shortly after Becket's death. Printed in color to show the pages as the artist created them.

Becket, Thomas. *The Correspondence of Thomas Becket, Archbishop of Canterbury.* Edited with a translation by Anne Duggan. London: Oxford University Press, 2001.

Staunton, Michael, ed. *The Lives of Thomas Becket.* Manchester: Manchester University Press, 2001. An invaluable resource on Becket. Includes a wide collection of primary translations of documents related to the events in his life and to Becket personally.

William of Newburgh. *William of Newburgh: The History of English Affairs, Books I and II.* Trans. by P. G. Walsh and M. J. Kennedy. Warminster, UK: Aris & Phillips, 2007. Written at the close of the 12th century, William's history covers England from 1066–1198.

Secondary Sources

Aurell, Martin. *The Plantagenet Empire 1154–1224.* Trans. by David Crouch. Harlow, UK: Longman, 2007. Aurell's thorough history of the triumphs and failures of the Plantagenet dynasty translated into English. Includes a lengthy chapter about Becket.

Barber, Richard. *Henry Plantagenet: A Biography of Henry II of England.* Boydell Press, 2001. Complete biography of Henry, including his relationships with Eleanor of Aquitaine and Becket.

Barlow, Frank. *Thomas Becket.* Berkeley: University of California Press, 1990. Comprehensive biography that relies heavily on primary sources and considers the divergent stories they tell.

Duggan, Anne. *Thomas Becket.* Oxford: Oxford University Press, 2005. Concentrates on the cult of Becket and investigates the man and the myth.

Urry, William. *Thomas Becket.* Stroud, UK: Sutton Publishing, 1999. Urry begins his book in November 1170, only one month before Becket's murder. He discusses the conflict between Henry and Becket, the murder, and the legacy of Becket's death.

World Wide Web

British History: The Middle Ages. http://www.bbc.co.uk/history/british/middle_ages/. Maintained by the British Broadcasting Corporation, this site has articles about Henry II, his disagreement with Becket, timelines, and interactive content.

The Medieval Sourcebook. http://www.fordham.edu/halsall/. Includes a number of documents from Henry II's reign such as the *Constitutions of Clarendon* in the section on Medieval Legal History. The section on English Angevins includes other documents relating to Henry and to Becket.

Sources of British History. http://www.britannia.com/history/docs/document.html. Site provides a great deal of information about British history and this page has primary source documents about Henry II and Becket.

Multimedia Sources

*Becket.*1964. Dir. Peter Glenville. Paramount Film. DVD. 150 minutes. A commercial film based on Jean Anouilh's play and starring Richard Burton as Becket and Peter O'Toole as Henry II.

*The Lion in Winter.*1968. Dir. Anthony Harvey. MGM. DVD. 134 minutes. A commercial film based on John Goldman's play about a Christmas reunion between Henry II and his estranged wife Eleanor of Aquitaine. Stars Peter O'Toole and Katherine Hepburn.

Martyrs. 1999. DVD. Films Media Group. 53 minutes. Examines the concept of martyrdom and the historical context of several Christian martyrs, including Becket.

61. Rule of Saladin and the Ayyubids (1169–1250)

In the 12th century, Islam faced a period of uncertainty. Turkish mercenary soldiers constituted the Islamic standing army in Baghdad, and rival Abbasid nobles plotted against one another for control of the caliphate. The ongoing struggle between Sunni and Shi'a factions of the faith continued, particularly because the powerful nation of Egypt was under Shi'a Fatimid rule. At the end of the century, Islam also saw repeated incursions on their easternmost lands by the Mongols. These internal struggles and external threats exposed Islam to the greatest possibility of defeat by the West that it had faced. Yet, one of the factors that helped to reunify Islam was the First Crusade and the establishment of Latin kingdoms within Islamic lands. Another source of reunification was the rise of powerful generals from Syria.

The greatest of these generals was Saladin, son of Najm al-Din Ayyub, and founder of the Ayyubid dynasty in Egypt. After spending 10 years in the court of the Syrian ruler Nur ad-Din, and accompanying his uncle

Shirkuh on military expeditions against Fatimid Egypt, Saladin had proven himself enough to be given command of the Egyptian city of Alexandria. When the Syrians took control of all Egypt, Saladin was named vizier. In that position, he was able to move against the Fatimid caliph and become governor himself. In 1175, Saladin's army marched into Syria, then ruled by Frankish Christians, took the country, and named himself Malik or king. His mentor, Nur ad-Din, had died a year earlier. When the Christian ruler of the Latin principality of Antioch, Reginald of Chatillon, captured a caravan in which Saladin's sister was traveling, Saladin's forces moved into the Holy Land. At Hattin, the Christian army was defeated, and Saladin, who was usually merciful to the defeated, had all the soldiers killed.

Saladin then moved on to a victory in Jerusalem, where he spared the lives of those who had fought him. Christians had held the city for 88 years, and its loss precipitated the Third Crusade, led ostensibly by three European kings, Richard I of England, Philip Augustus of France, and Frederick Barbarossa of Germany. Barbarossa died on route, and Philip Augustus was interested in returning home more than in fighting Muslims, so Richard the Lionheart emerged as the leader. The resulting battles between Richard and Saladin did much to make the men respect one another and make both legendary heroes of their cultures, but did not bring about a change in the political situation. On September 2, 1192, Saladin and Richard signed a peace treaty which left things very much as they had been before the Crusade. Richard returned to England, and Saladin continued to rule Egypt, Syria, and Palestine until his death the next year. His son, Al-Aziz Uthman followed him as emir.

TERM PAPER SUGGESTIONS

1. Compare the battle strategies and military tactics of Saladin and Richard the Lionheart. Which was the greater general? Why?

2. Saladin is considered one of Islam's greatest heroes, not only because he was a great warrior, but for other things he did. Are Saladin's military exploits or his generosity and kindness the greater of his accomplishments? What Islamic precepts did Saladin live by?

3. Compare and contrast the picture of Saladin from one of the Arabic primary sources and a Christian primary source.

ALTERNATIVE TERM PAPER SUGGESTIONS

1. With a partner, write and present a dialogue between Richard the Lionheart and Saladin as they work out the truce that ended the Third Crusade. Take care to refer to particular clauses of the truce.

2. In a group of three or four, create a readers' theater production from primary sources about the Third Crusade.

3. Create a series of maps showing the military campaigns of Saladin and the territories he conquered.

Primary Sources

Baha' al-Din Ibn Shaddad. *The Rare and Excellent History of Saladin.* Trans. by D. S. Richards. Burlington, VT: Ashgate Publishing, 2002. Biography of Saladin written by a close companion and judge of the army during the last years of Saladin's life.

Gabrieli, Fanncesco., ed. *Arab Historians of the Crusades.* London: Routledge & Kegan Paul, 1969. Contains an extensive section of translations of Arab works about Saladin and the third Crusade.

Imad al-Din. *The Autobiography of al-Imad al Din al Katib al-Isfahani.* Trans. by Dwight F. Reynolds in *Autobiography in the Arabic Literary Tradition.* Berkeley: University of California Press, 2001. Al-Din was Saladin's personal assistant and secretary and his autobiography concentrates on the time he spent with Saladin.

Joinville, Jean de, and Villehardouin, Geoffroy de. *Chronicles of the Crusades.* Trans. by Caroline Smith. London: Penguin Classics, 2009. Although these eye-witness accounts are from later Crusades, they give a great deal of insight into Western beliefs and motives.

Richard of Devizes. *Chronicle.* Trans. by J. A. Giles. Cambridge, OT: In Parentheses Publications, 2000. http://www.yorku.ca/inpar/devizes_giles.pdf. Scholars acknowledge some inaccuracies in English monk Richard's *Chronicle,* but it is especially valuable for his description of the events of Richard the Lionheart's preparation for the Third Crusade.

Secondary Sources

Al-Rahmaan, Abd. *The Book of the Islamic Market Inspector.* Oxford: Oxford University Press, 2000. Very detailed and descriptive account of the professions found in a typical Islamic marketplace. Notable for its perspective on common people rather than on rulers.

Azzam, Abdul Rahman. *Saladin*. New York: Longman, 2009. As much a history of the times as a story of Saladin, this book helps put the man in the context of the political and social upheaval of his times.

Highland, Ann. *The Medieval Warhorse from Byzantium to the Crusades*. Conshohocken, PA: Combined Books, 1996. Discusses ways horses were employed in medieval warfare and their importance in battle, particularly in the Crusades.

Hindley, Geoffrey. *Saladin: Hero of Islam*. Barnsley, UK: Pen and Sword Publishers, 2007. Biography of Saladin and historical study of the times in which he lived.

Imad al-Din. *The Pen and the Sword*. Trans. by Dwight F. Reynolds in *Autobiography in the Arabic Literary Tradition*. Berkeley: University of California Press, 2001. Imad al-Din's biography of Saladin written after Saladin's death. www.escholarship.org.

Maalouf, Amin. *The Crusades through Arab Eyes*. New York: Schocken Books, 1989. The author uses contemporary chronicles and eye-witness accounts to probe the Arab point of view during the Crusades.

Nicholle, David, and Hook, Christa. *The Third Crusade 1191: Richard the Lionheart, Saladin and the Battle for Jerusalem*. Oxford: Osprey Publishing, 2005. An examination of the campaign strategies and battle tactics of the leaders of important battles in the Third Crusade.

Reston, James. *Warriors of God: Richard the Lionheart and Saladin in the Third Crusade*. New York: Anchor Books, 2001. A highly readable account of two of the most outstanding warriors of the Crusades, showing them as complex men, not as legends.

World Wide Web

Crusades-Encyclopedia. http://www.crusades-encyclopedia.com/. A portal that links to an astonishing amount of information on the Crusades; primary sources, encyclopedia articles, secondary sources, women in the Crusades, and bibliographies.

De Re Militari: The Society for Medieval Military History. http://www.dere militari.org/. Includes articles on all aspects of medieval military operations, including the Crusades. Provides extensive bibliography of related materials. Also has some primary sources.

Multimedia Sources

Empires: Holy Warriors. 2005. DVD. National Geographic. 120 minutes. Tells the story of Richard the Lionheart's battle with Saladin over Jerusalem in the Third Crusade. Filmed in the Middle East; uses primary documents.

Islam: Empire of Faith. 2001. DVD. PBS. 180 minutes. Part of the *Empires* series; includes on-location filming, displays of period art and architecture and reinactments. Has a companion Web site: http://www.pbs.org/empires/ islam/index.html.

Warriors: Richard the Lionhearted. 2008. DVD. The Military Channel. 60 minutes. Dramatization of Richard's part in the Third Crusade and his meetings with Saladin.

62. Genghis Khan Establishes the Mongol Empire (1185)

In mid-12th century, Mongol tribes were nomadic groups that traded, fought, and intermarried with one another throughout the vast Asian steppe, but had no centralized government. That began to change around 1185 when a young man called Temujin began his ascent to power and in a few years established the largest empire in land area in history. Temujin joined a Mongol tribe led by Toghril and by 1196 had been chosen as overlord of the tribe.

As overlord, Temujin began a campaign of conquest against rival tribes. At the Battle of the Carts, Temujin defeated the Tanguts and boiled 70 captives alive. In 1201, he defeated the Tatars and slaughtered all the males over three feet tall. Continuing to attack rival tribes, by 1205 Temujin had defeated them all. At a congress of tribes at the Onon River in 1206, Temujin was named Genghis Khan, or universal monarch. From there, he led his forces to conquer the Chinese provinces Xi Xia and Chin. Other conquests included parts of Afghanistan, the land of Bokhara, and Smarkand.

Genghis Khan then turned his attention to his homeland where he built his capital city of Karakorum, developed a written legal code called the *Yassa,* and built a system of roadways to encourage trade. His army, however, under the leadership of his sons and generals, continued to invade and conquer additional lands. Even after the death of Genghis Khan in 1227, his son and the next khan, Ogedai, continued to expand the empire to almost twice the size it had been when Genghis died. Mongol forces eventually attacked and defeated the Abbasid Caliphate in Baghdad.

Genghis Khan's grandson, Mangu, inherited the empire from Ogedai. When Mangu died in 1259, his brother Kublai was named Great Khan of a kingdom that extended from the Pacific to the Black Sea. Kublai completed the conquest of China in 1279 and founded the Yuan dynasty there. Opening the door of China to visitors and to trade, Kublai welcomed the Venetian travelers Marco

Polo and his father to his court where they remained for 17 years. The Mongol Empire, which changed the course of world history, began to decline sometime in the late 13th century, when it was divided into four khanates.

TERM PAPER SUGGESTIONS

1. What methods did the Mongols use to control China? What were the positive and negative effects of the Mongol conquest of China?

2. Compare the law code of Ghengis Khan, the Yassa, to one or more of the following law codes: Justinian Code, the laws of William the Conqueror, the Salic law, or the Russian Pravda.

3. Analyze the treatment of conquered people by the Mongols. Were people assimilated into the Mongol culture? What was the Mongol attitude towards religious differences?

4. More than 30 films produced in several different countries are available about Genghis Khan. Choose at least three films, each from a different country, and analyze the way he is portrayed by the different cultures.

5. Analyze the military strategies and battle tactics utilized by the Mongols. How were they able to defeat armies much greater in size than they?

6. The Mongol Empire changed the course of world history. Evaluate these changes and discuss both positive and negative outcomes for at least two cultures.

ALTERNATIVE TERM PAPER FORMATS

1. Create a series of maps showing the extent of the Mongol Empire before and during Genghis Khan's rule and its division into the four khanates.

2. Create a multimedia presentation about the art, architecture, and culture of the Mongol Empire.

Primary Sources

Carpini, Giovanni Di Plano. *The Story of the Mongols Whom We Call the Tartar–Historia Mongalorum Quo s Nos Tartaros Appellamus: Friar Giovanni Di Plano Carpini's Account of His Embassy to the Court of the Mongol Khan.* Trans. by Erik Hildinger. Boston: Branden Publishing Company, 1996. In the mid-13th century Friar Carpini was sent on a missionary trip to convert the Mongols. This is his record of that journey.

Grigor of Akner. *History of the Nation of Archers (The Mongols).* Cambridge, MA: Harvard University Press, 1954. http://rbedrosian.com/hsrces.html. Translation of a 13th-century manuscript from Armenia.

Sauma, Bar. *The Monk of Kublai Khan: Emperor of China,* or *The History of the Life and Travels of Rabban Sawma, Envoy and Plenipotentiary of the Mongol Khans to the Kings of Europe and Markos Who as Yahbh-Allaha III Became Patriarch of the Nestorian Church.* Trans. by E. A. Wallis Budge. London: The Religious Tract Society, 1928. *Traveling to Jerusalem.* http://chass.colostate-pueblo.edu/history/seminar/ sauma.htm.

Secondary Sources

Alsen, Thomas T. *Commodity and Exchange in the Mongol Empire: A Cultural History of Islamic Textiles.* Cambridge: Cambridge University Press, 1997. Considers the economic and social importance of textiles created by Muslim weavers transported to China in the 13th century.

Behnke, Alison. *The Conquest of Genghis Khan.* Minneapolis: Lerner Publishing Group, 2008. After an introductory chapter on Mongol life, the text follows the course of Genghis Khan's victories and concludes with a discussion of the empire after his death. Includes a list of primary sources, a timeline, and a glossary.

Khan, Paul. *Origin of Chingis Khan.* Boston: Cheng and Tsui Company, 1998. An adaptation of the translation of one of the oldest texts in Mongolian *(Yuan Ch'oa Pi Shih),* written shortly after the death of Ghengis Khan.

Lane, George. *Genghis Khan and Mongol Rule.* Westport, CT: Greenwood Publishing, 2004. Tells the Mongol story from the rise of Genghis Khan to the end of the 14th century. Includes 21 primary documents and 15 biographies of notable Mongols.

Riasanovsky, Val. *Fundamental Principles of Mongol Law.* Bloomington: Indiana University Publications, 1965. A reprint of a 1937 classic publication on Mongol law.

Saunders, J. J. *The History of the Mongol Conquests.* Philadelphia: University of Pennsylvania Press, 2001. A carefully documented history of the Mongol empire. Includes two appendices, genealogical table, and extensive notes.

Turnbull, Stephe. *Genghis Khan and the Mongol Conquests 1190–1400.* Oxford: Osprey Publishing, 2003. Contains information about the battle strategies, training of horses, and extent of Mongol conquests.

World Wide Web

Asia for Educators. http://www.columbia.edu/itc/eacp/japanworks/mongols. Hosted by Columbia University, this site contains images, multimedia presentations, timelines, maps, primary sources, and articles.

Genghis Khan on the Web. http://www.isidore-of-seville.com/genghis/. Annotated Web directory to information on the great Mongol conqueror Genghis Khan.

Mongolian Culture. http://www.mongolianculture.com/. A wide collection of information on Mongolia, with images, extensive links to history resources, a bibliography, and excerpts from primary sources.

Multimedia Sources

China: Under the Mongols–A.D.1279–1368. 1977. VHS. Insight Media. 18 minutes. Examines the Mongol rule of China and the revolts that brought the empire to an end.

Genghis Khan: Rise of the Conqueror. 2003. DVD. Discovery Channel. 50 minutes. Basic biography of Khan.

Genghis Khan: Terror and Conquest. 2005. DVD. Arts and Entertainment Network. 50 minutes. Made for television and not entirely accurate, but gives a feel for the period.

Genghis Khan: To the Ends of the Earth and Sea. 2008. DVD. Funimation Productions. 136 minutes. Well researched and beautifully filmed. In Japanese with English subtitles.

Horsepower: Harnessed for War. 2009. DVD. Insight Media. 54 minutes. Examines the ways horses have been used in battle and their influence on the nature of warfare; includes the use of horses by the Mongol empire.

Mongol: The Rise of Genghis Khan. 2008. DVD. New Line Home Video. 126 minutes. A commercial film that covers the life of Genghis Khan from 1172 to 1206. In Mongolian with English subtitles.

Mongols: Storm from the East. 2006. DVD. Films Media Group. Four-part series. 50 minutes each. Includes *Birth of an Empire, World Conquerors, Last Khan of Khans,* and *Tartar Crusaders.* Traces the rise of Genghis Khan's empire, the reign of Kubla Khan, and the Western world's reaction to Mongol invaders.

63. Japanese Military Rule Begins (1185)

During the Heian period (c. 600–1185), Japan had attempted unsuccessfully to establish a centralized pattern of landholding. Instead, military families were able to expand their holdings and assemble well-trained armies of samurai. The word *samurai* originally meant "those who serve" and designated those who served as palace guards. Later, samurai was applied to the class of aristocratic warriors. When the royal succession was contested in 1156, both contenders turned to military families to aid their cause. Civil war between the Genji (Minamoto) and Heike (Taira) troops erupted, ending with a Heike victory. Kiyomori, the Heike leader, arranged a marriage between his daughter and the emperor. When she bore a son, Kiyomori proclaimed himself heir to the emperor.

As emperor, Kiyomori proved unpopular because of popular disapproval of the way he gained the throne and because of his ruthlessness. Genji forces rebelled against him, led by the sons of the man he had defeated earlier. In 1185, the Taira forces were defeated and a military administration was set up in Kamkura. The emperor remained on the throne, but the real power in the country was the Genji leader, who was given the title of Shogun (military leader).

In 1333, the Kamakura shogunate was replaced by rival samurai, the Ashikaga family, which moved the capital back to the city of Kyoto. Centralized government weakened under the Ashikaga, since local barons, *daimyo*, ruled provinces with dictatorial power and often fought against one another for land. The Ashikaga shogunate remained in power until 1600.

TERM PAPER SUGGESTIONS

1. Compare the feudal structures of medieval Japan with that of Western Europe in the 11th and 12th centuries. Consider political organization, bonds of loyalty, and the significance of religion in each society.

2. Compare Japan during the classical period (c. 600–1185) with medieval Japan under military rule.

3. How did samurai values developed during the medieval ages influence the Japanese cultural tradition?

4. Compare the emperor of Japan during the medieval period with the French king during the 11th and 12th century. What were their views on the monarchy? What kinds of powers were entailed in the position? What limitations were placed on their power?

5. Why did the practice of Zen Buddhism achieve popularity among the warriors of medieval Japan? What teachings were compatible with the warriors' life style and values? How was Zen Buddhism a religion of paradox in Japan?

6. How does the traditional Noh drama of the medieval period reflect the values of the culture? What is the importance of gesture and posture in the plays?

7. What was the position of women in medieval Japan? What factors most influenced their status in society?

8. Japan repulsed two Mongol invasions in the 13th century. What factors made this possible? What were the effects of the invasion attempts on the shogunate?

ALTERNATIVE TERM PAPER SUGGESTIONS

1. Discipline and meditation were important parts of the practice of Zen Buddhism. Prepare a multimedia presentation on Zen Buddhism which incorporates traditional Japanese music. Also demonstrate the tea ceremony ritual and explain its religious significance.

2. Prepare a multimedia presentation on the weapons, armor, and military strategies of the medieval samurai warrior. Concentrate your presentation on the period before 1600 when the Tokugawa period began and a number of traditions changed.

Primary Sources

DeBary, William Theodore, et al., eds. *Sources of Japanese Tradition, Volume One: From Earliest Times to 1600,* 2nd ed. New York: Columbia University Press, 2002. Documents included from literature, personal writing, and government until the 17th century. Each section is accompanied by an introductory commentary by one of the editors.

McCullough, Helen Craig, ed. and trans. *The Taiheiki: A Chronicle of Medieval Japan.* New York: Columbia University Press, 1959. A work of several authors, this chronicle is a contemporary account of events of the 13th and early 14th centuries in Japan.

Secondary Sources

Deal, William E. *Handbook to Life in Medieval and Early Modern Japan.* Oxford: Oxford University Press, 2006. Comprehensive resource on topics from everyday life and art, to warfare and geography.

Friday, Karl F. *Samurai, Warfare and the State in Early Medieval Japan.* New York: Routledge, 2001. Chapters on the culture, meaning, organization, tools, and science of medieval Japanese warfare.

Oyler, Elizabeth. *Swords, Oaths, and Prophetic Visions: Authoring Warrior Rule in Medieval Japan.* Honolulu: University of Hawaii Press, 2006. Oyler examines several medieval Japanese texts and their treatment of the civil war that led to shogunate rule in the nation.

Turnbull, Stephen. *The Warriors of Medieval Japan.* Oxford: Osprey Publishing, 2005. Discusses four types of warriors, including samurai, found in medieval Japan.

Yamamura, Kozo, ed. *The Cambridge History of Japan, Vol. 3: Medieval Japan.* Cambridge: Cambridge University Press, 1990. Contains 13 chapters, each written by a medieval scholar. Topics cover a wide range.

World Wide Web

About Japan: A Teachers Resource. http://aboutjapan.japansociety.org. This site is maintained by the Japan Society of New York and includes essays, lesson plans, historical documents, maps, and images.

Asia for Educators. http://www.columbia.edu/itc/eacp/japanworks/. Hosted by Columbia University, this site contains images, multimedia presentations, timelines, maps, primary sources, and articles.

Asian Art Collection at Princeton University. http://etcweb.princeton.edu/asianart/index.isp. An online exhibit with commentary on the 6,000 pieces of Asian art housed in the Princeton University Art Museum. One collection from Japan is called the "Age of Military Rule: Cycles of Restoration and Destruction."

Multimedia Sources

Acting Techniques of the Noh Theater of Japan. 1980. DVD. Insight Media. 30 minutes. A modern actor in Noh theatre demonstrates the historic postures and gestures of Noh.

China and Japan: 1279–1600. 1985. DVD. Insight Media. 26 minutes. Discusses Japanese history from the Kamakura through the Ashikaga shogunates.

Eastern Empires. 2001. DVD. Kultur Films. 50 minutes. Part of the *Story of Civilization Series.* Explores ancient and medieval Chinese and Japanese empires. Includes a segment on medieval military rule in Japan. Visits to ancient sites, reenactments, period images, and expert interviews.

Horsepower: Harnessed for War. 2009. DVD. Insight Media. 54 minutes. Examines the ways horses have been used in battle and their influence on the nature of warfare; includes the use of horses by Japanese samurai.

The Samurai. No date. DVD. The History Channel. 100 minutes. Historians discuss samurai training and the Bushido rituals. Filming on location; uses demonstrations of fighting skills expected of samurai.

Samurai Warrior. 2002. DVD. The History Channel. 50 minutes. Recounts how the samurai rose from the medieval feudal culture. Also traces samurai influences to the present.

64. City-State of Benin Rises to Power (c. 1200)

The kingdom of Benin and its capital city, also Benin, rose to power in the 13th century in what is today southern Nigeria. A group of autonomous villages, each surrounded by a moat, seems to have voluntarily formed an alliance under the leadership of Igodo, the *oba,* or king of Benin around 900. Igodo was a member of the Osigo dynasty that ruled until the late 12th century. By 1200, Edo kings were ruling, and the city had developed into a major trading, political, and religious center for the Edo people of the West African region. Benin confirms that significant urbanization occurred in subSaharan Africa during the Middle Ages.

Near the mouth of the Niger River, the city and surrounding kingdom were ideally situated for trade both by land and by sea. The aristocratic families grew wealthy from trade with the Sudanese cultures to the north. Palm oil, ivory, pepper, and beautifully designed cotton fabrics were exported. Later, Benin engaged in the slave trade. As early as 1500, Benin had entered into trade with the Portuguese.

Archeological study and descriptions by early European travelers reveal the city of Benin to have been carefully planned and constructed. Primary streets were straight and as much as 131 feet wide. Houses were built along side streets with front porches facing the street. The people living in Benin also seem to have been prosperous. The capital was well fortified with a system of moats and earthwork ramparts enclosures. Estimates suggest that the Benin wall enclosed as much as 2,000 square miles of land. Within the larger structure, a rampart more than 60 feet high surrounded Benin city. Ramparts and moats were constructed simultaneously; as the soil was removed from the ditch, it was used to build up the rampart, with the moat inside.

Oba Ewuare the Great (r. c.1440–c.1470) ordered further moats to be built within the city. Nine gates, which provided access to the city, were closed each night. The palace complex, with its living quarters for the king, reception courts, harem, and other royal structures, formed a large part of the city. Ewuare also began a campaign of conquest to increase Benin lands that continued under his successors. The kingdom stopped expanding and halted its slave trade in the mid 1500s, but remained a prosperous center for commerce until the British destroyed the city in the 19th century.

One of the greatest achievements of the people of Benin was their beautiful and sophisticated art works in bronze, ivory, and wood. Benin may have been doing bronze casting as early as 1200, and the works are considered among the finest examples of African art. Bronze bas relief plaques commissioned by the oba and royal court tell much of the history of the people. When the British destroyed the city, they seized more than 1,000 of the Benin bronzes, only about 50 of which have been returned to Nigeria.

TERM PAPER SUGGESTIONS

1. Most of the extant literature from ancient Benin is in the form of folktales. What do these tales reveal about the values and beliefs of the Benin culture?

2. Compare the folktales of Benin to those from another culture.

3. Compare the social and cultural structure of Benin to that of ancient Ghana or Mali.

4. How much responsibility did Benin have for the African slave trade in the 14th–18th centuries?

5. What happened to the Benin bronzes? What are the issues involved in having them returned to Nigeria? Take a position on the issue and support your opinion.

ALTERNATIVE TERM PAPER SUGGESTIONS

1. Benin (Nigerian) folktales are generally short, interesting stories. Prepare a storytelling event for the class using the Benin tales. Your presentation should be at least 20 minutes long, well prepared, and entertaining. You may work with another person for a longer presentation.

2. Create a multimedia presentation on Benin art. Since the people of Benin were also accomplished musicians and designed several instruments, include music in your presentation.

Primary Sources

Dayrell, Elphinstone. *Folk Stories from Southern Nigeria West Africa.* London: Longmans, Green and Co., 1910. http://www.sacred-texts.com/afr/fssn/fsn00.htm. More than 30 folk stories collected in the early 20th century.

Eden, Richard. *Decades of the New World.* Published in 1555. "*English Merchants at the Royal Court of Benin*" http://www.wsu.edu:8080/~wldciv/world_civ_reader/world_civ_reader_2/eden.html.

Eweka, Iro. *Dawn to Dusk: Folktales from Benin.* London: Routledge, 1998. The folktales collected here reveal the ancient Benin values and culture. The book also includes a collection of Benin proverbs in both Edo and English.

Secondary Sources

Falola, Toyin. *Key Events in African History: A Reference Guide.* Westport, CT: Greenwood Press, 2002. Develops 36 key events from African history that resulted in important changes. Includes cross-references, maps, illustrations, and suggestions for additional reading.

Okpewho, Isidore. *Once Upon a Kingdom: Myth, Hegemony, and Identity.* Bloomington: University of Indiana Press, 1998. Okpewho looks at the legacy of the Kingdom of Benin in the stories and legends of modern Africa.

Walthall, Anne. *Servants of the Dynasty: Palace Women in World History.* Berkeley: University of California Press, 2008. A collection of essays about palace women throughout history; includes a chapter about women in the royal harem of Benin and one about royal women and indigo dying in the palaces of Nigeria.

World Wide Web

The Ancient Web.org. http://www.ancientweb.org. This is a commercial site with books for sale, but it also has an abundance of free information about ancient civilizations, including flash essays, interactive maps, timelines, and essays.

Edo Arts and Culture Institute. http://www.edoartsandculture.org/Home.html. Dedicated to the preservation of the culture of ancient Benin, this site has images in a virtual museum, articles on culture, history, and social customs, a timeline, and maps.

Institute for Benin Studies. http://www.greatbenin.org/igodo.html. Images, links, and articles by scholars and from the current press.

Multimedia Sources

Benin: An African Kingdom. 1994. DVD. Films for the Humanities. Five-part series, 15 minutes each. Traces the influences of ancient Benin that have been preserved in the traditions of modern Nigeria. Documentary footage, dances, songs, and art work are presented.

The Glories of Ancient Benin: African Studies. 1997. DVD. Films for the Humanities. 15 minutes. Explores the Museum of Porto-Novo in the former city-state of Benin for insight into cultural, political, and economic life there.

65. Founding of Western Universities (c. 1200)

Institutions for advanced learning were established in Islamic countries in the 8th century and are responsible for the preservation of much classical learning, as well as for advancements in philosophy and the sciences. The exact history of the Western university is somewhat obscure, and several universities vie for the designation of *first*. Education was the prerogative of the church in the early Middle Ages, and almost every monastery had a school for both future clergy and for children of nobility. Tutors, who had received their training at the cathedral schools, were sometimes employed by the wealthy as well. If students at monastic and cathedral schools did not become monks or tutors, they were often employed as scribes, envoys, and administrators of royal business. By the 11th century, students who sought further knowledge than the monastic schools provided were traveling throughout Europe and the Islamic world to study with prestigious teachers. At the same time, Aristotle's work and Greek and Roman classics were finding their way into the hands of scholars.

Originally, students of one master lived together and pooled their resources in what they called *colleges*. Many of the most famous teachers such as Peter Abelard were first affiliated with the cathedral schools. However, as the church began to question the teaching of nontraditional subjects, such as Greek philosophy, sciences, and dialectics, it became more difficult for teachers to pursue new avenues of thought. Universities technically came about when a group of master teachers incorporated themselves into a guild or *universitas*. Universities developed rapidly throughout Europe, with Bologna and Paris being among the first cities to authorize the guilds of learning. In 1200, the king of France chartered the University of Paris in a document that also protected the faculty and students from the townspeople. In 1231, the pope issued a bull that ensured that the universities themselves had the right to control the examinations and conferring of degrees.

The basic curriculum of the universities throughout the Middle Ages consisted of the seven liberal arts, divided into the *trivium;* grammar, rhetoric, and logic; and the *quadrivium;* arithmetic, astronomy, geometry, and music. At the beginning, students had great power in the administration and governance of the university, but as time passed, secular and church authorities passed rules for the curriculum, professor qualifications, admission, and student behaviors. The Middle Ages witnessed the founding of some of the modern world's most respected universities, such as the Universities of Paris, Oxford, Cambridge, and Bologna.

TERM PAPER SUGGESTIONS

1. Universities developed from monastic and cathedral schools that had been the source of education for centuries. How did the founding of these new universities affect the education of women in the Middle Ages?

2. Compare the structure, curriculum, governance, and population of the modern university to that of a medieval university.

3. How did the reintroduction of Aristotelian philosophy affect the university? Why did authorities try to suppress Aristotelian teachings?

4. What was scholasticism? How did this theory influence the educational institutions of the Middle Ages?

5. What were the causes of the introduction of the study of law in medieval universities? How did this development affect society in general?

6. Define the Christian humanist thought that was developed by John of Salisbury in the 12th century. How did this philosophy influence the university and later scholars?

7. Discuss the structure of the medieval university and the effect this structure had on the reception of Aristotelian thought in the Latin West.

8. What were the causes of the 12th-century renaissance? What effect did it have on medieval thinking? What part did the university play in the renaissance?

ALTERNATIVE TERM PAPER SUGGESTIONS

1. Assume that you are a student just entering a major university in 1215. Write a series of letters home to your parents detailing what you are observing and learning about university life.

2. Reenact the trial of Peter Abelard for heresy. One person should take the role of Abelard and another St. Bernard of Clairvaux. What is at stake in this trial? Why is the trial an important landmark in medieval thought? You may present your trial before the class or prepare a video version.

Primary Sources

John of Salisbury. *The Metalogicon of John of Salisbury: A Twelfth-Century Defense of the Verbal and Logical Arts of the Trivium.* Trans. by Daniel D. McGarry. Berkeley: University of California Press, 1955. http://www

.questia.com/read. John of Salisbury's treatise on the educational system and his defense of the study of liberal arts.

Kirshner, Julius, and Morrison, Karl F., eds. *University of Chicago Readings in Western Civilization: 4, Medieval Europe.* Chicago: University of Chicago Press, 1986. Section entitled "Control of Learning" contains several primary documents dealing with the university.

Secondary Sources

Brundage, James A. *The Medieval Origins of the Legal Profession: Canonists, Civilians, and Courts.* Chicago: University of Chicago Press, 2008. Examines the Roman foundation of law, medieval society without lawyers, the revival of the legal profession by universities, and the practice of canon law.

Bullough, Vern L. *Universities, Medicine and Science in the Medieval West.* Aldershot, Hampshire, UK: Variorum, 2004. A collection of essays by Bullough on the development of medicine and science as professions and on how knowledge of these disciplines was transferred.

Cobban, Alan B. *English University Life in the Middle Ages.* Columbus: Ohio State University Press, 1999. Looks at the social and economic lives of students and teachers; discusses methods of teaching and learning and the curriculum.

Grant, Edward. *The Foundations of Modern Science in the Middle Ages: Their Religious, Institutional, and Intellectual Contexts.* Cambridge: Cambridge University Press, 1996. Has a chapter on how science influenced the medieval universities and several chapters on Aristotle and learning.

Jaeger, C. Stephen. *The Envy of Angels: Cathedral Schools and Social Ideals in Medieval Europe, 950–1200.* Philadelphia: University of Pennsylvania Press, 1994. Discusses education from Carolingian France to the 13th century and universities.

Janin, Hunt. *The University in Medieval Life, 1179–1499.* Jefferson, NC: McFarland, 2008. Provides an overview of the university and key figures in the Middle Ages. Traces the development of several medieval institutions. Maps and photographs included.

Kretzmann, Norman, et al. *The Cambridge History of Later Medieval Philosophy: From the Rediscovery of Aristotle to the Disintegration of Scholasticism, 1100–1600.* Cambridge: Cambridge University Press, 1988. A collection of essays on medieval philosophy. Includes essays on Paris and Oxford, scholastic logic, and the teaching of logic.

Rait, Robert S. *Life in the Medieval University.* Charleston, SC: BiblioBazaar, 2007. A facsimile reprint of Rait's 1912 study of the medieval university.

De-Ridder-Symoens, Hilde, ed. *A History of the University in Europe: Volume I, Universities in the Middle Ages.* Cambridge: Cambridge University Press, 1992. Collection of essays on such topics as the structure, management, teachers, and students found in medieval universities.

World Wide Web

Academic Apparel: College and University History. http://www.academicapparel .com/caps/College-University-History.html. Although this is a commercial site, there are several articles on the history of the university, caps and gowns, academic degrees, and academic dress.

The Medieval Sourcebook. http://www.fordham.edu/halsall. The section "Selected Sources: Intellectual Life" contains a number of primary documents about education and universities in the 11th–14th centuries.

Multimedia Sources

The History of Christianity: Universities and Monasteries. 2000. DVD. Insight Media. 30 minutes. Disk 2 in a set of six, this video explores the relationship between Christian monasteries and the establishment of universities.

The Monastics. 1988. VHS. Insight Media. 21 minutes. Discusses the importance of monasteries and convents in the development of universities and features the influence of individuals such as Abelard and Thomas Aquinas.

The Saint and the Scholar: Portrait of Abelard. 2003. DVD. BBC Production. 50 minutes. The story of Peter Abelard whose teaching led to his trial as a heretic.

66. Crusaders Sack Constantinople (1204)

In 1198, Pope Innocent III issued a call for the Fourth Crusade into Egypt, the center of Islamic power at that time. However, the Crusaders never made it to Egypt. As an army of primarily French knights prepared to make its journey, it contracted with Venetian merchants to provide passage on their ships. The Venetians insisted that an alternate route be taken by the army, one that would lead to profits for all who participated. This Crusade would be directed against Constantinople. The pope agreed with the plan, seeing a means to gain authority over the Eastern church and reunify it with the Latin church. The anti-Byzantine predisposition among the soldiers brought them around to the new plan easily. Little thought was given to the facts that the Crusades were instituted as holy wars to regain Jerusalem from Moslem control or that the Byzantines were fellow Christians.

The crusading army first sailed to the Dalmatian city of Zara, which Venice had lost and wanted to regain. In spite of specific orders from the pope not to attack the Christian city, more than 200 ships laden with soldiers entered the port at Zara on November 10, 1202. After a two-week siege, the city surrendered and the Crusaders spent the winter there. In April of 1203, they set sail again, stopping for the conquest of the island of Corfu, and arriving in Constantinople on June 24. After giving the city a chance to surrender, the attack began from both land and sea. The Byzantine capital had withstood five centuries of attacks on its battlements, but in July the Crusaders were able to drive out the emperor and install the prince who had asked for their help. They did not go home, or to Jerusalem. Instead, they wintered in Constantinople where they devised a new plan for the city, one which would install a Latin emperor, remove the Greek patriarch, and divide the wealth among themselves. This time, when they breached the walls on April 13, 1204, the Crusaders began three days of pillaging and killing unlike anything the city had ever seen. The Latin kingdom of Constantinople was formed, and for the next 60 years Latin nobles ruled the city. Some Crusaders remained in Byzantium on land they received as a reward, but most returned to Europe as very wealthy men. Although they had been excommunicated, when the pope received the gift of the Greek church, he rescinded the edict.

Additional Crusades followed, but not as multinational efforts. The church turned most of its crusading efforts into rooting out heretics within Europe itself, calling for the Albigensian Crusade into southern France in 1208, which resulted in another opportunity for French nobles to enrich their own pockets.

TERM PAPER SUGGESTIONS

1. Compare the sacking of Constantinople as recounted in one of the primary sources with that of modern historians, or compare the event as retold by one of the European Crusaders and a Byzantine historian.

2. Assess the internal political situation in Constantinople in 1204. Did the leaders of Byzantium contribute to their own downfall? How?

3. What part did the commercial interests of merchants play in the planning and the results of the Fourth Crusade?

4. Other than the loss of property and lives, what were the results of the Fourth Crusade for the Byzantine Empire?

5. What difficulties did the Crusaders face in transporting their equipment? Vast amounts of arms, horses, and supplies were needed for the Crusades. How did the Crusaders meet the demands of conveying their gear?

6. How much responsibility for the sack of Constantinople should rest on the church? Did the church know how the Crusade would end? Did the church try to stop the actions of the Crusaders? In addition to the letter calling for a Crusade, in what ways did Pope Innocent III participate in the effort?

7. There were no additional multinational Crusades after the Fourth, but their influence continued long after 1204. What effects did the Crusade ideal have on Western world thought and political action?

ALTERNATIVE TERM PAPER SUGGESTIONS

1. Using information from Gunter of Paris's *Hystoria Constantinopolitana,* from Pope Innocent III's call for the Crusade and his "Reprimand of Papal Legate," construct and record a podcast mock interview with a church official concerning the church's involvement in the Fourth Crusade.

2. Assume the persona of a Byzantine Christian who witnesses the sack of Constantinople and its aftermath. Write a series of diary entries about what you see happen.

Primary Sources

Choniates, Nicetas. *O City of Byzantium: Annals of Niketas Choniates.* Detroit: Wayne State University Press, 1984. The story of the sack of Constantinople as witnessed by a Byzantine historian.

De Clari, Robert. *The Conquest of Constantinople.* http://www.deremilitari.org/ RESOURCES/SOURCES/clari.htm. Complete translation of an eyewitness account from de Clari, a knight from Picardy who was part of the Fourth Crusade.

De Villehardouin, Geoffrey. *Memoirs or Chronicle of the Fourth Crusade* and *The Conquest of Constantinople.* Trans. by Frank T. Marzials. London: J. M. Dent, 1908. *Project Gutenburg.* http://www.gutenberg.org/. This is a first-hand account of the Crusade and is also the first prose history to be written in French.

Gunther of Pairis. *Hystoria Constantinopolitana.* Translation in Alfred J. Andrea, *The Capture of Constantinople: The Hystoria Constantinopolitana of Gunther of Pairis.* Philadelphia: University of Pennsylvania Press, 1997.

Gunther's work is his attempt to justify the clergy's participation in the sack of Constantinople in the Fourth Crusade.

Pope Innocent III. "Reprimand of Papal Legate." http://www.fordham.edu/halsall/source/1204innocent.html. The pope's angry letter to the legate after he heard the news of what had happened at Constantinople.

Secondary Sources

Bartlett, W. B. *An Ungodly War: The Sack of Constantinople and the Fourth Crusade.* Salem, MA: The History Press, 2001. Complete history of the Fourth Crusade. Includes extensive notes section and bibliography.

Munro, Dana Carleton. *The Fourth Crusade.* Whitefish, MT: Kessinger Publishing, 2004. A reprint of the classic 1896 University of Pennsylvania publication.

Phillips, Jonathan. *The Fourth Crusade and the Sack of Constantinople.* New York: Viking Penguin, 2004. Complete history beginning with the papal call for the Crusade, through the preparations and the arrival in Constantinople, to the resulting destruction.

Queller, Donald E., and Madden, Thomas F. *The Fourth Crusade: The Conquest of Constantinople.* Philadelphia: University of Pennsylvania Press, 1997. Another complete history of the Fourth Crusade with emphasis on the Byzantine reaction.

World Wide Web

Crusades-Encyclopedia. http://www.crusades-encyclopedia.com/. A portal that links to an astonishing amount of information on the Crusades; primary sources, encyclopedia articles, secondary sources, women in the Crusades, and bibliographies.

De Re Militari: The Society for Medieval Military History. http://www.deremilitari.org/. Includes articles on all aspects of medieval military operations, including the Crusades. Provides extensive bibliography of related materials. Also has some primary sources.

Medieval History Texts in Translation. http://www.leeds.ac.uk/history/weblearning/Medieval HistoryTextCentre/medievalTexts.htm. The University of Leeds has placed several documents from the Crusades online, including a collection related to the Fourth Crusade.

Multimedia Sources

The Crusades: The Holy Wars. 2007. DVD. Kultur Media. 50 minutes. Uses reconstructions and animation to retell the story of the Crusades.

The Sack of Constantinople. 2003. DVD. The Teaching Company. 30 minutes. Number 28 in the series of lectures called *The Era of the Crusades.*

67. Reconquista (1212–1347)

After the Muslim conquest of the Iberian Peninsula in the 8th century, a number of small Christian kingdoms remained in the northern mountain region. In the 11th century, some of these kingdoms began fighting against the Muslims and made small gains in territory. In 1067, the Spanish folk hero Rodrigo Diaz de Vivar (El Cid) was instrumental in a victory over the city of Saragossa. Over the next thirty years, El Cid fell in and out of favor with Spanish kings, and at one time fought for the Muslim kings. With El Cid's leadership in 1085, Toledo was recaptured, encouraging the Christians to continue their efforts. Valencia was captured by El Cid in 1094, and he ruled there as Alfonso VI's governor for the remainder of his life. The Christian successes in battle also laid the groundwork for Pope Urban II's call for the First Crusade to Jerusalem.

Although Christians kept up efforts to recover the lands captured by the Moors, the reconquest was not launched in full until the Battle of Las Navas de Tolosa in 1212, led by Alfonso VIII of Castille. Alfonso and his successors went on to win control of most of Andalusia. James I of Aragon seized Majorca in 1229. Cordoba fell into the hands of Ferdinand III and Alfonso X in 1236, and Cadiz was defeated in 1262. By the end of the 13th century, most of Spain had been wrested from Islamic rule. It was not until 1492, however, that the last Muslims were defeated in Granada and the entire country united under a Christian monarchy.

Islamic caliphates had allowed Jews and Christians to remain in Iberia and practice their religions, although they were subject to higher taxation. In the early years of the Reconquista, Christians continued the policy of religious tolerance. Sephardic Jews numbered well over one million in the late 12th century. A number of Jews rose to important administrative positions in the Iberian Christian government of the 13th and 14th centuries. Enormous pressure, and the economic and political advantages of Christians, influenced a large number of Jews to convert. By the end of the 14th century, however, anti-Semitism was rising, and in 1492 the 200,000 remaining Sephardic Jews were expelled from Spain.

TERM PAPER SUGGESTIONS

1. Compare the legal system of Spain under Islamic and Christian rule. How were religious minorities treated by each government?

2. Compare the position of women in Islamic Spain to their position in Christian Spain after the Reconquest.

3. Eleventh century Reconquista efforts served as an example for Crusades to the Holy Land. Why did the Crusade in Iberia succeed, but those to the Middle East fail?

4. What were the contributions of the Sephardic Jews to the culture of Christian Spain?

5. No one doubts El Cid's duplicity in fighting in both Muslim and Christian armies. Why is his story so attractive? How do you account for his being a national hero of Spain?

6. Analyze the effects of over 200 years of war on the Spanish national character.

7. Moorish rule extended throughout the Iberian Peninsula. How did two countries with two different languages develop there during the 11th and 12th centuries?

8. Compare the idea of kingship held by the Spanish monarchs with that of French or English monarchs.

9. Compare Sephardic folktales to those from another medieval culture.

ALTERNATIVE TERM PAPER SUGGESTIONS

1. Prepare a multimedia presentation on the Sephardic Jews and their artistic and creative contributions to medieval Spain.

2. Research the life of El Cid. Prepare a storytelling presentation to recount the facts and legends that surround him.

3. Prepare a storytelling presentation based on the large body of Sephardic folktales from medieval Spain.

Primary Sources

Alfonso the Emperor. *The Chronicle of Alfonso the Emperor.* Trans. and ed. by Glenn Edward Lipskey. http://libro.uca.edu/lipskey/chronicle.htm. Covers the reign of Alfonso VII, 1126–1157.

Barton, Simon, and Fletcher, Richard, eds. *The World of El Cid: Chronicles of the Spanish Reconquest.* Manchester: Manchester University Press, 2001. Includes translations of four chronicles written in Spain between 1110 and 1150. Three focus on the reigns of Spanish kings, and the fourth is a biography of Rodrigo Diaz, El Cid.

Constable, Olivia Remie. ed. *Medieval Iberia: Readings from Christian, Muslim, and Jewish Sources.* Philadelphia: University of Pennsylvania Press, 1997. Contains English translations of excerpts and entire documents on religious, political, and social issues.

Cuenca. *The Code of Cuenca: Municipal Law on the Twelfth-Century Castilian Frontier.* Trans. by J. F. Powers. Philadelphia: University of Pennsylvania Press, 2000. Translation of the royal charter granted by King Alfonso VII to the town of Cuenca after it was conquered by Christians.

Secondary Sources

Dillard, Heath. *Daughters of the Reconquest: Women in Castilian Town Society, 1100–1300.* Cambridge: Cambridge University Press, 1990. http://libro .uca.edu/dillard/daughters.htm. Using primary documents for his research, Dillard presents information about the variety of women in Spanish towns and discusses how urbanization and the Reconquest influenced their lives.

Gerber, Jane S. *Jews of Spain: A History of the Sephardic Experience.* New York: The Free Press, 1992. One of the most thorough histories of Sephardic Jews available. Begins with early Jewish history and continues until the Renaissance. Includes primary documents, maps, and population tables.

Lay, Stephen. *The Reconquest Kings of Portugal: The Creation of a Medieval Frontier Monarchy.* Hampshire, UK: Palgrave Macmillan, 2009. At the same time when Spain was taking back control from Islamic rulers, Portugal was asserting itself as a nation. This book traces that development.

Nicholl, David, and Mcbride, Angus. *El Cid and the Reconquista 1050–1492.* Oxford: Osprey Publishing, 1988. This short book focuses on the weapons, armor, and military tactics of the Reconquista.

O'Callaghan, Joseph F. *Reconquest and Crusade in Medieval Spain.* Philadelphia: University of Pennsylvania Press, 2002. Examines the Reconquest as an inspiration for and as an endeavor consistent with the papal Crusades to the Middle East. Also explores the rhetoric of the Spanish Crusade.

Reilly, Bernard F. *The Medieval Spains.* Cambridge: Cambridge University Press, 1993. Covers Spanish history from the fall of Rome to 1474. Extensive coverage of the *Reconquista.* Includes lengthy bibliography.

World Wide Web

De Re Militari: The Society for Medieval Military History. http://www.dere militari.org/. Includes articles on all aspects of medieval military operations. Has both primary and secondary sources online on war in medieval Spain. Provides extensive bibliography of related materials.

Internet Medieval Sourcebook. http://www.fordham.edu/halsall/sbook1p.html. Section entitled "Selected Sources: Iberia" has primary source documents from the Reconquista period.

The Library of Iberian Resources Online. http://libro.uca.edu/. Sponsored by The American Academy of Research Historians of Medieval Spain. Provides access to a number of out-of-print texts, essays, and monographs.

Multimedia Sources

Advance of the Reconquest. 2007. DVD. Films for the Humanities and Sciences. 25 minutes. Uses architectural case studies to highlight the growth of Christian influence in Spain. Discusses Fernando III's capture of Cordoba. In Spanish.

Christians, Jews, and Muslims in Medieval Spain. 1979. DVD. Insight Video. 33 minutes. Traces the history of Spain from 711 until the expulsion of the Jews.

The Conquerors: El Cid. 2005. DVD. The History Channel. 50 minutes. Uses reenactments, visits to actual sites, expert interviews, and primary documents to explore the story of El Cid.

El Cantar de Mio Cid. 1980. DVD. Films for the Humanities and Sciences. 60 minutes. Tells the story of El Cid while separating the man from the legend. In Spanish with English subtitles.

El Cid. 1961. Dir. Anthony Mann. DVD. Weinstein Company. 181 minutes. A commercial film starring Charleton Heston and Sophia Loren. Follows the story of El Cid from peacemaker to accused traitor to national hero. Not completely accurate historically, but provides visual context.

La Disgregacion del Islam Andalusi y el Avance Cristiano. 2004. DVD. Films for the Humanities and Sciences. 53 minutes. Traces the course of the reconquest from the death of Almazor, the Battle of Las Navas de Tolosa, and El Cid's involvement, to its conclusion. Dramatizations and maps. In Spanish with English subtitles.

First Steps Toward Reconquest. 2007. DVD. Films for the Humanities and Sciences. 25 minutes. Discusses the 11th-century beginnings of the Reconquest, the importance of the Druero River, and the relationship between Alfonso VI and El Cid. In Spanish.

Islam's Last Stand in Spain. 2007. DVD. Films for the Humanities and Sciences. 25 minutes. Explores the last Islamic military resistance to the Reconquest. Visits sites of the last battles. In Spanish.

The Middle Ages: From Anonymity to Authorship. 2005. DVD. Films for the Humanities and Sciences. 50 minutes. Examines the rise of Spain's national literature by comparing the works of authors in the 13th and 14th centuries and through dramatic readings. In Spanish with English subtitles.

La Peninsula de los cinco (The Peninsula of Five Kingdoms). 2005. DVD. Films for the Humanities and Sciences. 52 minutes. Explores the mix and clashes of cultures in Iberia using maps, reenactments, art, and architecture.

The Spanish Reconquista. 2004. DVD. Films for the Humanities and Sciences. 53 minutes. The film begins with the defeat of Islamic forces in the mountains of northern Spain and traces the return of Christian influence through the Reconquest. Explores how small principalities merged into one nation.

68. Magna Carta (1215)

Signed by King John (1167–1216) at the demands of his barons, the Magna Carta (Great Charter) is one of the most significant human rights documents in history. Although John and later monarchs upheld its provisions with varying degrees of enthusiasm—some ignoring them altogether—the English people, and later American colonists, continued to claim the civil rights outlined in Magna Carta. Primarily a feudal document regarding the responsibilities of a monarch to his subjects, Magna Carta had far greater implications.

Most significantly, Magna Carta placed the king under the same rule of law as his people. Other matters in the charter included the king's authority in church matters, his right to tax and use the royal treasury, and his specific obligations to his subjects. Among other things, the right to a speedy trial by a jury of one's peers, the right to petition, and the use of a grand jury were promised. Originally composed of 63 provisions, or chapters, the document was reissued with some revisions in 1217 and 1225. By the end of the 13th century, Magna Carta was firmly ensconced as the law of the land, and the precedents it set became the basis for English constitutional law.

When English monarch Richard the Lionheart died in 1199, his brother John ascended to the throne. Already unpopular with commoners and nobles, John made several disastrous decisions that further alienated him from those he ruled. His failure to meet financial obligations to Philip II of France caused him to lose much of his inherited French territory. He then instigated an expensive and unsuccessful conflict to regain this land. When he returned to England short of funds, he tried to collect scutage, a fee paid to be excused from military service, from the barons who had not fought with him. When some of the barons rebelled and captured London, John agreed to discuss a charter delineating his powers. Negotiations between the barons, led by the archbishop of Canterbury, Stephen Langton, and John eventually resulted in his signing Magna Carta at Runnymede in 1215. Signed copies of Magna Carta with the king's seal were distributed to every county and city in England and were read to assemblies of all freemen.

King John himself had no intention of abiding by Magna Carta and immediately petitioned Pope Innocent III to nullify it. The pope agreed, but the changes were already at work. English barons again rebelled because of John's attempts to reverse his agreement. John died in 1216 before the revolt had gotten very far, and Magna Carta was reissued in 1217 by King Henry III.

TERM PAPER SUGGESTIONS

1. Compare the Bill of Rights from the Constitution of the United States to the Magna Carta. What similar rights are guaranteed by both? Why were these rights important to both medieval Englishmen and 18th century Americans?

2. Choose one of the rights, such as the right to petition, mentioned in the Magna Carta. Thoroughly research it and how it has evolved in meaning to the way we view that right today. Be sure you discuss significant events and court cases that are related to the right.

3. The original Magna Carta contained two articles regarding Jews in England. These statements were not included in later versions. Research the reasons for both the inclusion and later exclusion of the articles. How did these articles reflect the power struggle between church and state?

4. Both Magna Carta and the Declaration of Independence were written in response to the excesses of the monarchy. Thomas Jefferson and the signers of the Declaration were certainly familiar with the previous document. What similarities are there in the details of the two documents?

5. The original Magna Carta is above all a feudal agreement between a king and his barons. "Freemen" are only mentioned twice in the document. Explain how Magna Carta in general, and these references in particular, were instrumental in the American Revolution.

ALTERNATIVE TERM PAPER SUGGESTIONS

1. Assume the role of Stephen Langton, archbishop of Canterbury and leader of the English barons. Write and deliver a prologue to the chapters of Magna Carta as you might have delivered it to King John when presenting the document for his signature. Be sure to explain fully the barons' position and the reasons for taking this action.

2. Both Magna Carta and the United States Constitution essentially outline the relationship that is to exist between a government and its people. Yet, neither document remained static. Imagine yourself as one of the founders of a new nation today. Write your own Great Charter or Bill of Rights that could be the basis upon which your country is built. Write a justification for each article you include.

Primary Sources

British documents at *Sources of British History*. http://www.britannia.com/ history/docs /document.html.

The Constitution of the United States and the *Bill of Rights,* http://www.archives .gov/exhibits/charters/constitution.html

The Declaration of Independence, http://www.archives.gov/exhibits/charters/ declaration.html

Henry I's *Coronation Charter of Baronial Liberties* (1100; a precedent for Magna Carta)

Henry II's *Constitutions of Clarendon* (1164; a precedent for Magna Carta)

John I's *Concessions of England to the Pope* (1213)

Magna Carta (1215)

Pope Innocent III's *Declaration that Magna Carta Is Null and Void* (1216)

Secondary Sources

Baker, J. H. *An Introduction to English Legal History,* 4th ed. New York: Oxford University Press, 2004. A well-known resource on the growth of legal institutions in England.

Brand, Paul. *Kings, Barons and Justices: The Making and Enforcement of Legislation in Thirteenth-Century England.* London: Cambridge University Press, 2003. Detailed history of English laws from 1259 to 1267. Includes the text of three important legislative documents.

Holt, J. C. *Magna Carta,* 2nd ed. Cambridge: Cambridge University Press, 1992. This revised edition of a classic study of the Magna Carta and its reissues places the document in context and discusses its historical implications. Appendices contain the charter text and several related primary documents.

Howard, A. E. Dick. *Magna Carta: Text and Commentary.* Charlottesville: University of Virginia Press, 1964. This short (68 pp.) book is an excellent place to begin study of Magna Carta. Howard explains the circumstances leading up to the Magna Carta, considers ten categories into which the

63 chapters fall, discusses the significance of the document, and provides a copy of the text.

Maitland, F. W., and Montague, F. C. *A Sketch of English Legal History.* Boston: Adamant Media Corporation, 2005. This is a facsimile reprint of the 1915 edition published by G. P. Putnam's Sons. Covering the period from 600 to the late 19th century, the work is a classic discussion of the development of the legal system in Britain.

Musson, Anthony. *Medieval Law in Context: The Growth of Legal Consciousness from Magna Carta to the Peasants' Revolt.* Manchester: Manchester University Press, 2001. Discusses justice and the law from the perspective of all social classes, and traces the development of the English judicial system.

Pennington, Kenneth. *The Prince and the Law, 1200–1600: Sovereignty and Rights in the Western Legal Tradition.* Berkeley: University of California Press, 1993. An investigation of the power of monarchs versus the rights of their subjects.

Thackeray, Frank W., and Findling, John E. *Events that Changed Great Britain, from 1066 to 1714 .* Westport, CT: Greenwood Press, 2004. A chapter on Magna Carta explores the immediate and lasting implications of the documents. Also provides an excellent bibliography for further research.

Thompson, Faith. *Magna Carta—Its Role in the Making of the English Constitution 1300–1629.* Minneapolis: University of Minnesota Press, 2004. A reprint of the 1948 classic reference, this volume still is valuable in a study of Magna Carta. The 12 chapters are divided into three chronological sections. Chapter V is an excellent discussion of how Magna Carta affected the church in England.

Turner, Ralph V. *Magna Carta.* London: Pearson Longman, 2004. Turner is one of today's leading authorities on Magna Carta and its implications. This book traces the continuing influence of the document on English history.

Turner, Ralph V. *History Today* Sept. 2003, 53.9(7): 29. Turner considers how and why Magna Carta became a beacon of liberty in Britain and, increasingly, in the colonies and United States.

World Wide Web

The Avalon Project: Documents in Law, History, and Diplomacy. http://www .avalon.law.yale.edu/default.asp. An extensive online document collection maintained by Yale Law School that includes Magna Carta and other legal texts.

BBC History: The Middle Ages. http://www.bbc.co.uk/history/british/middle _ages/. Site has articles, interactives, a timeline, images, and biographies. Several selections on King John and on Magna Carta.

English Legal History Materials. http://vi.uh.edu/pages/bob/elhone/elhmat
.html. This site is maintained by the Department of History at the
University of Houston. It contains the materials used in teaching the
English Legal History course, including Magna Carta and comments.

Internet Medieval Sourcebook. http://www.fordham.edu/halsall/sbook.html. This
site provides several versions of Magna Carta, along with a number of
other related documents, including Pope Innocent III's Declaration
voiding Magna Carta and a selection from Roger of Wendover's *Flowers
of History* discussing the charter. An invaluable resource for any student
of the Middle Ages.

Multimedia Sources

*Kings & Queens of England, Vol. 1: From the Dark Days of Anglo-Saxon Times to
the Glorious Reign of Elizabeth I.* 2000. Kultur Video. 50 minutes.
Includes footage concerning the rule of King John I.

The Magna Carta. 2002. DVD. Films for the Humanities and Sciences.
22 minutes. Discusses the conditions leading up to Magna Carta and its
importance in the history of human rights.

Medieval Realms: Britain from 1066–1500. 1996. CD-ROM. Films for the
Humanities and Sciences. Multimedia collection of original material
from sources in the British Library; includes literature, travel narratives,
illuminated manuscripts, writs, charters, wills, music, maps, and deeds,
along with images of buildings and artifacts.

The Western Tradition: Video 19, The Middle Ages. Annenberg. WGBH Boston.
1989. This video series is available on demand to registered (free) users.
http://www.learner.org/resources/series58.html. Both this and the next
video provide a context for the creation of Magna Carta.

The Western Tradition: Video 20, The Feudal Order. 1989. DVD. Annenberg.
WGBH Boston. This video series is also available on demand to
registered (free) users. http://www.learner.org/resources/series58.html.

69. Rise of the Aztec Empire (c. 1225)

According to Aztec (Mexica) history, originally, from the island Aztlan
somewhere in the north, people entered the Valley of Mexico in the middle of the 12th century. Toltecs had controlled the region for some time,
but their empire was in decline. In 1171, tribes under Toltec dominance,
including Aztecs, rebelled and overthrew the Toltec. For the next half

century, small independent states without the power to conqueror others formed throughout the Valley. For a while, the Aztecs seemed to be vassals of more powerful tribes including Culhuacan, but some left to settle on an island in Lake Texcoco near modern Mexico City. They called their settlement Tenochititlan.

By the middle of the 13th century, the Mexica were building a city on the island and on land they reclaimed from the lake. As they grew in power, they began to stage attacks on other tribes, primarily to capture individuals to use in sacrifice. Although human sacrifice was a key component of their worship, the Mexica culture was advanced in many ways. They developed a system of writing, instituted the Chinampa system of agriculture that produced an abundance of food, created a very accurate calendar, understood mathematical concepts, were skilled artists and craftsmen, and insisted that children receive an education.

Tenoch (r. 1325–1375) was considered the first Aztec emperor. It was he who directed the completion of Tenochititlan's ball courts, markets, and large ceremonial centers. He also established a very large army, both for his own use and to be hired out as mercenaries by neighboring peoples. Tenoch's successor, Acamapichtli (r.1372–1391) began the campaign of conquest that built the empire. By the time the fourth emperor, Iztcoatl (r. 1427–1440), came to power, the empire controlled the whole Valley of Mexico. Iztcoatl expanded the city, built roads, and constructed a large causeway to connect the island to the surrounding land. Later emperors continued with conquests until they ruled far beyond the Valley. Tenochititlan collected tribute from the conquered territories and continued to demand people for their sacrifices. In 1502, a rebellion by the conquered people began that had not been completely quelled when the Spanish conquistadors arrived in 1519 and destroyed the empire.

TERM PAPER SUGGESTIONS

1. Compare the process of collapse in the Mayan Empire and the Aztec Empire. Did they have similar causes? Was the process fundamentally the same in both cases?

2. What were the gender expectations for men and women in the Aztec culture? What was the position of women?

3. Compare the culture and achievements of the Aztecs in Mexico and the Inca in Peru.

4. How did the art and architecture in Tenochtitlan reflect the values and beliefs of the Aztec culture? Where can you see the purpose of human sacrifice revealed through art forms?

5. Analyze the Aztec economic system. Where did the wealth originate for the grandeur of the Aztec Empire? How important was trade?

6. Compare the agricultural system of the Aztec Empire to that in Europe in the 12th century.

ALTERNATIVE TERM PAPER SUGGESTIONS

1. Create a multimedia presentation concerning Aztec art and architecture. What spiritual or religious elements are incorporated into the art forms?

2. Create a replica of the Aztec calendar and explain its meaning in an oral presentation. How does the calendar reflect the religious beliefs of the culture?

Primary Sources

Burland, C.A., ed. *The Codex Fejérváry-Mayer*. London: Graz, 1971. One of the few pre-Spanish surviving codices. Named for two early European owners, this volume is a complete facsimile reproduction. The codex divides the world into five parts around a central tree representing the four compass points.

Keber, Eloise Quinones. *Codex Telleriano-Remensis: Ritual, Divination and History in a Pictorial Aztec Manuscript*. Austin: University of Texas Press, 1995. A complete facsimile reproduction of the 16th century codex with extensive commentary. Although produced after the Middle Ages, the codex contains the entire history of the nation.

Nutall, Zelia, ed. *The Codex Nutall*. Dover Publications, 1975. A full-color reproduction of a pre-Columbian Aztec codex with introduction.

Secondary Sources

Aghajanian, Alfred. *Chinampas: Their Role in Aztec Empire-Building and Expansion*, 2nd ed. Los Angeles: IndoEuropean Publishing Company, 2007. Describes the Chinampa agricultural system and explores how it influenced the settlement of tribes and the eventual rise of the empire.

Conrad, Geoffrey W., and Demarest, Arthur Andrew. Cambridge: Cambridge University Press, 1984. *Religion and Empire: The Dynamics of Aztec and Inca Expansionism*. Reviews the ideologies of the Aztecs and Incas and how they differ from modern political thought. Explores how ideologies led to expansionism.

Gruzinski, Serge. *The Aztecs: Rise and Fall of an Empire.* New York: Harry N. Abrams, 1992. Chapters on the mythical history of the Aztecs, the rise of the empire, and the conquest by Spain. Also includes documents, a chronology of rulers, maps, and further reading.

Hassig, Ross. *War and Society in Ancient Mesoamerica.* Berkeley: University of California Press, 1992. Study of the importance of warfare to the Mayan and Aztec cultures.

Jimenez, Randall C., and Graeber, Richard B. *Aztec Calendar Handbook,* 4th ed. Saratoga, CA: Historical Science Publishing, 2006. Using hundreds of sources, the authors created a lucid resource on the Aztec calendar. Contains 150 drawings, a glossary, and bibliography.

Leon-Portilla, Miguel. *Aztec Thought and Culture: A Study of the Ancient Nahuatl Mind.* Norman: University of Oklahoma Press, 1990. Includes chapters on Nahuatl philosophy, concept of the universe, theology, and way of life.

Walthall, Anne. *Servants of the Dynasty: Palace Women in World History.* Berkeley: University of California Press, 2008. A collection of essays about palace women throughout history; includes a chapter about women weavers in the Aztec palaces.

World Wide Web

The Ancient Web. http://www.ancientweb.org/. This is a commercial site with books for sale, but it also has an abundance of free information about ancient civilizations, including flash essays, interactive maps, timelines, and essays.

Archaeology: A Publication of the American Archaeological Institute. http://www.archaeology.org/. Search feature leads to many articles from *Archaelogy Magazine.*

Dumbarton Oaks Research Library and Collection. http://www.doaks.org/. Dumbarton Oaks is a Harvard University Research institute devoted in part to pre-Columbian studies. A large collection of scholarly papers on many topics is available. Also provides a searchable database with translations of some ancient texts.

Foundation for the Advancement of Mesoamerican Studies. http://www.famsi.org/. Drawings, photos, texts, videos, and other resources are accessible from this site. Available in both English and Spanish.

Multimedia Sources

Ancient Mysteries: Secrets of the Aztecs. 2006. DVD. Arts and Entertainment Production. 50 minutes. Discusses the archeological research going on in

Mexico City, beginning with the discovery in the 1970s of the Great Temple of Tenochtitlan.

Empires of America. 2001. DVD. The History Channel. 50 minutes. Volume 6 of *History's Ancient Legacies.* Compares the empires of the Aztecs and Incas in Meso-America.

Engineering an Empire: The Aztecs. DVD. The History Channel. 50 minutes. Considers the engineering and technological feats of the Aztecs, particularly in building their capital on reclaimed land.

The Fall of the Aztec. 2005. DVD. PBS Video. 50 minutes. Presents the invasion of Mexico by Conquistadors, but also looks at internal problems related to the fall of the Aztec empire.

History–Digging for the Truth: The Aztecs of Blood and Sacrifice. 2008. DVD. Arts and Entertainment Production. 50 minutes. Host Joel Bernstein visits Mexico to use forensic science to examine the bones of victims of sacrifice.

In Search of History: The Aztec Empire. 2005. DVD. The History Channel. 50 minutes. Traces the rise of the Mexica from a small tribe to the empire that controlled most of Mexico. Discusses how the Spanish were able to conquer the empire in only a few months.

Mayans and Aztecs: Ancient Lands of the Americas. 2000. DVD. Cromwell Production. 50 minutes. Graphics, computer animations, location footage, and expert interviews reveal the history of two great Mexican civilizations.

Secrets of the Dead: Aztec Massacre. 2008. DVD. PBS. 60 minutes. Explores a recent archeological find that contains bodies of Europeans and raises questions about the reputed acquiescence of the Aztecs to Spanish conquistadors.

70. Kingdom of Mali (c. 1240–1500)

The West African province of Mali was once part of the Kingdom of Ghana, and when Ghana's power declined, the Malinke people found themselves vassals of the larger, more powerful Sosso tribes. Each Malinke village was governed by a chief or *mansa* whose right to lead was predicated on his descent from the founder of the settlement. The *mansa* also acted as an intercessor between the people and their ancestral spirits, making clan membership essential. This practice kept the tribes autonomous and unorganized until the leader at Niani, Sundjata Keita (r. 1210–1260), brought them together.

Sundjata, the "Lion King," traveled from village to village and persuaded each *mansa* to join him in fighting the Sosso. As they did so, Sundjata assumed the title of *mansa* for that village so he could symbolically claim to be a descendant of all the founders of Malinke villages. In 1238, Sundjata's large Malinke army defeated the Sosso ruler Sumaguru at the battle of Kirina, laying claim to all Sosso lands. The Malinke continued to amass territory until the 14th century when the kingdom of Mali was a federation of twelve provinces and three states, extending from the Atlantic Ocean to the city of Gao, and from the Sahara to the gold fields in Bure.

Mali's rise to power was closely tied to the gold trade and the constant flow of caravans crossing its territory to get to Egypt and North Africa. Use of the Niger River encouraged a more versatile and stable economy than had been found in Ghana. River transport moved goods more safely and quickly along the trade route, but the fertile soil along the river also produced enough agricultural goods for Mali to sell.

In 1324, Mali's great king Mansa Musa (r. 1312–1337) made a pilgrimage to Mecca taking evidence of Malinke wealth with him in the form of hundreds of camels transporting gold and other valuables and traveling with 500 slaves. This display of wealth caught the attention of the Muslim world and increased interest in trade with Mali. Musa also built the trade centers of Djenne and Timbuktu, the latter becoming an important center for learning and religion.

Mali began to decline in the 15th century, in part a victim of its own success. The kingdom was so large that its army could not effectively police the borders and was increasingly attacked by Taureg Berbers to the north and Mossi to the south. Provinces within the kingdom began to call for their independence from Mali rule. In 1433, Taureg forces overran Timbuktu, and Mali could not regain its strength.

TERM PAPER SUGGESTIONS

1. One of the issues historians face in studying a topic such as the ancient kingdom of Mali is that there are so few indigenous written sources. Review the primary and secondary sources on Mali and write a paper on the types of resources that are most valuable to historians as they try to reconstruct the history of an ancient civilization.

2. Analyze Sundjata's ideology concerning kingship. How do his beliefs compare to those of another kingdom of the 13th century in Europe or the Muslim world?

3. Discuss the conversion of the kingdoms of Western Africa to Islam. How did this happen? Why were the native people open to this new religion?

4. The kingdoms of Mali and Ghana rose to great power in sub-Saharan Africa and were able to control trade across the Sahara. How were the kingdoms significant influences on world history? Why were they unable to sustain their power?

ALTERNATIVE TERM PAPER SUGGESTIONS

1. The story of Sundjata is legendary among West African people. Retell the story in the form of a movie created on software such as Moviemaker or I-movie, or in another multimedia format. Incorporate music from Mali in your product.

2. Timbuktu has become symbolic of any distant, exotic place. Research the city as it was at the height of its power and as it is today, and create a multimedia presentation on your findings.

Primary Sources

Farias, P. F. de Moraes. *Arabic Medieval Inscriptions from the Republic of Mali: Epigraphy, Chronicles, and Songhay-Tuareg History.* Oxford: Oxford University Press, 2004. Farias has catalogued and translated hundreds of inscriptions that tell the history of Mali. Text includes 250 illustrations.

Ibn Battuta. *Ibn Battuta in Black Africa.* Trans. by Said Hamdun and Noel King. Princeton, NJ: Markus Wiener Publishers, 2005. Battuta spent 29 years traveling through Africa in the 14th century. He recorded his impressions of the Mali kingdom in this volume.

Secondary Sources

Austen, Ralph A., ed. *In Search of Sundjata: The Mande Oral Epic As History, Literature and Performance.* Bloomington: Indiana University Press, 2000. The 14 essays in this work offer various perspectives on the most famous of African epics.

McKissack, Patricia, and McKissack, Frederick. *The Royal Kingdoms of Ghana, Mali, and Songhay: Life in Medieval Africa.* New York: Henry Holt, 1995. Written for middle school students, this book privides a good overview of the three kingdoms. Includes two chapters on Mali.

Oliver, Roland, and Atmore, Anthony. *Medieval Africa: 1250–1800.* Cambridge: Cambridge University Press, 2001. Chapter 5 concerns the area of Mali and the gold trade.

Oliver, Roland, and Fagan, Brian M. *Africa in the Iron Age: c.500 BC–1400 AD.* Cambridge: Cambridge University Press, 1975. Extensive history of many African cultures. Chapter 15 is entitled "Mali and its Neighbors."

Pancella, Peggy. *Mansa Musa: Ruler of Ancient Mali*. Portsmouth, NH: Heinemann, 2003. A full-length biography of the ruler often called the lion of Mali.

Quigley, Mary. *Ancient West African Kingdoms: Ghana, Mali, and Songhai*. Portsmouth, NH: Heinemann, 2002. Discusses the political, social, and economic facets of the three kingdoms.

Thobhani, Akbarall. *Mansa Musa: The Golden King of Ancient Mali*. Dubuque, IA: Kendall/Hunt Publishing Company, 1998. Short biography of the most famous king of Mali.

World Wide Web

The Ancientweb. http://www.Ancientweb.org. This is a commercial site with books for sale, but it also has an abundance of free information about ancient civilizations, including flash essays, interactive maps, timelines, and essays.

Collapse: Why Do Civilizations Fall? http://www.learner.org/interactives/collapse/past.html. Interactive Web resource provided by the Annenburg Foundation that contains information on Mali and Songali.

Mali: Ancient Crossroads of Africa. http://mali.pwnet.org/. Features history articles, images, a timeline, lesson plans, and a bibliography of resources. Prepared by the Virginia Department of Education.

The Story of Africa. http://www.bbc.co.uk/worldservice/specials/1624_story_of_africa/. Hosted by the BBC, this site has many resources on Africa from prehistory until today. Includes information on the ancient kingdom of Mali.

World's Most Endangered Sites. http://www.history.com/classroom/unesco/timbuktu.html. A cooperative project undertaken by UNESCO and The History Channel, a number of endangered historic sites are featured on the Web page. Timbuktu is one of the places presented through articles about its history and that of Mali, images, maps, and a bibliography.

Multimedia Sources

Africa. 1984. VHS. Home Vision. Set of eight programs, 57 minutes each. Program 3 *Caravans of Gold* follows the routes of gold traders across Africa and into the Far East. Program 4, *Kings and Cities*, travels to Kano in Nigeria to observe the king in his 15th century palace where government is much the same as it was in the medieval kingdoms.

The Bambara Kingdom of Segu. No date. DVD. Films Media Group. 19 minutes. Looks at the art and architectural achievements of the Mali civilization.

Early Empires. http://www.learner.org/vod/vod_window.html?pid=2154. 1992. Streaming video. Annenburg. Unit 11 of the Bridging World History course. learner.org. Individuals must register to view the videos, but there is no cost. Examines how empires are formed, legitimized, and how they fall using Mali as one case study.

How Samba Became Viceroy. 1995. DVD. Films Media Group. 26 minutes. Dramatization of a folktale from Mali.

71. Mamluk Sultanate in Egypt (1250–1517)

Around the 9th century, the rulers of the Islamic Abbasid dynasty initiated the policy of using Mamluks, or slaves from many regions who were trained to be soldiers, to manage affairs in the lands they conquered. The practice of relying on the slave soldiers spread throughout the Muslim world. By the late 12th century, the Ayyubid rulers of Egypt and Syria had come to depend almost entirely on the Mamluks, who were a growing segment of the population, for defense and expansion efforts. Because of their importance to the nation, Mamluk political influence grew. Those who served the sultan well could earn their freedom and rise to important positions. When al-Salih Ayyub (r. 1240–1249), sultan of Egypt and Syria, died in 1249 during the Sixth Crusade, Mamluk soldiers killed his son and selected one of their own generals as the new sultan.

Al-Mu'izz Aybak, (r.1250–1257) became the first sultan of the Mamluk dynasty, a designation that was adopted during the Renaissance, but was not used by the sultans themselves. The general Baybars led Mamluk forces to victory against Crusaders at al-Mansura in 1250 and against the Mongols in Syria in 1260. He then murdered the third Mamluk sultan, al-Muzaffar Qutuz (r. 1259–1260) and seized the throne himself. Over the next 17 years, al-Zahis Baybars I (r. 1260–1277) continued campaigns against the Latin Kingdoms in the East and kept the Mongols from invading Egypt. When Baghdad's caliph agreed to move to Cairo, the Islamic world effectively recognized the supremacy of the Mamluks, and the capital became the center for intellectual, commercial, and artistic growth.

The office of sultan was not hereditary until near the end of the dynasty. Slave-soldiers were given instruction in the Islamic faith, in warfare, and in Arabic, and when freed could assume administrative responsibilities. Mamluks also recruited slaves for the ruling class, and the most powerful soldier became the next sultan.

Control of trade routes through the Mediterranean and Red Seas produced great wealth for the sultanate. Pilgrims on their way to Mecca and Medina enriched the coffers of the nation. In turn, the sultans were generous patrons of the arts. Mamluk decorative objects such as enameled glass, inlaid metalwork, and textiles were sought throughout the world. Beginning with Qala'un (r. 1280–1290), Mamluk sultans endowed public works such as hospitals, mosques, minarets, and bridges. Under Qa'itbay (r. 1468–1496), the shrines of Mecca and Medina underwent marked restoration. The Mamluk empire engaged in extensive building until its absorption into the Ottoman empire in 1517.

TERM PAPER SUGGESTIONS

1. Compare the idea of kingship held by Mamluk leaders with that of leaders in at least two other 13th- or 14th-century kingdoms.

2. Mamluk agricultural policy divided land among the army officers or *amirs* as a reward for their service. How does this policy compare with the feudal system of granting fiefs? Were there similar obligations and privileges that accompanied the grant of land?

3. Analyze the concept of the institution of slavery in Muslim society. How is this different from your own understanding of involuntary servitude? What are the implications of the Mamluk perception of slavery on the relationship between slave and master?

4. Mamluks were originally slave-soldiers. How did this identity affect their philosophy of government and their culture?

5. What genres of writing flourished under the Mamluks? How did these genres reflect the values of the culture?

6. Compare the rule of the Mamluk dynasty with the rule of one of the following: the Ayyubid dynasty, Norman England, Yuan Dynasty in China.

7. Analyze the Mamluk treatment of religious and ethnic minorities in their empire. What reasons can you give for their policies regarding minorities?

ALTERNATIVE TERM PAPER SUGGESTIONS

1. Prepare a multimedia presentation on the architecture and art of the Mamluk dynasty.

2. Prepare a podcast on the life and accomplishments of al-Zahis Baybars I.

Primary Sources

Gabrieli, Fanncesco., ed. *Arab Historians of the Crusades.* London: Routledge & Kegan Paul, 1969. Includes translations from the works of 17 Arab historians on the Crusades, with Part 4 containing 12 documents from the Mamluk era.

Stillman, Norman A., ed. *Jews of Arab Lands: A History and a Sourcebook.* New York: The Jewish Publication Society of America, 1979. Includes "The Jews Oath in Mamluk Egypt," "Traveling Incognito with a Mamluk Caravan," and 10 other texts written by or about Jews in Mamluk Egypt.

Secondary Sources

Amitai-Preiss, Reuven. *Mongols and Mamluks: The Mamluk-Ilkhanid War, 1260–1281.* Cambridge: Cambridge University Press, 1995. A detailed history of the 20-year war between Mongols and Mamluks; includes maps, a glossary, illustrations, and genealogical tables.

Behrens-Abouseif, Doris. *Cairo of the Mamluks: A History of Architecture and Its Cultures.* New York: I. B. Tauris, 2007. Basing her research on extensive archival research, the author discusses 60 monuments in Cairo. Color photos, architectural drawings, and isometric images are included.

Broadbridge, Anne F. *Kingship and Ideology in the Islamic and Mongol Worlds.* Cambridge: Cambridge University Press, 2008. Explores the ideas of kingship held by medieval Arabic rulers and how they used diplomacy to promote their own ideologies.

Goitein, S. D., and Lassner, Jacob. *A Mediterranean Society: The Jewish Communities of the Arab World as Portrayed in the Documents of the Cairo Geniza: An Abridgement in One Volume.* Berkeley: University of California Press, 1999. Based on the Cairo *geniza* documents, Goitein published a six-volume study of the everyday lives of Jews under Muslim rule. Lassner edited and abridged these texts.

Irwin, Robert. *The Middle East in the Middle Ages: The Early Mamluk Sultanate 1250–1382.* Carbondale: Southern Illinois University Press, 1986. History of the first Mamluk rulers; includes maps, chronology, and bibliographies of primary Arabic and non-Arabic sources.

Sabra, Adam. *Poverty and Charity in Medieval Islam: Mamluk Egypt, 1250–1517.* Cambridge: Cambridge University Press, 2001. Examines the attitude of Muslims in Egypt toward poverty and the poor and the way *waqfs* (pious gifts) were used to help the poor.

World Wide Web

The Art of the Mamluk Period (1250–1517). http://www.metmuseum.org/toah/ hd/maml/hd_maml.htm. Part of the Metropolitan Museum of Art's online exhibition. Features information as well as pictures of Mamluk objects.

Cairo: Living Past, Living Present. http://menic.utexas.edu/cairo/main.html. An interactive teaching site that features information, maps, and images from throughout Cairo's history, including during the Mamluk period.

Eternal Egypt. http://www.eternalegypt.org/EternalEgyptWebsiteWeb. A fascinating site with articles, video segments, animations, images, and virtual tours from 5,000 years of Egyptian history, including the Mamluk era.

Museum with no Frontiers. 1993. http://www.discoverislamicart.org/exhibitions/ISL/the_mamluks%20/introduction.php. Information and illustrations from the Mamluk sultanate, as well as of Mamluk influences that remain.

MuslimHeritage.com. http://www.muslimheritage.com/Default.aspx. This site contains articles, biographies, a timeline, interactive map, book reviews, and links to additional resources.

Petrie Museum of Egyptian Archaeology. http://www.petrie.ud.ac.uk/index2.html. Lists the caliphs for the 877-year Islamic rule in Egypt. Provides access to thousands of images, part of which are from the Islamic period.

72. Roger Bacon Writes the *Opus Maius* (1265)

The rediscovery of the work of Aristotle unsettled the world order of medieval Europe so much so that in 1231 teaching Aristotle was forbidden in Paris. In spite of opposition, scholars adamant about the new learning continued to press forward. The philosopher Roger Bacon, who had been at Oxford and studied the work of Robert Grosseteste, was the first to lecture on Aristotle's writing in Paris after it had been condemned. Bacon challenged the old dialectic pedagogy of memorizing arguments and repeating them. He believed that true learning should be based on empirical evidence, that observation of phenomena was as important as being told about them. He advocated a universal science that would combine Christian theology, scientific experience, and human advancement; science, he believed, should be a tool used by Christianity. By the middle of the 13th century, for unknown reasons, Bacon had returned to England.

Shortly after his return, Bacon became a Franciscan. Again, for reasons that are not clear, he was taken back to France around 1257 and was confined for a time. Information about where he was held and for how long is also lacking, but it is known that he contacted Cardinal Guy Le Gros Foulques and offered to write a new philosophical work for him. When Foulques was elected Pope Clement IV, he instructed Bacon to write the work and send it directly to him without seeking approval from his superiors in the order. In 1265, Bacon sent this work, *Opus maius (Major Work)* along with *Opus minus (Minor Work)* to Clement. *Opus maius,* written in six parts, combines scientific information from past writers, along with Bacon's thoughts, in order to persuade the pope that experimentation and empirical knowledge could be of service to the church. *Opus minus* is a continuation of the first work, which also contains a discussion of alchemy and a critique of universities. Bacon's *Opus tertium (Third Work)* was not sent to the pope.

Bacon continued to produce a large number of works, including a treatise on the science of optics *(Perspectiva),* until his death in 1292. Although not a scientist in the strictest sense—he made no discoveries and conducted no experiments—Bacon is still a major figure in the development of scientific thought. His insistence on inductive reasoning and empirical evidence represents the beginning of the fight for intellectual freedom.

TERM PAPER SUGGESTIONS

1. Why do you think Bacon became a Franciscan? Were there qualities of the Franciscan order and the philosophy of St. Francis that encouraged the development of scientific thought? If not, what could have induced Bacon to choose this path for his life?

2. Explain the concepts of "natural sciences" and "natural philosophy." What is the significance of these ideas in the development of intellectual thought?

3. Medieval science is generally pictured as a product of the reintroduction of Aristotle and other Greek writers to the Western world. What prior scientific knowledge did the West have when these writers were reintroduced? What were the main institutions in both the West and in the Islamic world that led to the rediscovery of these writers? How were the ideas of the "new learning" received?

4. According to historian A. C. Crombie, science in the Middle Ages was more concerned with the practical than with speculative or theoretical thinking. Do you agree with this assessment? Why or why not? Use examples from writers from the sixth through 14th centuries to support your opinion.

5. How did the scientific thinkers of the 12th through 14th century try to assimilate the "new learning" from the Greeks into their theological framework of beliefs?

6. What is science? What was the Greek and Roman conception of science? Did this conception change in the Middle Ages? How? Is the modern conception of science the same as that of the Middle Ages?

7. One of the conflicts between science and religion is the tension between the idea of an omnipotent God who can change nature at his will and the evidence

of patterns of change and development in the natural world. What influence did this issue have on Islamic and Western thought? What influence did this issue have on universities?

8. Consider Bacon's emphasis on mathematics as a science that supports all other sciences. Explain his position. Do you agree with his analysis? Why or why not?

9. Although Bacon did not invent anything himself, he wrote about a number of possibilities for the future, including glasses, a telescope, and a reformed calendar. Research these ideas in his writings and compare them to the actual inventions.

ALTERNATIVE TERM PAPER SUGGESTIONS

1. Bacon wrote extensively about alchemy, which the modern world does not consider a science. In the 13th century, alchemy, which was more than trying to turn other metals into gold, was a common practice. Prepare a multimedia presentation about medieval alchemy and its influences on later science.

2. In 1278, Bacon was accused of sorcery, condemned by the church, and imprisoned for two years. Assume the persona of Bacon and prepare a speech in your own defense to deliver before the church court.

Primary Sources

Bacon, Roger. *Opus Majus of Roger Bacon, Vol. I and II.* Trans. and ed. by Robert Belle Burke. Whitefish, MT: Kessinger Publishing, 2005. Modern translation of Bacon's best-known work.

Bacon, Roger. *Roger Bacon and the Origin of Perspective in the Middle Ages: A Critical Edition and English Translation of Bacon's* Perspectiva *with Introduction and Notes.* Trans. by David C. Lindberg. Oxford: Oxford University Press, 1996. Printed in both Latin and English on facing pages with extensive notes and analysis.

Dales, Richard C., ed. *The Scientific Achievement of the Middle Ages.* Philadelphia: University of Pennsylvania Press, 1973. Includes translations of works by several medieval scientists. Bacon is not included, but this volume provides context for his writing.

Grant, Edward, ed. *A Sourcebook in Medieval Science.* Cambridge: Harvard University Press, 1974. More than 80 authors are represented in translations of 180 works on science in the Middle Ages. Some were not available in English before this volume. Includes several excerpts from Bacon.

Lerner, Ralph, and Mahdi, Muhsin, eds. *Medieval Political Philosophy: A Sourcebook.* Ithaca: Cornell University Press, 1995. Translations include works of Bacon, Aquinas, and others, plus Jewish and Islamic philosophers.

Secondary Sources

Bartlett, Robert. *The Natural and the Supernatural in the Middle Ages.* Cambridge: Cambridge University Press, 2008. A collection of four essays, one of which is about Bacon's *Opus Maius.*

Clegg, Brian. *The First Scientist: A Life of Roger Bacon.* New York: Avalon Publishing Company, 2004. Biography of Bacon emphasizing his contributions to scientific thinking. Includes translated excerpts from Bacon's work, a list of Bacon's books, and extensive notes and bibliography.

Easton, Stewart Copinger. *Roger Bacon and His Search for a Universal Science: A Reconsideration of the Life and Work of Roger Bacon in Light of His Own Stated Purposes.* New York: Columbia University Press, 1952. Respected evaluation of the life and works of Bacon.

Evan, Gillian Rosemary. *Fifty Key Medieval Thinkers.* London: Routledge, 2002. Contains a chapter concerning each of 50 influential medieval intellectuals from all walks of life, including Roger Bacon.

Grant, Edward. *The Foundations of Modern Science in the Middle Ages: Their Religious, Institutional and Intellectual Contexts.* Cambridge: Cambridge University Press, 1996. Study of how the philosophy, theology, and natural philosophy of the Middle Ages made the scientific revolution of the Renaissance possible.

Lindberg, David C. *The Beginnings of Western Science: The European Scientific Tradition in Philosophical, Religious, and Institutional Context, Prehistory to A.D. 1450.* Chicago: University of Chicago Press, 2007. The last half of this book discusses medieval science and helps put Bacon's thinking in context of the time in which he lived.

World Wide Web

Epact: Scientific Instruments of Medieval and Renaissance Europe. http://www.mhs.ox.ac.uk/epact. Epact is an electronic catalogue of more than 500 scientific instruments housed in four European museums. Each instrument has a picture, description, use, and, if known, information about its creator. Has an introductory essay and bibliography.

Faith and Reason. http://www.pbs.org/faithandreason/stdweb/welcome.html. The PBS companion Web site to the video of the same name has additional articles, images, audio files, and links.

Multimedia Sources

Medieval Conflict: Faith and Reason. 1986. DVD. PBS. 55 minutes. Examines how the West tried to reconcile faith with the new scientific reasoning gained from access to Greek and Islamic texts.

73. St. Thomas Aquinas Writes *Summa Theologia* (1267–1273)

Thomas Aquinas was one of the most influential writers and philosophers of the Middle Ages. His works covered a broad spectrum of subjects, including theology, science, education, and politics. *Summa Theologia (Comprehensive Theology),* written between 1267 and 1273, integrates the Christian world view and the ideas of Aristotelian science. This masterpiece contains about two million words that must be printed in several volumes today. Aquinas contended that reason and science do not contradict faith, but instead may be used to strengthen faith. In *Summa,* Aquinas raised more than 3,000 questions in the format used in the universities of his time. First, he listed every possible challenge to the answer he wished to consider. He then cited an authority who corroborated his position and explained his own response to the question. Finally, his argument refuted each of the opposing statements he initially raised. With this method, Aquinas provided rational arguments for the existence of God, arguments for the nature of the soul, and arguments to answer other theological questions.

Aquinas was the son of the Count and Countess d'Aquino and was sent to the Benedictine monastery of Monte Cassino at the age of five for an education. Around 1240, he went to Naples to study at the new university. While there, he came under the influence of the Dominicans and joined them in 1244. His family was so upset with this decision that they kidnapped him and held him for a year, trying to convince him to renounce his vows. When he would not, the family relented and let him return to his order. Aquinas spent the remainder of his life lecturing in Paris and Italy and producing a vast body of writing. He was well known in his own lifetime, but not all opinions of his work were favorable. In 1273, the Bishop of Paris condemned Aquinas for his *Summa Theologia,* and Aquinas died in 1274 at the age of 49.

The chief detractors of Aquinas after his death were fellow philosophers John Duns Scotus and William of Ockham. But only four years after his death, the works of Aquinas were accepted as the official doctrine of the Dominican order. In 1323, Pope John XXII canonized Aquinas, and the church declared him a Doctor of the Church in 1567, recognizing him as one of the leading church fathers.

TERM PAPER SUGGESTIONS

1. Aquinas offers five proofs for the existence of God. Evaluate the reasoning used in each of these proofs. How does Aquinas use the philosophy of Aristotle in his reasoning? How are faith and reason reconciled by Aquinas?

2. Review the principles of a just war as outlined by Aquinas. How have these principles influenced modern philosophies of war? How have views of war shifted since Aquinas's time?

3. Thomas Aquinas argues that there are four types of laws. Explain each of these and relate them to the legal and judicial systems of the Middle Ages.

4. What is the relationship between the political philosophy of Thomas Aquinas and the development of a liberal parliamentary system? Consider Magna Carta in your discussion.

5. How did Aristotelian philosophy conflict with Christian theology on the subject of eternity? On the subject of the soul? How did Aquinas resolve these conflicts?

6. The principle political theory of the medieval period was Augustinian, derived from St. Augustine's *City of God* (c. 420), which saw the state as a servant of the church. Compare this ecclesiastical political theory to that of St. Thomas.

7. Was Aquinas's ideal of the relationship between church and state a radical departure from the reality of his age or a confirmation of what was happening in the West?

8. Compare Aquinas's proof of the existence of God to St. Anselm's earlier argument. How was Anslem influenced by Augustine and Aquinas by Aristotle?

9. Compare Aquinas's argument that faith and reason were compatible to the earlier arguments of Averroes and Maimoides. With whom does Aquinas agree?

10. Chose one of Aquinas's opponents—Duns Scotus, William of Ockham, or Suger of Brabant—and compare that individual's philosophy with Aquinas's.

11. Did the texts of Aquinas affect the attitude toward and treatment of Jews in a positive or negative manner?

ALTERNATIVE TERM PAPER SUGGESTIONS

1. Choose a war from the 20th century. With a partner, prepare a debate on whether the conflict met Aquinas's principles of a just war. Be sure to include a discussion of more than one position. For instance, you might argue that

participants in the Vietnam War on one side were involved in a just war, but that for others it was not a just war.

2. Select significant quotations from the works of St. Thomas Aquinas. Match these quotations to images from the modern world. Present the images and quotations in a multimedia presentation. The purpose of the presentation should be to stimulate thought in your audience about what you consider the important questions of existence.

Primary Sources

Aquinas, Thomas. *Selected Writings of St. Thomas Aquinas.* Ed. by Ralph McInery. London, Penguin Classics, 1999. Contains a large collection of Aquinas's writings with notes and commentary.

Duns Scotus, John. *Duns Scotus–Philosophical Writings: A Selection.* Trans. by Alan P. Wolter. Indianapolis: Hackett Publishing, 1987. Includes excerpts from several of Duns Scotus's most significant works.

Kreeft, Peter. *A Shorter Summa: The Essential Philosophical Passages of Saint Thomas Aquinas' Summa Theologica.* San Francisco: Ignatius Press, 1993. Kreeft has selected passages from the five volumes of the *Summa Theologica* along with detailed commentary on each. A good place to start research on the philosophy of Aquinas.

Ockham, William. *Ockham–Philosophical Writings: A Selection.* Trans. by Philotheus Boehner. Indianapolis: Hackett Publishing, 1990. Includes excerpts from several of Ockham's most significant works.

The Sophia Project. http://www.molloy.edu/sophia/sophia_texts.htm. Translations of several excerpts from Thomas Aquinas.

Secondary Sources

Copleston, F. C. *Aquinas: An Introduction to the Life and Work of the Greatest Medieval Thinker.* London: Penguin Books, 1955. This book contains a lucid explanation of the philosophy of Aquinas and its impact on the modern world.

Evan, Gillian Rosemary. *Fifty Key Medieval Thinkers.* London: Routledge, 2002. Contains a chapter concerning each of 50 influential medieval intellectuals from all walks of life, including Thomas Aquinas.

Hood, John Y. B. *Aquinas and the Jews.* Philadelphia: University of Pennsylvania Press, 1995. Analyzes Aquinas's comments on the relationship between Jew and Christian found in several of his treatises.

Pasnau, Robert, and Shields, Christopher. *The Philosophy of Aquinas.* Boulder, CO: Westview Press, 2004. Begins with a brief biography and discussion of the age in which Aquinas lived and devotes the remaining chapters to aspects of his philosophy such as "The Goal of Human Life" and "The Order of the Universe."

Selman, Francis. *Aquinas 101: A Basic Introduction to the Thought of St. Thomas Aquinas.* Notre Dame: Ave Maria Press, 2007. Selman discusses Aquinas's beliefs on topics such as the soul, good and evil, creation, and the emotions in easy-to-understand language.

World Wide Web

Corpus Thomisticum. http://www.corpusthomisticum.org/index.html. Available in several languages, this site has full texts of the works of Aquinas, a bibliography of research concerning Aquinas, and a searchable database.

Thomas Instituut te Utrecht: Thomas Aquinas. http://www.thomasinstituutorg/ thomasinstituut/scripts/index. A large selection of texts by Thomas Aquinas either in the original Latin or translated into English or French.

The Window: Philosophy on the Internet. http://www.trincoll.edu/depts/phil/ philo/index.html. Features links to many other resources, a timeline, and information about individual philosophers. As with many gateways, some of the links are no longer active, but the site is still worth visiting.

Multimedia Sources

Hermits, Monks, and Madmen. 1996. DVD. Discovery Channel. 53 minutes. Looks at saints that were able to forgo earthly desires to improve their souls. Includes Thomas Aquinas.

Medieval Philosophy: Thomas Aquinas. 1987. DVD. BBC. 45 minutes. Discusses the foundations of the philosophy of Aquinas and how he is a forerunner of modern scientific methods.

The Monastics. 1988. VHS. Insight Media. 21 minutes. Discusses the importance of monasteries and convents in the development of universities and features the influence of individuals such as Abelard and Thomas Aquinas.

Philosophy of Religion. 2004. DVD. Films for the Humanities and Sciences. 44 minutes. Renown scholars explore religious questions regarding evil, the nature of God, and the rational basis for belief in God, using texts by Thomas Aquinas and other philosophers.

Reason and Faith: Philosophy in the Middle Ages. 2007. DVD. Insight Media. A series of 30-minute lectures by Thomas Williams. One program concerns Thomas Aquinas.

Thomas Aquinas: The Angelic Doctor. 2000. VHS. Insight Media. Set of twelve 30-minute lectures by Jeremy Adams covering the life of Aquinas, his writing, the controversy over his philosophy, and the influence he has had on later philosophers.

74. Marco Polo Travels to China (1271–1295)

The Venetian traveler Marco Polo is one of the most famous individuals from the Middle Ages, and his *Book of Marvels: The Travels of Marco Polo* is one of the best known texts. In 1271, Marco began a 25-year journey through the Far East with his father Nicolo and his uncle Maffeo. The two older men had already been on a journey to Bejing, and the pope desired for them to return bearing a message to Chinese emperor Kubla Khan. Two Dominican friars set out on the expedition with them, but returned before they had traveled very far. The three Polos made the 9,000-mile journey alone, traversing terrain that would not be seen again by Europeans for 500 years.

The Polos were welcomed back by Kubla Khan, and Marco became an emissary for the court, traveling across the vast empire and reporting back to the khan. Marco's copious notes of his journeys became the basis for his *Book of Marvels: The Travels of Marco Polo* when he returned to Venice.

In 1292, the Polo family was asked to escort a Mongolian princess to Persia to be married. At the end of their two years of difficult travel, they learned the Kubla Khan had died. Aware that a civil war usually followed the death of a khan, they decided to return to Venice instead of going back to China. They arrived in Italy in 1295, where Marco soon gained renown for the fabulous stories he told. Marco was captured by a ship from Genoa during a sea battle and was imprisoned for a year. During his imprisonment, he formed a friendship with the writer Rusticello who assisted him in compiling his notes into the *Book of Marvels*. After his release from prison, Marco Polo returned to Venice where he married, had children, and ran a successful business until his death.

Some historians have doubted that Marco Polo went to China or spent time in Kubla Khan's court. The basis for this argument is that he does not mention the Great Wall, drinking tea, women with bound feet, and other unusual aspects of the culture. Historians who believe he did complete the journey, although he did exaggerate the events, counter that he would not have been able to write in such detail or at all about many of the things he did without having seen them. Whatever the truth behind the journey might be, the *Book of Marvels* encouraged Western imagination and curiosity about the vast Mongol empire in the East. The work also fueled the desire of others to travel. Christopher Columbus owned a copy of the *Book of Marvels* in which he made notes. That manuscript, with marginal notes that may or may not have been written by Columbus, is owned by the *Biblioteca Colombina* in Seville, Spain.

TERM PAPER SUGGESTIONS

1. What influences did the return of Marco Polo and the publication of his travel story have on European society?

2. Compare at least three mass media representations of Marco Polo with his own story of his travels. How have the creators of the products manipulated the story for their own ends? Include Polo's own distortion of truth in your discussion. What purposes could he have had for embellishing the truth?

3. Choose a subject written about by Marco Polo and by a medieval historian. Compare their treatments of the subject.

4. What is the role of women in the *Travels of Marco Polo?* Who are the people Polo seems to admire? How are women portrayed?

5. What is Marco Polo's attitude toward faiths other than Christianity? How does he portray individuals of other religions?

6. Compare the writing style and subject matter of the *Travels of Marco Polo* with *The Travels of Sir John Mandeville,* printed about 50 years later.

ALTERNATIVE TERM PAPER SUGGESTIONS

1. Create an interactive map of Marco Polo's journey. Hyperlink information about people and places and use quotations from *The Travels of Marco Polo.*

2. Write a six to eight page imitation of Marco Polo's travel book describing the American landscape, architecture, culture, and social habits as if you are traveling here for the first time. Suggest things that should be seen, and relate some of the things that happen to you as you journey through the country.

3. Prepare a podcast interview with Marco Polo upon his return to Venice. Include some of his own words from his *Travels.*

Primary Sources

Manderville, Sir John. *The Travels of Sir John Manderville.* Another example of medieval travel writing printed about 50 years after *The Travels of Marco*

Polo. Full text translation at http://www.romanization.com/books/manderville.

Manuel, Komroff, ed. *Contemporaries of Marco Polo.* New York: Liveright, 1928. Reprinted by W. W. Norton and Company, 1980. The text includes an introduction and translations of works by four travelers to the East before Marco Polo: Friar John of Pian de Carpini, Friar Willian of Rubruck, Friar Odoric, and Rabbi Benjamin of Tudela.

Polo, Marco. *The Customs of the Kingdoms of India.* Trans. by Ronald Latham. London: Penguin Books, 2007. A reprint of a 1958 translation by Latham, this text by Polo includes some of his most amazing descriptions.

Polo, Marco. *The Travels of Marco Polo.* Trans. by Manuel Komroff. Middlesex, UK: Penguin Classics, 1958. A well-known translation of Polo's work.

Polo, Marco. *Travels in the Land of Kubla Khan.* Trans. by Ronald Latham. London: Penguin Books, 2005. A reprint of a 1958 translation.

Secondary Sources

Akbari, Suzanne Conklin, and Iannucci, Amilcare, eds. *Marco Polo and the Encounter of East and West.* Toronto: University of Toronto Press, 2008. Collection of essays that consider Polo's travel narrative in several medieval languages, as influenced by contemporary travel literature and illuminated manuscripts, and in the many transformations of the text in print and on film.

Bergreen, Laurence. *Marco Polo: From Venice to Xanadu.* New York: Vintage Books, 2008. Comprehensive biography includes 16 pages of photos, illustrations, and several maps.

Clements, Jonathan. *Marco Pole: Life and Times.* London: Haus Publishers, 2007. Biography of Polo that seeks to determine whether he actually traveled to China.

Haw, Stephen. *Marco Polo in China: A Venetian in the Realm of Khublai Khan.* New York: Routledge, 2006. Haw revisits Polo's text to refute the assertion that Polo never traveled in China.

Larner, John. *Marco Polo and the Discovery of the New World.* New Haven: Yale University Press, 1999. Examines the influence of Marco Polo's writing on exploration and geography.

World Wide Web

In the Footsteps of Marco Polo: A Journey Through the Met to the Land of the Great Khan. http://www.metmuseum.org/explore/Marco/index.html. This interactive site has images, brief articles, and maps that create a virtual journey along the Silk Road.

The Marco Polo Odyssey. http://www.nationalgeographic.com. A nine-minute slide show narrated by Mike Edwards who traveled the same route as Marco Polo. Current images of the route.

The Humanities Exchange. http://www.humanities-exchange.org/marcopolo.htm. This site features digital exhibits from worldwide museums, including the Marco Polo exhibit organized by Contemporanea Progetti in Florence, Italy.

Multimedia Sources

History's Mysteries: The True Story of Marco Polo. 2005. DVD. The History Channel. 50 minutes. Searches for the truth behind Marco Polo's story of his travels.

Mysterious China: The Marco Polo Collection. 2006. DVD. PBS Production. Includes three programs: *Marco Polo's Silk Road,* which travels the 5000 mile-long route retracing the journey; *Marco Polo's Shangri-La;* and *Marco Polo's Roof of the World.* 90 minutes each.

Marco Polo. 2007 (DVD release date). Rhi Entertainment. 176 minutes. This is a made-for-TV miniseries about the adventures of Marco Polo.

Marco Polo. 1982. DVD. Versatil Studio. 483 minutes. 3 disks. Made-for-TV miniseries on the life of Marco Polo.

Biography: Marco Polo: Journey to the East. 2008. DVD. A&E Entertainment. 50 minutes. Uses reenactments and interviews with historians to tell the story of Polo's journey.

75. Habsburg Dynasty Begins (1273)

In 1273, the German nobility elected Rudolf (r. 1273–1291) emperor, ending the Great Interregnum, the period from 1254–1273 when no ruler was in power. For most of the next 600 years, the Habsburg dynasty held the throne of Germany as the Holy Roman Emperors.

The Habsburgs rose to power through faithful service to the Hohenstaufen dynasty, becoming so close to the monarchs that Emperor Frederick II (r. 1214–1250) served as Rudolf's godfather. When Frederick died, his young son Conrad succeeded him, but he died four years later. This began the 19-year period known as the Great Interregnum. There were two rulers during the time, but they had very little power. Rudolph had been gradually amassing more land during the Interregnum, so that by 1273 the Habsburgs were the most powerful family in the kingdom. The German princes had been glad to endorse a new emperor whom they hoped would advance German interests abroad while serving their own interests within Germany. Contrary to the intentions of his electors, Rudolf devoted a great deal of his attention to solidifying his own dynasty.

Although frequent internal and external conflicts marked their reign, the Habsburg dynasty kept the crown and continued to expand their holdings. Some of the Swiss cantons revolted shortly after Rudolf's death. His son Conrad did not have the support of the German nobility and was murdered in 1308. During the next two decades, the Habsburg kings lost Swiss territory and the German crown, which they did not recapture until 1438. After losing Germany, the Habsburgs relocated to Austria and made Vienna their new capital. From there, they slowly managed to gain additional land and to recapture what they had lost, some by legitimate means, and some through deceit. Rudolf IV (r. 1358–1365) wanted Germany back. He forged documents claiming that the Habsburgs had a right to participate in the elections of German kings. More intrigue and conflicts caused the borders of the Habsburg holdings to shift frequently over the next 100 years. Frederick V (r. 1452–1493) began to alter this trend when he arranged a marriage between his son and Mary of Burgundy, and the Habsburgs gained the Low Countries. Additional advantageous marriages brought more land under Habsburg control, until by the 16th century they ruled European territories from Spain to Hungary and Bohemia, and from the Low Countries to Northern Italy.

TERM PAPER SUGGESTIONS

1. While England and France were developing as nations, Germany was splintered into an assortment of principalities, duchies, and municipalities. Discuss the government of Germany during the 12th century and trace its consolidation into a nation during the 13th through 15th centuries.

2. What were the purposes of the Hanseatic League? Was it successful in achieving these purposes? What led to its eventual decline?

3. What were the principal issues involved in the conflict between the German monarchy and the church during the 13th and 14th centuries?

4. Was the Holy Roman Empire holy? Was it Roman? Was it an empire?

5. Would you characterize the German monarchy between 1250 and 1440 as weak or powerful? What were the major causes of its weakness or power?

6. Some German municipalities became centers for innovative visual arts between c.1250–1450. What were the reasons for the prolific production of art in these areas?

7. By what means was power acquired and exercised in German towns in the late Middle Ages?

8. What were the main factors affecting relations between peasants and their landlords in German-speaking Europe?

ALTERNATIVE TERM PAPER SUGGESTIONS

1. Create a series of maps showing the changing borders of the Hapsburg lands from 1273 to 1500. Indicate how the land was annexed or lost from one map to another.

2. Political figures can never please all their constituents. However, the many conflicting interests in late medieval Germany increased the emperor's difficulty in establishing a stable central government. Design an interactive, multimedia, graphic organizer that shows the kinds of issues at least five of the following groups pressed for that advanced their own interests: princes, knights, Church in Rome, local bishops, serfs, towns, small independent territories within Habsburg borders, merchants.

Primary Sources

Charles IV. "The Golden Bull of Charles IV, 1354 A.D." http://avalon.law .yale.edu/subject_menus/medmenu.asp. *The Avalon Project: Documents in History, Law, and Diplomacy,* maintained by Yale Law School. English translation of this significant Habsburg document.

John of Paris. "On Royal and Papal Power," in Schoedinger, Andrew B., ed., *Readings in Medieval Philosophy.* Oxford: Oxford University Press, 1996. John of Paris wrote this treatise around 1306. The preface and first three chapters are included.

Salimbene, Adam. *From St. Francis to Dante: Translations from the Chronicle of the Franciscan Salimbene, 1221–1288.* Trans. by George Gordon Coulton. Whitefish, MT: Kessinger Publishing, 2007. A facsimile reproduction of a rare translation of Salimbene's contemporary history.

Secondary Sources

Aram, Bethany. *Juana the Mad: Sovereignty and Dynasty in Renaissance Europe.* Baltimore: Johns Hopkins University Press, 2005. Discusses the life of Juana "the mad" Queen of Castile and her role in establishing the Habsburg Dynasty.

Arnold, Benjamin. *Princes and Territories in Medieval Germany.* Cambridge: Cambridge University Press, 1991. Looks at reasons for the failure of Germany to develop a nation state in the 11th and 12th centuries. Discusses the many types of regional authority that developed.

Griffin, Nigel, Griffin, Clive, and Thompson, Eric Southworth Colin, eds. *Culture and Society in Habsburg Spain.* Rochester, NY: Boydell and Brewer, 2001. A collection of essays regarding life in Spain under Habsburg rule.

Hunt, Edwin S., and Murray, James. *A History of Business in Medieval Europe, 1200–1550.* Cambridge: Cambridge University Press, 1999. Discussion of medieval business is divided into two sections: before and after the Black Death.

Unowsky, Daniel. *Limits of Loyalty Imperial Symbolism, Popular Allegiances, State Patriotism,* Vol. 9. Oxford: Berghahn Books, 2007. Focuses on the state and ruling dynasty, verses the national movements and ethnic conflicts of the Habsburg Monarchy.

Wheatcroft, Andrew. *The Habsburgs.* London: Penguin Books, 1996. Describes the Habsburg family and how they ruled their empire, and the effect that empire had on later historical figures, including Freud and Hitler.

World Wide Web

The Medieval Sourcebook. http://www.fordham.edu/halsall/sbook1n.html. The section called "Empire and the Papacy" has translations of several documents from the 13th and 14th century.

Monumenta Germaniae Historica. http://www.mgh.de/dmgh/. These documents are in German, but for students who have knowledge of the language, the extent of what is offered is great: letters, laws, edicts, diplomatic documents, and church documents, all from the Middle Ages.

Multimedia Sources

The Dream of an Empire. 1998. DVD. Films for the Humanities and Sciences. 53 minutes. Traces the background of the power struggle that resulted in Rudolph von Hapsburg receiving the crown and establishing the Hapsburg dynasty in Austria and Spain in 1273.

The Holy Roman Empire. 2002. DVD. Schlessinger Media. 30 minutes. Traces the empire from Charlemagne to the French Revolution. Contains segments concerning the relationship between papacy and empire.

76. English Conquest of Wales (1283)

The western part of Britain known as Wales was part of the Roman province of Britannia. When Anglo-Saxons invaded Britain in the fifth century, they drove the Celtic Briton natives to the west and north where they remained protected and isolated from the Saxons by mountains. Those who settled in the west became the Welsh. The people were organized into several small kingdoms, most of which unified sometime around the late ninth century. Raids into Anglo-Saxon territory were common at this time, and the Mercian king Offa ordered a 120-mile protective wall built between his kingdom and Wales, known as Offa's Dyke.

When Hywel Dda (r. c. 910–950) became king, he gained the Dyfed territory through marriage, uniting all the Welsh Britons. Hywel's reign was stable enough that he was able to issue the first Welsh coinage and record the first law code. After Hywel's death, however, internal disputes and Viking and English raids kept the country distressed. Gruffydd ap Llywelyn (r. 1039–1063) succeeded in reuniting most of Wales and began invasions of England. Even though Edward the Confessor felt Gruffydd was a serious enough threat that he traveled to the border to arrange a peace agreement personally, Gruffydd was assassinated by fellow Welshmen.

After the invasion of 1066, Norman lords were given estates in Wales and, by the end of the 11th century, held most Welsh land. With the Normans came monks and bishops tied to the church in Rome and to Canterbury. The Welsh had always maintained the Christian faith brought to Britain by the Roman Empire. Although Wales did not submit easily to the archbishop of Canterbury, the Welsh church of St. David eventually became subordinate to the English church.

Over the next century, some Welsh lords became powerful enough to challenge the English. In 1199 Llywelyn ap Iorwerth (r. 1194–1240) was able to seize the English fortress at Mold and declare himself "Prince of Wales." He paid homage to the English king for all the Welsh barons. When the barons forced King John to sign the Magna Carta in 1215, Llywelyn was influential enough to ensure that his rights and those of the Welsh people were recognized. Under his leadership, Norman castles throughout Wales, which served as points from which the English could launch attacks, were destroyed. He continued to labor for the independence of Wales from England until his death, as did his successors.

Llywelyn's grandson Llywelyn ap Gruffyd (r. 1263–1282) fought against Henry III and in the Treaty of Montgomery (1267) received formal recognition for the principality of Wales. When Henry's successor, King Edward I, came to power, Llywelyn refused to pay homage to him, would not attend his coronation, and ignored royal summonses to London. Edward launched an invasion in 1276, took most of Llywelyn's land, and imposed crushing terms on the Welsh in the Treaty of Conway the next year. Llywelyn gathered enough support to begin another rebellion in 1282. He and his brother David were killed in battle and their heads displayed on poles at the Tower of London as a warning to all traitors. The Statue of Rhuddlan in 1284 placed Wales under the authority of England forever.

Edward I named his own son Prince of Wales, began building castles for the garrisoning of English troops, and encouraged the emigration of English people to Wales. The conquest of Wales allowed Edward to turn his attention to Scotland and continue efforts to unite the kingdom of Britain.

Wales has not been an independent nation since 1283, but is an integral part of the United Kingdom. Two hundred years after losing its independence, Wales produced the king who would replace the last of the Plantagenet line and begin the Tudor dynasty. The Welsh language, stemming from Celtic ancestors, is still spoken by many people living there and is reflected in place names throughout the country.

TERM PAPER SUGGESTIONS

1. What were the accomplishments and failures of Edward I in his attempts to unite the British Isles under a single monarchy? Why was Wales important to him?

2. What were the contributions of the Welsh to the Hundred Years War between England and France?

3. What contributions have the Welsh made to modern English culture, economics, and society?

4. Compare Christianity as practiced by the Welsh in 1066 with that introduced after the Norman invasion.

5. Discuss the effects of the physical environment (geography, climate, natural resources) on the development of Wales as a distinct nation.

6. How did the Welsh military forces compare to those of other nations in the Middle Ages? What was the composition and purpose of the *Teulu* (king's guard)? Did the *Teulu* give the Welsh an advantage or disadvantage in battle?

ALTERNATIVE TERM PAPER SUGGESTIONS

1. Although many Norman castles were destroyed in Wales, the countryside still has many of the most remarkable castles in the world. Create a multimedia presentation about Welsh castles. Indicate why the choice of sites for the castles was significant in maintaining power.

2. The patron saint of Wales is St. David. Research the life and legends of St. David and prepare either a storytelling presentation or a multimedia presentation based on the information you discover.

Primary Sources

Giraldus Cambrensis. *The Description of Wales*. Detailed description of the geography, social, and economic aspects of Wales in the last part of the 12th century. http://www.visionofbritain.org.uk/text/contents_page.jsp?t_id=Cambrensis_Desc

Price, Huw, ed. *The Acts of Welsh Rulers, 1120–1283*. Cardiff : University of Wales Press, 2005. Contains 444 documents, primarily in Latin, but with English summaries and notes, from 12th- and 13th-century rulers.

"The Statute of Rhuddlan" in Blakely, Brian L., and Collins, Jacquelin, eds. *Documents in British History, Volume I: Early Times to 1714,* 2nd ed. New York: McGraw-Hill, 1993, 74–76. This is the document that declared England's sovereignty over Wales.

Secondary Sources

Davies, R. R. *The Revolt of Owain Glyn Dwr*. New York: Oxford University Press, 1997. A history of Wales in the 15th century. Contains pictures, maps, and genealogical tables.

Morris, John Edward. *The Welsh Wars of King Edward: A Contribution to Military History Based on Original Documents*. Oxford, Clarendon Press, 1968.

Morris, Marc. *A Great and Terrible King: Edward I and the Forging of Britain*. London: Windmill Books, 2009. This highly readable biography of Edward shows a balanced picture of the man who brutalized Wales and Scotland, but who erected the Eleanor Crosses in memory of his beloved wife.

Platt, Colin. *The Castle in Medieval England and Wales*. New York: Scribner, 1982. Filled with illustrations of architectural plans and with photos of the castles.

World Wide Web

BBC Cymru. http://www.bbc.co.uk/cymru/. The Web site for the Welsh BBC network. In Cymric, but has an English dictionary feature that can be activated. Good place to see the language.

British History: The Middle Ages. http://www.bbc.co.uk/history/british/ middle_ages/wales_conquest_01.shtml. This site has articles, interactive content, a timeline, Web links, and information about historical figures.

Castles of Wales. http://www.castlewales.com/home.html. Information on Welsh castles; also includes history articles, abbeys and monasteries, images, maps, and a glossary of castle terminology.

Digital Mirror. http://www.llgc.org.uk/index.php?id=digitalmirror. The digital library of The National Library of Wales. Contains images, biographies, manuscripts, and maps.

Mapping Medieval Townscapes: A Digital Atlas of the New Towns of Edward I. http://ads.ahds.ac.uk/. Looks at the layout and characteristics of 13 Welsh towns established by Edward I after his conquest of Wales; examines commonalities and decision-making processes involved in their design. Part of the Archaeology Data Service Web site.

Wales History. http://www.bbc.co.uk/wales/history/. BBC Wales. Provides a variety of information ranging from the Celtic past to modern events. Access to archived video segments is provided.

Wales. http://www.nationalarchives.gov.uk/utk/wales/. An online exhibit from Britain's National Archives. Images, documents, searchable database.

Multimedia Sources

Celtic Britain: Wales, a Nationhood. 2006. DVD. Kultur Media. 50 minutes. Filmed in the countryside and villages of Wales, the video highlights important historical events and examines the nation's culture.

The Genius of Wales: From the Age of Saints to the Industrial Revolution. 2007. DVD. Ryko Distribution. 71 minutes. A series of brief biographies of significant men and women from Welsh history.

A Spiritual Journey. 1998. VHS. Pembrokeshire County Council. 40 minutes. A tour of St. Davids Cathedral, the mother church of Welsh Christianity.

77. England Establishes Parliament (1295)

For many years, English monarchs had summoned men to "parley." Advisory councils of the country's leading figures had been traditional, and sometimes also included county knights. Edward I (r. 1239–1307) had held several parleys beginning in 1274. But when Edward I summoned clergy, lords, and men of the shires to a parliament in 1295, he was setting in motion a significant change in English politics and government. He was beginning an institution, not simply calling a meeting.

The early parliaments were irregular, held in different locations, and had no set requirements for who might attend. By the time Edward II became king in 1307, the representatives were much more regularized. After 1325, no Parliament was called without delegates from commoners, one from each borough and two from each shire, constituting what would become the House of Commons. About seventy barons and upper-level clergy made up the lords in Parliament. The power of the medieval monarchs lessened in some areas, but they remained the head of government and, more often than not, continued to have their own way. Still, this model of government was unique for its time and set a precedent for all future English governments.

Slowly, over the next three or four centuries, Parliament appropriated more and more of the duties and powers of the king and his council until the role of monarch became ceremonial. The model of Parliament was adopted by the United States and has been instituted in other countries as well.

TERM PAPER SUGGESTIONS

1. What factors were significant causes for the development of Parliament as an independent institution with broad political, legislative and financial powers by the end of the Middle Ages?

2. How was Parliament used during Henry III's reign? How did Parliament differ from other assemblies? What was the purpose of the Great Council?

3. How did Parliament develop during Edward I's reign? How did the Statutes differ from common law? Did the Statutes solve problems or cause problems? How did the king use Parliament? What powers had Parliament acquired by the end of Edward's reign?

4. How did Parliament develop during the reign of Edward II? What powers did it aquire and how did it exercise them? What was the significance of Keighley's petition and the commune petitions? Of Edward's Coronation Oath?

5. What is the "Doctrine of Capacities?" Why did it develop during the reign of Edward II? What is the relationship between this doctrine and the Statute of York of 1322? What is its relationship to English constitutional history?

6. Did Parliament or the king control finance and money during the reign of Edward III? What were the functions of the Estate of Merchants and the Staple? Who controlled them?

7. What was the function of the *commons* in medieval Parliament? Who attended the commons? How were they selected? At what point is it possible to identify an actual House of Commons?

8. What is the significance in Parliament of the hereditary peerage that was adopted during the late Middle Ages?

9. How can the liberal parliamentary movement be traced to the writings of St. Thomas Aquinas?

ALTERNATIVE TERM PAPER SUGGESTIONS

1. Assume the persona of Edward II. Write a series of diary entries concerning what happens to you after c. 1320.

2. Create a multimedia presentation concerning the history of Parliament. Include such topics as the development of elections for representatives, the formation of political parties, and the office of prime minister.

Primary Sources

Acts of the English Parliament. http://en.wikisource.org/wiki/Category: Acts_of_the_ English_Parliament. A source for translations of many of the acts of Parliament from 1295 until 1707 when, under the Act of Union, the governing body became the Parliament of the United Kingdom.

"The Manner of Holding Parliament." http://www.avalon.law.yale.edu/ medieval/manner.asp. A document from the time of Edward outlining the procedures for summoning Parliament, what offices should be appointed, and the regulations for the conduct of members.

"Summonses to Parliament, 1295." http://www.britannia.com/history/docs/. *Britannia History* site has a number of primary source translations, including Edward I's three separate summonses of churchmen, barons, and men of the shires to the Parliament of 1295.

Secondary Sources

Dodd, Gwilym. *Justice and Grace: Private Petitioning and the English Parliament in the Late Middle Ages.* Oxford: Oxford University Press, 2007. History of the custom of private petitions to Parliament and their effects on the British parliamentary and legal system.

Harding, Alan. *Medieval Law and the Foundations of the State.* Oxford: Oxford University Press, 2002. A history of law, the judicial system, the monarchy, and parliamentary government in England and France.

Goldsworthy, Jeffrey. *The Sovereignty of Parliament: History and Philosophy.* Oxford: Oxford University Press, 1999. Chapter 2 deals with the establishment of Parliament and its development until the Reformation.

Keen, M. H. *England in the Later Middle Ages,* 2nd ed. London: Routledge, 2003. Includes several sections dealing with the development of Parliament throughout the last two centuries of the medieval period.

Prestwick, Michael. *The Three Edwards: War and State in England,* 2nd ed. London: Routledge, 2003. Study of political developments in England during the reign of the three Edwards. Includes a chapter on the establishment of Parliament.

Tuck, Anthony. *Crown and Nobility: England 1272–1461,* 2nd ed. Oxford: Blackwell Publishers, 1999. Chapter 1 concerns the reign of Edward I and discusses his relationship with various sessions of Parliament in depth.

World Wide Web

Florilegium Urbanum. http://www.trytel.com/~tristan/towns/florilegium/flor00 .html. Large selection of excerpts from primary sources on various aspects of medieval urban life; includes a section on government. Some items that are rarely in translation.

United Kingdom Parliament. http://www.parliament.uk./index.cmf. From this home page, select the About Parliament tab. This will take you to a page with other links, including one about the history of Parliament with images, articles and documents.

Multimedia Sources

The House of Lords. No date. DVD. Films for the Humanities and Sciences. 64 minutes. Examines the history, function, and modern role of the House of Lords.

Medieval Realms: Britain from 1066–1500. No date. CD-ROM. Films for the Humanities and Sciences. Multimedia collection of original material from sources in the British Library; includes literature, travel narratives, illuminated manuscripts, writs, charters, wills, music, maps, and deeds, along with images of buildings and artifacts.

78. Ottoman Empire Begins (1299)

By 1299, a small group of Turks, under the leadership of Othman, had taken over most of Anatolia and formed a confederation of local Turkish tribes. Othman I (r. 1280–1324) established his capital in the city of Bursa and began a campaign of conquest that would eventually lead to his successors controlling one of the largest empires in history. The Ottoman dynasty he began ruled longer than any other dynastic family.

The Ottoman's were skilled fighters, and Othman's vast army was composed in large part of volunteers from throughout the Islamic world. They were attracted by the promise of sharing in the wealth of conquered territories and by their belief in Islam's spread throughout the world. Expansion continued after Othman's death under his son Orkhan (r. 1324–1359) and achieved dramatic gains under the third ruler Murad I (r. 1359–1389). He seized Greece, Thrace, and northwest Turkey. In 1389 at the Battle of Kosovo, Ottoman forces defeated the Serbs and were able to quickly advance through the reminder of the Balkan territories. The Empire continued to grow through the reign of Mehmed II (r. 1451–1481) with his troops achieving the greatest victory of all, the capture of the Byzantine capital of Constantinople in 1453. Later rulers concentrated on the administration and consolidation of the Empire instead of taking new territory.

Ottoman Turks exhibited relative tolerance toward other religions in their conquered territories, allowing Jews and Christians to continue to live and worship in these lands. They did face high taxation, were not allowed to arm themselves, and sometimes were treated brutally. The Sultan also extracted a "child tax" or "blood levy" against some families. A male child was taken as a small child, brought up as a Muslim, and became one of the exclusive military forces called the *janissaries*. These foot soldiers swore their loyalty directly to the sultan, and their large numbers gave the military more flexibility than cavalry alone would have provided.

Some of the Christians and Jews converted to Islam, either out of changed beliefs or to escape the penalties they had to pay. Bitter resentment grew from Christians and Jews against the converts, as well as against the Turks themselves. Some of the regional ethnic conflicts today are a result of the divisions that occurred under Ottoman rule.

By the end of the 15th century, the Ottoman Empire controlled the entire Silk Road, allowing it to levy taxes on all the goods transported through its territory and to grow extremely wealthy. Sultans became great patrons of the arts and built beautiful buildings as monuments or memorials. The wealth the Ottomans gained from the Silk Road encouraged the growth of exploration in the Renaissance. By the 16th century, European nations were seeking ways to bypass the Ottoman Empire and continue to trade.

There was no direct succession to the Ottoman sultanate, leading to power struggles that at times threatened the Empire itself. Close family members of the dead sultan fought most vehemently for the throne.

Mehmed II felt he came up with a solution to this issue. Once a new sultan was enthroned, all other candidates for the position were to be murdered. This meant siblings, not only of the new ruler, but those of the dead sultan as well. This policy remained in effect for about 150 years.

The Ottoman Empire declined in the 1800s when it lost trade revenue and then land to Russia, England, and Italy. Final removal of the Ottoman sultan did not occur until the end of World War I when Turkey was declared a republic.

TERM PAPER SUGGESTIONS

1. How do you account for the rise of the Ottoman Empire and its expansion into southeastern Europe in the 14th and 15th centuries? Was it more the strengths of the Ottomans or the weaknesses of their adversaries?

2. Compare the causes and effects of the invasions in the 11th century by the Seljuk Turks and those in the 15th century by the Ottoman Turks. What impacts did these invaders have on their conquered lands?

3. Discuss the role of the sultan in Ottoman society. How did his role compare to that of a European monarch?

4. Describe the development, achievements, and key contributions of the Ottoman and the Byzantine cultures, noting similarities, differences, and connections.

5. How do you account for the success of the Ottoman Empire in its conquest of the Balkans? Was it due to their strengths or weaknesses of the conquered cultures?

6. The Ottoman Empire extended over quite a large land area and encompassed people with different ethnic backgrounds and languages, yet it managed to rule at least some of its territory for over 600 years. What challenges did the empire face in administration under these circumstances? How did it deal with them? What advantages did these circumstances give the Ottomans?

7. Compare Islam under the Ottomans to Islam in one of the earlier caliphates such at the Fatamids, Ayyubids, or Mongols.

ALTERNATIVE TERM PAPER SUGGESTIONS

1. Create a multimedia presentation on the art and architecture of the Ottoman Empire.

2. Create a series of podcast "news" reports about the growth of the Ottoman Empire.

Primary Sources

Al-Ghazali, abu Hamid. *The Path of Sufism: An Annotated Translation of al-Ghazali's al-Munqidh min al-dalal.* Trans. by Richard Joseph McCarthy. Louisville, KY: Fons Vitae Publishing, 2000. Written before the Ottoman expansion but gives valuable insight into Muslim philosophy.

Ibn Khaldun. Selections from *A Universal History.* http://www.humanistic texts.org/ibn_khaldun.htm. Ibn Khaldun (1332–1406) was an Arab historian from Tunis. He wrote primarily about Africa and Spain.

Tabib, Rashid al-Din. *A Compendium of Chronicles: Rashid al-Din's Illustrated History of the World (Jami al-Tawarikh).* Trans. by Sheila Blair. London: Nour Foundation, 1995. Originally intended to be a history of the Mongols, Tabib expanded his chronicles and included information from the creation of Adam to his own time.

Secondary Sources

Faroqhi, Suraiya. *The Ottoman Empire and the World Around It.* London: I. B. Tauris, 2007. Features multiple illustrations and is divided into two separate sections, the Ottoman Empire in Asia and Africa and the Ottoman Empire in Europe.

Finkle, Caroline. *Osman's Dream: The History of the Ottoman Empire.* New York: Basic Books, 2005. A complete, well researched history of the Ottoman Empire from its inception to collapse.

Goodwin, Jason. *Lords of the Horizons: A History of the Ottoman Empire.* New York: Pacador, 1998. Chapter 17 discusses the expansion and maintenance of the empire throughout its history.

Jackson, Sherman A. *On the Boundaries of Theological Tolerance in Islam: Abū Hāmid al-Ghāzalī's Faysal al-Tafriqa Bayna al-Islām wa al-Zandaqa.* Oxford: Oxford University Press, 2003. A close textual analysis of al-Ghasali's work.

Imber, Colin. *The Ottoman Empire, 1300–1650: The Structure of Power.* New York: Palgrave Macmillan, 2002. Uses multiple resources, including previously untranslated sources, to document the rise of the empire.

Inalcik, Halil. *The Ottoman Empire: The Classical Age 1300–1600.* London: Phoenix Press, 1975. Features a history of the Ottoman Empire, as well as a discussion of its politics, religion, and economics.

Kafadar, Cemal. *Between Two Worlds: The Construction of the Ottoman State.* Berkeley: University of California Press, 1995. Traces the rise of the Ottoman Empire from its beginnings as a tiny state to its eventual control of the Islamic world and the Eastern Roman Empire.

World Wide Web

Museum With No Frontiers: Discover Islamic Art in the Mediterranean. http://www.discoverislamicart.org/exhibitions/ISL/. This page has a number of links to Islamic art exhibits, including one to the Ottomans and one to Western influence in Ottoman lands.

The Ottomans.org. http://www.theottomans.org/english/history/history1600_2 .asp. Includes information on various periods of Ottoman history, including Islamic forerunners of the empire, maps, a glossary, images, and an extensive list of references.

Multimedia Sources

The Glories of Islamic Art: The Ottomans and Their Capital Istanbul. 2007. DVD. Insight Media. 45 minutes. Explores the Ottoman city, the legacy of the Byzantine Empire, and the introduction of their own culture into art and architecture.

The Ottoman Empire. 1996. DVD. Films Media Group. 47 minutes. Includes interviews with scholars and other resources to probe the military power and social structure of the Ottomans. Includes a discussion of *doshan* (Christian peasant boys taken and trained to serve the sultan), the role of women, religion, and family life.

The Ottoman Empire: 1280–1683. 1984. DVD. Landmark Films. 26 minutes. Short overview of the four centuries of Ottoman rule.

79. Peak of Medieval Pilgrimages (c. 1300–1450)

The faithful had been making pilgrimages for centuries. Early Christians emulated Jews and traveled to Jerusalem. They visited other Holy Land sites as well. In the late seventh century, Muslims began making pilgrimages to Mecca, Medina, and Jerusalem. Pilgrimages, considered acts of penance, could be difficult journeys, particularly if the penitent walked barefooted or took no money or food. Travel along unprotected roads presented another danger, and sea voyages were also unsafe. Therefore, early pilgrims had generally considered the journey carefully beforehand and were serious in their intent.

As more churches, cathedrals, and mosques were built, often at great expense, there were more places for pilgrims to visit. Places of worship soon realized that they could increase their income if pilgrims visited. By the 13th century, travel had become safer as well. There were still dangers, but if one traveled in a group, safety increased. Taverns were built along the most traveled routes and near sacred sites to care for the pilgrims. Before too many years, a kind of tourist industry had burgeoned. Enterprising individuals even arranged for groups of pilgrims to travel together and planned their trip. Pilgrimage destinations began to manufacture items such as badges for pilgrims that indicated they had been there. Guidebooks were printed and sold, and merchants closest to the sites sold trinkets and "holy" relics.

For Christians, a church where the bones of a saint were buried meant special blessings. If a miracle had been reported there, the church was even more appealing. Other relics soon began to appear in the churches and monasteries throughout Europe, adding to the appeal of certain sacred places.

By the 14th century, the number of pilgrimages had increased drastically. Many social and religious circumstances contributed to this. The church encouraged pilgrimages. Penance was necessary for forgiveness; going on a pilgrimage was an act of penance. Credit for penitent actions could even be built up to use against later sins. In addition, famine and the plague had not only decreased the population but had made people very aware of the brevity of life. The fear of being unforgiven and the fear of dying were powerful motivators. Some individuals made the journeys to ask the local saint to intercede for them, truly believing it would happen. Others who were ill made trips to places where miracles had taken place as soon as the sufferer drank the water or touched a holy relic, hoping they too would be healed. The belief in the power of relics also lured the vulnerable to buy relics from professional pilgrims. If one could not make the journey personally, perhaps some of the blessings could be had through owning a relic.

People also wanted to go on a pilgrimage for the joy of traveling. Few opportunities existed for travel for most individuals in the Middle Ages. A pilgrimage gave them a legitimate reason to leave their homes and take a trip. Most of author Geoffrey Chaucer's fictional pilgrims going to Canterbury fall into the latter category, which he satirizes in his work. Religious reformists such as the Lollards fervently objected to pilgrimages for just this reason, but the church was not interested in discouraging pilgrims. One of the most popular sites with pilgrims, and most lucrative for the church, was Rome itself.

TERM PAPER SUGGESTIONS

1. Trace the evolution of the pilgrimage in medieval society.

2. What reasons did the medieval church have for promoting pilgrimages?

3. A significant portion of medieval literature, particularly during the earlier centuries, was hagiography (saints lives). Hagiography was interwoven into chronicles and histories and miraculous events presented as fact. What was the relationship among the profusion of hagiography, the adoration of relics, and pilgrimage?

4. What were the social and economic results of the large number of pilgrims who traveled through the Western and Islamic world?

5. Islam encourages its followers to undertake a pilgrimage known as the Haj. This duty is described in the Qur'an XXII, 27–38. Read these verses and compare them to a primary source (several are listed here) from a Western pilgrim about why he or she undertook the journey. Are the reasons similar? Do pilgrims of both faiths expect the same outcomes?

6. Consider the use of pilgrimage in literature after the Middle Ages. Choose two works from the Renaissance or later in which characters undertake pilgrimages, either physical or spiritual, and compare those two works.

ALTERNATIVE TERM PAPER SUGGESTIONS

1. Research popular places for pilgrims in the Middle Ages from all three major religious traditions. Prepare a multimedia presentation about these sites. What were pilgrims visiting at the site? What was the religious attraction?

2. Choose a site you would like to visit today; it may be a religious site but does not have to be. Plan your trip by any means other than a direct flight. Write a series of journal entries (a travelogue) about the journey to reach the site, what you see and do when you arrive, and how you return home. Include specific details (hotels, streets, sights, etc.) and discuss the people you meet during your journey.

Primary Sources

Anonymous. *Guidebook to Palestine.* Trans. by J. H. Barnard. London: Palestine Pilgrims' Text Society, 1894. http://chass.colostate-pueblo.edu/history/seminar/anonymous.htm. This work from around 1350 was probably composed by several authors.

Benjamin of Tudela. *The Itinerary of Benjamin of Tudela.* Trans. by Marcus Nathan Adler. New York: B & R Samizdat Express, 2008. Tudela's personal account of his 12th-century pilgrimage to the Holy Land.

Fabri, Friar Felix. *The Book of Wanderings of Felix Fabri (Circa 1480–1483 A.D.).* Trans. Aubrey Stewart. London: Palestine Pilgrims' Text Society, 1896.

http://chass.colostate-pueblo.edu/history/seminar/fabri.htm. Translation of Fabri's personal account of his pilgrimages to the Holy Land.

Fabri, Friar Felix. *Once to Sinai: The Further Pilgrimage of Friar Felix Fabri.* Trans. H. M. F. Prescott. Cambridge: Macmillan, 1947. http://www.archive.org/details/oncetosinaithefu008226mbp. Detailed first-person account of Fabri's second pilgrimage.

Kempe, Margery. *The Book of Margery Kempe.* Trans. by Lynn Stanley. New York: W. W. Norton & Company, 2000. Although Margery Kempe never learned to write, two scribes wrote the story she dictated describing her pilgrimage to Jerusalem. A number of other translations are available, and parts of the text can be found online.

Poloner, John. *Description of the Holy Land.* Trans. by Aubrey Stewart. London, 1894. http://chass.colostate-pueblo.edu/history/seminar/poloner/poloner.html. Poloner traveled to Jerusalem in the early 15th century and published this work around 1421.

Webb, Diana. *Pilgrims and Pilgrimage in the Medieval West.* London: I. B. Tauris, 1999. West includes translations of a variety of primary sources including personal accounts, guidebooks, and state documents along with her expert commentary on each section.

Secondary Sources

Birch, Debra J. *Pilgrimage to Rome in the Middle Ages: Continuity and Change.* Rochester, NY: Boydell & Brewer, 2000. Discusses the journey to Rome, the cult of saints, and the obligations, privileges, and provisions for welfare of the pilgrims.

Netton, Ian Rich. *Golden Roads: Migration, Pilgrimage and Travel in Medieval and Modern Islam.* Richmond, UK: Curzon Press, 1993. 1995. A collection of scholarly essays on Islamic pilgrimage, its significance and influence.

Sumpion, Jonathan. *The Age of Pilgrimage: The Medieval Journey to God.* London: Faber and Faber, 1975. Examines the people from all walks of life who went on pilgrimages and their reasons for leaving behind their familiar worlds, and how and where they traveled.

Ure, John. *Pilgrimages: The Great Adventure of the Middle Ages.* New York: Carroll & Graf Publishers, 2006. Discusses motivation for pilgrimages, major sites, specific individuals who traveled, and how a profitable tourist business arose from pilgrimage.

Webb, Diana. *Medieval European Pilgrimage, c. 700–c. 1500.* Hampshire, UK: Palgrave, 2002. Discusses motives and varieties of pilgrimages, the geography of pilgrimage, and how the pilgrimage influenced medieval culture.

Webb, Diana. *Pilgrims and Pilgrimage in the Medieval West.* London: I.B. Tauris, 1999. Deals with pilgrimage from the 7th to 16th centuries. Utilizes wide variety of primary source documents for research.

Weber, Elka. *Traveling through Text: Message and Method in Late Medieval Pilgrimage Accounts.* London: Routledge, 2005. Compares how writers from the Jewish, Christian, and Islamic faith structure personal accounts of pilgrimages.

World Wide Web

European Medieval Pilgrimage Project. http://www.internationalschooltoulouse .net/vs/pilgrims/index.htm. Part of the European Virtual School, this Web site provides images, history, interactive activities, maps and more.

The Medieval Sourcebook. http://www.fordham.edu/halsall/sbook1s.html. Has a large number of primary sources on church relics and medieval pilgrimages.

Pilgrimage and Pilgrims. http://courseweb.stthomas.edu/medieval/chaucer/pilgrim .htm. Four medieval personages guide viewers through the medieval church and its focus on pilgrimages. Articles, link, images.

Multimedia Sources

Chaucer: The General Prologue to "The Canterbury Tales." DVD. Films Media Group. 20 minutes. Audio of brief excerpts of the prologue text, discussion of the pilgrimage and pilgrims, skit performed by students.

Pilgrimages of Europe. 2004. DVD (set of six). Janson Media. 540 minutes. Visits 12 medieval sites popular with medieval pilgrims and examines the motives the pilgrims had for travel.

80. Avignon Papacy Begins (1305)

The long struggle between pope and king reached grim heights under Innocent III (r. 1160–1216). A devout and well-educated man, Innocent made it more difficult for individuals to get a divorce and ordered the laity to respect church property and submit to ecclesiastical courts. Innocent also instituted reforms within the church itself, requiring the clergy to set a better example for the laity. The task to which he devoted most energy was that of freeing the papacy from secular influence and reinforcing the church's supremacy over the state, angering France and England in his efforts.

By the time Boniface (1294–1303) became pope, England and France had developed strong national identities and were not inclined to submit to the pope. King Philip the Fair and England's Edward I both imposed taxes on clergy. Boniface ordered them to cease or be excommunicated. Philip struck back by refusing to allow the exportation of silver or gold. Edward turned down requests to protect clergy summoned to Rome, making it impossible for them to travel. Philip then arrested two highly placed clergy and tried them for treason. When they were found guilty, Boniface declared that the state had no jurisdiction over clergy. On November 18, 1302, Boniface issued the *Unam Sanctam,* declaring papal supremacy. The French burned it. Boniface planned to depose Philip and place the country under an interdict; the Estates General, an assembly of the lords of France, countered with a declaration that the pope had no civil authority, and that the king was responsible only to God.

In 1303, Philip sent troops to capture and hold Boniface. Within a few days, the townspeople of Anagni rescued the pope, but he was so badly shaken that he died within weeks. Benedict IX replaced him, but only for nine months, at which time someone poisoned him. After almost a year of careful consideration, the cardinals chose Clement V (1305–1314) as the new pope. Clement traveled to France for his investiture and decided that it would not be expedient for him to return to Rome. He, therefore, moved the entire papal court to Avignon, a papal territory that was presumably outside French control.

The seat of the papacy remained in Avignon for the next 70 years, a period when it was dominated by the French. All the popes during this time were French. Both Clement and his successor John XXII (1316–1334) lived very extravagantly at Avignon. John required that one-tenth of all salaries of the clergy be sent to him. He claimed the lands and property of any bishop who died. He also instituted Peter's Pence, the payment of one penny per household throughout Europe.

While Avignon was thriving, Rome was deteriorating. The population shrank, buildings went unrepaired, and politics worsened. In 1365, Pope Urban V (r. 1362–1370) ordered repairs on the Vatican in preparation for his return to the city. After three years in Rome, he returned to Avignon to arbitrate disagreements between France and England. He became ill and died within three months of his arrival. The new pope, Gregory XI (r. 1370–1378) remained in Avignon until 1377. When he returned to Rome, the "Babylonian captivity," as the Avignon Papacy is sometimes called, ended.

TERM PAPER SUGGESTIONS

1. Discuss the major problems the Avignon papacy faced and the ways in which it responded to those problems.

2. What was at stake for popes and for monarchs in this controversy over papal supremacy?

3. What were the qualifications one needed in order to be a bishop, an archbishop, cardinal, or pope in the 14th century? What was the relationship between papal qualifications and papal authority in the eyes of the monarchs?

4. In what ways did Clement V acquiesce to the demands of Philip of France? Was this a matter of compromise or were his actions self-serving?

5. What effect did the 70 years at Avignon have on the power and prestige of the papacy?

6. The monarchs of the 14th century, particularly Philip the Fair of France, leveled repeated charges of corruption against the papacy. Were these charges justified or were they propaganda tools of the monarchy?

ALTERNATIVE TERM PAPER SUGGESTIONS

1. As King Philip the Fair, write a series of letters to your leading minister, William de Nogaret, detailing your plans and giving him instructions for dealing with Pope Boniface VIII. Your last letter should discuss the death of Boniface.

2. Use both primary and secondary sources to prepare a dialogue between Philip the Fair and Boniface VIII to be presented to your class. Your discussion should reveal the attitudes of the two men toward one another and include some of the same language they used.

Primary Sources

Henderson, Ernest F. *Select Historical Documents of the Middle Ages.* New York: Biblo and Tannen, 1965. The majority of selections translated here are church documents or related to the church.

Kirshner, Julius, and Morrison, Karl F., eds. *University of Chicago Readings in Western Civilization: 4, Medieval Europe.* Chicago: University of Chicago Press, 1986. Contains a section called "Storm over the Papacy" with primary sources from the early 14th century.

Secondary Sources

Collins, Roger. *Keepers of the Keys of Heaven: A History of the Papacy.* New York: Basic Books, 2009. Contains a chapter on the Avignon papacy.

Mullins, Edwin. *The Popes of Avignon: A Century in Exile*. New York: Blue Bridge, 2008. Narrative history describing the secularization and materialism of the papacy.

Plogger, Karsten. *England and the Avignon Popes: The Practice of Diplomacy in Late Medieval Europe*. London: Legenda, 2005. Discusses diplomatic relations between England and the papacy, with examples drawn from multiple unpublished sources.

Wood, Diana. *Clement VI: The Pontificate and Ideas of and Avignon Pope*. Cambridge: Cambridge University Press, 1989. Compares and contrasts Clement's personal views with his official actions while pope.

World Wide Web

History of Western Civilization: The Late Medieval Church. http://history. boisestate.edu/westciv/babylon/. This is a course Web site developed by E. L. Skip Knox of Boise State University. There are 19 short articles on "Crisis in the Medieval Church." Site is searchable.

The Medieval Sourcebook. http://www.fordham.edu/halsall/sbook.html. The section entitled "Papacy and Empire" provides a number of translated documents related to the Avignon papacy, including a copy of Boniface's *Unam Sanctum*.

Multimedia Sources

The Popes: The Legacy of Peter. 2004. DVD. Arts and Entertainment Home Video. 120 minutes. Discusses the history of the papacy from earliest times until John-Paul II's tenure.

Sectarianism and Schism in Europe: Christianity in the 15th and 16th Centuries. 1999. DVD. Films for the Humanities and Sciences. 48 minutes. Part I discusses the efforts of popes to achieve political independence and the Great Schism. Part II concerns later church developments.

81. Dante Composes *The Divine Comedy* (1306–1321)

Dante Alighieri (1265–1321) composed one of the great works of literature during the last fifteen years of his life. A Florentine native, Dante had been exiled from the city for life because of involvement in political affairs and his refusal to pay a fine. He traveled for a few years after his exile and then settled in Ravenna.

The Divine Comedy is constructed in three parts, the Inferno, Purgatory, and Paradise, and is a combination of fantasy and fact, real and mythological characters, and symbolism. Dante himself is the main character, who on Good Friday in 1300, is guided through Hell, Purgatory, and Heaven by the epic poet Virgil, St. Bernard of Clairvaux, and his deceased love Beatrice.

The Inferno, with its nine increasingly horrific circles, is the most well known of the three sections. Throughout the poem, Dante makes comments on contemporary events and people, reveals his own political views, and consigns his enemies to hell and friends to heaven. Dante structures the poem into 100 cantos of *terza rima*, three line stanzas with an interlocking rhyme scheme, a verse form he invented. There is one introductory canto and each section has thirty-three cantos. By using himself as the central character, Dante also transformed the conventions of an epic.

The Divine Comedy placed Dante among the greatest literary geniuses of the world.

TERM PAPER SUGGESTIONS

1. Does *The Divine Comedy* support or subvert 14th-century Christian theology? What was the reaction of the church to the work?

2. Analyze the effects of *The Divine Comedy* on our modern world view and collective psyche.

3. In Dante's fictional world, one receives just punishment for evil deeds. Was this true in Dante's real world? Did the laws of medieval Italy reflect justice for all?

4. Compare Dante's portrayal of his contemporaries and the events of his time with the same people and events described in an historical source.

5. Analyze Dante's portrayal of women. It has been said that he idealizes Beatrice. Do you agree? Many 14th and 15th century writers revealed a strong misogynist vein in their work. Is Dante typical of the time? Is he a misogynist?

6. How was a work such as Dante's prepared and disseminated before the invention of the printing press?

7. What was Dante's involvement in the civil war between the Guelphs and the Ghibellines? How do you think this conflict may have influenced his writing?

ALTERNATIVE TERM PAPER SUGGESTIONS

1. Create a multimedia presentation of the various visual representations of Dante's work by such artists as Botticelli, William Blake, and Rossetti. Include quotations from Dante and music that is based on his work.

2. Create your own series of illustrations for one part of Dante's *Divine Comedy*. Use the work itself as the source of your ideas; do not use the work of other artists.

3. Write a canto in *terza rima* about a modern event on which you would like to comment.

Primary Sources

Alighieri, Dante. *Alighieri, Dante: Four Political Letters.* Trans. by Claire E. Honess. London : Modern Humanities Research Association, 2007. Provides a view of Dante's political involvement in the affairs of his time. Includes commentary.

Alighieri, Dante. *The Divine Comedy: The Inferno, The Purgatorio, and The Paradiso.* Trans. by John Ciardi. New York: New American Library, 2003. A modern translation by a renowned writer.

Alighieri, Dante. *Selections from the Vita Nuova (New Life).* Trans. by Joanna Finn-Kelsey and Thomas Okey. Maidstone: Crescent Moon, 2008. A series of poems and essays by Dante celebrating Beatrice, the woman he loved.

Secondary Sources

Chiarenza, Marguerite Mills. *The Divine Comedy: Tracing God's Art.* Boston: Twayne Publishers, 1989. A guide to teaching *The Divine Comedy*, including its themes, a chronological history of the author, the historical context, critical reception, and multiple primary and secondary sources for further research.

Dameron, George W. *Florence and Its Church in the Age of Dante.* Philadelphia: University of Pennsylvania Press, 2004. Chapters on the institutions, piety, vocations, and economy of the medieval Florentine church. Includes extensive supplemental material.

De Rooy, Ronald, ed. *Divine Comedies for the New Millennium.* Amsterdam: Amsterdam University Press, 2003. A collection of essays regarding translations of Dante's work, including discussion of the methods used to translate this piece.

Evan, Gillian Rosemary. *Fifty Key Medieval Thinkers.* London: Routledge, 2002. Contains a chapter concerning each of 50 influential medieval intellectuals from all walks of life, including Dante.

Gallagher, Joseph. *A Modern Reader's Guide to Dante's the Divine Comedy.* St. Louis: Liguori Publications, 2000. Although designed for first-time readers, this book also has a strong basis in scholarly fact.

World Wide Web

Bishop Pilla Program in Italian American Studies: Dante Studies. http://www
.jcu.edu/pilla/*dantestudies.htm.* Site hosted by John Carroll University
serves as a gateway for a large number of online translations, works in
Italian, illustrations, and other materials on Dante.

Dante Resources on the Internet. http://www.wisdomportal.com/Dante/
DanteResources.html#Poems. An amazingly comprehensive portal with
links to everything from lectures to quotations to stamps bearing Dante's
image.

The Divine Comedy: Research Edition. http://www.divinecomedy.org/divine_
comedy.html. This site features more than 20 full texts of the work in
several languages. Texts can be viewed in a variety of parallel formats and
are fully searchable. The first stop for any critical analysis of the work.

Princeton Dante Project. http://etcweb.princeton.edu/dante/pdp/. Contains texts
in Italian and English of *The Divine Comedy* and Dante's minor works.
Texts are searchable; site includes commentary, audio in both languages,
images, and a biography.

Multimedia Sources

The Circles of Light: The Divine Comedy. 1995. DVD. BBC Production. 50 minutes.
Dramatizations of scenes from Dante concerning the variations of love.

Dante's Inferno. 1993. DVD. Films Media Group. Eight segments, 11 minutes
each. Moves through the poem's first eight cantos in short segments.

Dante: Visions of the Inferno. 2006. DVD. Films Media Group. 74 minutes. Animated sequences, expert interviews, and an examination of Dante's purposes. Portions in Italian and French with English subtitles.

The Divine Comedy: Visions of Violence and Beauty. 2001. Films Media Group.
60 minutes. Examines Dante's text along with Botticelli's 92 surviving
illustrations completed 200 years after the poem's publication. Also considers the impact of the two artist's work on the imagination of the West.

Pioneers of the Spirit. 2002. DVD. VisionVideo. 55 minutes each. Set of seven
disks, with the fifth about Dante Aligheri.

82. Great Famine (1311–1317)

Between 800 and 1300, agricultural production had grown at a pace that
kept up with population growth. New technologies, new crops introduced from other lands, and new farming techniques all led to more food
being produced on less land. There were occasional food shortages in

some areas, and the poor often went hungry in the spring before crops were harvested, but the death of large numbers of people from starvation was rare. By the beginning of the 14th century, the population had increased to the point that producing crops on all arable land in optimal conditions was critical. At the same time, Europe was undergoing a slight shift in climate.

Beginning around 1311, a series of wet springs that prevented planting and early winters that shortened the growing season lessened food production. Although they were malnourished during the next two or three years, not many people died. The year 1315, however, was especially wet, and seeds that were planted rotted in the ground. The winter of 1315–1316 brought starvation to large numbers of people. Peasants, who were hardest hit by the famine, were too weakened to plant and care for crops in the spring, even if the weather improved, which it did not. The crops of 1316 were meager. By now, people had turned to eating their draft animals, and there were even some reports of cannibalism. Small children and infants were abandoned because parents could not feed them. Older people, especially women, sometimes starved themselves so that younger family members could survive.

In 1317, the weather normalized somewhat, but little planting was done. Draft animals were gone. People had eaten the grain they had set aside for planting and had no seed. About ten percent of the population had died of starvation. As much as ten percent more died of pneumonia, bronchitis, and other illnesses that were fatal in their malnourished state. The people who remained were simply too weak and had too few tools to make a rapid recovery. Slowly, however, food became more abundant, in part because there were many fewer people to feed. It was not until around 1325, however, that food production was sufficient enough for the population to begin to rise again.

TERM PAPER SUGGESTIONS

1. Compare the Great Famine of the 14th century to another famine such as the Potato Famine in Ireland in the mid-1800s, the engineered famine in Ukraine, or another 20th- or 21st-century famine. Are the causes comparable? What solutions were tried in each case? What were the consequences? What is your conclusion about famine?

2. During the Great Famine, a number of folktales developed, the best known of which is "Hanzel and Gretel." Another is "The Mouse Tower of Bingen." Research the stories that arose during this age and analyze their content and themes.

3. According to agricultural historians, at the time of the Great Famine, one bushel of grain seed was required to produce four bushels of grain. The medieval diet, especially among the poor, consisted almost entirely of grain. Research other factors related to food production and consumption, including the typical rent a farmer had to pay in food for the use of the land. How difficult was it for a farmer to feed his family in a good growing season?

4. Analyze the political, social, and economic consequences of the Great Famine.

5. Both poor and rich died during the Great Famine, although the poor suffered more. How did the monarchies deal with the famine in their countries? Were there any positive actions that helped their people survive?

6. There is still hunger in the world, and people die every day of starvation. Research this issue and analyze a specific problem you see in the production or equitable distribution of the food supply.

7. We hear a great deal about sustainable agriculture in the media. What is sustainable agriculture? How does it differ from earlier agricultural practices? What opinion do you have about this topic and why?

ALTERNATIVE TERM PAPER SUGGESTIONS

1. Create a multimedia presentation about the devastation caused by historic famines.

Primary Sources

de Venette, Jean. *The Chronicle of Jean de Venette,* ed. by Richard A Newhall, trans. by Jean Birdsall. New York: Columbia University Press, 1953. De Vennet writes about the events in France, including famine and plague, during the first half of the 14th century.

de Trokelowe, Johannes. "The Famine of 1315." *Medieval Sourcebook.* http://www.fordham.edu/halsall/source/famin1315a.html. Contemporary account of the famine.

Goodrich, Michael, ed. *Other Middle Ages Witnesses at the Margins of Medieval Society.* Philadelphia: University of Pennsylvania Press, 1998. A collection of translations of rare documents written by marginalized people in the Middle Ages.

Secondary Sources

Aberth, John. *From the Brink of the Apocalypse: Confronting Famine, War, Plague, and Death in the Later Middle Ages.* New York: Routledge, 2002. Divided into four sections based on the four horsemen of the apocalypse mentioned in the Book of Revelation. Section one focuses on famine in the Middle Ages.

Dyer, Christopher. *Making a Living in the Middle Ages: The People of Britain, 850–1520.* New Haven: Yale University Press, 2002. Discusses economic changes in medieval England, including the growth in industry, the rise of towns, and the effects of the Great Famine.

Fagan, Brian M. *The Little Ice Age.* New York: Basic Books, 2000. Chapter two discusses how climate changes caused the Great Famine.

Jordan, William Chester. *The Great Famine.* Princeton: Princeton University Press, 1996. Divided into three sections, the first discusses the events that led to the famine, with the others describing the situation in both rural and urban societies.

Mingay, G. E. *A Social History of the English Countryside.* London: Routledge, 1990. Describes changes that occurred in the English country from the feudal system to the mid-1800s. Chapter 3 deals with changes brought about by disease and famine.

World Wide Web

Imaging Famine. http://www.imaging-famine.org/. This Web site has no information about the European famine of the 14th century; however, the images shown and the questions that are asked about these images are thought provoking and can raise some of the same questions about earlier written reports of famine.

The Quality of Meat in the Medieval Home. http://kitchenhistorian. thecompendium.info/meat_and_spice.pdf. Discusses the varieties of meat available to medieval households and how meat was prepared and preserved,

Multimedia Sources

Common Life in the Middle Ages. DVD. Annenburg. Video 21 in a series of 25. learner.org. Individuals must register to view the videos, but there is no cost. Considers how the short life expectancy, famine, and disease influenced medieval thought.

Medieval Europe: Crisis and Renewal. 1996. DVD set. Insight Video. Professor Teofilo F. Ruiz leads viewers through the period between 1300 and 1500 and the series of calamities that plagued Europe. Includes footage on famines.

83. Battle of Bannockburn (1314)

Even before his conquest of Wales, England's Edward I (r. 1239–1307) had launched plans to bring Scotland under his control. At first, he had hoped to gain the crown peacefully by arranging a marriage between his son Edward and the only legitimate Scottish heir, the princess Margaret. Margaret's untimely death foiled this plan; however, Edward looked at the ensuing quarrel over the throne as an opportunity for him to gain sway over his northern neighbor. To prevent civil war, the Scottish Guardians (temporary ruling council) asked Edward I to serve as arbitrator between the opposing sides. Edward agreed on the condition that he be named overlord until the new government could be installed. After lengthy deliberations, Edward decided in favor of the Balliol candidate.

Yet no sooner was the decision made than Edward made it clear that he intended to continue as the Scottish overlord. Balliol was forced to agree to this and to accept decisions from the English regarding his country. In 1296, when Edward was ready to go to war with the French and demanded Scottish support troops, the Scottish rebelled. Edward's retaliation was swift and brutal. His troops swept through Scotland killing thousands on the march to Edinburgh. On the way back to England, Edward seized the Stone of Scone and took it to Westminster. Balliol was imprisoned in the Tower of London. Edward garrisoned English troops throughout the country and greatly curtailed Scottish liberty.

Opposition to Edward was led by William Wallace and Andrew de Moray, who gathered an army to meet the approaching English forces. Despite the English army being approximately five times larger, the Scots achieved a decisive victory at the Battle of Sterling Bridge in September 1297. The Scots continued to fight against the English and the following year at Falkirk the armies met again. Although the English were victorious, the Scots had practiced a scorched earth policy that left Edward's men without food, and they were forced to withdraw to English lands. Other battles followed with the Scots, who even crossed into English lands to attack. However, England was strong enough to force a truce with the Scots in 1302.

In 1305, Edward's forces captured and publicly executed William Wallace, a major blow to Scottish morale. In addition, Robert the Bruce was driven into hiding. When he came out of hiding in 1307,

Bruce renewed the fight against the English. His forces grew, especially when news of Edward I's death reached Scotland. It was not until 1314, however, that he was able to achieve the victory at Bannockburn that led to Scottish independence. In 1320, the Bruce sent the Declaration of Arbroath to the pope in Rome, formally declaring that Scotland was a free nation. Scotland remained a separate nation until 1603 when James VI of Scotland also became James I of England, uniting the two countries. The Stone of Scone was not returned to Scotland until 1997.

TERM PAPER SUGGESTIONS

1. Discuss the importance of national symbols such as the Stone of Scone to a people. Why did Edward take the stone? Why were the English so slow to return it? What similar symbols have played a part in international warfare?

2. What factors within Scotland itself made it easier for the English to conquer them? Have similar factors in other places led to conquests?

3. Compare an English historian's and Scottish historian's accounts of events in Scotland's war to achieve independence.

4. Analyze the relationship between Scotland and France during the early 14th century. What were the outcomes for both nations of their relationship?

5. Scotland underwent a long period without a king. What were the social and political consequences of an extended lack of leadership? How do consequences in Scotland compare to another nation that experienced similar circumstances? What was the importance of a king in the Middle Ages?

6. Some historians believe the Scottish national identity formed during its struggle for independence from England. Do you agree? What do you consider to be the characteristics of the national identity of the nation? How would the fight to remain a free nation have built these characteristics? What part do you think geography and physical features of the land play in developing a national identity?

ALTERNATIVE TERM PAPER SUGGESTIONS

1. Many Scots still speak Gaelic, the native language of Scotland. Create a multimedia presentation in which you compare English to Gaelic. Include brief audio segments of Gaelic.

2. Create an interactive map of Scotland with links to some of its most famous landmarks and historical sites.

Primary Sources

Anonymous. *Vita Edwardi Secundi*. Trans. by Wendi R. Childs. Oxford: Oxford University Press, 2005. Concerned with the reign of Edward II, this contemporary chronicle reports at length on the war with Scotland.

The Chronicle of Lanercost 1272–1346. Trans. by Herbert Maxwell. Somerset, UK: Lanerch Press, 2001. Probably compiled by monks at Lanercost Priory from a variety of sources, this volume shows a clear bias against the Scots. Facsimile reproduction of 1913 edition.

The Chronicler of Bury St. Edmonds. "Edward I and the Scottish Crown," in Archibald R. Lewis, ed. *The High Middle Ages: 840–1300*. Englewood Cliffs, NJ: Prentice-Hall, 1970. Recounts the issue of kingship in Scotland beginning with Margaret's death and tells of Edward's subsequent actions.

The Declaration of Arbroath in Brian L. Blakely and Jacquelin Collins, eds. *Documents in British History, Volume I: Early Times to 1714*. New York: McGraw-Hill, 1993. This document, written by Robert the Bruce, was sent to Pope John XXII, asking for his favor and help against England.

Herton, Thomas Gray of. *Scalacronica: A Chronicle of England and Scotland 1066–1382*. Whitefish, MT: Kessinger Publishers, 2008. Facsimile reprint of an 1836 edition. Includes descriptions of battles in the Scottish war for independence.

Stones, E. L. G., ed. *Anglo-Scottish Relations 1174–1328: Some Selected Documents*. Oxford: Oxford University Press, 2002. A number of documents from this period in a facing-page publication of both Latin and English versions.

Secondary Sources

Armstrong, Pete, and Turner, Graham. *Bannockburn 1314*. Oxford: Osprey, 2002. The story of Robert the Bruce's capture of the English-held castles in Scotland and the battle that won Scotland's independence.

Barrow, Geoffrey. *Robert Bruce: And the Community of the Realm of Scotland*. Edinburgh: Edinburgh University Press, 2005. Covers Scottish history from 1286–1329. Chapter 12 deals with the battle of Bannockburn and its importance to the nation.

Brown, Michael. *Bannockburn*. Edinburg: Edinburg University Press, 2008. Discusses not only the events leading up to and during the battle of Bannockburn, but also the aftermath for the British Isles as a whole.

Bingham, Caroline. *Robert the Bruce*. London: Constable, 1998. Biography of the Bruce that looks for the man behind the myths.

Magnusson, Magnus. *Scotland: The Story of a Nation.* London: HarperCollins Publishers, 2000. A complete history of Scotland from the Roman occupation until James VI. Includes chapters on William Wallace and Robert Bruce.

Nusbacher, Aryeh. *Bannockburn: 1314.* Glouchestshire: Tempus, 2004. Discusses not only the legendary figures of the war, but also the common soldiers and knights who helped win Scotland's freedom.

Reese, Peter. *Bannockburn.* Edinburg: Canongate Books, 2000. Battle history with multiple illustrations divided into three parts: the path to battle, the contenders, and Bruce's masterstroke.

Sadler, John. *Bannockburn: Battle for Liberty.* South Yorkshire: Pen and Sword Books, 2008. Focuses on the entire Scottish battle for liberty rather than just the battle of Bannockburn, but does feature a 32-page long description of the battle.

World Wide Web

De Re Militari: The Society for Medieval Military History. http://www.deremilitari.org/. Includes articles on all aspects of medieval military operations. Has both primary and secondary sources about fighting between England and Scotland. Provides extensive bibliography of related materials.

Scotland's History. http://www.bbc.co.uk/scotland/history/. This BBC site has pages on all eras of Scottish history, many images, timelines, interactive features, maps, and timelines.

Multimedia Sources

Heroes of Scotland: The Bruce of Bannockburn. DVD. Kultur Video. 50 minutes. Includes reconstructions, reenactments, primary sources, interviews; filmed in Scotland.

Heroes of Scotland: William Wallace–The True Story. DVD. Kultur Video. 50 minutes. Includes reconstructions, reenactments, primary sources, interviews; filmed in Scotland.

The History of Warfare: The Battle of Bannockburn, 1314–The Lion Rampart. 2009. DVD. Allegro Studio. 55 minutes. Reconstruction of the Battle of Bannockburn with actors and with special effects. Includes interviews with historians.

History's Mysteries: The True Story of Braveheart. 2005. DVD. The History Channel. 50 minutes. Examines the historical truth and the legend of William Wallace.

84. Hundred Years War (1337–1453)

The roots of the Hundred Years War go back to the Norman Conquest. William I of England was also duke of Normandy, with a kingdom on both sides of the English Channel. William split his French and English holdings between two sons, but during the next 250 years, English monarchs maintained or amassed territory in France. Periodic conflicts over these lands on the continent were common. At the beginning of the 14th century, tensions began to grow. English monarchs found the taxes imposed by the French king objectionable. Paying homage to the French king humiliated the English, and the French monarch was beginning to exercise greater power over the feudal principalities.

Tempers flared when in the 1330s Philip VI of France (r. 1328–1350) ignored his promise to restore English territory in Guienne taken by his father, Charles IV, and he gave French support to Scotland in its war against England. England also began to strengthen its power in Flanders, an important market for English wool. When Edward III (r. 1327–1377) asserted his claim to be the king of France and invaded the Low Countries in 1337, the Hundred Years War began. In 1340, Edward defeated the French fleet at Sluis, and in 1346 won the Battle of Crecy and besieged Calais. By 1360, England possessed Calais, and almost all of Aquitaine, and received a large ransom for having captured the king.

Around 1369, the French renewed the wars and won back most of the territories under the leadership of their able general Du Guesclin. In 1415, Henry V of England (r. 1413–1422) won at Harfleur and at the well-known Battle of Agincourt. After more victories, Henry forced Charles VI of France (r. 1380–1422) to recognize him (Henry) as heir to the French throne. The English continued to gain French land and by 1429 held almost all of Northern France. However, after Joan of Arc led the French in battle at Orleans, Charles VIII (r. 1422–1461) was able to be crowned. Joan's capture and death only fueled French resolve, and their victories continued. By 1453, England retained only their hold over Calais.

Over 100 years of war, the Great Famine, and the Black Death caused great harm to France and its social system. Yet, Charles VIII and later monarchs were able to rebuild the French nation from the ruins. Most of the powerful principalities had been destroyed, allowing the monarchy to unite the regions more cohesively under royal power.

TERM PAPER SUGGESTIONS

1. Analyze how the Hundred Years War affected the development of strong central monarchies in France and England.
2. What were the positive effects of the Hundred Years War for England?
3. How was the war financed in England? What effect did the war have on the English constitutional government and Parliament?
4. How were the armies raised for the war? What is meant by *indentured retinues?* What was the role of mercenaries? What were the Free Companies? What problems were created by the soldiers of these types?
5. Why were the English able to win significant victories over the French and overrun the countryside, but were not able to take the kingdom of France?

ALTERNATIVE TERM PAPER SUGGESTIONS

1. Create an interactive map showing the major battles of the Hundred Years War. Include a variety of information in the links you establish such as the number of troops on each side, leaders, outcome, and military strategies.
2. Create a board game based on the events and people involved in the Hundred Years War.
3. Create a blog on which you assume the persona of a soldier during one segment of the Hundred Years War. Post information about your life during your service to the king. Or choose to be one of the kings and post information for your countrymen.

Primary Sources

de Charny Geoffroi. *A Knight's Own Book of Chivalry*. Trans. by Elspeth Kennedy. Philadelphia: University of Pennsylvania Press, 2005. Fourteenth-century text advising knights on proper conduct as soldiers for God and king.

Gesta Henrici Quinti: The Deeds of Henry the Fifth. Trans. by Frank Taylor and John S. Roskel. New York: Oxford University Press, 1975. Translation of a contemporary history of Henry V.

Given-Smith, Chris, ed. *Chronicon Anonymi Cantauriensis (The Chronicle of Anonymous of Canterbury, 1346–1365)*. Oxford: Oxford University Press, 2008. The first complete translation of this chronicle of mid-14th century England.

Froissart, Jean. *The Chronicles of Froissart*. Trans. by John Bourchier. London: G. C. Macaulay, 1924. http://ehistory.osu.edu/osu/.Complete translation.

Froissart lived in the late 14th and early 15th centuries and traveled widely throughout Europe. He witnessed many of the events he records.

Knighton, Henry. *The Chronicle of Henry Knighton 1337–1396.* Trans. by G. H. Martin. New York: Oxford University Press, 1996. Contemporary narrative of English history during the early period of the Hundred Years War.

Rogers, Clifford J. ed. *The Wars of Edward III: Sources and Interpretations.* Woodbridge, UK: Boydell Press, 1999. Includes royal documents, military papers, and excerpts from chronicles to tell the story of Edward's military failures and his rise to success as a commander.

Secondary Sources

Allmand, Christopher. *The Hundred Years War: England and France at War c. 1300–c.1450.* Cambridge: Cambridge University Press, 1979. Features a special section on French geneology discussing the succession of the crown. Discusses the causes and progress of the war, approaches, conduct, and institutions of war, as well as the war's affect on society.

Burne, Alfred H. *The Crecy War: A Military History of the Hundred Years War from 1337 to the Peace of Bretigny, 1360.* Sacramento: Combined Publishing, 1999. As a British military tactician, Burne uses research, personal knowledge, and storytelling to describe the English campaigns in France during the war.

Crane, Susan. *The Performance of Self: Ritual, Clothing, and Identity during the Hundred Years War.* Philadelphia: University of Pennsylvania Press, 2002. Just at the time national identity was emerging, Crane argues that personal identity was also developing and can be seen through medieval costume and ritual.

Curry, Anne. *The Hundred Year's War.* New York: Palgrave Macmillan, 2003. Written by one of England's foremost experts on the Hundred Year's war, but it differs from other histories of the war in that it also contains portraits of soldiers, a discussion of the war's cruelties, and portraits of civilians.

Nicolle, David. *French Armies of the Hundred Years War: 1328–1429.* Oxford: Osprey Publishing, 2000. Well-illustrated with maps, diagrams, and other artwork; describes the history, organization, uniforms, and equipment of the French military force during the conflict.

Seward, Desmond. *The Hundred Years War: The English in France 1337–1453.* New York: Penguin, 1978. Lengthy, well-researched book focusing mostly on the characters central to the conflict.

Vale, Malcolm. *The Origins of the Hundred Years War: The Angevin Legacy, 1250–1340.* Oxford: Oxford University Press, 1996. Traces how the actions of earlier Anglo-French nobility led the two countries to war.

World Wide Web

BBC History: The Middle Ages. http://www.bbc.co.uk/history/british/middle _ages/. Site has articles, interactives, a timeline, images, and radio links. Includes extensive section on the HundredYears War.

British Battles. http://www.britishbattles.com/100-years-war/. Extensive information on British warfare from 1066 on. Images, timeline, anecdotes, informative articles.

De Re Militari: The Society for Medieval Military History. http://www.dere militari.org/. Includes articles on all aspects of medieval military operations. Has both primary and secondary sources on the Hundred Years War. Provides extensive bibliography of related materials.

"Hundred Years' War 1337–1453." *French-at-a-Touch.* http//:www.french-at-a-touch.com/French_History/. This is a commercial site but it has an extensive section on French history with timelines, maps, articles, and links.

"Hundred Years' War 1337–1453." *The Other Side.* http://www.theotherside. co.uk/. This Web site has a wide variety of information on Europe, including current events. Also has historical sections with articles, links, maps, and images.

Multimedia Sources

The Late Middle Ages. DVD. Annenburg. Video 23 of 25 in *The Western Tradition* series. Deals with the Hundred Years War and plague. learner.org. Individuals must register to view the videos, but there is no cost. Considers how the constant warfare and plague weakened Europe.

The Kings and Queens of England: 1216 to 1471. 2005. DVD. Cromwell Productions. 50 minutes. Brief biographies and discussion of major events in the monarchs' reigns.

85. Black Death (1347–1350)

Bubonic plague had stricken limited areas of the world for centuries. Athens was afflicted in the fifth century BCE. The Byzantine capital, Constantinople, suffered a serious outbreak during the sixth century and again in the eighth century. However, the outbreak that occurred in the mid-1300s spread from China through Asia into Europe and caused millions of deaths, as much as one-third to one-half of the population. According to contemporary accounts, the Black Death reached the port of Kaffa on the Black Sea in 1346. Legend says Tartar soldiers catapulted the dead bodies of plague victims over the walls of the city in an attempt to capture it, but the plague may have been transmitted by rats. Ships from Kaffa then carried the pestilence to Sicily and Genoa, and travelers spread it over land.

The Black Death is believed to have been carried by rats and the fleas they harbored. When the fleas migrated to humans, they infected people with the plague bacillus. Medical researchers estimate that at its height, the disease traveled as rapidly as eight to twelve miles a day. Because of this extremely rapid spread, the plague may have been present in a pneumonic form as well as being transmitted from person to person. The term *bubonic* comes from the buboes or swellings that formed in the lymph nodes of the armpit and groin areas. Other symptoms included profuse sweating, general weakness, fever, and for the pneumonic form, severe coughing. A majority of the diseased died within two to three days of developing symptoms; some lingered for as long as two to three weeks.

Reactions to the plague were varied. Some tried to flee areas where plague was present. Frightened people tried to seclude themselves from other individuals, but, of course, could not stop the movement of rats and fleas. In addition, a person could be a carrier for several days before he or she developed symptoms. A group known as the flagellants believed the plague was a punishment from God; they therefore beat themselves to show their suffering and penance. AntiSemitic pogroms were common as Christians blamed Jews for bringing the disease. Few stopped to think that the Jews were suffering as badly as any other group, In 1348, Pope Clement VI issued a bull, *Quamvis Perfidiam,* in which he condemned the persecution of Jews and the belief they had caused the plague, saying that the pestilence was everywhere, afflicting "Jews and many other nations." Writing about his experience during the plague, the physician Konrad of Megenberg said that so many Jews had died in Vienna that they had to increase the size of their cemetery. So many people were dying at the height of the plague that the pope announced a world indulgence, which allowed laity to perform the last rites and bury people.

When the worst of the outbreaks were over around 1351, some towns had been depopulated by plague or flight. Some areas had only 10 to 20 percent of their former populations. A few areas were almost unscathed, including some Jewish ghettoes, but the general decrease in population created a labor shortage, freed land from the need for agricultural production, and effectively destroyed the feudal system, allowing for the development of a middle class. The plague also severely curtailed trade, adversely affecting the economies of cities and nations. Psychological, religious, and sociological effects of the plague were long-lasting, but some historians credit the Black Death with bringing about changes such as the rise of secular education, industrialization, and vernacular literature.

TERM PAPER SUGGESTIONS

1. Trace the path of the Black Death along the trade routes between east and west. Analyze in detail the economic impact of this movement.
2. What were the social, political and economic consequences of the plague?
3. How did the economic and demographic forces present after the plague lead to a weakening of the feudal system?
4. What problems confronted kings after the plague and how did they respond?
5. Which societies were losers and which were winners as a result of the plague years? How did their experiences during these years differ?
6. What were the effects of the plague on literature and the arts during and immediately following its outbreak?
7. After the Black Death epidemic, diseases continued, and still continue, to play an important role in human history. What are some examples of current concerns about the effects or potential effects of diseases on societies?

ALTERNATIVE TERM PAPER SUGGESTIONS

1. You are a young person who works on the docks in Italy when the galleys come into port carrying the Black Death. Write a series of journal entries about what you see happening over the next two or three months in your city and to people you know.
2. Create an interactive map showing the path the plague followed from 1346–1350.
3. Many artists created visual images of the Black Death. Create a multimedia presentation using these images. Find appropriate music to accompany the images.

Primary Sources

Aberth, John, ed. *The Black Death: The Great Mortality of 1348–1350: A Brief History in Documents.* New York: Bedford/St. Martins, 2005. A collection of documents from Christian, Islamic, and Jewish writers throughout Europe on the course of the Black Death.

Clyn, John. *The Annals of Ireland.* Trans. by Bernadette Williams. Dublin: Four Courts Press, 2007. Clyn wrote his chronicle between 1333 and 1349 and includes reports of how the Black Death affected his monastery and surrounding regions.

Given-Smith, Chris, ed. *Chronicon Anonymi Cantauriensis (The Chronicle of Anonymous of Canterbury, 1346–1365).* Oxford: Oxford University Press, 2008. The first complete translation of this chronicle of mid-14th century England.

Herton, Thomas Gray of. *Scalacronica: A Chronicle of England and Scotland 1066–1382.* Whitefish, MT: Kessinger Publishers, 2008. Facsimile reprint of an 1836 edition. Tells the story of Britain before, during, and after the plague years.

Horrox, Rosemary, ed. *The Black Death.* Manchester: Manchester University Press, 1994. A very large collection of documents from throughout Europe written during and after the Black Death by ordinary citizens, governments, church authorities, and physicians.

Knighton, Henry. "Description of the Black Death from Chronicles" in Brian L. Blakely and Jacquelin Collins, eds. *Documents in British History, Volume I: Early Times to 1714,* 2nd ed. New York: McGraw-Hill, 1993, 90–92.

Marcus, Jacob Rader, and Saperstein, Marc, eds. *The Jew in the Medieval World: A Sourcebook, 315–1791.* Documents include those written by Jews during the plague and official documents written against the Jews.

Ordinance of Labourers (1349) and *Statute of Labourers* (1351). http://www .britannia.com/history/docs/. The first document represents Edward III's attempt to hold wages for laborers at their preBlack Death levels. The second is an attempt to enforce the first ordinance.

Secondary Sources

Bynum, Caroline Walker, and Freedman, Paul, eds. *Last Things: Death and the Apocalypse in the Middle Ages.* Philadelphia: University of Pennsylvania Press, 1999. A collection of scholarly essays concerning the medieval conception of death.

Byrne, Joseph P. *The Black Death.* Westport, CT: Greenwood Press, 2004. Discusses the spread of the Black Death, including its likely causes as determined then and now, and its affect on society, cities, individuals, and art.

Cantor, Norman F. *In the Wake of the Plague: The Black Death & the World it Made.* New York: The Free Press, 2001. Discusses facts and myths surrounding popular knowledge of the Black Death, with a lengthy section on "the Jewish Conspiracy," which was believed by many at the time as the cause.

Cohn, Samuel K. *The Black Death Transformed: Disease and Culture in Early Renaissance Europe.* New York: Oxford University Press, 2003. A revisionist history that examines a widespread array of primary and secondary sources that reevaluate the causes and impact of the Black Death.

Dyer, Christopher. *Making a Living in the Middle Ages: The People of Britain, 850–1520.* New Haven: Yale University Press, 2002. Discusses economic changes in medieval England, including the growth in industry, the rise of towns, and the effects of the Black Death.

Gottfried, Robert S. *The Black Death: Natural and Human Disaster in Medieval Europe.* New York: The Free Press, 1963. Broken into seven chapters, this book covers the history of the plague, the environment in Europe, the plague's beginnings and progress, its immediate consequences, the beginning of modern medicine, and the transformation of Europe.

Herlihy, David. *The Black Death and the Transformation of the West.* Cambridge: Harvard University Press, 1997. Short, but well researched volume discussing the plague and the technological and social advances that occurred in its wake.

Ziegler, Philip. *The Black Death.* New York: Harper & Row, 1969. Lengthy discussion of the origins of the Black Death, its spread throughout Europe, the death toll, and the effect on society, economics, education, agriculture, architecture, and the church.

World Wide Web

BBC History Online: The Middle Ages. http://www.bbc.co.uk/history/british/middle_ages/black_impact_01.shtml. Has articles, images, an animated population map, and other resources.

Secrets of the Dead: Mystery of the Black Death. http://www.pbs.org/wnet/secrets/previous_seasons/case_plague/index.html. The companion site for the PBS series includes articles, images, and a list of other informative websites.

The Decameron Web. http://www.brown.edu/Departments/Italian_Studies/dweb/dweb.shtml. Since *The Decameron* takes place during the plague, this site has a page with links to information on the Black Death.

Multimedia Sources

The Black Death. 2003. DVD. The History Channel. Part of the *History's Turning Points* series. 50 minutes. Traces the story of the Black Death from Venice in 1347 as it spread through Europe.

The Black Death: 1347 A.D. 2002. DVD. Transatlantic Films. 75 minutes. Begins with the ship that entered the harbor of Venice in 1347, and follows the trail of the plague throughout Europe, killing a third of the population.

Cataclysm: The Black Death Visits Tuscany. 2004. DVD. Films for the Humanities and Sciences. 49 minutes. Historians discuss the aftermath of the Black Death in the cities of Sienna and Florence.

Common Life in the Middle Ages. DVD. Annenburg. Video 21 in a series of 25. www.learner.org. Individuals must register to view the videos, but there is no cost. Considers how the short life expectancy, famine, and disease influenced medieval thought.

Heresy, War, and the Black Death: Christianity in the 13th and 14th Centuries. 1999. DVD. Films Media Group. 48 minutes. Considers two medieval reactions to the Black Death: to see the plague as a punishment from God or to place blame on the Jews.

In Search of History: Scourge of the Black Death. 2005. DVD. The History Channel. 50 minutes. Examines recorded outbreaks of the Black Death from Justinian's Plague in 542 until modern times; includes discussion of treatment and new understandings of how the disease spreads and affects the body.

Medieval Europe: Crisis and Renewal. 1996. DVD set. Insight Video. Professor Teofilo F. Ruiz leads viewers through the period between 1300 and 1500 and the series of calamities that beset Europe. Includes segment on the plague.

86. *The Decameron* is Published (1348)

In the midst of the Black Death, Giovanni Boccaccio created his literary masterpiece *The Decameron,* which begins with a vivid eye-witness description of the plague. The work is also one of the first to be written in vernacular Italian instead of Latin. Seven young Italian ladies and three gentlemen decide to leave the city of Florence for their country estates, hoping to escape the Black Death. In the country, they continue their carefree lifestyles and meet each day to tell stories on a theme determined by the king or queen chosen for that day. Each character tells 10 stories, for a total of 100 tales in the volume.

Boccaccio's tales vary from the comic to tragic, ancient to contemporary, and moral to amoral. The author does not judge the stories or their tellers; he is simply a storyteller himself. Boccaccio, who was influenced by both Dante and Petrarch, set the standard for Italian prose for centuries in this work. Later in life, he is said to have regretted writing *The Decameron,* but by that time it was being read throughout Europe.

In 1350, Boccaccio and Petrarch began a lifelong friendship characterized by extensive correspondence between the two. Petrarch is largely responsible for Boccaccio turning toward a more humanistic philosophy. In the same year, Boccaccio began his 15 volume Latin work on mythological science, *De genealogiis deorum gentilium,* a work indicative of his great learning on many subjects. Other works included *Corbaccio,* a misogynist rant caused by his being rejected by a woman he admired, *De casibus virorum illustrium,* in which men from Adam to Petrarch tell of their falls from fortune, and *De claris mulieribus,* biographies of 104 famous women. Boccaccio continued to write until his death in 1375, producing an incredible volume of work that influenced writers for centuries.

TERM PAPER SUGGESTIONS

1. How does Boccaccio portray women? Many medieval male writers were clearly misogynists. Does Boccaccio fit this category? Why or why not? Consider the women in *The Decameron, The Elegy of Lady Fiammetta,* and the biographies of famous women written by Boccaccio.

2. Using evidence from *The Decameron,* summarize what Boccaccio seems to believe about religion in general and the Catholic church in particular.

3. What customs, beliefs, and ideas popular in his own time does Boccaccio satirize or critique?

4. Numbers are often highly symbolic in literature. What meaning do you assign to the fact that there are 100 tales, 10 tales told for 10 days? How could storytelling help individuals deal with the emotional and societal instability they faced as a result of the plague?

5. Compare the fiction of Boccaccio to the historical *Chronicles of Froissart.* What do the two writers say about the crisis of the 14th century in Europe? Is there an apocalyptic tone in their writings, or do they depict events that they see as normal occurrences?

6. Compare and contrast the ways in which Boccaccio and Dante represent human sin or misconduct.

7. Analyze the influence the poet Petrarch had on Boccaccio's work. Examine the correspondence between the two men in your discussion.

ALTERNATIVE TERM PAPER SUGGESTIONS

1. Boccaccio's *Decameron* has inspired painters, illustrators, and musicians. Create a multimedia presentation using the visual images, Boccaccio's text, and music inspired by the work.

2. Create a storytelling performance using one of the stories from *The Decameron*. You should assume the persona of the character from the text.

Primary Sources

Boccaccio, Giovanni. *The Decameron.* Trans. by Jonathan Usher and Guido Waldman. Oxford: Oxford University Press, 1998. Includes introduction and bibliography.

Boccaccio, Giovanni. *The Elegy of Lady Fiammetta.* Trans. by Mariangela Causa-Steindler and Thomas Mauch. Chicago: University of Chicago Press, 1990. An innovative first person novel related by the female protagonist.

Boccaccio, Giovanni. *The Esposizioni.* http://www.brown.edu/Departments/Italian_Studies/dweb/dweb.shtml. This is Boccaccio's unfinished lecture on Dante's *Divine Comedy.*

Boccaccio, Giovanni. *Famous Women.* Trans. by Virginia Brown. Cambridge: Harvard University Press, 2003. Latin text and English translation on facing pages; this is the first collection of women's biographies in the West. 106 women are included.

Froissart, Jean. *The Chronicles of Froissart.* Trans. by John Bourchier. London: G. C. Macaulay, 1924. http://ehistory.osu.edu/osu/. Complete translation. Froissart lived in the late 14th and early 15th centuries and traveled widely throughout Europe. He witnessed many of the events he records.

Petrarch, Francesco. *Petrarch, the First Modern Scholar and Man of Letters: A Selection from His Correspondence with Boccaccio and Other Friends, Designed to Illustrate the Beginnings of the Renaissance.* Trans. by James Harvey Robinson. New York: G. P. Putnam, 1898. A number of these letters are available at *Francesco Petrarch and Laura de Nouves,* http://petrarch.petersadlon.com/index.html.

Secondary Sources

Hastings, Robert Alistair Bartley Gordon. *Nature and Reasoning in the Decameron.* Manchester: The University Press, 1975. A religious and secular discussion of morality as presented in *The Decameron.*

Kuhns, Richard. *Decameron and the Philosophy of Storytelling.* New York: Columbia University Press 2005. Discusses the method of storytelling in *The Decameron* from literary, philosophical, and historical perspectives.

Lee, A. C. *The Decameron: Its Sources and Analogues*. New York: Haskell House Publishers Ltd, 2005. Originally written in 1909, still the most popular handbook for *The Decameron* studies.

Migiel, Marilyn. *Rhetoric of the Decameron*. Toronto: Toronto University Press, 2005. Denounces masculine readings of *The Decameron* and also critiques previous feminine viewpoints, offering a modern feminist review of the classic text.

Weaver, Elissa B. ed. *The Decameron: First Day in Perspective*. Toronto: University of Toronto Press, 2004. A collection of scholarly essays on the first set of tales in The Decameron, sponsored by the American Boccaccio Association.

World Wide Web

The Decameron Web. http://www.brown.edu/Departments/Italian_Studies/dweb/dweb.shtml. A very helpful site; images, analysis, information on social context, a full-text translation, and a concordance.

Heliotropia: Forum for Boccaccio Research and Interpretation. http://www.heliotropia.org/index.shtml. *Heliotropia* is the official journal of the American Boccaccio Association. PDF files of the current issue and archives of past articles are available.

Multimedia Sources

Tales from the Decameron. 1988. VHS. Celeste Productions Ltd. for Channel 4. 71 minutes. Uses shadow puppet animation to retell six of Boccaccio's stories.

87. Ming Dynasty (1368–1644)

For almost a century, China was under the Mongol Yuan dynasty that began with Kublai Khan's ascent to the throne. Kublai's descendants had lived their entire lives in China and gradually lost interest in the Mongol-controlled lands. In 1356, the Chinese began a rebellion against the Yuan dynasty, and a leader soon came to the fore. Chu Yuan-Chang was orphaned at the age of 16 and became a Buddhist monk. But when drought and famine caused widespread hardship for the people in north and central China, he left the monastery to join a band of rebels. Contemporary texts report that Chu's band stole from the wealthy and spread their spoils among the needy. Considered a talented military leader, Chu and his army swept through China, bringing most of it under their control by 1368.

Chu proclaimed himself emperor when he captured the Yuan capital of Khanbligh (Beijing), but he established his capital in Nanjing (Nanking). Here, he took the imperial name of Hong-wu and established the Ming (Brilliance) dynasty. Hong-wu, now with an army of over 200,000, drove the Mongol artistocrats and their army out of China and pursued them until they reached the Mongol capital of Karakoum, which the Chinese destroyed.

Hong-wu now turned his attention to consolidating his power and the administration of the country. He began a series of reforms that organized the government into six boards, each with administrative powers, but each directly responsible to him. Rebels, and even his own generals whom he might suspect of disagreeing with him, were quickly executed. Hong-wu issued laws himself and eliminated the office of prime minister. The new emperor also established schools and encouraged farmers to grow cotton. Chu took an inventory of his nation. Administrators documented the size of all land holdings and used these for taxation purposes. A system of population registration called the *li-chia* organized every 10 households into a *chia* with a leader, and every 10 *chia* into a *li* with a group of ten *chia* chiefs. Labor needs and security issues were easily controlled with the system. People were classified into three groups, military, civil, and crafts and were not allowed to move from one class to another.

Under Chu, the civil service system was revived and government bureaucracy grew to become more important than the military. In 1382, Chu established the Embroidered-uniform Guard, which functioned as a kind of secret police with law enforcement and judicial powers over every individual in the nation. Hong-wu was noted for his kindness to the peasants, but his distrust of the educated and wealthy led him to treat them ruthlessly at times, including carrying out three purges. The third Ming emperor, Chu's son Yung-lo (r. 1403–1424) rebelled against his nephew who had been appointed emperor by *Hung-wu* before his death. After five years, Yung-lo desposed the emperor and took over the throne. At the time of Yung-lo's reign, the Chinese were among the world's best shipbuilders. The emperor ordered the eunuch Chen Ho (Zheng) to embark on seven voyages, taking as many as 300 ships and 28,000 sailors throughout Southeast Asia, along the Persian Gulf, and to the coast of Somalia. These expeditions were halted in 1433. Yung-lo undertook several construction projects such as dredging the Grand Canal and rebuilding Peking, where he moved the capital. He also commissioned the compilation of the Yung-lo *Tatien* (1403–1408), a collection of 11,915 volumes of literary, scientific, and religious works. About 800 chapters out of the more than 22,000 are extant.

During the 272 years of the Ming dynasty, government administration improved, building increased, and foreign trade developed. In spite of the violent beginning, the age was predominantly one of prosperity and peace. Arts, literature, science, and medicine grew rapidly during the age. Ming porcelain is often considered the finest of Chinese ceramic art. Painting flourished, four great novels were written, drama reached its heights, and architecture was at its zenith.

TERM PAPER SUGGESTIONS

1. How did the administration function under the six ministries established by Hong-wu? What checks and balances were part of the system? How did the ministries consolidate Hong-wu's power?

2. What effect did the seven exploratory voyages led by Zheng (Chen Ho) have on the culture and level of tolerance and open-mindedness of China? Why do you think these voyages were stopped? Were the voyages detrimental or helpful to China? How are the legends of Sinbad connected to the voyages of Zheng?

3. Sort through the conflicting narratives about Hong-wu. Was he a great leader? Was he a compassionate ruler? Was he a cruel despot? Did he have more positive or negative leadership qualities?

4. What roles did eunuchs fulfill in the Ming Dynasty?

5. The Forbidden City in Bejing was constructed under Ming emperors. What were the purposes of this enterprise? How did the City reflect the cultural values of the Chinese?

6. Hong-wu instituted a number of agricultural reforms throughout the Chinese countryside, many of which were continued and added to by his successors. What were the effects of these reforms? How did Chinese agriculture change under the Ming dynasty? Were these changes positive or negative for the populace?

7. Compare the siege warfare of medieval China with that of medieval Europe.

8. Compare the justice and legal system in Ming China to that of another medieval culture.

9. How did the Ming emperors use art as propaganda?

ALTERNATIVE TERM PAPER SUGGESTIONS

1. Create a multimedia virtual tour of the Forbidden City. Include a map of the structure, links to additional information, and medieval Chinese music.

2. Create a multimedia presentation on Ming art and architecture. Incorporate medieval Chinese music.

Primary Sources

Chu Yuan-Chang. *Manifesto of Accession as First Ming Emperor.* http://www
.fordham.edu/halsall/eastasiasbook.html. This letter was sent to the
Byzantine Emperor in 1372.

Ebrey, Patricia Buckley. *Chinese Civilization: A Sourcebook,* 2nd ed. New York:
The Free Press, 1993. Contains 60 pages of translations of Ming documents on a number of subjects.

Primary Source. *The Enduring Legacy of Ancient China.* Boston: Cheng & Tsui,
2006. Printed text plus CD, designed for teachers and students. Includes
primary documents and guides for using them.

Secondary Sources

Andrew, Anita M., and Rapp, John A. *Autocracy and China's Rebel Founding
Emperors: Comparing Chairman Mao and Ming Tatzu.* Lanham, MD:
Rowman and Littlefield, 2000. Offers a comparison of Mao Zedong and
Ming Tatzu, describing the similarities between the founding of the
Ming Dynasty and the Cultural Revolution.

Dreyer, Edward L. *Zheng He: China and the Oceans in the Early Ming Dynasty,
1405–1433.* Upper Saddle River, NJ: Longman, 2006. Describes the
voyages of explorer Zheng He during the early portion of the Ming
Dynasty, including how they affected China's world view during that
period and thereafter.

Gascolgne, Bamber. *The Dynasties of China: A History.* Philadelphia: Running
Press, 2003. A history of the various dynasties of China, it focuses not
only on general history, but also on the personalities that affected
each era.

Hucker, Charles O. *The Ming Dynasty: Its Origins and Evolving Institutions.* Ann
Arbor: University of Michigan, Center for Chinese Studies, 1978. Discusses the organization of the beginning of the Ming Dynasty, as well as
the dynasty in its maturity.

Menzies, Gavin. *1421: The Year the Chinese Discovered America.* New York:
HarperCollins. 2003. Basis for a PBS series, this book explores the idea
that Zheng's voyages may have taken him to the shores of North America
70 years before Columbus.

Mote, Frederick W., Twitchett, Denis, and Fairbank, John K. *The Cambridge
History of China: The Ming Dynasty, 1368–1644, Part 1.* Cambridge,
UK: Cambridge University Press, 1988. Chapters 2 and 3 in
particular focus on the rise of the Ming Dynasty, including its military
origins.

World Wide Web

Asia for Educators. http://www.columbia.edu/itc/eacp/japanworks/cosmos. Hosted by Columbia University, this site contains images, multimedia presentations, timelines, maps, primary sources, and articles.

Ebrey, Patricia Buckley. *A Visual Sourcebook of Chinese Civilization.* http://depts .washington.edu/chinaciv/index.htm. A wide variety of images and information grouped into 10 categories.

Chinese Siege Weapons. http://www.grandhistorian.com/chinesesiegewarfare/. Images, information, and timeline for Chinese siege warfare. In Chinese and English.

James P. Geiss Foundation. http://www.geissfoundation.org. The Geiss Foundation is dedicated to promoting the study of Ming China. The resources are somewhat limited here, but there are some unusual and rare images and information on the site.

Society for Ming Studies. http://www.colby.edu/ming. This site maintains a list of links to Web information about Ming China.

Multimedia Sources

Ancient Treasures: Imperial Art of China. 1998. DVD. Films Media Group. 9 minutes. Short overview of art created for China's rulers. Includes Ming art.

Emperor of the Seas. 2008. DVD. Razor Digital. 52 minutes. Traces the seven ocean voyages of Zheng and his men.

1421: The Year China Discovered America. 2004. DVD. PBS. 120 minutes. Explores the controversial idea that Zheng's voyages may have taken him to the shores of North America 70 years before Columbus.

Wonders of the Ancient Worlds: Ancient China. 2002. DVD. Schlessinger Media. 50 minutes. Video tour of four of China's most spectacular structures, including the Forbidden City.

88. *The Catalan Atlas* and Developments in Cartography (1375)

The medieval advancements in human understanding of geography and how to accurately represent it made the exploration of the Renaissance possible. *The Catalan Atlas*, published in 1375, is a landmark in this advancement. Abraham Cresques, a Jewish mapmaker at the Catalan school of cartography, created the atlas at the request of Charles V of France, and it was drawn and colored by hand.

Cresques integrated several traditions in this atlas that is three meters high and 65 centimeters wide. The images were drawn on parchment that was attached to six panels of wood. The medieval mappamundi tradition accepted the Christian worldview of the age and was often more theological than geographic representations. These maps usually placed Jerusalem near the center of the world and were filled with religious imagery. Cresques drew on this tradition and used religious imagery, but only in the nonEuropean sections of the atlas, which were the lesser known areas. The farther away from the Christian center, the more fantastical the images became. He also drew on the tradition of portolan charts of the sea that provided valuable navigational information for medieval ships. Cresques's panel representing the Atlantic Ocean and Black and Mediterranean Seas have rhumb lines first used in the portolan charts. Rhumb lines marked the compass directions of winds and assisted sailors in plotting the ship's course. The African area of the atlas not close to the Mediterranean is filled with fanciful images such as the mythical east to west flowing River of Gold that carried the riches of the interior continent to the Atlantic. Asia has drawings of camel caravans, a female warrior, and pearl divers.

The European and Mediterranean sections of the atlas indicate how cartography advanced since the earlier T-O mappamundi. The maps are detailed and highly accurate and much more useful to a monarch than the remainder of the atlas. More than 1,000 places were identified throughout Europe and the Mediterranean with flags indicating the political power in the area. Correct place names are situated at right angles to the coast line of the Mediterranean and the Atlantic. Crosses for churches indicate large cities, but nothing marks the favorite spots for pilgrimage. Few illustrations appear in this area of the atlas, but rivers and mountains are clearly marked.

The Catalan Atlas marks the first use of a compass rose, but it is not aligned with the rhumb lines as later roses are. A great deal of text is also found on the atlas, but like the symbols, there is no definite orientation. Parts of the map can be read regardless of the point from which one is viewing it. A calendar wheel is marked with 1375 so that the atlas can be accurately dated. Cresques has interwoven Biblical tradition, Marco Polo's and Ibn Battuta's travel accounts, Greek and Roman myths, popular literature, and earlier maps to create a map that gives insight into the European worldview of the time and to indicate what is to come.

TERM PAPER SUGGESTIONS

1. Analyze the relationship between map making, expanding travel, and navigational technology such as astrolabes and sextants.
2. What effects did the "new learning" based on Greek scholarship have on the development of cartography?
3. How do cartographic projections reflect the cosmology and ideology of their creators?
4. In what ways does a historian use maps as primary documents from a time period? What "readings" of a culture can be made using maps? Why are the distortions important?
5. Evaluate the usefulness of medieval maps. In what ways did the maps make travel easier? What problems would travelers encounter when using the maps?
6. How does the Catalan Atlas differ from modern world maps in technique, content, and intended use?

ALTERNATIVE TERM PAPER SUGGESTIONS

1. Create a multimedia glossary of cartography terminology using public domain images to illustrate each term. Be sure to include terms from maps of the Middle Ages, although you may also use modern map terminology.
2. Medieval maps are sometimes viewed as primitive attempts at modern mapping with geographical and topographical features. However, these early maps often had quite different purposes. Research the varied purposes of medieval maps and create a multimedia presentation that groups images of the medieval maps under those purposes.

Primary Sources

The Catalan Atlas, 14th Century. http://www.bnf.fr/eluminures/manuscripts/aman6.htm. The site is maintained by The Bibliotheque Nationale de France and includes other manuscript images as well.

Chekin, L. S. *Northern Eurasia in Medieval Cartography: Inventory, Texts, Translation, and Commentary.* In addition to Chekin's commentary and translations of medieval maps, this book contains 100 reproductions of early maps.

Vigra, Vincent, and The Library of Congress. *Cartographia: Mapping Civilizations.* New York: Little, Brown, 2007. Collection of historic maps selected from the more than 4 million in the Library of Congress.

Secondary Sources

Buisseret, David. *Monarch, Ministers, and Maps: The Emergence of Cartography as a Tool of Government in Early ModernEurope.* Chicago: University of Chicago Press, 1992. Although this collection of essays deals with the centuries immediately following the Middle Ages, it provides understanding of just how important medieval developments in cartography were to become.

Ditchburn, David, MacLean, Simon, and MacKay, Angus. *Atlas of Medieval Europe.* London: Routledge, 2007. Covers the entire medieval period from the Atlantic to the Russian steepes. Maps are used to discuss issues or series of events in medieval history. 180 maps, commentary, and bibliography.

Edson, Evelyn. *The World Map, 1300–1492: The Persistence of Tradition and Transformation.* Baltimore: Johns Hopkins University Press, 2007. Contains discussion of Andrea Bianco's three maps, mappamundi of the 13th and 14th centuries, and the influence of travel and exploration on cartography.

Ehrenberg, Ralph E., ed. *Mapping the World: An Illustrated History of Cartography.* Washington, D.C.: National Geographic, 2005. Chronologically arranged collection of maps covering thousands of years.

Goffart, Walter. *Barbarians, Maps, and Historiography: Studies in the Medieval West.* Toronto: University of Toronto, 2009. A collection of Goffart's previously published essays on medieval narrative and printed maps and history.

Harley, J. B., and Woodward, David, eds. *The History of Cartography: Cartography in Prehistoric, Ancient, and Medieval Europe and the Mediterranean, Vol. I.* Chicago: University of Chicago Press, 1987. Comprehensive resource on early maps with contributions from a variety of scholars on their areas of expertise.

Haywood, John. *Historical Atlas of the Medieval World: AD 600–1492.* New York: Metro Books, 2000. A useful reference for maps and medieval history. Shows how political divisions were constructed throughout the Middle Ages.

Talbert, Richard J. A., and Unger, Richard, eds. *Cartography in Antiquity and the Middle Ages: Fresh Perspectives, New Methods.* Leiden: Brill Academic Publishers, 2008. Thirteen experts contribute to the discussion of the history of mapmaking.

Thrower, Norman J. W. *Maps and Civilization: Cartography in Culture and Society.* Chicago: University of Chicago Press, 2008. Discusses mapping from prehistoric times until the present. Chapter 4 is about cartography in medieval Europe and the Islamic world.

Whitfield, Peter. *New Found Lands: Maps in the History of Exploration.* New York: Routledge, 1998. Explores the way individuals used maps as an expression of the power of conquest and annexation. 150 illustrations.

World Wide Web

Early Medieval Maps. http://www.henry-davis.com/MAPS/EMwebpages/EM1.html. This site includes a timeline of medieval cartography, images of medieval maps, reconstructed images where needed, and an extensive bibliography.

Europeana: Think Culture. http://www.europeana.edu/portal/index.html. This site produced by the European Union allows visitors to search for many items of cultural significance. There are about 70 images of medieval European maps on the site. New information is added frequently.

Map History/History of Cartography. http://www.maphistory.info/index.html. This site does not appear impressive when opened, but it is a very helpful portal to bibliographic essays, map images, and free Web texts on cartography.

Periodic Historical Atlas. http://www.euratlas.com/summary.htm. Online collection of maps of Europe from the years 1 to 2000. May zoom in and out to search for features. Has links and a bibliography.

Perry-Castañeda Library Map Collection. http://www.lib.utexas.edu/maps/historical/history_middle_east.html. A large collection of historic maps of the Middle East.

Multimedia Sources

The Face of the World: A History of Human Exploration. 2004. DVD. Films for the Humanities and Sciences. Three 30-minutes programs. The story of mapmaking from prehistory until the 20th century. Includes *First Steps into the Unknown.* An introduction to humanity's development of geographic understanding from prehistory until the Portuguese explorations during the Renaissance.

Bridging World History: Unit 1. Maps, Time, and World History. 2004. DVD. Annenberg. 30 minutes. Part of a 26 part set. http://www.learner.org/. Examines how historians use geographic and chronological frameworks to study world history. Viewers must register and log in, but the service is free. Has a companion Web site with additional material.

89. John Wycliffe Translates the Bible into English (1376)

Oxford professor John Wycliffe was one of many individuals who criticized the church for the Great Schism that resulted in the election of two popes. Early in his career, Wycliffe received several church offices and was chosen to go to Rome to negotiate the payment of tribute to the papacy. Like some other devout individuals of his time, he attacked the priesthood for corruption and the accumulation of worldly goods, questioned doctrine such as transubstantiation, and asserted that the essential authority on matters of faith was the Bible, not the priesthood or the pope. Wycliffe encouraged his followers to read the Bible, and in order to make this happen, he began the first full translation of the Bible into English, probably completed primarily by his assistants. The Council of Toulouse in 1299 had expressly forbidden the laity to possess scripture other than Psalms and forbade the Bible's translation "into the vulgar tongue."

Wycliffe's actions and beliefs were in violation of canonical law and were threatening to the hierarchy of the church. Pope Gregory XI ordered Wycliffe to appear before the bishop of London in 1377 to answer charges of heresy. General rioting in London at the time enabled Wycliffe to escape, and he was placed under the protection of the Queen Mother. A second hearing in 1378 aroused such negative public opinion against the church that Wycliffe was not sentenced. He continued to teach and to write against the church until 1380 when he was forced to retire from Oxford. His works were condemned by the London synod in 1382 and many were burned. By this time, however, many individuals had copies of the English Bible, his pamphlets, and other works, and Wycliffe's influence on his followers, called the Lollards, had spread far beyond England, paving the way for the Protestant Reformation. Wycliffe died in 1384.

TERM PAPER SUGGESTIONS

1. Why is John Wycliffe sometimes called "the Morning Star of the Reformation"? What are some doctrines he shared with later reformers?

2. Research the church's objections to having the Bible translated into the vernacular. Why did the church take this position? What was to be gained by keeping ordinary people from reading the Biblical text?

3. Wycliffe was highly critical of the practice of excommunication, which had been threatened or imposed on individuals from the poorest serf to the mightiest of monarchs. Considering Wycliffe's beliefs about the relationship of an individual to God, what were his objections to this policy? Why was the church so adamant about retaining the policy?

4. The Hebrew Bible (Torah) is the basis for the Old Testament of the Christian Bible, but there are differences, particularly in the organization of the books. Why do you think Christians rearranged the order of the books? What purposes did these changes serve?

5. Compare the contents of the Christian Bible and the Qu'ran.

6. Trace the development of the Lollards in England and throughout Europe and their influence on the Protestant Reformation.

ALTERNATIVE TERM PAPER SUGGESTIONS

1. In the character of Wycliffe, prepare and present a speech in your own defense against the charge of heresy before the bishop of London.

2. Prepare a multimedia presentation about the history of the Christian Bible. Include information from early Christian history when the church decided upon the Biblical canon, until the discovery of the Dead Sea Scrolls and modern translations.

Primary Sources

Powell, Edgar, and Trevelyan, George Macaulay, eds. *The Peasants' Rising and the Lollards: A Collection of Unpublished Documents Forming an Appendix to "England in the Age of Wycliffe."* Whitefish, MT: Kessinger Publishing, 2009. Facsimile reproduction of an 1899 edition of these primary source documents.

Wycliffe, John. *An Apology for Lollard Doctrines.* Trans. by James Henthorn Todd. Charleston, SC: BiblioLife Reproduction Series, 2009. Wycliffe's explanation of his beliefs.

Wycliffe, John. *The English Works of Wyclif Hitherto Unprinted.* Boston: Adamant Media Corporation, 2005. Unabridged facsimile of an 1880 edition published in London. Contains a large number of documents on a variety of topics.

Wycliffe, John. *Tracts and Treatises of John de Wycliffe, D.D. with Selections and Translations from his Manuscripts, and Latin Works.* Ed. for The Wycliffe Society by the Rev. Robert Vaughan, D.D. London: Blackburn and Pardon, 1845. *Online Library of Liberty.* http://oll.libertyfund.org/index .php?option=com_content&task=view&id=380.

Wycliffe's translation of the Bible into English is available free from several Web sites.

Secondary Sources

Cadman, Samuel Parkes. *The Three Religious Leaders of Oxford and Their Movements.* New York: The MacMillan Company, 1916. http://books.google .com/. Book I focuses on Wycliffe and later medievalism through chapters such as "Heralds of Reform," "Sources of Wycliffianism," "The Quarrel with the Papacy," and "Princes and People."

Evans, Gillian Rosemary. *Fifty Key Medieval Thinkers.* London: Routledge, 2002. Contains a chapter concerning each of 50 influential medieval intellectuals from all walks of life, including Wycliffe.

Evans, G. R. *John Wyclif: Myth & Reality.* Downers Grove, IL: Intervarsity, 2006. Offers a well-researched, up-to-date biography of Wycliffe that attempts to dispel some of the myths regarding his life's work.

Kenny, Anthony. *Wyclif in His Times.* New York: Clarendon Press, 1986. Features articles from multiple contributors discussing Wycliffe's influence on multiple disciplines.

McFarlane, Kenneth Bruce. *John Wycliffe and the Beginnings of English Nonconformity.* London: English Universities Press, 1952. Describes how John Wycliffe's translation of the Bible helped spread Protestantism throughout England.

Stacey, John. *John Wyclif and Reform.* Philadelphia: The Westminster Press, 1964. Discusses Wycliffe and his affect on the reformation through his translation of the Bible.

Tyndale, William. *The Obedience of a Christian Man.* Trans. by David Scott Daniell. London: Penguin Books, 2000. A biography of Wycliffe by later reformer Tyndale.

World Wide Web

English Bible History. http://www.greatsite.com/timeline-english-bible-history/ index.html. This is a commercial site, but it has information about Wycliffe and other reformers and interesting images of early Bibles.

The History of the Bible: Part VI: John Wycliffe. http://www.ancientpage.com/museum/history/englishbible/english2.htm. Information posted by the Wycliffe Society.

The Lollard Society. http://lollardsociety.org/. Has a large number of texts by Wycliffe and Hus, scholarly articles, and extensive bibliographies of resources.

Multimedia Sources

The Battle for the Language of the Bible. 2003. DVD. Films for the Humanities and Sciences. 52 minutes. Traces the difficulty in gaining acceptance for a Bible in the English language. Wycliffe, Caxton, Tyndale, and the KJV are included.

The Dissenter. 1993. VHS. New Dimensions Video. 57 minutes. Features stories of Wyclif, John Hus, and Martin Luther as they endeavored to reform the church.

John Wycliffe: The Morning Star. No date. DVD. CF Media. 75 minutes. Video biography of Wycliffe; focuses on the response to his translation of the Bible and his fight against abuses such as the sale of indulgences.

90. Great Schism (1378–1415)

In 1377, Pope Gregory XI (r. 1370–1378) moved his court from Avignon back to Rome, thus ending the Avignon papacy. However, the controversy the church faced did not end. When Gregory died, the new pope, Urban VI (r. 1378–1389), an Italian, was elected by the cardinals in Rome. He hated the French and immediately began to attack the French cardinals. The cardinals left Rome, denied the legitimacy of Urban's election, and chose their own pope for Avignon. Now, not only was the church itself split, but all of Europe began to take sides and support one pope over the other.

Church leaders tried unsuccessfully, in 1409 at the Council of Pisa, to reach an agreement that would mend the schism, but they only made matters worse. Declaring that neither Pope Gregory XII in Rome nor Pope Benedict XIII was the rightful heir, they elected a third pope, Alexander V. Alexander died shortly after his election, but his successor, John XXIII, won allegiance from much of Europe. Then, in 1415, the Council of Constance met, determined to reunite Catholics under one pope. The Council asked all three popes to resign; only Gregory complied. The other two were deposed and a new pope, Martin V (r. 1415–1431), was elected.

The Council of Constance met 45 times during its three-year session and dealt with a number of other church issues, including Conciliar rights, John Hus, and the Lollards. Lollards were the followers of John Wycliffe who had died in 1384. His ideas, however, did not die with him. In fact, the movement had spread and grown in strength. In Bohemia, under the leadership of John Hus, the movement had grown especially strong and threatening. Hus and his fellow reformer Jerome of Prague were called before the Council to answer charges of heresy, were found guilty, and were condemned to be burned at the stake. The Council also ordered the bones of Wycliffe disinterred and burned.

The Council of Constance achieved its primary goal of ending the Great Schism, but it was unable to stop the spread of dissent that would grow into the Reformation.

TERM PAPER SUGGESTIONS

1. What were the effects of the Great Schism on the European balance of power?

2. Explain the Conciliar Movement within the church. What were its aims? What effect did it have on papal power?

3. Medieval Europe experienced several crises in the 14th century, some natural and some caused by man. What connections can you make between three or more of the following crises: the Black Death, the Babylonian Captivity, Great Schism, the Hundred Years' War, the Peasant Revolts, and the rise in heresy? Which of the events do you think caused the greatest disruption to society and why?

4. Both heresy and schism represent a break within the structure of the church. In the 14th century, how were the two different and how did the church react to each? What were the long-term effects of each?

5. Compare Western Roman Catholicism with Eastern Orthodox Christianity in the 14th century. What has each retained from early Christianity? How has each changed? On what points of doctrine are they together, and where have they drifted apart?

6. Discuss the outcomes of the Council of Constance on the papacy and on the other matters it discussed.

7. Was John Hus a heretic? How did his work change Christianity?

ALTERNATIVE TERM PAPER SUGGESTIONS

1. By the time the Council of Constance met in 1415, there were three European popes. With a partner, or in a group of three, assume the personas

of two of the three popes and present debate arguments that you might deliver before the Council as to why you should be the only pope.

2. Write a series of diary entries that might have been written by John Hus between the time he is ordered to appear before the Council of Constance and his death.

Primary Sources

Peters, Edward, ed. *Heresy and Authority in Medieval Europe: Documents in Translation*. Philadelphia: University of Pennsylvania, 1980. Contains a translation of the edict from the Council of Constance, excerpts from John Hus's treatise "On Simony," and a contemporary report of the trial and execution of Hus written by Peter of Mladonovice.

Speed, Peter, ed. *Those Who Prayed: An Anthology of Medieval Sources*. New York: Italica Press, 1997. A large collection of translated documents on medieval spiritual and religious life from 600–1500.

The Council of Constance. http://www.piar.hu/councils/ecum16.htm. Some sections of the documents produced by the Council of Constance are translated; other sections are summarized, but the entire substance of the meetings is covered.

Secondary Sources

Blumenfeld-Kosinski, Renate. *Poets, Saints, and Visionaries of the Great Schism, 1378–1417*. University Park: The Pennsylvania State University Press, 2006. Discusses the discord created by the existence of three popes and the letters, allegorical and polemical texts, prophecies, and images created by those attempting to offer hope and solutions.

Creighton, Mandell. *A History of the Papacy from the Great Schism to the Sack of Rome*. London: Longmans, Green, 1897. Volume I, Book I discusses the three popes of the Great Schism as well as the conflict itself in great detail.

Gail, Marzieh. *The Three Popes*. New York: Simon and Schuster, 1969. Describes the effects of the three popes in Rome, Avignon, and Pisa, as all attempted to control Christianity.

Lea, Henry Charles. *A History of the Inquisition of the Middle Ages:* Vol II. New York: Harper & Brothers, 1887. "Convocation of the Council of Constance" gives a brief history of the Council of Constance, including the trial of John Hus.

Lewin, Alison Williams. *Negotiating Survival: Florence and the Great Schism, 1378–1417*. Cranbury, NJ: Rosemont, 2003. Discusses the effects of the Great Schism on life in Florence both during and after the conflict.

Salembier, Louis. *The Great Schism of the West*. London: Kegan Paul, Trench, Trubner, 1907. A classic and authoritative work on the causes of the Schism.

Stump, Phillip H. *The Reforms of the Council of Constance (1414–1418)*. Leiden: E. J. Brill, 1994. Divided into three parts, The Context, The Reform, and The Ideas and Images;this text discusses the goals, achievements, and failures of the Council of Constance.

Thatcher, Oliver J., and McNeal, Edgar H. *A Source Book for Medieval History*. New York: Charles Scribner's Sons, 1905. Sections 171–173 focus on the Council of Constance, beginning with the council's claim of supreme authority in 1415, the reforms demanded by the council, and the meeting of general councils and their power in the church. Digital copy at http://www.archive.org/details/sourcebookformed00thatuoft.

Wilks, Michael. *The Problem of Sovereignty in the Later Middle Ages: The Papal Triumph with Augustinus Triumphus and the Publicists*. Cambridge: Cambridge University Press, 1963. A discussion of the development of stable secular governments alongside the decline in the church's political control.

Wylie, James Hamilton. *The Council of Constance to the Death of John Hus*. London: Longmans, Green,. 1900. This book, divided into lectures, focuses on the trial and execution of John Hus, but lectures II and III give an exhaustive history of the Council of Constance.

World Wide Web

Christian Classics Ethereal Library. http://www.ccel.org/. This searchable site has translations of both primary and secondary sources.

The Lollard Society. http://lollardsociety.org/. Has a large number of texts by Wycliffe and Hus, church documents, scholarly articles, and extensive bibliographies of resources.

Multimedia Sources

John Hus. DVD. CF Media. 55 minutes. Story of Hus's fight to bring the Bible to people in their own language, his trial, and death at the stake.

Sectarianism and Schism in Europe: Christianity in the 15th and 16th Centuries. 1999. DVD. Films for the Humanities and Sciences. 48 minutes. Part I discusses the efforts of popes to achieve political independence and the Great Schism. Part II concerns later church developments.

Truth Prevails: The Undying Faith of Jan Hus. 2007. DVD. Vision Video. 60 minutes. On location filming, interviews with historians; CD has extended interviews, timeline, and teaching resources.

91. Peasants' Revolt (1381)

After the reduction of the population by the Black Death (1347–1350), agricultural workers were in short supply, but landlords did not want to pay higher wages or allow workers to move to other areas. Periodic rebellions broke out when the nobility tried to reduce peasants' already limited rights. In England, in 1351, the Statute of Labourers attempted to keep wages at preplague levels. The statute was not effective at holding the wages down and created anger among the peasants. The Jacquerie revolt took place in France in 1358, as peasants protested the pillaging of their land by the mercenary soldiers of the Hundred Years War (1337–1453) and the nobility's excessive demands for rent. When the leader, Guillaume Karle, was captured and beheaded, the remainder of the protesters went home, but the nobles still killed thousands of the poor in retribution.

In 1380, the English crown increased the poll tax to one shilling per person. This so angered poor workers that they revolted. The rebellion began in Essex and Kent with Wat Tyler as the leader. The rebels quickly seized Canterbury and then converged on London, increasing their numbers along the way. Rebels requested that Richard II (r. 1367–1400) meet with them to discuss their demands. When he refused, they swept through the streets, burning homes and buildings, including two prisons. The peasants then stormed the Tower of London and killed several prominent individuals. On June 14, Richard agreed to a meeting. The king agreed to abolish serfdom, reduce taxes, and change laws concerning the buying and selling of goods. The next day, in another meeting, Tyler was stabbed by the mayor of London and died soon after. Richard II successfully defused the situation by promising concessions, but as soon as the rebels dispersed, reprisals followed and all the concessions were reversed.

In 1382, further revolts in England led to the execution of 10 men. The 14th-century revolts did not immediately end serfdom, but they did weaken it and the power of the nobles to control the lives of their workers.

TERM PAPER SUGGESTIONS

1. A number of peasant revolts occurred throughout Europe in the late Middle Ages. What social and economic factors ignited these revolts? Discuss general conditions and the causes of particular revolts.
2. What sort of obligations did the early and mid-medieval peasant have to his lord? How were these determined? Was there a distinction between free and

unfree peasants? What other categories of people might you expect to find living in medieval villages? What was the mayor's role in the village?

3. How did the obligations of peasants to their lords change during the late Middle Ages? How did the "chronology of labour services" affect these obligations?

4. How did the nobility and landowners adapt to the changed economic circumstances of the late 14th century?

5. Compare the causes, tactics, and results of two or more of the 14th-century peasant revolts.

ALTERNATIVE TERM PAPER SUGGESTIONS

1. With a partner, reenact the meeting between Richard III and Wat Tyler at the end of the Peasant's Revolt.

2. Create a multimedia presentation about the life of the poor after the Black Death swept through Europe. Include information about the kinds of agreements that were made between landowners and tenants.

Primary Sources

Froissart, Jean. *The Chronicles of Froissart.* Trans. by John Bourchier. London: G. C. Macaulay, 1924. http://ehistory.osu.edu/osu/. Complete translation. Froissart lived in the late 14th and early 15th centuries and traveled widely throughout Europe. He witnessed many of the events he recorded, including "Wat Tyler's Rising."

Ordinance of Labourers (1349) and *Statute of Labourers* (1351). http://www.britannia.com/history/docs/. The first document represents Edward III's attempt to hold wages for laborers at their preBlack Death levels. The second is an attempt to enforce the first ordinance.

Peasant's Revolt, 1381. Britannia History. http://www.britannia.com/history/docs/. A contemporary account of the meeting between Richard II and Wat Tyler, the leader of the Peasant's Revolt.

Walsingham, Thomas. From *English History.* "*John Ball and the Peasants' Revolt, 1381*" in Brian L. Blakely and Jacqeulin Collins, eds. *Documents in British History, Volume I: Early Times to 1714,* 2nd ed. New York: McGraw-Hill, 1993, pp. 102–104.

Secondary Sources

Aston, T. H. *Landlords, Peasants and Politics in Medieval England.* Cambridge: Cambridge University Press, 2006. A collection of 12 essays on the relationships between peasants, landlords, and the political tensions between them.

Bennet, H. S. *Life on the English Manor: A Study of Peasant Conditions 1150–1400.* Cambridge: Cambridge University Press, 1989. First published in 1937. Includes chapters on the church, manorial courts, the administration of manors, the peasants' year, rents, and services.

Dunn, Alastair. *The Great Rising of 1381: The Peasants' Revolt and England's Failed Revolution.* Gloucestershire, UK: Tempus Publishing, 2004. A complete history of the Peasant's Revolt.

Hanawalt, Barbara A. *The Ties that Bound: Peasant Families in Medieval England.* New York: Oxford University Press, 1989. Argues that family ties and interactions remained much the same before and after the Black Death killed a significant proportion of the population.

Harriss, Gerald. *Shaping the Nation: England 1360–1461.* Oxford: Oxford University Press, 2005. Includes a large section on agrarian life, the church, and the nobility.

Hilton, Rodney. *Bond Men Made Free: Medieval Peasant Movements and the English Rising of 1381.* New York: Routledge, 2003. First half of this volume discusses the general problems of the peasantry and the second half the Peasant Revolt itself.

O'Brien, Mark. *When Adam Delved and Eve Span: A History of the Peasants' Revolt of 1381.* New Clarion Press, 2004. History of the revolt looking at the effects of feudal, religious, and heretical influences.

Shahar, Shulamit. *Fourth Estate: A History of Women in the Middle Ages.* New York: Routledge, 2003. Includes discussion of public and legal rights, women peasants, and heretical movements.

Steven, Justice. *Writing and Rebellion: England in 1381.* Berkeley: University of California Press, 1994. Examines the short texts written by six of the rebels in the revolt of 1381 and concludes that the revolt was a well-planned and disciplined attempt to gain rights, rather than the spontaneous outburst it is often portrayed as.

Waugh, Scott L. *England in the Reign of Edward III.* Cambridge: Cambridge University Press, 1991. Part II concerns the economic challenges faced by the peasantry in the 14th century.

World Wide Web

Brittania History. http://www.britannia.com/history/index.html. Site has a collection of primary documents, including a contemporary description of the Peasants' Revolt and articles on the revolt and people involved.

Voices of the Powerless: The Peasants' Revolt. http://www.bbc.co.uk/radio4/history/voices/voices_revolt.shtml. A digitalized copy of a radio program aired on August 1, 2002. Melvin Bragg explores the history of the Peasants' Revolt.

Multimedia Sources

Medieval England: The Peasants' Revolt. 1984. Video. Learning Corporation of America. 31 minutes. Looks at the reality of the life of the lower classes by focusing on the Wat Tyler revolt.

Medieval Europe: Crisis and Renewal. 1996. DVD set. Insight Video. Professor Teofilo F. Ruiz leads viewers through the period between 1300 and 1500 and the series of calamities that plagued Europe. Includes footage on popular revolts.

The Peasants' Revolt 1381. 2005. DVD. Cromwell Productions. 43 minutes. Uses reenactments and readings from eye-witness accounts to tell the story of the revolt.

The Peasants' Revolt: The Castle. 1993. DVD. BBC Production. 44 minutes. Shows the living and working conditions of 14th-century peasants.

92. Rise of the Inca Empire (c. 1390)

Around 1100, a small band of Inca warriors from the mountains above the present Peruvian city of Cuzco began to conquer the tribes in the valley. By 1200, the ruler Manco Capac had consolidated power in the Cuzco valley. Over the next two centuries, they continued their conquests until the Inca became the wealthiest and largest of the pre-Columbian civilizations in America. Inca Roca (r. c. 1350–1380) added land until the Inca territory stretched for about 2,500 miles along the coast of South America through a diverse landscape of desert, mountains, lush valleys, and tropical forests, containing tribes that spoke a variety of languages. Inca-controlled lands reached about 500 miles inland.

Inca civilization was rigidly structured under a powerful ruler called the *Inca* who was considered a god. The emperor's family, priests and other nobles, government officials, warriors, and the common people comprised the levels of society. The rulers maintained strict control of the lives of their citizens, but they also saw that they were protected, had food in times of shortage, and had materials they needed for their work. The Inca had domesticated several animals and had a sophisticated agricultural system. Part of the produce each year belonged to the government, which stored it in large warehouses for distribution when the people needed it.

Although they had no written language, the Inca developed mathematical recordkeeping using *quipu,* a system employing a series of knotted strings. Skilled artisans, the Inca created ornamental works of silver and gold, metal tools and weapons, jewelry, and skillfully woven blankets and garments. The people were also talented architects and builders who constructed beautiful temples and large cities such as Machu Picchu. Canals and aqueducts carried water throughout the city. Massive white granite blocks weighing 10–15 tons were used in the buildings, but the Inca had no wheeled vehicles for moving these stones. In addition, these blocks are carefully sculpted and fitted so that mortar was not needed to hold them together. The Inca also built a system of roadways and bridges.

The Inca had a very accurate calendar based on the movements of the sun and stars. Their religion was based on worship of the sun, and the emperor was considered to be a direct descendent of the sun god. After their deaths, the emperors and their wives were mummified. Archeologists still have many unanswered questions about the Inca, particularly since they had no written records of their own and most early information comes from the Spaniards. In 1532, Francisco Pizarro and a small band of about 180 soldiers conquered the vast Inca Empire and destroyed many of the civilization's artifacts.

TERM PAPER SUGGESTIONS

1. Compare the Inca civilization to that of the Maya or Aztec.

2. Discuss agricultural production by the Inca. What particular problems did they face? How did they deal with these problems? What crops were produced?

3. The Inca vastly outnumbered the Spanish. Why were the Spanish able to defeat them, instead of the other way around?

4. Investigate the communication system the Inca rulers used to administer their vast empire. How did it operate? What additional uses did the system have beyond conveying the emperor's orders?

5. How do the cities and temples constructed by the Inca embody their religious beliefs and values?

6. Compare the Inca concept of kingship to that of European or Islamic rulers in the 14th century.

7. Assess the contributions of the Inca to the culture of modern Peru.

ALTERNATIVE TERM PAPER SUGGESTIONS

1. Create a 3-D model of the city of Machu Picchu, either as a miniature or digitally.
2. Create a multimedia presentation on the art and architecture of the Inca civilization.
3. Create a multimedia presentation showing the roadway system of the Inca and the bridges they constructed. Discuss the engineering methods that were used.

Primary Sources

The Inca had no written language. Some of the earliest Spanish chronicles are listed here.

Cobo, Father Bernabe. *Historia del Nuevo Mundo (History of the New World: Inca Religion and Customs)*. Trans. by Roland Hamilton. Austin: University of Texas Press, 1990. Father Cobo published this work containing much information about the Inca religion in 1653.

de Ayala, Felipe Guaman Poma. *The First Chronicle and Book of Good Government (Neuva chronic y buen gobiemo)*. Trans. by Daniel L. Frye. Indianapolis: Hackett Publishing Company, 2006. Written between 1600 and 1616. Spanish and English versions are online at http://www.kb.dk/permalink/2006/poma/info/en/frontpage.htm.

de Gamboa, Pedro Sarmiento. *History of the Incas and the Execution of Tupac Amaru*. New York: Cosimo Classics, 2007. De Gamboa spent 20 years in Peru interviewing the Inca and listening to their stories, but he attempts to portray the people as savage tyrants who deserved the treatment they received by the Spanish. The work was originally published in 1972; this is a facsimile reproduction of a 1907 British translation.

de la Vega, Garlicaso. *The Royal Commentaries of the Incas and General History of Peru*. Trans. by Harold V. Livermore. Indianapolis: Hackett Publishing Company, 2006. An abridgement of Livermore's two-volume translation, this text includes the historical sections of de la Vega's work. De la Vega, born in 1539, was the son of a Spanish nobleman and an Inca princess. His *Commentaries,* published in 1609 in Lima, are considered the most reliable of the colonial sources.

Secondary Sources

Calvert, Patricia. *The Ancient Inca.* New York: Scholastic, 2004. Topics include farming, nobility, medicine and healing, warriors, and builders.

Canseco, María Rostworowski de Diez. *History of the Inca Realm.* Trans. by Harry B. Iceland. Cambridge: Cambridge University Press, 1999. Uses information from early European chronicles and records and archeology to reconstruct the history of the Inca.

de Gamboa, Pedro Sarmiento. *History of the Incas.* Trans. by Clements Markham. Cambridge: The Hakluyt Society, 1907. Online at Project Gutenberg http://www.gutenberg.org/etext/20218. A classic study of Inca civilization.

Malpass, Michael A. *Daily Life in the Inca Empire.* Westport, CT: Greenwood Press, 1996. Topics include politics, private life, religion, and science. Includes a timeline, glossary, and the contributions of Inca to modern Peru.

McEwan, Gordon. *The Incas: New Perspectives.* New York: W. W. Norton & Company, 2006. McEwan introduces the various sources of information on Inca culture, discusses the Inca civilization in detail as revealed in those sources, and then looks at current evaluations of and issues in the study of the Inca.

World Wide Web

About Peru History. http://www.about-peru-history.com/. Topics include Inca civilization, Machu Picchu, and Inca art. Articles and images.

Destination Machu Picchu. http://www.peru-machu-picchu.com/index.php. A virtual tour of Machu Picchu.

The Inca. http://incas.perucultural.org.pe/english/index.htm. Many brief articles on all aspects of Inca civilization.

Maya-Inca-Aztec. http://mayaincaaztec.com/index.html. A commercial site where postings are not peer-reviewed but has many articles on the history of the Inca and many images.

Peruvian National Anthropology, Archaeology and History Museum. http://museonacional.perucultural.org.pe/. In Spanish. The National Museum of Peru. A number of exhibits.

Multimedia Sources

Ancient Inca. 2004. DVD. Schlessinger Media. 23 minutes. A brief overview of Inca civilization and customs. Partially animated.

Death Cult of the Incas. DVD. History Channel. 55 minutes. Examines the Inca practice of mummification and the exalted place the dead retained in Inca culture long after they were mummified.

Great Inca Rebellion. 2007. DVD. National Geographic Television and Film. 55 minutes. Tells the story of Manco Capac's rebellion against Spanish rule and the long siege that left the city of Cuzco in ruins.

Inca Mummies: Secrets of a Lost World. 2002. DVD. National Geographic Productions. 53 minutes. Explores the Incan mummification process and considers the cultural significance of the mummies that have been discovered.

Lost Cities of the Incas. DVD. 2001. National Geographic Television. 55 minutes. Examines the ruins of cities abandoned by the Inca or destroyed by European conquistadors in order to help answer questions about Inca culture.

Machu Picchu: Lost City of the Inca. 2007. Arts and Entertainment Home Video. 55 minutes. Host Josh Bernstein leads viewers in the footsteps of explorer Hiram Bingham who discovered Machu Picchu in 1911. Also looks at ancient manuscripts and archeological evidence to determine the purpose of the city.

Peru: Kingdom in the Clouds. 1996. DVD. Films for the Humanities and Sciences. 26 minutes. Overview of the nation of Peru and its Inca heritage.

93. Chaucer Writes *The Canterbury Tales* (c. 1400)

Geoffrey Chaucer began his masterpiece *The Canterbury Tales* sometime after his wife Phillipa's death in 1385. Obviously influenced by Boccaccio's 100-story work *The Decameron,* Chaucer intended to write a collection of 124 stories told by different individuals who were making a pilgrimage to the Shrine of St. Thomas Becket at Canterbury Cathedral. He died before the work was finished, but that part which he wrote is one of the most famous works of English literature and the Middle Ages. The work begins with a general prologue that reveals why the diverse group is traveling together and introduces each pilgrim separately to the reader. Agreeing to participate in a story-telling contest, the pilgrims plan to entertain and instruct one another with stories, two each on the way to Canterbury and two each on the return journey, all to be judged by the innkeeper of the Tabard Inn.

Like Boccaccio in *The Decameron,* Chaucer chooses to write in the vernacular. *The Canterbury Tales* is one of the first works of English literature to be written in English. Unlike Boccaccio, however, Chaucer provides a cross-section of 14th-century England in his characters, everyone from a poor plowman to a wealthy knight, with various motives for and experiences in travel and from all walks of life. All of Boccaccio's characters are young, wealthy ladies and gentlemen who leave the city to escape the Black Death. They all have the luxury of not being required to stay to work, and they have a comfortable place to go and the means to travel there.

Chaucer himself had opportunity to meet all sorts of people during his life. His father was a successful wine merchant, and as a youth, Chaucer would have met many of the people with whom his father dealt. When Chaucer was about 17, he became a page in the household of the Duke of Clarence. He later fought in the army of Edward III against the French in the Hundred Years War. When Chaucer was captured and held for ransom, Edward himself paid the ransom. John of Gaunt, the son of Edward III, became Chaucer's patron, and during the next several years, Edward and John sent Chaucer on a number of diplomatic missions to the continent. When Chaucer was in Italy, he may have met Boccaccio and Petrarch, but there is no direct evidence that he did so.

Chaucer's early writing was typical of the age: courtly love poems. He was fluent in several languages and completed several translations of works into English. He then turned to more original work, completing *The Book of the Duchess, The House of Fame,* and *The Parliament of Fowls.* After 1374, when he was named customs controller for the port of London, Chaucer had more time for writing and more opportunities for meeting individuals who were not from the nobility.

Chaucer died in 1400 and was buried in Westminster Abbey. The area near his tomb is known as The Poets' Corner because a number of other English writers have been buried nearby. Chaucer's masterful command of the language, his broad knowledge of the people of his age, and his ability as a storyteller in a variety of genres make him one of the most important of English writers. *The Canterbury Tales* reveals much about the entire culture of late 14th-century England.

TERM PAPER SUGGESTIONS

1. Several of Chaucer's pilgrims and characters in the tales take vows. Explain the significance of vows in the Middle Ages to all levels of society. How were vows made? By whom? What kinds of conflict did the vows engender? Did vows strengthen or weaken the prevailing social order?

2. Examine *The Canterbury Tales* for evidence of antiSemitism. Analyze whether it is Chaucer who is antiSemitic or whether he is reporting common medieval attitudes that he does not hold himself.

4. What changes in the social order of 14th-century Europe are evident in Chaucer's *Canterbury Tales?* Who benefits from these changes?

5. Who was harmed or suffered losses as a result of the changes? Chaucer created pilgrims with distinct characters and then selected appropriate tales for them to share with the other pilgrims on their way to Canterbury Cathedral. Select a tale and explain how this tale is particularly appropriate to the pilgrim who tells it. Consider the life style, occupation, values, behavior, and personality of the pilgrim in this explanation.

6. How is the position of women portrayed in *The Canterbury Tales?* How accurate a picture of women's status and rights is this portrayal? Evaluate Chaucer's general opinion of women as seen both in his characters and in the stories they tell.

7. What is Chaucer's opinion of the church in the late 14th century? Are his sentiments those of the general public? Does he break with established teachings? Are the criticisms he makes valid, or is he unfair in making some of the accusations he does? How important is religion in the work? Can you read the *Tales* as a religious work?

8. Categorize the Canterbury pilgrims into classes or groups that existed in 14th-century England. Are there any pilgrims that don't fit into a group or class? Look at the pilgrims you group together. Are they representative of that group or class? Does Chaucer exaggerate the characteristics of any group? Other than royalty, are there any groups he leaves out of the general prologue? How accurate a picture of 14th-century life does Chaucer provide through his characters?

9. Compare *The Decameron* to *The Canterbury Tales,* considering such topics as style, author's purpose, audience, range of genres, and characterization.

ALTERNATIVE TERM PAPER SUGGESTIONS

1. Choose one of the stories from *The Canterbury Tales.* Assume the persona of the character who tells the story. Introduce yourself using information from the general prologue and from the prologue to the story, then tell the story. This should be a storytelling performance.

2. Create a multimedia presentation using 14th-century images on the people and places of Chaucer's time. Use 14th-century music to accompany your presentation.

3. Prepare a presentation on dress or costume of the 14th century. Include information on fabric, color, and style, especially that referred to by Chaucer.

Primary Sources

Chaucer, Geoffrey. *The Canterbury Tales.* Modern English translations are available from many sources.

Furnival, Frederick J. *Fifty Earliest English Wills in the Court of Probate, London: A. D. 1387–1439.* Ann Arbor, MI: University of Michigan Humanities Text Initiative, 1999. http://name.umdl.umich.edu/ EEWills. These early wills give insight into the lives of individuals in Chaucer's time.

Goldie, Matthew Boyd, ed. *Middle English Literature: A Historical Sourcebook.* Hoboken, NJ: Wiley-Blackwell, 2003. Contains 14th- and 15th-century primary documents that give insight into the age in which *The Canterbury Tales* was written.

Gower, John. *Confessio Amantis, or Tales of the Seven Deadly Sins.* Oxford: Clarendon Press, 1899–1902. http://name.umdl.umich.edu/Confessio. A poetic frame story surrounding shorter poems written by Chaucer's contemporary and friend.

Secondary Sources

Bisson, Lillian M. *Chaucer and the Late Medieval World.* New York: St. Martin's Press, 1998. Places the work of Chaucer in the context of his own time and experiences.

Lambdin, Laura C. *Chaucer's Pilgrims.* Westport, CT: Greenwood Press, 1996. Discusses the occupation of each of Chaucer's pilgrims in three parts: the daily routine, how the occupation affects the story told by the pilgrim, and how the occupation and tale relate to the "General Prologue."

McKisack, May. *The Fourteenth Century: 1307–1399.* Oxford: Oxford University Press, 1959. A standard and complete history of the 14th century.

Patterson, Lee, ed. *Geoffrey Chaucer's The Canterybury Tales.* New York: Oxford University Press, 2007. Features 10 essays focusing on the most popularly taught *Canterbury Tales* with full annotations.

Phillips, Helen. *An Introduction to the Canterbury Tales.* New York: St. Martin's Press, 2000. Features the historical and literary background for each tale, as well as evaluations using modern theoretical perspectives.

Russell, J. Stephen. *Chaucer and the Trivium: The Mindsong of the Canterbury Tales.* Gainesville: University Press of Florida. Describes the trivium of medieval education (logic, grammar, and rhetoric) and how Chaucer's education under this system influenced *The Canterbury Tales.*

Thompson, N. S. *Chaucer, Boccaccio, and the Debate of Love.* London: Somerset, 1996. Compares and contrasts *The Canterbury Tales* and *The Decameron* on the subject of love.

World Wide Web

Geoffrey Chaucer Online: The Electronic Canterbury Tales. http://www.kankedort .net/. Annotated links to translations and resources on Chaucer.

The Geoffrey Chaucer Page. http://www.courses.fas.harvard.edu/~chaucer. Contains a translation of *The Canterbury Tales* and other works, a glossary, information about Middle English, a concordance, and more.

The Online Medieval and Classical Library. http://omacl.org/author.html. Provides translations of several of Chaucer's works.

Multimedia Sources

The Canterbury Tales. 1998. DVD. Insight Media. 30 minutes for each of three CDs. Animated adaptations of the *Tales* voiced by members of the Royal Shakespeare Company.

Chaucer: The General Prologue to "The Canterbury Tales." 2001. DVD. Films Media Group. 20 minutes. Middle English reading of the prologue and short dramatization by students of part of "The Pardoner's Tale."

Chaucer Reads Chaucer: "The Miller's Tale." 1998. DVD. Films Media Group. 80 minutes. Costumed actor plays the role of Chaucer telling "The Miller's Tale" to a group of his contemporaries. In Middle English with Modern English subtitles.

Geoffrey Chaucer: The Canterbury Tales. 1998. CD-ROM. Films Media Group. Printable texts in Middle and Modern English; interviews with scholars; facsimile reproductions; all 24 tales, and more.

Geoffrey Chaucer: Poet and Pilgrim. 1998. VHS. Guidance Associates. 25 minutes. On-location filming; narrative, dramatized readings, retelling of "The Nun's Priest's Tale."

A Prologue to Chaucer. 1986. DVD. Films Media Group. 30 minutes. Retraces through film reenactments the journey made by Chaucer's pilgrims. Relates characters and themes to the reality of 14th-century life.

94. Christine de Pisan Publishes *The City of Ladies* (1405)

French author Christine de Pisan's (c. 1364–1430) publication of *The City of Ladies* brought public attention to the misogynist attitude prevalent among male writers and church officials in the Middle Ages. Pisan first broached the subject in 1399 when she wrote *L'epistre au dieu d'amours*

(The Letter of Cupid), which decried the negative depiction of women in the highly popular *Le roman de la rosa (The Romance of the Rose)*, a work begun by Guillaume de Lorris and completed by Jean de Muen around 1280. When Pisan's contemporary, Jean de Montreuil, wrote *La Querelle de la Rose*, she replied with *The Letter of Cupid* and a famed literary debate concerning the portrayal of women ensued. Pisan amplified her arguments in *The City of Ladies* and its sequel, *The Book of the Three Virtues* (1409).

Pisan was the first European woman to make her living as a writer. Her writings covered a wide spectrum of genres including poetry, history, politics, education, military science, and feminist issues. Although few women were educated in the 14th century, Pisan's father, chief physician for King Charles V of France, insisted on a rigorous curriculum for her. She spoke several languages and was well read in many disciplines by the time she was 15 and married to Etienne de Castel. When both her father and husband died, Pisan had to provide for herself, her three children, mother, siblings, and other relatives in the household. Some wealthy friends encouraged her to publish her poetry, which she did, to critical and financial success.

As a woman supporting herself and her family, Pisan was naturally interested in the position of women in medieval society. Both her father and husband had left small estates, but Pisan's repeated court appeals to obtain what she considered rightfully hers and her family's were dismissed because she was a woman. During the next few years, Pisan wrote extensively on political, historical, military, and educational matters and continued to labor for the recognition of women. Her most widely read work is *Le livre de la cite des dames (The Book of the City of Ladies, 1405)*.

TERM PAPER SUGGESTIONS

1. Research Christine de Pisan's military manual, *The Book of Deeds of Arms and of Chivalry*, written around 1410. Evaluate the work considering such questions as How accurate is her depiction of warfare? How valuable was the book to medieval military strategists? What does she mean by a "just war"?

2. Consider Christine de Pisan both as a feminist in her own time and as a forerunner of modern feminists. What feminist principles did she hold? How might she have shaped later thinking about women's roles in society.

3. De Pisan was the first woman to make her living from writing, a fact that is especially remarkable in an age of patrons. How did the patronage system encourage and control artistic endeavors? How did Pisan manage to both utilize and subvert the patronage system?

4. Research women's legal rights in France or in another country during the Middle Ages. Compare what you learn to common conceptions of women's rights.

ALTERNATIVE TERM PAPER SUGGESTIONS

1. Prepare a debate between Guillaume de Lorris, author of the first part of *The Romance of the Rose,* and Christine de Pisan concerning the depiction of women in literature of the Middle Ages.

2. Study the illustrations from de Pisan's works. Prepare a multimedia presentation showing how these illustrations are or are not representative of illustrations and illuminations from other medieval manuscripts. How are the illustrations related to Pisan's themes in writing?

Primary Sources

De Pisan, Christine. *The Book of the Body Politic.* Ed. by Kate Langdon Forhan. Cambridge: Cambridge University Press, 1994. Written during the Hundred Years War, this text considers the roles of princes, nobility, and commoners in the state.

De Pisan, Christine. *The Book of Deeds of Arms and of Chivalry.* Trans. by Sumner Willard. University Park: Pennsylvania State University Press, 1999. This edition of de Pisan's volume includes corrections from earlier translations and comments, notes, and an introduction by editor Charity Cannon Willard.

De Pisan, Christine. *Selected Writings of Christine de Pisan:* Norton Critical Edition. Trans. by Renate Blumenfeld-Kosinski and Kevin Brownlee. New York: W. W. Norton, 1999. Blumfeld-Kosinski also edits this book, which includes seven critical essays on Pisan's work.

De Pisan, Christine. *The Treasure of the City of Ladies: or The Book of Three Virtues.* Trans. by Sarah Lawson. London: Penguin Books, 1985.

Most of de Pisan's other works are available in translation and easily accessible.

Secondary Sources

McGrady, Deborah L., and Altmann, Barbara K., eds. *Christine de Pisan: A Casebook.* London: Routledge, 2002. Extensive collection of essays on the work of de Pisan.

Quilligan, Maureen. *The Allegory of Female Authority: Christine De Pizan's Cite Des Dames.* Ithaca, NY: Cornell University Press, 1991. An in-depth analysis and interpretation of Pisan's *City of Ladies.*

Shahar, Shulamit. *Fourth Estate: A History of Women in the Middle Ages.* London: Routledge, 2003. First published in 1983, this work has become a classic in the study of medieval women. Contains an excellent chapter on women's legal rights.

World Wide Web

Internet Women's History Sourcebook. http://www.fordham.edu/halsall/women/womensbook.html. Provides links to articles, Web pages, and general information about women in the Middle Ages.

Medieval Illuminated Manuscripts. http://www.kb.nl/manuscripts. A Web collection of images from medieval manuscripts. Has a good search feature.

NYPLDigitalGallery. http://digitalgallery.nypl.org/nypldigital. Contains more than 2,000 digital images of pages and illuminations from medieval manuscripts.

Other Women's Voices: Translations of Women's Writing before 1700. home.infionline.net/~ddisse. Site serves as a clearinghouse for access information to a wide variety of women's early writing, both in the original language and in translations. Provides a number of links for de Pisan's works.

Multimedia Sources

Manuscripts in Medieval Europe. 2008. Number 201 in *A Journey through Aesthetic Realms* series on Supreme Master TV, Available for streaming at http://www.suprememastertelevision.com/bbs/board.php?bo_table=ajt. Short video discussing how manuscripts were manufactured during the Middle Ages.

Socio-historic Gender Roles: Medieval History. 1994. DVD. School Media Associates. 10 minutes. Explores gender roles in medieval England.

Sybils! An Interactive Exploration of Women in the Middle Ages and the Renaissance. 1997. CD-ROM. Films for the Humanities and Sciences. Texts, images, articles, music, biographies, and a bibliography of additional resources.

95. Battle of Agincourt (1415)

The Battle of Agincourt, which took place on October 25, 1415, ended in a British victory over the French. England had gained extensive territory during the first half of the 14th century and lost most of it again in the last part of the century. Early in the 15th century, the French lands of Burgundy and Armagnac were engaged in conflict and gave Henry V (r. 1413–1422) the opening he needed in 1415 to reassert his right to large parts of France.

Henry probably did not intend to take the campaign deep into France. He began the invasion by putting Harfleur under siege and using his new guns to hammer the town until it surrendered; some historians say until he butchered the population. The English also suffered heavy losses during the five-week siege, mostly from dysentery. From Harfleur, Henry proposed marching to Calais and sailing home, but as he began the march to the port, he met the French army at Agincourt. Henry gave the French the opportunity to surrender, which they of course refused to do because they thought they could defeat the small English force.

Estimates of the numbers of troops at Agincourt on each side vary from historian to historian, but all agree the English were greatly outnumbered, by as much as six to one. But as the French soldiers readied for battle, they began to argue among themselves as to which units should be in the van and which should not. The French did not have a leader, and Henry was a seasoned king commander. Henry's archers, armed with longbows, were able to turn the French cavalry, which collided with the advancing foot soldiers, causing confusion in the French lines. The armored French quickly became bogged down in the mud on the field and were easy targets for the unarmored English. Approximately 6,000 French troops were killed, including 600 nobles. More than 1,000 nobles were captured. Henry V ordered his men-at-arms to kill the prisoners. When they refused, he ordered the archers to fire on the prisoners and kill them all.

The English then continued to Calais and sailed for home. The loss of so many knights was a devastating setback for France, and in a few years Henry was able to negotiate the Treaty of Troyes, which made him the heir of the French king Charles VI.

TERM PAPER SUGGESTIONS

1. In what ways was Agincourt typical of feudal warfare? At the same time, how did it help point to the future of war?

2. What innovations in military strategy at Agincourt changed the nature of warfare?

3. Analyze the Agincourt campaign as an example of chivalry in battle.

4. Compare Shakespeare's depiction of the battle of Agincourt in *Henry V* to historical documents about the battle. What did Shakespeare change? Why?

5. How do you explain the success of the English against such overwhelming odds at the Battle of Agincourt?

6. Historically, there is often a profit made from war. Who profited from the Hundred Years War? How did they profit?

7. Analyze the importance of the Battle of Agincourt within the history of the Hundred Years War.

ALTERNATIVE TERM PAPER SUGGESTIONS

1. Create a series of drawings showing the progress of the Battle of Agincourt.

2. Memorize and perform at least 35 lines spoken by Henry V in Shakespeare's drama.

Primary Sources

Usk, Adam. *The Chronicle of Adam Usk: 1377–1421*. Trans. by C. Given-Wilson. New York: Oxford University Press, 1997. Adam Usk wrote extensively about the Hundred Years War and witnessed several battles.

Thompson, Peter E., ed. *Contemporary Chronicles of the Hundred Years War: From the Works of Jean Le Bel, Jean Froissart & Enguerrand de Monstrelet*. New York: The Folio Society, 1966. Includes translations from three important historians of the 100 Years War.

Secondary Sources

Barker, Juliet. *Agincourt*. Manchett, UK: Little, Brown, 2006. A description of how England's outnumbered archers defeated the French Army. Well illustrated with details of life in medieval Europe.

Curry, Anne. *Agincourt: A New History*. Gloucestershire: Tempus, 2006. Discusses the battle from both the English and French viewpoints, with a special section on what went wrong for the French.

Hibbert, Christopher. *Agincourt*. Oxford: Windrush Press, 1995. Details both the massive preparations for and the actions during the battle of Agincourt.

Keegan, John. *The Face of Battle: A Study of Agincourt, Waterloo, and the Somme*. London: Pimlico, 2004. In the section focusing on Agincourt, Keegan describes the battle, but also focuses intently on what happens to soldiers during war.

Seward, Desmond. *Henry V as Warlord*. London: Penguin Classics, 2002. Examines Henry's blind ambition, cruelty, and desire to win at any cost.

Sumption, Jonathan. *The Hundred Years War, Volume I: Trial by Battle*. Philadelphia: University of Pennsylvania Press, 1992. Traces the Hundred Years War from Edward III, the Battles of Crecy and Portiers, and the capture of the French king.

Sumption, Jonathan. *The Hundred Years War, Volume II: Trial by Fire.* Philadelphia: University of Pennsylvania Press, 1999. Covers the Hundred Years War from the death of Charles IV to the surrender of Calais to the English in 1347.

Rothero, Christopher. *The Armies of Agincourt.* Oxford: Osprey, 1981. Part of the Men-at-Arms Series, packed with illustrations and research describing the history, organization, uniforms, and equipment of the English and French at the Battle of Agincourt.

World Wide Web

BBC History: The Middle Ages. http://www.bbc.co.uk/history/british/middle _ages/. Site has articles, interactives, a timeline, images, and radio links. Includes extensive section on the 100 Years War.

British Battles. http://www.britishbattles.com/100-years-war/. Extensive information on British warfare from 1066 on. Images, timeline, anecdotes, informative articles.

De Re Militari: The Society for Medieval Military History. http://www.deremilitari.org/. Includes articles on all aspects of medieval military operations. Has both primary and secondary sources on the 100 Years War. Provides extensive bibliography of related materials.

Multimedia Sources

Agincourt. 2005. DVD. Films for the Humanities and Sciences. 52 minutes. Interviews with historians, on-location filming, and dramatic readings of first-hand accounts.

Medieval Warfare: Agincourt. 2007. DVD. Kultur Media. 50 minutes. Reconstruction of battle and dramatic readings of first-hand accounts.

Henry V. 1990. DVD. Films for the Humanities and Sciences. 176 minutes. Film adaptation of Shakespeare's dramatic history. Not entirely historical, but provides insight into why the nations are at war.

96. Career and Death of Joan of Arc (d. 1431)

When English king Henry V (r. 1413–1422) renewed fighting in the Hundred Years War, his Agincourt campaign captured almost all of northern France for England. Then, with the Treaty of Troyes in 1420, Henry was acknowledged as the heir of Charles VI (r. 1380–1422) of France.

Henry died before he could assume the French throne, but the dauphin had not been crowned. The French people believed that their new king should be French, not English, but their forces were weakened from the losses of the Agincourt campaign.

At this time, an unlikely leader stepped forward. When the young peasant girl Joan of Arc was about 12, she reported that she heard angelic voices telling her that the English had no right to the French throne and that she must help ensure that they were driven out of France. At 17, Joan persuaded soldiers from a local garrison to escort her to see the dauphin, whose ineffective government was operating in exile. During the 11-day journey, Joan dressed as a soldier. When she met the future king Charles VII (r. 1422–1461), Joan asked him to allow her to save the French. At the end of a three-week investigation of Joan, Charles armed her and gave her command of a large military force he was sending to fight the English at the besieged city of Orleans.

Joan met the English at Orleans and offered them the chance to lift their siege and leave. They did not take a peasant girl's warning seriously, but Joan engineered a plan that freed the French city and sent the English into retreat. The Maid of Orleans continued to pursue the English and fought through to Reims where Charles VII was crowned in July 1429. Joan's victories had turned the tide for the French, and the nation was jubilant. However, once Charles had his crown, he began to distance himself from Joan. When Joan was captured by English allies, Charles refused to ransom her. She was sold to the English who put her on trial charged with heresy and witchcraft.

The verdict had been determined before the trial began. Joan was denied counsel, and her judges focused on her dressing in male attire and the voices she purported to hear. After months of mistreatment and isolation, a sick Joan made the confession the English sought. She put on women's clothing and was sentenced to life in prison. Joan soon retracted her confession and donned her soldiers clothing, angering the court, which then condemned her to death. Standing at the stake in Rouen, Joan asked for a cross to be held before her so that she could focus on it as she died. Joan died on May 30, 1431. Twenty-five years after her death the pope overturned her guilty verdict, and, in 1920, Joan was canonized.

TERM PAPER SUGGESTIONS

1. Why was the 17-year-old peasant girl such a threat to the English? What did they hope to gain by sentencing her to death?

2. People in the Middle Ages had long accepted that mysticism experienced by women was a gift from God. For example, Hildegard of Bengin, Catherine of Siena, Birgitta of Sweden, and Ludwina of Schiedam all experienced mystical visions and revealed them to church authorities. Study the mysticism of at least two of these women and compare their visions and actions to those of Joan. Why were Joan's visions called witchcraft?

3. What basic changes in the nature of medieval warfare does Joan's involvement indicate? Joan, a female soldier, remained an anomaly, but what had happened to war during the Hundred Years' War that would involve a peasant girl at all? Why would she have cared who was King of France? What does this indicate about commoner and nobility alike that changed during the course of the war?

4. One of the major charges brought against Joan was that she dressed in male clothing. Why was the court concerned with this? What were the medieval attitudes toward dressing in clothes designed for the other gender?

5. How did the leadership of Joan of Arc affect the French forces at Orleans? Did her leadership have any effect on the outcome of the war? Why or why not?

ALTERNATIVE TERM PAPER SUGGESTIONS

1. Research the artistic representations of Joan of Arc since her death. Prepare a multimedia presentation detailing the ways in which her image has been altered. Discuss the purposes of the variations.

2. Using information from the letters of Joan of Arc and from the transcript of her trial, create a 30-minute reader's theatre presentation with two to four participants.

Primary Sources

Joan of Arc's Letter to Henry VI, 1429. http://www.britannia.com/history/docs/. A translation of the letter sent by Joan to King Henry VI while he was laying siege to the French city of Orleans.

Primary Sources and Context Concerning Joan of Arc's Male Clothing. Historical Association for Joan of Arc Studies, http://primary-sources-series.joan-of-arc-studies.org/. Translations of excerpts and complete documents about Joan's insistence on wearing male clothing.

Saint Joan of Arc's Trial of Condemnation. http://www.stjoan-center.com/Trials/. English translations of the transcripts from Joan's trials.

Secondary Sources

Adams, Jeremy duQuesnay, trans. *Joan of Arc: Her Story*. New York: St. Martin's Press, 1998. Translated from French, features a detailed narrative of Joan of Arc's life, as well as lengthy quotations from multiple historic documents.

Brooks, Polly Schoyer. *Beyond the Myth: The Story of Joan of Arc*. New York: Houghton Mifflin Company, 1990. Not only a historical biography of Joan of Arc, it also features descriptions and interpretations of her visions.

Fraioli, Deborah A. *Joan of Arc: The Early Debate*. Rochester, NY: Boydell Press, 2002. While most biographies of Joan of Arc focus on her actions as those of a political figure, this work reviews those actions on the basis of the Catholic doctrine of *discretion spirituum* (the discernment of spirits).

Fraioli, Deborah A. *Joan of Arc and the Hundred Years War*. Westport, CT: Greenwood Press, 2005. Interwoven history of the Hundred Years War and biography of Joan of Arc, which discusses how her belief in a sacred kingdom helped bring the conflict to its end.

Pernoud, Regine. *Joan of Arc: By Herself and Her Witnesses*. Chelsea, MI: Scarborough House, 1969. After an introduction to the environment in France during Joan of Arc's life, this biography covers Joan's early years, her meeting with the dauphin, her military campaigns, her trial and execution, and her trial of rehabilitation after her death.

World Wide Web

De Re Militari: The Society for Medieval Military History. http://www.deremilitari.org/. Includes articles on all aspects of medieval military operations. Has both primary and secondary sources on the 100 Years War. Provides extensive bibliography of related materials.

Historical Association for Joan of Arc Studies. http://www.joan-of-arc-studies.org/. Provides several translations of primary documents as well as other works on Joan of Arc.

The International Joan of Arc Society. http://smu.edu/ijas/index.html. Has several works related to Joan of Arc available, including the entire transcript of her 1431 trial and condemnation. Also has teaching resources, an interactive map, and images.

Multimedia Sources

Joan of Arc. 1999. DVD. Hallmark Entertainment. 140 minutes. A very elaborate television production of Joan's story featuring well-known actors.

Joan of Arc: Child of War, Soldier of God. 2000. DVD. Hallmark Channel. 56 minutes. Critically acclaimed program filmed in France and the Czech Republic; uses Joan's own words to tell her story.

Joan of Arc: The Maid of Orleans. 2002. DVD. Films Media Group. 49 minutes. Dramatization filmed in Joan's native village. An actress reads from Joan's letters and her testimony. Scholars also discuss the issues involved in her trial and the myth that has grown around her.

Joan of Arc: Virgin Warrior. 1998. DVD. A & E Home Entertainment. 50 minutes. Biography Channel production of the life of Joan of Arc.

Jeanne d'Arc. 2000. DVD. Films for the Humanities and Sciences. 270 minutes. French miniseries about Joan of Arc. In French with English subtitles.

Mystic Women of the Middle Ages. 2002. DVD. Films for the Humanities and Sciences. Six segments, 24 minutes each, one on Joan of Arc.

97. Fall of Constantinople (1453)

The Ottoman Empire rose from tribes in Anatolia led by Osman-ghazi I (r. 1280–1324) and was involved in a campaign of conquest that seized lands in Thrace, Bulgaria, and Turkey. After the capture of Thrace, Pope Gregory XI (r. 1370–1378) called for a crusade against the Ottomans to gain back Christian territory and defend Constantinople. The crusade only led to further expansion by the Ottomans into Serbia and the remainder of Bulgaria.

When Sultan Mehmed II (r. 1451–1481) came to power, he began another push for territory that captured Constantinople in 1453, Athens in 1456, and Otranto in Italy in 1480. The fall of Constantinople meant the end of the Byzantine Empire, the bastion of Christianity in the East. Although there had been a breach with the Western church for centuries, Constantinople had remained a Christian capital and had halted Muslim inroads into Europe.

Mehmed carefully crafted his plan to conquer the great city. First, he signed treaties with the Venetians and Hungarians that allowed him to move freely about the Mediterranean. His next step was to isolate Constantinople. He built a fortress called Rumeli Hisar on the European side of the Bosphorus. The Ottomans already had a fortress on the opposite shore only a few miles from Constantinople. Together, these fortresses could close off entrance to the Black Sea. The Ottomans sank a Venetian ship in the strait in 1452, sending a warning to the West, which did not react forcefully.

When Rumeli Hisar was completed and manned in August, the emperor of Constantinople realized the siege was about to begin. He was cut off from help from the sea, and he had no land surrounding the city from which to seek help. The emperor ordered the city's gates closed around its 50,000 citizens. A small group of ships with 700 men made it through to help defend Constantinople in January of 1453, and some 400–500 men from other areas of the Mediterranean arrived soon after.

In the first week of April, the Ottomans set their plan in motion. As many as 150,000 troops gathered on the plains near the city. Approximately 200 ships entered and lined the harbor. Mehmed brought a large cannon and installed it in front of one of the city's gates. He then sent an offer to the city saying that if it surrendered, he would spare its occupants and respect their property. The emperor refused the offer and the attack was ordered. On April 20, four large European ships laden with provisions for the city arrived at the Bosphorus. In one of the most spectacular naval battles of the Middle Ages, these four ships pushed their way through the smaller ships to the city's port.

The siege continued, marked by several failed attempts by the Ottomans to enter the city. On May 25, Mehmed received word that the Venetians were amassing their fleet to come to Constantinople's aid. Shortly after midnight on May 29, Mehmed launched a full-scale attack by land and sea. He sent wave after wave of soldiers in to breach the walls. By early morning, Ottoman flags were flying over Constantinople.

TERM PAPER SUGGESTIONS

1. Compare the descriptions written by Benjamin of Tudela and by Ibn Battuta of Constantinople during its last years as the Byzantine capital.

2. Compare the opinions expressed by Barbaro, Gennadios, Kritovoulos, and Sphrantzes about the Ottoman conquest of Constantinople.

3. Discuss the Byzantine defense of Constantinople against the Ottomans. Compare it to the earlier defense against the Fourth Crusade. Why did attempts to save the city fail?

4. Analyze the effects of gunpowder and cannon on warfare in the mid- to late-15th century and beyond. How did the nature of warfare change?

5. What were the results of the loss of Constantinople to the church and Western culture?

6. Analyze the battle strategies of Mehmed II. Was his victory one of military genius, luck, or both?

ALTERNATIVE TERM PAPER SUGGESTIONS

1. You are an elderly person in 1454, almost 100 years old, who has always lived in Constantinople. Talk to your great-grandchild about the changes you have seen in the city during your lifetime. What familiar elements of the city from your childhood and youth remain?

2. The last Byzantine emperor, Constantine XI Palaeologus (r. 1449–1453), met the people of his city when they knew the final assault was about to begin and delivered an impassioned speech. Using information from primary sources, reconstruct this speech and deliver it to the class. Use costuming to set the mood.

3. Prepare a physical or digital model of the siege of Constantinople, placing the Ottoman forces and the Byzantine defenses in their proper positions.

Primary Sources

Baker, Ernest. *Social and Political Thought in Byzantium. From Justinian I to the Last Palaeologus. Pages from Byzantine Writers and Documents.* Oxford: Oxford University Press, 1961. Includes documents from shortly before the fall of Constantinople.

Barbaro, Nicolo. *Diary of the Siege of Constantinople, 1453.* Jericho, NY: Exposition Press, 1969. A translation of Barbaro's eye-witness account of Constantinople's fall to the Turks.

Gunther of Pairis. *The Capture of Constantinople: The "Hystoria Constantinopolitana" of Gunter of Pairis."* Trans. by Alfred J. Andrea. Philadelphia: University of Pennsylvania Press, 1997. A contemporary account of the fall of Constantinople.

Medieval and Renaissance Studies: Primary Sources: Byzantine History. http://apps.carleton. edu/curricular/mars/Translations/primary_sources. Maintained by Carleton College, this site has translations of eight contemporary documents about the fall of Constantinople.

Sphrantzes, George. *George Sphrantzes: The Fall of the Byzantine Empire: A Chronicle by George Sphrantzes 1401–1477.* Boston: University of Massachusetts Press, 1980. Translation of eye-witness account of the fall of Constantinople.

Secondary Sources

Bartusis, Mark C. *The Late Byzantine Army: Arms and Society, 1204–1453.* Philadelphia: University of Pennsylvania Press, 1992. History divided into two parts: Army as an Instrument of Policy and Army as an Institution.

Crowley, Roger. *1453: The Holy War for Constantinople and the Clash of Islam and the West.* New York: Hyperion, 2005. Focuses on the dissonance between Islam and Christianity that caused the fall of Constantinople, and studies the effect on interactions between the two religions today.

Feldman, Ruth Tenzer. *The Fall of Constantinople*. Minneapolis: Twenty-First Century Books, 2008. Discusses the effect of the fall of Constantinople on European history, particularly the end of the dark ages.

Nicolle, David MacGillivray. *The Last Centuries of Byzantium, 1261–1453*. New York: St. Martin's Press, 1972. Discusses the government, commerce, and culture of the last 200 years of Byzantine power.

Nicolle, David, Haldon, John F, and Turnball, Stephen R. *The Fall of Constantinople*. New York: Osprey Publishing, 2007. Part III, written by David Nicolle, focuses entirely on Constantinople in 1453.

Pears, Edwin. *The Destruction of the Greek Empire and the Story of the Capture of Constantinople by the Turks*. Whitefish, MT: Kessinger Publishing, 2004. Indepth description of the region after the Latin conquest, leading to 1453 and the destruction of Constantinople. Includes multiple maps and illustrations.

Runciman, Steven. *The Fall of Constantinople, 1453*. Cambridge: Cambridge University Press, 1965. Detailed description of the fall of Constantinople, from background information to preparations for and the timeline of the siege.

Wells, Colin. *Sailing from Byzantium: How a Lost Empire Shaped the World*. New York: Delacorte Press, 2006. Reviews the cultural, social, and economic influences of the Byzantine Empire that survived the empire.

World Wide Web

Byzantium: Faith and Power (1261–1557). http://www.metmuseum.org/special/Byzantium/byzantium_splash.htm. Digital exhibit from Metropolitan Museum of Art. Examines the art and culture of the last three centuries of Byzantine influence. Extensive collection of images of artifacts from world museums. Helen C. Evans edited a companion book published by Yale University Press in 2004.

De Re Militari: The Society for Medieval Military History. http://www.dere militari.org/. Includes articles on all aspects of medieval military operations. Has both primary and secondary sources on the Crusades. Provides extensive bibliography of related materials.

Dumbarton Oaks Research Library and Collection. http://www.doaks.org/. Dumbarton Oaks is a Harvard University Research institute devoted in part to Byzantine studies. A large collection of scholarly papers on many topics is available online. Also provides a searchable database with translations of some texts.

Multimedia Sources

The Fall of Byzantium. DVD. Annenburg. Video 16 in a series of 25. learner.org. Individuals must register to view the videos, but there is no cost. Examines the fall of the Byzantine Empire to Islam.

The Siege of Constantinople. 2003. DVD. The History Channel. Part of the *History's Turning Points* series. 50 minutes. Story of the Ottoman Turks' capture and destruction of the Byzantine capital.

98. Gutenberg's Printing Press Revolutionizes Book-Making (1455)

In 1452, Johannes Gutenberg, working in his workshop in Mainz, Germany, put together a wine press, oil-based ink, paper, and his own idea of moveable type and revolutionized the manufacture of books. Most medieval books in Europe and the Islamic world were painstakingly copied by hand, often by monks in scriptoriums. The Chinese had invented a method of block printing 600 years before Gutenberg; however, because their language contained many more characters than the Western alphabet, the process was very labor intensive. Marco Polo brought this knowledge back from his journey to China in the 13th century, but little was done with it at that time. In addition, the paper-making techniques of China were known in Europe, yet paper was thought unsuitable for books, which were copied on more durable vellum.

As a businessman, Gutenberg realized the potential for a more rapid way to meet the 15th-century demand for printed documents. More documentation was needed for secular concerns than in the past when monks copied texts and few of the laity could read. Gutenberg's major contribution to printing was moveable metal letters. The letters needed for a book page could be placed in the tray, inked, and all the copies of that page needed could be printed. Then the tray could be reset with the reusable letters and another page printed. Gutenberg also realized that vellum would be too expensive for the production of large numbers of copies of books and used paper.

The church quickly took advantage of the new technology. One of the most profitable print ventures was making copies of indulgences that the church could sell. Press runs of up to 200,000 indulgences were common. Theological texts and manuals for inquisitions were also popular.

Gutenberg's most famous work is the Latin Bible, of which he printed 300 copies in 1455. The church found it could not control the printing of texts, however, and a wide variety of popular texts began to be copied and sold. In 1476, William Caxton brought the printing press to England and began producing popular literature in the English language.

Print spread rapidly throughout Europe. Estimates vary as to how many texts might have been printed in the first 50 years after the introduction of the press, but the number was probably larger than the total number of hand copied texts that existed in 1455. The printing press increased the literacy rate in Europe, encouraged learning, and was a major factor in the Renaissance.

TERM PAPER SUGGESTIONS

1. What was the reaction of the Islamic world to the invention of the printing press? Why? How did this affect the Islamic position as leader in the sciences?

2. What effect did the printing press have on the church? On the Reformation?

3. Compare the arrival of the printing press in Germany with its arrival in England. Did Gutenberg and Caxton face similar problems? How did the general public react to the printing press and the rapid production of text?

4. What issues did printers face as they produced works from other languages? How accurate were their reproductions?

5. Analyze the issue of property rights as it applied to literary works in the 15th century. Who owned the copyright of a work? Explain how the concept of copyright developed.

ALTERNATIVE TERM PAPER SUGGESTIONS

1. Create a multimedia presentation showing the history of text from the illuminated manuscript through to the 20th century. Use public domain images of pages of print. Consider the materials used in making books and the size and shape of texts.

2. With a partner, develop a debate between a printer and an author over who owns the right to sell copies and profit from a literary work.

Primary Sources

Weissbort, Daniel, and Eysteinsson, Astradur, eds. *Translation: Theory and Practice: A Historical Reader.* Oxford: Oxford University Press, 2006. A collection of documents written by translators on the process of translation. Includes work from Caxton, who translated many of the works he printed.

Carruthers, Mary, and Ziolkowski, Jan M., eds. *The Medieval Craft of Memory: An Anthology of Texts and Pictures.* Philadelphia: University of Pennsylvania Press, 2003. A collection of translated texts and pictures examining the ways medieval individuals remembered texts, including puns and clues in pictures.

Secondary Sources

Echard, Sian. *Printing the Middle Ages.* Philadelphia: University of Pennsylvania Press, 2008. Detailed history of print, looking not only at the classics that were preserved in print, but also at the vast amount of subcanon literature that was printed in medieval Britain.

Eisenstein, Elizabeth L. *The Printing Press as an Agent of Change.* Cambridge: Cambridge University Press, 1979. Examines the standardization, preservation, and dissemination of text after the printing press, and looks at the influence of print on the church, science, and issues of censorship.

Eisenstein, Elizabeth. *The Printing Revolution in Early Modern Europe.* Cambridge: Cambridge University Press, 1983. This volume is organized in two sections: the emergence of print culture and the interaction of print with other developments.

Gillespie, Alexandra. *Print Culture and the Medieval Author: Chaucer, Lydgate, and Their Books, 1473–1557.* Oxford: Oxford University Press, 2006. Studies Caxton and printing in the 15th century; looks at the various editions of Chaucer and Lydgate as they were assembled and printed.

Hotchkiss, Valerie, and Robinson, Fred C. *English in Print from Caxton to Shakespeare to Milton.* Urbana: University of Illinois Press, 2008. Thorough discussion of the history of print in England. Includes more than 130 photos of early manuscripts.

Man, John. *Gutenburg: How One Man Remade the World with Words.* Indianapolis: Wiley, 2002. Both a biography of Gutenberg and his struggles to make printing a profitable business and a discussion of the technical and theological problems with printing the Bible.

Zieman, Katherine. *Singing the New Song: Literacy and Liturgy in Late Medieval England.* Philadelphia: University of Pennsylvania Press, 2008. Most studies of early print focus on the change from oral to written text. Zieman's study examines the ways print changed liturgy as it became an orally read text.

World Wide Web

The American Printing History Association. http://www.printinghistory.org/htm/misc/links.html. Has a large number of links to additional resources.

The Atlas of Early Printing. http://atlas.lib.uiowa.edu/index.html. Graphically presents the spread of printing throughout the West; includes an animation of the early press in operation and a description of book-making in the 15th-century.

Educator Resources: Teaching Gutenberg. http://www.hrc.utexas.edu/educator/modules/gutenberg/. Hosted by the University of Texas at Austin, this site has a great deal of information about the history of print, Gutenberg, and the Gutenberg Bible. Images and primary source material.

Gutenberg Museum Mainz. http://p25338.typo3server.info/index.php?id=29&L=1. The Web site for the museum in Gutenburg's hometown. Has images, articles, and digital exhibitions. English version available.

The Schoyen Collection. http://www.schoyencollection.com/Pre-Gutenberg.htm. Digitalized images from much of the Schoyen collection of manuscripts covering 5,000 years of text production. Section 21 includes examples of a variety of preGutenberg printing.

Multimedia Sources

Gutenberg: The Birth of Printing. 1989. DVD. Clearvue & SVE. 24 minutes. Traces printing from the Chinese use of block print to Gutenburg to modern printing presses.

History of Printing. 2005. DVD. Films for the Humanities and Sciences. 28 minutes. Brief overview of the history of printing from the invention of movable type to the development of newspapers and magazines.

Printing Transforms Knowledge. DVD. 1986. Clearvue & SVE. 54 minutes. Explains the importance of the printing press in the spread of learning and explores how print influenced the Renaissance.

99. Spanish Inquisition Begins (1478)

In 1478, Spanish monarchs Ferdinand II (r. 1479–1516) and Isabella I (r. 1474–1504) asked for and received permission from Pope Sixtus IV to reinforce the efforts of the church to maintain orthodoxy by naming inquisitors within their territories. This renewed Inquisition would be directly under their control, not under the authority of the church. The Spanish Inquisition was not completely dismantled until the 19th century.

The monarchs ordered their new appointees to boldly defend the Catholic faith by cleansing their dioceses of all heresy. Tribunals were created in all major towns and cities and a rigid bureaucracy established to conduct investigations of all suspected of veering from the true path. A general council of priests called the *suprema*, who were appointed directly by the monarch, administered the bureaucracy in Europe and the Spanish colonies. Extensive transcripts of the courts of Inquisition provide a vivid record of the abuses of the trials.

A number of Jews and Muslims living in Iberia had converted to Christianity after the Reconquest was completed when Fredinand and Isabella captured Granada from the Muslims. The king and queen gave them the choice of conversion, exile, or worse. Some individuals had already converted because of the discrimination they faced. Sometimes, these *conversos* truly accepted Christianity; sometimes they conformed in public and continued their religious practices in private. All conversos, however, were under the authority of the Inquisition which was determined to rid the church of hypocritical Christians. Monarchs, who saw themselves as ruling with direct authority from God, seized on the opportunity of the Inquisition to charge that those who were disloyal to God were also disloyal to their Christian rulers. The expansion of the Inquisition allowed the king and queen to eliminate almost anyone they saw as a threat and to control the population through fear.

Even if Jews and Muslims did convert, they were considered second-class citizens, not pure-blooded Christians. Marriage between a Christian and a Jew, Muslim, or converso was forbidden. Yet, a number of the conversos had risen to positions of importance in finance and government by the end of the 15th century. In addition, Jews still controlled a large portion of the banking and financial industry. The Jews and Muslims faced growing resentment from the Christians that sometimes turned to violence against them. Ferdinand and Isabella were able to channel this resentment into popular support for their own religious fanaticism. A conviction for heresy also gave the crown justification for seizing the property of the individual and his or her family.

Tomas de Torquemada, a Dominican friar, was appointed Grand Inquisitor in 1478 and remained in the position until his death in 1498. More than 2,000 individuals were found guilty of heresy and executed under Torquemada's administration. Torquemada was also primarily responsible for engineering the expulsion of the Jews and Muslims from Spain in 1492. When the Spanish colonized New World territories, they took the Inquisition with them. Large numbers of indigenous peoples were killed as heretics when they did not convert to Christianity or if they returned to their own religious practices. The fervor with which the Inquisition was carried out varied in different places and times, but for over 300 years, monarchs held the threat of its possibility over the heads of the population of Spanish territories.

TERM PAPER SUGGESTIONS

1. Compare the Spanish Inquisition to the earlier persecution of heretics that took place throughout Europe.
2. The Spanish Inquisition was part of Ferdinand and Isabella's strategy for increasing their royal power. In what ways did the Inquisition aid their plan?
3. What were the effects of the Inquisition on the social fabric of life in Spain and later in the colonies?
4. What techniques did the Grand Inquisitor Torguemada develop to ferret out heretics and elicit confessions from them? What was the purpose of the *auto de fe*?
5. How do you explain the fact that the clergy, followers of Christ, whose teaching was based on love and forgiveness, could accept the practices of the Inquisition such as persecution, torture, and execution so enthusiastically?
6. What was the relationship between the Inquisition and censorship of speech and print?

ALTERNATIVE TERM PAPER SUGGESTIONS

1. Create a multimedia presentation using images and text created during the Spanish Inquisition in Europe and in the New World.
2. Using primary source transcripts of Inquisition trials, create a readers' theater presentation.

Primary Sources

Edwards, John, ed. *The Inquisitions, Series 1: Manuscripts of the Spanish, Portuguese and French Inquisitions in the British Library, London.* London: Primary Source Microfilm, no date. A very large collection of letters, transcripts, statutes, and other documents written during and about the Inquisition on microfilm.

Homza, Lu Ann, ed. *The Spanish Inquisition, 1478–1614: An Anthology of Sources.* Indianapolis: Hackett Publishing Company, 2006. A collection of newly translated documents concerning the Inquisition; includes court transcripts, descriptions of prisons, and letters. With introduction and commentary.

Secondary Sources

Ames, Christine Caldwell. *Righteous Persecution: Inquisition, Dominicans, and Christianity in the Middle Ages.* Philadelphia: University of Pennsylvania Press, 2008. Explores the ways in which the church and Dominicans specifically found support for their persecution in theological texts so that they believed they were acting on behalf of their faith.

Griffin, Clive. *Journeymen-Printers, Heresy and the Inquisition in Sixteenth-Century Spain.* New York: Oxford University Press, 2005. Examines the Inquisition's persecution of those who printed and distributed unorthodox texts. Through careful study of archival records, Griffin reveals an underground of Protestant-leaning printers in Spain.

Haliczer, Stephen. *Inquisition and Society in the Kingdom of Valencia, 1478–1834.* Berkeley: University of California Press, 1990. Follows the Inquisition during the Renaissance through the 19th century.

Lambert, Malcolm. *Medieval Heresy: Popular Movements from the Gregorian Reform to the Reformation.* Oxford: Blackwell Publishers, 1992. A good general study of heresy in the Middle Ages.

Longhurst, John Edward. *The Age of Torquemada.* Sandoval, NM: Coronado Press, 1962: Carrie, 2003. http://vlib.iue.it/carrie/texts/carrie_books/longhurst2/. Longhurst discusses the history of Jewish persecution in Europe from the First Crusade until the Spanish Inquisition.

Rawlings, Helen. *The Spanish Inquisition.* Oxford: Wiley-Blackwell, 2006. A comprehensive history of the Inquisition from its beginnings through the 19th century. Includes maps, a glossary, and a chronology.

Roth, Cecil. *The Spanish Inquisition.* New York: W. W. Norton, 1996. Discusses the history of the Inquisition from its authorization by the pope until it was canceled in the 19th century. Looks carefully at some of the major personalities of the persecution.

World Wide Web

"How the Spanish Inquisition Worked." http://history.howstuffworks.com/european-history/spanish-inquisition.htm. Includes articles, streaming video, and images.

Nos Los Inquisidores: The Harley L. McDevitt Collection on the Spanish Inquisition at the University of Notre Dame. http://www.rarebooks.nd.edu/exhibits/inquisition/. A large collection of Inquisition primary documents in Spanish, a number of which have been digitalized.

Multimedia Sources

The Fires of Faith: Dissidents and the Church. 2000. DVD. BBC. 50 minutes. The video does not directly discuss the Inquisition; however, it sets the stage by presenting church reactions to earlier conflicts of faith.

History's Mysteries: The Inquisition. 2005. DVD. The History Channel. 50 minutes. Traces the history of the crusade against heresy, from Pope Gregory IX's establishment of the court of inquisition in 1231, to the end of the Middle Ages.

Kill Them All: Christian Crusaders Against Christian Heresy. 2006. DVD. Insight Media. 60 minutes. Tells the story of the Catholic Church's attempt to obliterate any variations in religious practice and belief during the Middle Ages. Includes footage on the Spanish Inquisition.

Secret Files of the Inquisition: The Complete Series. 2007. DVD. PBS. Four episodes, 60 minutes each. Uses documents from the Vatican and other archives to trace the history of the Catholic church's attempts to enforce orthodoxy throughout Europe.

100. Wars of the Roses End (1485)

Before England could enjoy peace with France following the battle of Castillon (1453) that ended the Hundred Years' War, the nation was embroiled in a series of bitter civil wars. England's King Henry VI (r. 1422–1461, 1470–1471), from the House of Lancaster, had made some disastrous decisions in the war against France that led nobles to rebel against him. The leader of the revolt was Richard of York. The ensuing conflicts were known as the Wars of the Roses because the Lancastrian emblem was a red rose and that of the Yorks a white rose. Although the first major battle did not take place until 1455 at St. Albans, the dispute had started earlier. In 1450, Richard of York forced Henry VI to acknowledge him as the heir to the throne, passing over his own son. In 1453, Henry became insane when he heard his forces had lost the territory of Bordeaux, and Richard was appointed protector. However, when Henry recovered the next year, he excluded Richard from the royal council. An angry Richard opted for combat.

At the battle at St. Albans, the Lancastrians were defeated, and Richard again became protector for a brief time during 1455–1456. Both sides were in combat again in 1459. The next year, the Yorkists captured the king at Northampton, and Richard rushed to London to claim the throne. However, the lords devised a compromise that allowed Henry to remain king, Richard would continue in an important position, and the Yorkists would be the successors to Henry. Queen Margaret, Henry's wife, the power behind the throne and the mother of Henry's disinherited son, raised her own army and defeated the Yorkists at Wakefiled in 1460. Richard was killed in the battle, but his son, Edward continued to claim to be the heir. Margaret rescued Henry in 1461 at the second battle of St. Albans. Meanwhile, Edward won a battle at Mortimer's Cross and marched into London unopposed to claim the crown as Edward IV. Henry regained the throne in 1470, and Edward deposed him again in 1471. Similar hostilities and transfers of power continued periodically for the next two decades.

Finally, in 1485, Richard III (r. 1483–1485), who had usurped the throne from his nephew, was defeated at Bosworth Field in the last battle of the wars. Just as important in bringing the fighting to an end, Henry Tudor married the Princess Elizabeth of York. Nobles accepted Henry as their king and the Tudor dynasty began. The ease with which the new king was accepted was in part because 30 years of fighting had extracted heavy tolls from the nobility, more so than from the middle and lower classes. Approximately 90 individuals of noble birth were killed during the 30 years of war. Although many more common soldiers died, the percentage of upper class deaths was larger. In addition, many of the dukes had spent vast fortunes fighting one another, diminishing their economic power. With an end to the long years of fighting, England was ready to enter the Renaissance.

TERM PAPER SUGGESTIONS

1. Analyze the effects of the Wars of the Roses on the common people in England.

2. Unlike the Hundred Years War, the Wars of the Roses were civil wars fought only on English soil. Contrast the effects of this series of Civil Wars on England with the effects of the international conflict of the Hundred Years War.

3. How did the problems faced by the English nation—loss of the Hundred Years War, unrest in Scotland, Ireland, and Wales, economic problems, weak leaders—contribute to the Wars of the Roses?

4. Compare contemporary historical accounts of the English kings Henry VI and Richard III to the characters in Shakespeare's plays about them.

5. Richard III had been accused of the murderer of the two young sons of Edward IV, but some people, including those who belong to the Richard III Society, believe this is a false accusation. What do you think? On what evidence do you base your belief?

ALTERNATIVE TERM PAPER SUGGESTIONS

1. Create a board game based on the events and people involved in the Wars of the Roses.

2. Assume you are a member of the lesser nobility in England during the period from 1453–1485. You are involved enough in the troubles to know what is going on, but you are neither a York nor a Lancaster. Write a series of journal entries about what is happening to your country.

3. Create an interactive media presentation about the Wars of the Roses. Include links to battle sites, people, and events of the civil war.

Primary Sources

Anonymous. *Croyland Chronicle.* http://www.r3.org/bookcase/index.html. This is a contemporary history of the Wars of the Roses.

The Battle of Bosworth: August 22, 1485. http://www.r3.org/bosworth/chronicl .html. Has a large collection of primary sources from the Wars of the Roses period.

Benet, John. *John Benet's Chronicle for the Years 1400 to 1462.* Ed. by Gerald Leslie Harriss and M. A. Harriss. London: Royal Historical Society, 1972. Benet, who wrote this history, was a clergyman in London.

Mancini, Dominic. *The Usurpation of Richard III.* Trans. by C. A. J. Armstrong. Oxford: Oxford University Press, 1969. Mancini was an Italian traveler and writer who visited England in 1480–1483 and wrote about what he saw there, including a description of the English soldier in the Wars of the Roses.

Hardyng, John. *The Chronicle of John Hardyng.* Trans. and ed. by Henry Ellis. London: Woodfall, 1812. John Hardyng died in 1465 while still working on his *Chronicles.*

Secondary Sources

Carpenter, Christine. *The Wars of the Roses: Politics and the Constitution in England, c. 1437–1509.* Cambridge: Cambridge University Press, 1997. Carpenter positions her discussion of the Wars of Roses within the context of what they meant for the concept of kingship in England.

Gillingham, John. *The Wars of the Roses: Peace & Conflict in the 15th Century.* New York: Pheonix Press, 2001., Gillingham discusses not only the battles and soldiers, but the lives of those not involved in the conflict.

Harriss, Gerald. *The Wars of the Roses: Politics and the Constitution in England, c.1437–1509.* Cambridge: Cambridge University Press, 2005. Looks at the political ramifications of the Wars of the Roses on the English monarchy.

Hicks, Michael. *The Wars of the Roses 1455–1485.* London: Routledge, 2003. Includes a detailed chronology, as well as chapters on life in England apart from the war and an analysis of the effects of 30 years of fighting.

Lander, J. R. *The Wars of the Roses.* Charleston, SC: The History Press, 2007. Lander, a scholar of 15th-century England, relies heavily on primary source documents to tell the story of the conflict between the Yorks and Lancasters.

Royle, Trevor. *Lancaster Against York: The Wars of the Roses and the Foundation of Modern Britain.* London: Palgrave-MacMillan, 2008. Examines each of the Lancastrian and Yorkish kings and the part they played in the war and in establishing a more powerful monarchy.

Weir, Allison. *The Wars of the Roses.* New York: Random House, 1995. The first half of the book is devoted to the circumstances leading up to the war; the second deals with individuals who played a significant part in the conflict.

Winstead, Karen. *John Capgrave's Fifteenth Century.* Philadelphia: University of Pennsylvania Press, 2006. Using the works of writer and theologian John Capgrave, Winstead draws a picture of the late medieval English culture, including the political turmoil of the Wars of the Roses.

World Wide Web

The Richard III Society: American Branch. http://www.r3.org/intro.html. Extensive online primary documents related to Richard III, the Wars of Roses, and the Battle of Bosworth. Links to other resources and some online texts.

De Re Militari: The Society for Medieval Military History. http://www.deremilitari .org/. Maintained by an international association of scholars, the site offers articles on many aspects of medieval warfare, links to other sites, a bibliography, and book reviews.

Luminarium Encyclopedia Project: Wars of the Roses. http://www.luminarium.org/ encyclopedia/houseoflancaster.htm. Provides a genealogical table for the houses of York and Lancaster and links to many articles about the people and events of the Wars of the Roses.

Military History Encyclopedia on the Web. http://www.historyofwar.org/index.html. Has a large section on the Wars of the Roses.

Société de l'Oriflamme. 2005. http://xenophongroup.com/monctjoie/oriflam.htm. This site devoted to medieval warfare provides links to many other sites and articles on the subject.

Wars of the Roses.Com. http://www.warsoftheroses.com/index.htm. Easy to navigate Web site that has maps, biographical information, a timeline, and information about battles.

The Wars of the Roses. http://www.wars-of-the-roses.com/. Provides information about individual battles, links to other sources, maps, and the individuals involved.

Multimedia Sources

Medieval Realms: Britain from 1066–1500. No date. CD-ROM. Films for the Humanities and Sciences. Multimedia collection of original material from sources in the British Library includes literature, travel narratives, illuminated manuscripts, writs, charters, wills, music, maps, and deeds, along with images of buildings and artifacts.

Medieval Warfare: The Wars of the Roses: To Bosworth Field. 2001. Video. Kultur Video. 50 Minutes. The story of the Wars of the Roses is told through reenactments, computer-generated effects, contemporary accounts and images, and interviews with historians.

The Missing Princes of England. 2001. DVD. A&E Entertainment. 50 minutes. Explores the story of Richard III's two nephews who were imprisoned in the Tower of London and never seen again.

Shakespeare, William. *The Tragedy of Richard III.* 2001. DVD. BBC. 120 minutes. Film version of Shakespeare's drama.

The Yorks and Lancasters. 2004. DVD. Films Media Group. 47 minutes. Examines the growth of English nationalism during the Wars of the Roses.

Wars of the Roses. 2008. DVD. Eagle Rock Entertainment. Three 50-minute episodes: "The Two Roses," "The Kingmaker," and "One Perfect Rose." Covers entire history of the War of the Roses.

The Wars of the Roses. 1998. DVD. Films Media Group. 30 minutes. Military historian David Chandler discusses the Wars of the Roses using reenactments, graphics, and maps.

Index

About the Author

Jean S. Hamm is an assistant professor in the Department of English at Radford University.